About the Author

David Hamblin was born in 1935, and has a degree in Classics from Oxford University. For many years he was a Lecturer in the School of Management at Bath University, but he took early retirement in 1985 to work as a psychotherapist, having been trained at the Psychosynthesis and Education Trust and at the Bath Centre for Psychotherapy and Counselling. After taking up astrology in the 1960s, he became a Tutor for the Faculty of Astrological Studies and was also Chairman of the Astrological Association of Great Britain in the 1980s. His book *Harmonic Charts* (Aquarian Press) was published in 1983. Since his retirement as a psychotherapist in 2000, he has written several articles, and has also (his proudest achievement) walked the 630-mile South West Coast Path. He is married, with two daughters and two granddaughters. His email address is pigleystair@yahoo.co.uk and his website is www.davidhamblin. net.

The cover design is a reproduction of the design of a crop circle which appeared at Etchilhampton, Wiltshire, England, in 2004. It shows a seven-pointed star inside an eleven-pointed star inside a thirteen-pointed star: three of the prime numbers that are discussed in this book.

THE SPIRIT OF NUMBERS:

A New Exploration of

Harmonic Astrology

David Hamblin

The Wessex Astrologer

Published in 2011 by
The Wessex Astrologer Ltd
4A Woodside Road
Bournemouth
BH5 2AZ
England

www.wessexastrologer.com

ISBN 9781902405537

A catalogue record of this book is available at The British Library

Cover design by Tania at Creative Byte, Poole, Dorset

Contents

Author's Note

Since the first publication of this book, a computer programme has been created which produces a Table of Aspects similar to that shown on pages 266-7, and so greatly simplifies the task of identifying harmonic aspects as described in Appendix I. This is the Kepler 8 program, which is available through www.astrosoftware.com.

The charts in this book were calculated using the Astrocalc program. There are some discrepancies between the positions of Chiron given by Astrocalc and those given by other programs, and these discrepancies may affect the pattern of harmonic aspects involving Chiron, especially for charts from before the twentieth century.

Preface

I am now in the autumn of my life, and I do not intend to do any more writing after I have finished this book. So I would like to begin the book with a very personal statement.

I will start with a quotation from Iain McGilchrist's brilliant book about the two hemispheres of the brain:

> "Certainty is the greatest of all illusions: whatever kind of fundamentalism it may underwrite, that of religion or of science, it is what the ancients meant by *hubris*. The only certainty, it seems to me, is that those who believe they are certainly right are certainly wrong".[1]

It follows from this that I am not *certain* that the statements I will make in this book about the meaning of numbers are true, and I am not even *certain* that astrology as a whole is, in any ultimate sense, 'true'. If it is true, it is the most extraordinary and wondrous thing. How can it be that those rocks and gaseous masses up there in the sky (including some quite small ones, like Pluto and Chiron) affect our behaviour here on Earth? How can it be that the pattern which the planets form at the moment that we emerge from our mother's womb becomes imprinted on our consciousness, so that it influences our behaviour until the day of our death? We may believe this to be true, but we cannot be certain; and we should never forget what an outlandish thing it is that we are believing.

Some readers of this book may be aware that I went through a period in which I doubted the truth of astrology, to such an extent that I was unable to practise it. I set out my reasons for this in Garry Phillipson's book *Astrology in the Year Zero*.[2] However, I have now reached a position where I feel that it is worthwhile to practise astrology, because, even though it may possibly not be true, it most certainly *seems* to be true. In the process of researching for this book I have looked at more than a thousand charts, and I have been constantly amazed at how the birth chart does in fact describe people as they are. (There are a few exceptions where the birth chart does *not* seem to encapsulate the person's individuality, but for me these are the exceptions that prove the rule. Maybe in these cases there has been some mistake about the person's time of birth?)

However, for me, this *appropriateness* of the birth chart is far more striking if one focuses mainly on harmonic aspects rather than on signs and houses. There is a certain flatness about a signs-and-houses interpretation of the birth chart: each planet occupies one sign and one house, and all the signs and houses are equally significant, so no chart emerges as more distinctive than any other chart. This is very democratic, but I feel that it is not true to life. The reality of life is that some people have very much more striking and distinctive personalities than some other people. (I am not saying that they are better than other people, just more distinctive.) If we look at the harmonic aspects of people with very distinctive personalities, we tend to find that they have very striking and unusual clusters of harmonic aspects, more so than people whose personalities are more 'ordinary', more self-contradictory, more blurred. This is one of the reasons why I feel that the study of harmonic aspects is valuable.

And another reason why I value the study of harmonic aspects is that, for me, they are beautiful. (Maybe this is the answer to the question about 'truth'. John Keats said, "Beauty is truth, truth beauty: that is all ye know, and all ye need to know".) For me, the study of the inner meanings of the prime numbers (as set out in Chapter 17) is beautiful, and says something about the workings of the universe that was not clear before. Although Sevenness is not particularly strong in my own chart, I have tried to write this book in the spirit of Sevenness: that is, in an intuitive and inspirational way, in search of the hidden meanings that lie behind appearances. (At the same time, I have tried to be true to the spirit of Fiveness, by favouring precise and accurate calculation of aspects. Both Fiveness and Sevenness have a part to play in the act of creativity.)

I do not want my comments on the meaning of numbers (especially of the higher numbers, from Eleven onwards) to be taken as gospel truth; but nor do I want them to be cast aside or ignored. I would prefer them to be regarded as pointers towards the truth. I hope that other astrologers (perhaps using different methods from the ones I am using in this book) will investigate further, and will further enhance our knowledge of the mysterious ways in which the universe operates. But the full truth will never be known, for it is beyond human understanding.

I would have been unable to write the book without the co-operation of AstroDatabank, from whose huge collection of astrological data most of my examples have been drawn, and my immense thanks go to Pat Taglilatelo of AstroDatabank, and to Richard Smoot (formerly of AstroDatabank), for giving me permission to use their data, and for all the help that they have given me.

Also my heartfelt thanks go to Michael Harding, who has given me unstinting support, encouragement and practical help; to Grethe Hooper Hansen, who has supported me in my darkest moments, and has constantly re-affirmed how important it was for me to press on with the book; and above all to my wife Helen, who has tolerated the thousands of hours that I have spent locked away researching and writing the book, and has read the proofs and provided many valuable suggestions. For me, she has been both a tower of strength and a fountain of love.

1

An Introduction to Harmonics

What a wonderful thing is an astrological chart. It is a map of the solar system in relation to the Earth, *as it really is* at a particular time. If an astrologer opens his or her computer programme and clicks on the button for 'Now', a chart is revealed which shows the planets as they really are *now*. If the chart shows that the sun is setting, the astrologer can go into the garden and see that the sun is setting now. If it is night time and the chart shows Moon and Venus close together in the upper half of the chart, the astrologer can go out and see Moon and Venus close together in the sky. Many of the other planets are invisible to the naked eye, and yet the astrologer knows, from looking at the chart, that this is where they are *now*.

It is important to keep reminding ourselves that the chart represents reality on a grand scale. The planets are not just pinpricks in the sky. They are huge bodies that are circling the Sun, each in its own way and at its own speed. Each of these bodies is a unique world, with a distinctive chemical composition and a distinctive character. As they move around the sky, they form different relationships with one another and with the Earth. All of the different interplanetary relationships add up to form a pattern which is unique to this particular moment. The pattern of relationships which the planets form in the sky *now* has never occurred before, and will never occur again.

But the pattern keeps changing. If we click the 'Now' button and then allow the programme to 'run', we can see how the planets gradually move, breaking up the existing pattern and creating new patterns. They move so slowly that watching them move on the computer screen is rather like watching paint dry, and yet we know that, if we were to leave the programme running until tomorrow, a new pattern will have emerged. Some of the outer planets will have stayed virtually in the same place, but other planets will have moved, and so will have come into new relationships, not only with each other but also with the planets that have not moved.

For me, this pattern of *interplanetary relationships* is the most important thing to observe, and to try to interpret, in an astrological chart. But it is not what most astrologers have concentrated on. For most astrologers, the most important thing has been to divide the sky (in two ways) into twelve segments, and to call these segments 'signs' and 'houses'. Mars, they say, is in Gemini in the fifth house. Certainly this says something about where Mars is in the sky, but it says nothing about its *relationship* with other planets. Moreover, we should note that the system of signs and houses is essentially a man-made system or theory, rather than a description of cosmic reality as it has always been. We cannot go into the garden and *observe* Gemini or the fifth house (especially since the signs no longer correspond to the constellations after which they were named). Why twelve segments? Why not some other number? How do we know where the boundaries between the segments are? (In the case of the houses, it would seem that we *don't* know, since there are so many conflicting systems of house division.)

But of course, this is not the only thing that astrologers have done. They have also looked at interplanetary relationships, and have called this the study of *aspects*. Traditionally, seven types of aspect have been recognized: conjunctions, oppositions, trines, squares, sextiles, semi-squares and semi-sextiles, corresponding respectively to the numbers 1, 2, 3, 4, 6, 8 and 12. If Venus is sextile to Mars (that is, if the angular distance between Venus and Mars is one-sixth of the circle), then the relationship between Venus and Mars has the quality of the number 6.

This is certainly a start in looking at interplanetary relationships, but it is very far from being the whole story. For instance, what if there were five planets forming the pattern of a pentagram (a five-pointed star) in the sky. Wouldn't this be important? And what if, between two of these planets (A and B), there was another planet (C) equidistant from both of them, so that the angular distance from A to C and from C to B was one-tenth of the circle? Wouldn't this too be important? Wouldn't it be right to say that, if we ignored this, we would be ignoring a very significant feature of the pattern which the planets were forming in the sky at this moment?

And if we were to look at the 'Five' series of aspects (5, 10, 15…), then why not look also at the 'Seven' series (7, 14, 21…)? Why not look also at the higher powers of Two and Three (16, 32, 9, 27) which have been ignored in traditional astrology? Why not look at Eleven and Thirteen?

Thoughts like these inspired John Addey in 1976 to write his ground-breaking book *Harmonics in Astrology*.[1] In 1983 I followed him by writing a book, *Harmonic Charts*,[2] in which I described a method of identifying and interpreting many of these aspects which are ignored in traditional astrology. In this method, these aspects are revealed by drawing a number of harmonic charts. Thus, we can draw a fifth-harmonic chart, in which quintiles are shown as conjunctions, deciles (tenths) are shown as oppositions, and so on. In the same way, we can draw a seventh-harmonic chart, or an eighth-harmonic chart, or a ninth-harmonic chart. Each of these charts will reveal a different pattern of aspects.

But these harmonic charts can themselves be a stumbling block. If we draw harmonic charts (even if we have a computer programme that calculates them for us), we end up with several charts, each with a different Ascendant and a different pattern of planets, and we can easily make the mistake of thinking that each of these charts is a separate entity, when really it is just an artificial way of presenting some features of the original chart. If we use the harmonic charts to interpret the original chart, we find ourselves constantly switching our attention between the different charts, and this can be a laborious and confusing process. I believe this is the main reason why harmonic charts are not used by many astrologers.

Because of this, I felt it was important to develop a method of identifying the non-traditional aspects *without having to draw the harmonic charts*. This is the method which I will use in this book. For the benefit of astrologers who want to use the method themselves, I will describe the technique in detail in Appendix I ("How to Do It"). (I am hoping that before long a computer program replicating this technique will be available.) In the main book, I will focus on the ways in which I have used the method myself, for the purpose of interpreting astrological charts, and for identifying and clarifying the essential meaning of each of the numbers.

In harmonic astrology (as first developed by John Addey), the basic principle is that *each of the prime numbers (1, 2, 3, 5, 7 etc.) represents a different quality*, and that this quality is indicative of the inner essence, or spirit, of that number. Most people would agree that, if a person displays the quality of Oneness in his or her life, he or she is acting in the spirit of Oneness: that is, in accordance with the spirit, or spiritual essence, of the number One. The argument of this book is that, in the same way, each of the other numbers has its own spirit, or spiritual essence, which we can call Twoness, Threeness, and so on. Hence the title: *The Spirit of Numbers*.

So what is the spiritual essence of the numbers beyond One? In traditional astrology it is known that Twoness represents opposition, struggle, conflict, and Threeness represents pleasure, ease, harmony; but in harmonic astrology it is also believed that Fiveness is to do with building, structure, rationality, and Sevenness is to do with inspiration, wildness, intuition. Numbers which are squares (or higher powers) of prime numbers represent the quality of the prime number in a higher or more refined form. Composite numbers, such as 15 which is 5 x 3, represent combinations of qualities: thus, 15 is to do with pleasure in rationality.

My belief is that *every planet is aspected to every other planet*. The idea of an 'unaspected planet' is a nonsense, since all the planets have to work together, and the nature of this co-operation will have the quality of the particular numbers by which they are linked. For instance, if the angular distance between two planets is one-eleventh (or two, three, four or five elevenths) of the circle, then it is likely that their interaction will have the qualities of the number Eleven: that is to say, it will have the quality of Elevenness. Our task is to discover what this quality of Elevenness is, and how it is different from Thirteenness and from all the other prime numbers.

In this book I will look at all the numbers up to 32. This includes twelve prime numbers (1, 2, 3, 5, 7, 11, 13, 17, 19, 23, 29 and 31), seven numbers which are squares or higher powers of prime numbers (4, 8, 16, 32, 9, 27 and 25), and thirteen numbers (6, 10, 12, 14, 15, 18, 20, 21, 22, 24, 26, 28 and 30) which are products of more than one prime number. (Why stop at 32? The basic answer to this is that one has to stop somewhere. My feeling is that, when we get to 32, we are approaching a kind of 'vanishing point', beyond which we are looking at divisions of the circle which are so small that one cannot identify them with sufficient accuracy. 32, which is 2 x 2 x 2 x 2 x 2, seems to me a good round figure at which to stop.) We will try to identify and describe the distinctive qualities of each prime number, and also to look at the ways in which these qualities are manifested in squares, cubes and composite numbers. We will do this mainly by finding charts which are especially strong in a particular number, and seeing what these charts have in common. (For instance, a chart which is strong in Elevenness is one in which there are many pairs of planets which are linked by Elevenness aspects – one-eleventh, two-elevenths, and so on – and also possibly some pairs which are linked by Twenty-twoness aspects, since 22 is 11 x 2).

Mostly I will be using natal charts, so that we can investigate whether the owners of these Elevenness charts have personality characteristics in common, but I will also be using some mundane charts (charts for the time of events other than births), in the hope that this will shed further light on the meaning of the numbers. In the case of the first five prime numbers we can draw on the work of previous astrologers, but when we get to the higher prime numbers (starting with Eleven) we are moving into uncharted territory.

This brings me to the second purpose of this book, which is to explore the meaning of numbers for their own sake. Although our conclusions will be based on astrological evidence, I am hoping that they will be of interest and value beyond astrology. In investigating the meaning of numbers, we are looking at one of the central mysteries of the universe. Pythagoras said that "all things are number," and Ward Rutherford, in writing about Pythagoras, has said that "number and mathematics have the character of immutable truths," and that "numbers have about them the attributes of absolutes and of the gods themselves".[3] Mathematics has been described as a 'universal language', and a scientist has said on television that he expected that, when extra-terrestrials succeed in communicating with us on Earth, they will do so using the language of mathematics. (I believe that extra-terrestrials may already be communicating with us by means of crop circles, which are complex geometrical patterns, one of which is reproduced on the front cover of this book.) But, if mathematics is a language and numbers are its words, *what do the numbers mean?* Is it possible to translate the language of numbers into English or any other terrestrial language? If we can make some tentative steps in this direction, we will be making a start towards unlocking some of the basic secrets of the universe.

I would hope also that we will be making a start towards bringing *poetry* into the study of numbers, and bringing the world of the mathematician and the world of the creative artist closer together. Mathematics has always been seen as a dry intellectual study; even though mathematicians talk of the beauty of their craft, it is a peculiarly pure and virginal beauty, the beauty of pure form, without any apparent connection with the messiness, fluidity and emotionality of the real world in which we live. It reminds me of the beauty of an Arctic landscape, where there are no colours except white, and where no living things can grow. By discussing the meaning of numbers in terms that make sense within our world, we may be helping to bring colour and warmth into mathematics and to make it relevant to our everyday lives.

It is true, of course, that numerologists have for centuries been describing the meaning of particular numbers. Numerology, when it is used intelligently and sensitively, can certainly yield valuable insights (I am thinking especially of Shirley Gotthold's *The Transformational Tarot*[4]), and yet I am suspicious of traditional numerology because it is based on the decimal system, which is a man-made invention and so is not part of the 'universal language'. Thus, for numerologists, the important thing about the number 27 is that it is 20 + 7; but it is only the decimal system that makes this significant. For me, the important thing about 27 is the immutable and universal fact that it is 3 x 3 x 3.

I need also to say a word here about the way in which I am looking at numbers. My interest is in *numbers as divisions of a circle*.

We tend to think of numbers in terms of the number of things in a line. "Nine green bottles standing on a wall; if one green bottle should accidentally fall, there'd be eight green bottles standing on a wall". Looked at in this way, One is the smallest number, and Nine is a much larger number, but these are not the numbers with which we are concerned. I do not believe that the nine green bottles have the quality of Nineness, or that, when one bottle falls, this is transformed into a quality of Eightness.

Also we are not concerned with numbers denoting positions in a sequence (so-called *ordinal* numbers). Thus, I do not believe that the *first* green bottle has a quality of Oneness, or that the *second* bottle has a quality of Twoness.

Rather, we are concerned with numbers as divisions of a circle. Everything in nature is built out of spheres, circles, and cycles (which are circular movements in time). The Sun, the Earth and the planets are spheres. The Moon follows a circular path around the Earth, the Earth does the same around the Sun, and the Sun does the same around the galaxy. Einstein says that space itself is curved, which implies that the universe itself is somehow spherical, though this is a sphere too large for us to comprehend. In the same way, time proceeds in cycles: the cycles of the day, of the seasons, and so on.

In a circular system, numbers refer to the number of segments into which the circle is divided. Looked at in this way, One is not the smallest number, but the largest number. One is all-inclusive: it refers to the Whole, the entirety. As we proceed from One to Two to Three to Four, we are looking at the division of the circle into smaller and smaller segments. These are the numbers with which we shall be concerned in this book.

Our focus will be on investigating the prime numbers and seeing if we can identify their distinctive meanings. Each prime number is divisible only by itself and One; therefore, each prime number introduces a new quality, which, although it is part of the universal Oneness, is in every other respect different from the qualities of all the other prime numbers.

In the following chapters (starting with Chapter 3) I will look in turn at each of the prime numbers from One to Thirty-one. In each chapter I will present examples of charts which are exceptionally strong in that particular number. For instance, all charts contain some Twoness, but some charts contain very much more Twoness than others, and so can be expected to display the qualities of Twoness to a much higher degree. I have selected these charts from more than a thousand I have analysed. Most of them are the birth charts of famous (or fairly famous) people, but a few are of well-known and important events. The great majority of these charts are taken from the huge collection of birth data gathered by AstroDatabank, but there are also some charts from other sources, especially from *A Multitude of Lives*[5] by Paul Wright and from Frank Clifford's books *British Entertainers*[6] and *The Astrologer's Book of Charts*[7].

In the case of mundane charts, most of the data is from the internet.

With only one or two exceptions, I have only used charts where the time of birth comes from a reputable source and is known with reasonable accuracy. AstroDatabank have developed their Rodden Rating (RR) system (named after Lois Rodden, the founder of AstroDatabank), in which 'AA' means that the time comes from a birth certificate or official birth records; 'A' means that the time comes from the person whose chart it is, or from people close to that person; 'B' means that it comes from a biography; 'C' means there is some doubt about the reputability of the source so the data should be used with caution; 'DD' means 'Dirty Data'. I have only used charts with a rating of AA, A or B. If the time of birth is unknown or uncertain, then the methods employed in this book cannot be used, because some of the planets (especially the Moon) move so fast that the pattern of interplanetary aspects in a morning chart will be quite different from the pattern in an evening chart on the same day.

An important principle of harmonic astrology is that *the closer an aspect is to exactitude, the stronger it is.* Hence I will say a great deal about 'close' aspects and 'very close' aspects, because the importance of an aspect is very dependent on its closeness. And another principle is that *the permissible orb for any aspect is the orb for the conjunction, divided by the number of the aspect.* Thus, if we say that the maximum orb for a 'very close' conjunction is 2 degrees (= 120 minutes), then the maximum orb for a very close quintile is 120 divided by 5, i.e. 24 minutes, and the maximum orb for a very close 'twentieth' aspect is 120 divided by 20, i.e. 6 minutes.

In this book I have set the maximum orb for a conjunction at 12 degrees; for a 'close' conjunction at 6 degrees; and for a 'very close' conjunction at 2 degrees. If I was asked why I have settled on these figures, I would have to say, "Because I have to set the limit somewhere". In fact, of course, there is no fixed point at which an aspect ceases to be 'close', and no fixed point where it disappears altogether: rather, there is a gradual falling away of the intensity of an aspect on either side of the point of exactitude. But, from my experience in interpreting these aspects, I feel that these limits are about right.

I need at this point to explain the way in which the data will be presented. In each case I will present the time and place of the birth (or other event), the source of the data, and the Rodden Rating (RR). After the time (e.g. 13.30 = 1.30 p.m.), the Time Zone will be given in brackets (e.g. +08.00 means 8 hours west of Greenwich; –01.00 means 1 hour east of Greenwich). In the 'Source' notes, the abbreviation 'ADB' shows that I have obtained the data from AstroDatabank, and the abbreviation 'FCC' shows that I have obtained the data from one of Frank C. Clifford's books (named above).

I will then present the most important harmonic aspects in the chart (arrived at by the method which I will explain in Appendix 1). These aspects will be described by placing the number of the harmonic between the letters that signify the planets. Thus SO –4 –MO signifies Sun square Moon (since 4 is the harmonic number of the square). But also, we can often find clusters of three or more planets, and these are very important for interpretation. Thus, (SO–4–MO)–5/20–JU shows that:

(a) Sun is square Moon;

(b) Sun is quintile (or bi-quintile) Jupiter;

(c) The angular distance from Moon to Jupiter is one-twentieth (or a higher number of twentieths) of the circle.

If the number is <u>underlined</u>, this shows that the aspect is 'close'. Thus, SO–<u>4</u>–MO shows that Sun is closely square to Moon. If the number is in ***<u>bold underlined italics</u>***, this means that the aspect is 'very close'. Thus, SO–***<u>4</u>***–MO shows that Sun is very closely square to Moon.

If the planetary letters are *<u>italicized and underlined</u>*, this shows that the planet is within 8 degrees of one of the Angles of the chart (Ascendant, Descendant, Midheaven, I.C.) (since I believe that proximity to the Angles makes the planet more prominent in the subject's personality). Thus, *<u>SO</u>*–4–MO shows that Sun (but not Moon) is within 8 degrees of one of the Angles.

Sometimes there is a cluster of planets which is separately aspected to more than one planet (or to more than one cluster of planets), and I have shown this by means of indentations. For instance, in the harmonic aspects for Josemaria Escriva de Balaguer (page 19),

(SO–1–MO–1–SA)–1–(ME–1–JU)
                    –1–CH

shows that Chiron is conjunct to Sun, Moon and Saturn, but not to Mercury and Jupiter. Similarly, in the harmonic aspects for Frida Kahlo (page 40),

    (SO–2–MA)–8–MO
             –16–ME
             –32–CH

shows that Sun and Mars have separate harmonic links to Moon, Mercury and Chiron (but Moon, Mercury and Chiron are not linked to each other by harmonic aspects).

In the chapters dealing with particular numbers, I will not attempt to analyse the charts as a whole, as my purpose will be only to look at the strength of the chart in this particular number. Therefore, I will only present the aspects that pertain to that number. (For instance, in the chapter dealing with Oneness, I will only present conjunctions, which are Oneness aspects.) However, for the benefit of readers who wish to analyse the whole chart, the other harmonic aspects are listed in Appendix III.

I will not be presenting the actual birth charts (except in Chapter 18, where we will look at the interpretation of the whole chart). Some readers may be surprised by this (how can we have an astrological book without charts?), but charts take up a lot of space; and I am aware that, nowadays, virtually all astrologers have access to a computer programme which enables them to print out the charts within seconds if they wish to do so. Moreover, the purpose of this book is to show that valid information can be obtained simply from the harmonic aspects, without the need for the additional information (especially about signs and houses) that can be obtained from the actual chart wheel.

However, I need to stress that I am not trying to belittle or debunk traditional astrology. I do believe that important insights can be gained by looking at the signs in which the planets are placed (and, in particular, I think that the Ascendant sign is very important). Also (with more reservations) I think that a study of the houses can yield useful insights. Thus, my aim is not to persuade astrologers to give up their existing methods, but rather to enable them to use an additional tool which (I believe) will help them to make their interpretations more rounded and complete.

2

The Planets

Before we look at the links between the planets, we must first look at the planets themselves. In interpreting the planets I am not departing from astrological tradition, but it still feels important to summarize my own beliefs about the significance of each of the planets. I will do this mainly in the context of birth charts, but I will also say a word about the interpretation of the planets in mundane charts.

Firstly, the question of what the birth chart can tell us, and what can it not tell us. I do not believe that the birth chart can tell us *who we really are*. In common with spiritual teachers from all traditions, I believe that who we really are is pure undiluted consciousness and awareness. We are a facet of the universal Oneness.

However, in this incarnation we come into the world occupying a particular bodily form. The particular form which the body takes is of course influenced by the genes which we inherit from our ancestors, and may also be affected by environmental factors. I do not believe that it is influenced by the birth chart. To take one example: Robert Wadlow[1] became the tallest person in history (he reached a height of 8 feet 11 inches), due to a rare genetic disorder (hypertrophy of the pituitary gland). If the birth chart influenced the body, one would expect Wadlow's chart to contain some exceptional features, but in fact I can see nothing in his chart that would help to explain his tallness.

As well as having a body, we also develop a thinking and feeling mind. The mind, like the body, is influenced by genetic and environmental factors, and in one sense I think that it, too, is not influenced by the birth chart. For instance, AstroDatabank have the birth chart of a boy[2] whom they describe as "a genius with an IQ of over 180", but, once again, I can see nothing in this chart that would explain the exceptional quality of the boy's mind. At the other extreme, the Earl of Arundel (only son of the Duke of Norfolk)[3] was "born blind, deaf, dumb, lame, and never came to the use of his faculties"; but this could not be deduced from studying his birth chart.

However, the mind is not just a thinking machine. It is also the source of the ego, which has been described as "not who we are, but who we think we are". In the course of our lifetimes, we build stories around ourselves. We see ourselves as being a particular kind of person, and this influences our choices about how we think, how we feel and how we act. We develop a *personality* that makes us different from other people.

It is at this level (the ego level) that I believe that the birth chart exercises an influence. It seems to be the case that, at the moment when we emerge from the womb, the umbilical cord is cut, and we embark on life as an independent person, the pattern which the planets form in the sky at that moment imprints itself upon our virgin mind, and affects the way in which our ego develops. We tend to develop a personality which accords with the messages which the planets sent to us at the time of our birth. It is as though there was a consciousness in the planets themselves, which communicates to the consciousness that is present in us.

And it also seems to be the case that, throughout our lives, we are influenced by the patterns which the planets form in the sky. In studying mundane charts (the charts for events other than births), I am impressed by the fact that the chart is often descriptive of the mindset of the person (or people) who caused the event to occur. For instance, in the case of air and rail crashes, the chart often gives indications of the state of mind (e.g. negligence, stress, foolhardiness, deliberate sabotage) of the people who caused the crash. (I will give some examples of this later in the book.) It seems, for instance, that, if the chart for a particular time contains a very high level of Twoness (which is indicative of stress), then people in general will tend at that time to feel more stressed than at other times, and this will sometimes lead to dramatic events that are caused by high stress levels.

However, if the crash was caused not by human action but by technical problems, there is no indication of this in the chart. Similarly, if we look at charts of volcanic eruptions[4] or of earthquakes[5], which again are events not caused by human action, the chart seems to give no clear indication of the nature of the event. So it seems that the influence which the planets exert is not physical, but exists only at the level of *consciousness.* (Of course we know that the movements of the Sun and the Moon affect the Earth physically, for instance by creating the tides. But it would seem that the influence of the other planets is more subtle, and cannot be detected at the physical level.[6])

Thus, the planets affect us mainly at the level of the ego. But the ego can be transcended, and this implies that the influence of the birth chart can also be transcended. We can learn to grow beyond the ego, and to realize our true nature as pure consciousness and Oneness. An example of someone who achieved this completely is Ramana Maharshi, whom we will consider in Chapter 18. Not many people have transcended the ego as fully as Ramana Maharshi, but many people have achieved it partially, not destroying the ego but developing the ability to witness it from outside and to realize that it is "not who we are, but who we think we are". The study of the birth chart can help us to do this: it is, in a sense, a 'map of the ego', which we can witness from outside.

So we can now look at the part played by each of the planets in constructing this 'map of the ego'.

The Sun and the Moon

The Sun and the Moon together represent the ego itself: how the person sees himself or herself. The Sun represents the *proactive* side of the ego, and the Moon represents the *reactive* side. The difference between the Sun and the Moon is like the difference between *yang* and *yin*.

The Sun is oriented towards the future. It says not only "This is how I am", but also "This is how I want to be, in order to be fully myself". It shows the person striving to make a success of his or her life, and to find happiness and self-fulfilment. It shows the ways in which the person wants to affect other people and to change the world. Aspects to the Sun show the opportunities and challenges which the person faces in his or her path towards fulfilment.

It has been said that the ego is never satisfied: it always wants more. Negatively, we could say that the Sun represents this restless seeking for a goal that can never be attained. However, we should not be too dismissive about it. The Sun represents the life-force, the burning heart of individuality. It is the desire to *shine* in the world. Even though this desire is doomed to failure (we will fail to reach our goals, and then we will die), and even though it can lead to terrible acts of inhumanity as we struggle to overcome those who stand in our way, it is still in itself a beautiful thing: maybe we can learn to use it benevolently, using our shining light to bring warmth and colour into the lives of others.

The Moon is oriented towards the past. It says not only "This is how I am", but also "This is how I have become what I am". It is concerned with the ways in which the person feels he or she has been treated by the world. It shows the ways in which he or she responds to events in the present (which is of course influenced by events in the past). It shows especially the *feelings* which the person has about his or her life.

We could say that the Moon is concerned with 'the ego as victim'. It is the side of the ego that tends to say, "Poor me: look at how badly the world has treated me: there's nothing I can do about it". But again, we should not be too dismissive. The positive side of the Moon is to do with *acceptance*: the capacity to be intensely aware of one's environment, to have strong feelings about what is happening, and yet to be aware that this is how life is and that nothing needs to change. Happiness can come from simply being present in the world and feeling oneself to be an integral part of it.

Aspects to the Sun (especially when they are close) are always very important for the interpretation of the chart. The same is potentially true of aspects to the Moon, but here we have a problem, due to the speed with which the Moon moves through the zodiac. Within a single hour, the Moon moves more than half a degree, and this half-degree is enough to radically alter the Moon's harmonic links with other planets. Therefore, unless we know that we have a very accurate time for the birth or other event, the Moon's aspects should be treated with caution. (I will say more about this in Appendix 1.)

Mercury, Venus and Mars

These three inner planets are concerned with the goals of the ego, and with its ways of acting in the world and interacting with other people. To put it simply, we can say that Mercury is about the desire for understanding, Venus is about the desire for love, and Mars is about the desire for power.

Mercury wants to believe that it is wise and intelligent; Venus wants to believe that it is beautiful, attractive, and worthy of love; and Mars wants to believe that it is strong and powerful.

Mercury interacts with other people by communicating with them and trying to persuade them that what it says is right. Venus interacts by trying to attract other people towards it. Mars interacts by trying to exercise power over them.

All of these are the ways in which the ego strives to get what it wants and so gain happiness and self-fulfilment. So far, there is no morality in the picture. Mercury, Venus and Mars (and also Sun and Moon) are essentially a-moral.

The Outer Planets

When we come to the outer planets, we start to deal with morality. Jupiter, Saturn, Uranus, Neptune, Pluto and Chiron are all concerned with *moral principles*. Each believes that certain things are right, and other things are wrong.

Jupiter believes in the principle of growth and freedom. It believes that it is right to grow and expand as much as possible and to overcome all obstacles and difficulties. It believes that everything is possible.

Saturn believes in the opposite principle of control and limitation. It believes that it is right to accept one's limitations and to be realistic about what one can achieve. It believes in tackling life's problems in a controlled and disciplined way.

Uranus believes in the principle of individuality and originality. It believes it is right to try to express, as clearly and sharply as possible, one's uniqueness and one's difference from other people. It believes in establishing sharp boundaries between Self and Other.

Neptune believes in the opposite principle of universality and idealism. It believes it is right to throw one's lot in with the common lot of humanity and to work towards common goals. It believes in blurring the boundaries, and in minimizing the difference between Self and Other.

Pluto believes in the principle of dedication and single-mindeness. It abhors vacillation and indecision. It believes it is right to work steadfastly and ruthlessly towards one's goals.

Chiron believes in the principle of service. It believes it is right to try to find one's place in the world, and to find how best to be of service to humanity.

Despite its self-centredness and its overriding concern with its own survival and its own happiness, the ego is a moral entity. It wants to do right, and it blames and judges itself if it does wrong. It admires others who do right, and judges others who do wrong. But what is right and what is wrong? The interaction between the different moral principles represented by the outer planets, and also their links with the inner planets, can tell us much about the moral path which a particular individual will choose to follow.

And yet it is perhaps surprising that there is no planet which unequivocally represents the principle which I see as being at the heart of morality. I am told that there is a Native American tribe which believes that the whole of morality can be summed up in one sentence: "Nothing shall be done to harm the children". This principle – that one should help and protect, rather than harming, those who are weaker than oneself – is not clearly represented by any planet in the chart (although Neptune and Chiron carry a little of its flavour). Maybe this is because it is overriding and all-inclusive, and because the realization of its importance comes not from any one factor, but from one's overall awareness of the human condition and the human predicament.

Other Planets?

Astronomers now tell us that Pluto is not a planet after all, and Chiron, which is a maverick asteroid, was never categorized as a planet by astronomers. Yet these two bodies appear to exercise a power within the chart that is comparable even to that exercised by the giant planets Jupiter and Saturn. Clearly the astrological power exerted by a planet is not directly related to its size.

And this makes one wonder whether there are other heavenly bodies that should also be included in the chart. Probably the strongest candidates for inclusion are Ceres, Pallas, Vesta and Juno, which are the four largest of the asteroids within the asteroid belt between Mars and Jupiter. The astrological meanings of these asteroids are discussed by Demetra George and Douglas Bloch in their book *Asteroid Goddesses*.[7] Recently I have started to include these four asteroids in the chart, and I feel that they are potentially very valuable in chart interpretation. However, I have not included them in this book, as I do not yet have enough experience of using them in harmonic astrology.

3

Oneness

We can now start on our journey through the prime numbers, starting with the number One.

We all think we know what Oneness means, and yet there is a paradox at the heart of the meaning of the number One. On the one hand, One stands for isolation and separation; in the words of the song, "One is One and all alone and evermore shall be so". But on the other hand, when we are talking about Two (or a higher number) coming together into One, then we are talking not about isolation but about its opposite, which is unity and at-Oneness. In the words of Jesus in the Gospel of Thomas, "When the Two shall become One … then shall you enter the Kingdom".

The same paradox is present if we look at the number One in a more strictly numerical sense. On the one hand, One is entirely separate and distinct from all other numbers. If you multiply Two by Two, or Three by Three, you get a new number; but if you multiply One by One, and even if you continue to do so an infinite number of times, you still get One. But on the other hand, One is intimately linked to all other numbers, since every number is a multiple of itself and One. One can in fact be seen as the glue that binds all the other numbers together, since they are all linked by being multiples of One.

Another (related) paradox is that, although One is the smallest number, it refers to the largest reality. Oneness carries the idea of 'everything brought together into One', and thus of enormous size and power. Oneness is about *inclusiveness:* everything is included within it. (The word 'universe' comes from the Latin for One.) When Gandalf, in *The Lord of the Rings*, says "This is the One Ring that rules them all," he is not saying that there are no other rings; he is saying that the powers of all the other rings are included in the power of this One Ring.

All this makes One a truly mystical and magical number, in a way that no other number can aspire to be. Mystics have always seen Oneness (Oneness with God, or with the whole universe) as the goal, and also as the only true reality, with everything else as an illusion. In many psychologies the goal is internal Oneness: thus in Psychosynthesis, the goal is synthesis, which means the bringing together of the warring elements of the psyche (sub-personalities) into a state of Oneness or absence of conflict, unified by the 'I', which is the awareness of one's essential Self. The idea of Oneness is closely associated with the idea of peace, since peace is the absence of division, separation and conflict. It is also associated with the ideas of stability, constancy, and permanence.

In astrology, the conjunction (which is the aspect of Oneness) has always been seen to represent union between the planets involved: the two (or more) planets merge into One, and so become one united force. Most charts contain at least one conjunction of two planets, but conjunctions of three or more planets are comparatively rare. In order to find out more about the meaning of Oneness, we need to look at those charts which have the largest (or closest) conjunctions, so as to identify the people (or events) that have the greatest concentration of Oneness in their charts.

In this chapter we will look at some examples of people who have exceptionally high levels of Oneness in their birth charts. What do these people have in common? My suggestion is that they all have a core of stillness, solidity and permanence at the heart of their personality. The planets that are in conjunction have merged into One, and so are at peace with one another and have no need to act out their differences.

We can imagine that if a person had all eleven planets in conjunction (which is theoretically possible but in practice never happens), they would be in a state of pure Beingness and enlightenment, in which no action (or at least no ego-driven action) was necessary. They would have transcended the ego, or perhaps we could say that there would be no ego to transcend. If a person has four or five planets in conjunction, there are still conflicts, desires and stresses arising from the other planets that are outside the conjunction, but these stresses take place against a background of peacefulness and inner certainty that is represented by the conjunction. Moreover, the conjunction itself can act as a very powerful force, stimulating the person into action, the nature of which will depend on the relationship between the conjunction and the other planets in the chart.

Hence it seems to me that these people with very high levels of Oneness are all very *singular* people, who did their own thing and did it in a unique and individual way, apparently uninfluenced by the people around them, and often in defiance of the conventions of their society. Often there is a sense of great powerfulness, which I believe to be related to a quality of straightforwardness, single-mindedness and one-pointedness. With these people, one does not feel a need to say "On the one hand this, but on the other hand that". There is an absence of contradiction and paradox, and a sense that these people are 'all of a piece' and are at One with themselves.

Padre Pio, Josemaria Escriva, and Pierre Teilhard de Chardin

Padre Pio
Born 25 May 1887, 17.00 (–00.50) (birth name: Francesco Forgione)
Pietrelcina, Italy (41N12. 14E51).
Source: Birth certificate, via Bordoni (ADB). RR: AA.

((SO–_1_–PL)–1/_1_–ME)–1/1/1/_1_/_1_/1–(MA–_1_–NE)
MO–1–VE
VE–_1_–SA

Josemaria Escriva de Balaguer
Born 9 January 1902, 22.00 (+00.00)
Barbastro, Spain (42N02. 0E08).
Source: Baptismal certificate given by A.C. Borbon in *Opus Judei* p.123 (ADB). RR: AA.

(SO–_1_–MO–_1_–SA)–_1_–(ME–_1_–JU)
               –1–CH

Pierre Teilhard de Chardin
Born 1 May 1881, 07.00 (–00.12)
Orcines, France (45N46. 3E04).
Source: Birth certificate, via Gauquelin (ADB). RR: AA.

((VE–_1_–NE)–_1_–SO)–1–(JU–_1_–SA)
               –_1_/_1_/1–CH

We will start by looking at three spiritual leaders who all had quintuple conjunctions (all involving the Sun) in their charts, and so were exceptionally strong in Oneness. All of them were Catholic priests, but they each pursued their own paths. Two of them (Pio and Teilhard) were vilified by the Vatican in their lifetime; and yet two of them (Pio and Escriva) have now been pronounced to be saints.

Padre Pio was possibly the most saintly person to have lived in the twentieth century. He bore the stigmata of the Cross for fifty years, and was credited with innumerable miracles of healing and also with powers of prediction (he told Karol Wojtyla, when the latter was a young man, that one day he would be Pope). He often went into an ecstatic trance, and was credited with 'bilocation' (the ability to be seen in more than one place at the same time). He was in continuous pain, and was also constantly reviled and attacked by the Church, but he was sustained by the love of the people who flocked to him and supported him. It has been said that "over and over, Padre Pio kept stressing Christ's love".[1] He founded a hospital which he called the House for the Relief of Suffering, and he said that he wanted this hospital to be a place where "patients, doctors and priests will be reservoirs of love which will be more abundant in as much as it will be shared with others".

Padre Pio's quintuple conjunction brings together the Sun (representing the Self), Mercury and Mars (which together represent forceful communication), and Neptune and Pluto (the principle of reaching out to others, and the principle of single-minded dedication). The Sun-Pluto conjunction is especially close. We can see here the origins of Padre Pio's extraordinary powers. We must remember that, because these planets come together in Oneness (rather than in some other number), there is no conflict between them: there is not even any sense of pleasure or of creative effort in bringing them together: they are simply merged into One single united – and we could say irresistible – force, which (in Padre Pio's case) enabled him to withstand all of his physical pain and all the attacks against him by people who were afraid of his powers. This force can be used for either good or evil, and I think it is not always possible to tell from the birth chart in what direction it will be used. In Padre Pio's case it was used for good.

Josemaria Escriva was the founder of the Catholic order called Opus Dei ('The Work of God'). Both Opus Dei and its founder have attracted a great deal of hostility, mainly because of accusations of elitism, so it is important to assert that Escriva's intentions were not at all elitist. His goal can be summed up in the words "Everyone can be a saint". On his website [2] there is a moving description of the vision which inspired him to found Opus Dei: a vision of ordinary people, of every nation and race, devoting their lives to God and so being transformed into saints.

Escriva was a deeply devout man who pursued his goals with passionate and single-minded intensity throughout his life, overcoming many obstacles and setbacks. Like Padre Pio, he was racked by physical pain, but learnt to accept the pain and convert it into compassion for the suffering of others. Like Padre Pio, he was inspired by the example of Christ's love, and he himself inspired passionate love among his followers.

Escriva has a quintuple conjunction of Sun, Moon, Mercury, Jupiter and Saturn, including an exact Mercury-Jupiter conjunction and a Sun-Moon-Saturn conjunction which is very nearly exact. The coming together of Sun and Moon (so that there is no separation between his proactive and reactive selves) suggests an even more intense Oneness. When Jupiter and Saturn come together, there is an ability to pursue expansive goals in a controlled and disciplined manner, which was certainly true of Escriva.

The third of our Catholic visionaries is Pierre Teilhard de Chardin. Teilhard was not only a Jesuit priest but also a palaeontologist, biologist and philosopher, whose aim was to integrate religious experience with natural science, and in particular to reconcile Darwin's theory of evolution with Christian theology. He believed that this "convergence of systems" would lead to a "new state of peace and planetary unity". [3]

As with Padre Pio, Teilhard's spirituality was centred on Love. He wrote: "Some day after we have mastered the winds, the waves and gravity ... we will harness for God the energies of love, and then, for a second time in the history of the world, man will have discovered fire". In one of his rare personal statements, he wrote: "However far I go into my memories ... I can distinguish in myself the presence of a strictly dominant passion: the passion for the Absolute". [4] We can perhaps see the Absolute as a synonym for Oneness.

Teilhard's quintuple conjunction involves Sun, Venus, Jupiter, Saturn and Neptune, with very close conjunctions of Venus and Neptune and of Jupiter and Saturn. The Venus-Neptune conjunction is very strongly suggestive of his love for the Earth and for the whole of humanity.

We can note also that both Escriva and Teilhard have Chiron in conjunction with some of the planets in the main conjunction. This is suggestive of their desire to be of service to humanity.

Helen Duncan, Meurig Morris and Matthew Manning

Helen Duncan
Born 25 November 1897, 03.00 (+00.00)
Callander, Scotland (56N16. 4W14).
Source: Birth certificate, via Caroline Gerard (ADB). RR: AA.

(SO–1–MA–1–SA)–1–(MO–1–ME)
                    –1–UR)–1–CH

Meurig Morris
Born 17 November 1899, 14.30 (+00.00)
London, England (51N30. 0W10).
Source: from her, via *Scientific Astrology* 7/1931 (ADB). RR: A.

(((VE–1–MA)–1–UR)–1/1/1–CH)–1/1/1/1–ME
((ME–1–CH)–1/1–VE)–1/1/1–SA
SO–1–JU

Matthew Manning
Born 17 August 1955, 16.15 (–01.00)
Redruth, England (50N13. 5W14).
Source: from his personal assistant, via Frank C. Clifford (ADB). RR: A.

((SO–1–MA)–1–(MO–1–VE))–1/1/1/1–JU
                          –1/1/1/1–PL
(SO–1–PL)–1–ME

Our next cases are three people who (like Padre Pio) had remarkable psychic powers.

Helen Duncan was the last person to be convicted as a witch in Britain. In her séances she allegedly emitted from her nose a white liquid, 'ectoplasm', from which would emerge the solid shape of a deceased person, who would then converse with his or her loved ones in the audience. In her trial the prosecution did not deny that these things appeared to happen, but they claimed that the ectoplasm was cheesecloth which she had regurgitated (though an X-ray revealed her intestines to be normal). Helen Duncan had (and still has) many supporters, including Winston Churchill, who visited her in prison and then repealed the Witchcraft Act at the earliest opportunity. It seems that Duncan was a self-effacing person, not seeking anything for herself through her work, and carrying it out purely for the benefit of the people who were helped.

Meurig Morris was a trance-medium who, according to her AstroDatabank biography, "exhibited her skills in public halls with a trance guide named 'Power'. While on stage her soprano voice changed to baritone, her body stiffened with dignity and command, and she was able to preach for 45 minutes without faltering". So powerful was her oratory as 'Power' that she was called "one of the greatest woman orators of today," yet she herself was described (admittedly in a patronizing way which reflects the gender and class prejudices of the writer) as "a charming yet extremely simple West-country woman" with "a sterling character".[5]

Matthew Manning is well-known as a healer who, as a teenager, exhibited extraordinary psychic powers. Perhaps the most remarkable of these powers was his ability to produce automatic drawings: by focusing on the name of an artist, he produced drawings that were so much in the style of that artist that many art experts were fooled. In scientific tests it was discovered that Manning was producing a brain wave pattern that had never previously been reported, and that originated in the oldest, most primitive part of the brain. Manning's book *The Link* became a best-seller, and he was in danger of becoming a celebrity: but in 1977, as a result of a spiritual experience in the Himalayas, he resolved to withdraw from the public eye and to devote himself only to healing and to work which was of benefit to others.

All of these three people have a massive multiple conjunction in their birth chart (the details of which are listed above), and it would seem that – although not all psychics are strong in Oneness, and not all people strong in Oneness are psychic – strength in Oneness is very conducive to the development of psychic powers. My own belief is that this is linked to the one-pointedness, and also to the powerfulness, of

Oneness. People with high levels of Oneness are able to focus powerfully on one particular goal or activity, and to pursue this steadfastly throughout their lives. They may wish to help other people, but they have little need to be helped: they *know* what their lives are about. In Manning's case I believe that his Oneness is linked to his decision to forgo personal fame and to use his gifts in the service of others. He has stuck to this decision with the steadfastness, single-mindedness and inner certainty which seem to be characteristic of people with high levels of Oneness.

We can note also that in Meurig Morris's case (unlike all the other cases that we have so far considered) the Sun is not involved in the conjunction. This suggests that, although she knew that she had within herself this extremely powerful force, it was separate from her sense of her own identity – it was not who she believed herself to be. So she had to create an 'alter ego', an alternative personality that could express all the power that she believed that she herself lacked.

Lucky Luciano
Born 24 November 1897, 12.00 (–01.00)
Lercara Friddi, Sicily (37N45. 13E36).
Source: Birth certificate, via Bordoni (ADB). RR: AA.

$$((\underline{SO}\text{–}\mathbf{1}\text{–}\underline{MO}\text{–}\mathbf{1}\text{–}\underline{MA}\text{–}\mathbf{1}\text{–}\underline{SA})\text{–}1\text{–}\underline{UR})\text{–}1\text{–}CH$$
$$\text{–}1\text{–}\underline{ME}$$

Lest we should think that people with strong Oneness charts are all 'good' people working selflessly for the benefit of mankind, we can move now to the other end of the moral spectrum and look at the Mafia boss Charles 'Lucky' Luciano. Luciano was born in Sicily but moved to New York with his parents at the age of ten. By ruthless elimination of his rivals, he eventually became the super-boss of the American Mafia. He was nicknamed Lucky because he had survived a murder attempt in which his throat was cut and he was left for dead. He lived in a suite at the Waldorf Astoria, from where he controlled "bootlegging, narcotics, prostitution, the waterfront, the unions, food marts, bakeries and the garment trade ... infiltrating and corrupting legitimate business, politics and law enforcement".[6] He was always expensively dressed, with a beautiful woman on his arm, and he was a friend of celebrities including Frank Sinatra.

Eventually Luciano was charged with multiple counts of compulsory prostitution and sentenced to 30 to 50 years in prison, but continued to rule his empire from his cell. During World War II he helped the US Government by giving the orders that tightened security in the docks and ended the possibility of sabotage. As a result of this he was let out of prison and deported to Italy, where he continued to direct narcotics operations, and where he died.

Luciano has perhaps the strongest Oneness chart that I have seen, involving seven planets. We can note that he was born just 14 hours before Helen Duncan, and his Sun-Mars-Saturn-Uranus conjunction is the same as hers, but in Luciano's case the Moon is also involved. So what does a flamboyant character like Luciano have in common with a self-effacing person like Duncan? The answer, I believe, is that they both have the one-pointedness and inner certainty that is characteristic of Oneness. Both of them devoted their whole lives to a single cause, in defiance of the society in which they lived, and persisted in their activities in spite of imprisonment and other severe setbacks. We can note also that in Luciano's case all the planets in the conjunction are close to the Midheaven, causing him to act them out in the world to a far greater extent than Duncan.

Henri Landru

Born 12 April 1869, 06.00 (–00.09)
Paris, France (48N50. 2E20).
Source: Birth records, via T. Pat Davis (ADB). RR: AA.

((SO–**1**–MO)–1/**1**–JU)–1/**1**/1/1/1/1–(VE–**1**–NE)
(ME–**1**–CH)–1–VE

The French serial killer Henri Landru, known as 'Bluebeard', was a smooth talker who developed a formidable skill in swindling people out of their money. More than 300 people (most, but not all, of whom were women) are thought to have suffered financially at his hands. He killed his victims only when he felt it desirable to do so for self-protection. Eleven women and one boy (and two dogs) 'disappeared' after meeting him. His method of killing is unknown, but he is thought to have burnt their bodies. He appears to have had absolutely no remorse for his actions.

Landru has a quintuple conjunction of Sun, Moon, Venus, Jupiter and Neptune, with Venus also widely conjunct to Mercury and Chiron. He displays all of the inner certainty of Oneness, doing just what he wanted to do (we can note that he is also very strong in the Threeness principle of pleasure) and caring nothing for what other people thought of him. Like Luciano, he shows how Oneness can lead to 'evil' as well as good actions.

Charles Baudelaire and Algernon Swinburne

Charles Baudelaire
Born 9 April 1821, 15.00 (–00.09)
Paris, France (48N52. 2E20).
Source: Birth certificate, via Gauquelin (ADB). RR: AA.

(VE–**1**–JU–**1**–CH)–1–(SO–**1**–SA)
                                        –1–(MA–**1**–PL)
(ME–**1**–PL)–1/**1**–MA)–1–VE
UR–**1**–NE

Algernon Swinburne
Born 5 April 1837, 05.00 (+00.00)
London, England (51N30. 0W10).
Source: From biography by J.O. Fuller, via Gene Lockhart (ADB). RR: B.

(SO–**1**–MO–**1**–PL)–1–(ME–**1**–_VE_)
MA–**1**–JU

These two poets, both very strong in Oneness, have many similarities to each other: the adjective 'decadent' is often applied to both of them. Swinburne, who was the younger by 16 years, was in fact a great admirer of Baudelaire, and translated many of his poems into English.

Baudelaire's Oneness is exceptionally strong: he has a conjunction of SO–1–VE–1–JU–1–SA–1–CH, with Venus also –1–ME–1–MA–1–PL, and also an almost exact conjunction of UR–**1**–NE. Thus, the Moon is the only one of his eleven planets which is not part of a conjunction. Baudelaire was a mystic who was in love with the beauty of amorality or of evil: his collection of poems is called _Les Fleurs du Mal_ or _The Flowers of Evil_. He called himself a Satanist, and saw himself as a fallen angel.

He spent money wildly, dyed his hair green, and resolutely refused to do anything conventional. His lifelong liaison was with a drug-addicted prostitute, who was the "Black Venus" of his poems. He died of syphilis at the age of 46.

Swinburne has SO–1–MO–1–ME–1–VE–1–PL, with SO–**1**–MO–**1**–PL very close and ME–**1**–VE also very close, and in addition a very close MA–**1**–JU. He was in many ways a similar character to Baudelaire. According to one website,[7] he was "an excessive and passionate personality" who "had a craving for what was sensational and exotic". He "appeared to be a bisexual masochist who read and admired the work of the Marquis de Sade". William Rossetti said of him,[8] "No man living has a more vigorous command of the powers of invective", but also said, "No one can be more affectionate, sweet-natured and confiding, than Algernon Swinburne". Like Baudelaire, Swinburne sought to create beauty in his poetry, but sought the beauty in what the world sees as evil or, at least, as amoral. We should remember that Oneness is the level at which everything is at One and there is no good and bad, no right and wrong. Maybe we can say that both Baudelaire and Swinburne were in touch with this Oneness and sought to express the beauty and love which are in all things, in the dark as well as the light.

Eva Marie Saint
Born 4 July 1924, 17.25 (+04.00)
Newark, NJ, USA (40N44. 74W10).
Source: Birth certificate, via Gauquelin Book of American Charts (ADB). RR: AA.

(SO–**1**–ME–**1**–PL)–1–VE

Eva Marie Saint, the star of *On the Waterfront* and *North by Northwest*, has a quadruple conjunction of Sun, Mercury, Venus and Pluto. She has, in my perception, a quality of inner stillness, which gives her a great cinematic presence. She has never been part of the Hollywood 'jet set', but nor has she rebelled against it: she lives quietly in California, she loves the sea, she has been happily married for fifty years, and she is proud of having been part of cinematic history.

Other women who, in my view, have this same quality of inner stillness include **Pauline Collins**,[9] the star of *Shirley Valentine*, who has conjunctions of Sun-Mercury-Mars and Jupiter-Saturn, and the tennis star **Chris Evert**,[10] who has conjunctions of Sun-Mercury, Moon-Venus-Saturn, and Jupiter-Uranus. It seems possible that this quality – which cannot be discerned from a biography, but can be detected if one has seen the person in the flesh or on film or television – is common to all or most of the people who have strong Oneness charts. If so, we can say that this inner stillness is close to the essence of Oneness.

Sabine Dardenne
Born 28 October 1983, 09.20 (–01.00)
Tournai, Belgium (50N36. 3E23).
Source: Birth certificate, via Petitallot (ADB). RR: AA.

(SO–<u>1</u>–ME)–<u>1</u>–SA)–<u>1/1</u>/1–PL
<u>VE</u>–<u>1</u>–<u>MA</u>

At the age of 12, Sabine Dardenne was kidnapped by the notorious paedophile Marc Dutroux and held in a dungeon for 80 days, during which time she was repeatedly raped and sexually abused. However, she stood up to him as best she could, constantly pestering him, complaining, badgering, demanding. Since her release she has persistently refused to be cast as a victim or to be the object of pity and compassion, preferring to put the past behind her and to get on with her life. She has, however, written a book, *I Choose to Live*, "in order to get people off her back". She has said "I'm very strong-willed … In his cellar, I knew what was important for me was to see my family again. So I didn't give up, I kept going".[11] Jon Henley, who interviewed her for *The Guardian* nine years after her release, said: "In her determination, her detachment and her lucidity, the girl is extraordinary".[11] Dardenne has a quadruple conjunction of Sun, Mercury, Saturn and Pluto, together with a very close conjunction of Venus and Mars on the Midheaven, and I believe that this very large dose of Oneness helped to give her the inner certainty and self-assurance which enabled her to survive her ordeal with so little trauma.

Mata Hari
Born 7 August 1876, 13.00 (–00.23)
Leeuwarden, Netherlands (53N12. 5E46).
Source: Birth certificate, via Steinbrecher (ADB). RR: AA.

((SO–**1**–MA)–<u>1</u>/<u>1</u>–ME)–<u>1</u>–UR
MO–<u>1</u>–<u>SA</u>

Another person with great charisma and single-mindedness, and with a
close quadruple conjunction in her chart, was Margaretha Zelle, known
as Mata Hari, who has been called the world's first striptease dancer.
After leaving her violent husband she obtained work first as a circus
horse rider, then as an artist's model, and finally as an exotic dancer, in
which role she was an instant success. She had relationships with many
high-ranking military officers in several countries, and during World
War I she was accused (rightly or wrongly) of being a double agent, and
was put to death by firing squad. On the morning of her execution she
dressed up in her finest clothes: "this lady knows how to die," said the
sergeant-major who helped her.

Christine Keeler
Born 22 February 1942, 11.15 (–01.00)
London, England (51N30.0W10).
Source: "Abayakoon in *AQ* 12/1963 vouches for the accuracy of the
data" (ADB). RR: A.

(MO–<u>1</u>–UR)–1–(MA–<u>1</u>–SA)   (MA–<u>1</u>–SA is exact)
ME–1–<u>VE</u>

Christine Keeler, whose simultaneous affairs with a British cabinet
minister and a Russian (alleged) spy nearly caused the downfall of the
British government, has a quadruple conjunction of Moon, Mars, Saturn
and Uranus (and also a wide conjunction of Mercury and Venus near the
Midheaven). However, we should note that, unlike most of the other
cases that we have considered in this chapter, Keeler's Oneness links do
not include the Sun. The Sun, as I see it, represents a person's perception
of their purpose in life, or their view of their identity. Thus, Keeler's
charisma and sexual powerfulness belong to her instinctive Moon-
nature, and not to her purposive Sun-nature. This may be why Keeler,

despite having achieved a reputation as a *femme fatale* comparable to that of Mata Hari, has sought in later life to distance herself from this and to say, in effect, "That wasn't the real me".

King George III
Born 4 June 1738, 06.30 (+00.00)
London, England (51N30. 0W10).
Source: From Pamela Clark, Deputy Registrar of the Royal Archives ("between 6.00 and 7.00 a.m.") (ADB). RR: A.

((VE–**1**–SA)–**1/1**–ME)–**1/1/1**–NE

King George III may seem an odd person to include in this discussion of Oneness, but he has a strong quadruple conjunction and so cannot be ignored. However, we should note that George's conjunction – of Mercury, Venus, Saturn and Neptune – does not include either the Sun or the Moon. It seems possible (although this is pure speculation) that such a strong union of planetary forces, if it is separate both from one's purposive Sun-personality and from one's instinctive Moon-personality, may have a destabilizing effect on the personality as a whole, and so may have been a contributory cause of the unusual form of madness to which George eventually succumbed.

The Storming of the Bastille and the Breach of the Berlin Wall

Storming of the Bastille
14 July 1789, 13.30 (–00.09)
Paris, France (48N52. 2E20).
Source: Wikipedia. (This was the time when "the crowd surged into the undefended outer courtyard, and the chains on the drawbridge to the inner courtyard were cut. About this time gunfire began").

SO–**1**–ME–**1**–CH
(<u>VE</u>–**1**–UR)–**1**–<u>JU</u>

Breach of the Berlin Wall
9 November 1989, 22.30 (–01.00)
Berlin, Germany (52N31. 13E23).
Source: Wikipedia. (This was the time when East Germans first walked freely through the checkpoint.)

(SO–**1**–ME)–1/**1**–PL
(VE–**1**–UR)–1/**1**/1/1–(SA–**1**–NE)
JU–1–CH

Finally in this chapter, we will look at three mundane charts. The first two of these are the charts for two very similar events, 200 years apart, both of which changed the course of history: the storming of the Bastille, which precipitated the French Revolution, and the breach of the Berlin Wall, which precipitated the end of Communist rule in Eastern Europe. In both cases, a huge crowd of angry civilians had gathered, and this crowd, by its sheer force and determination, was able to break through and destroy the structures which represented the oppressive regime.

We can see that in both charts there are two multiple conjunctions: in one case SO–**1**–ME–**1**–CH, in the other case (SO–**1**–ME)–1/**1**–PL; in one case (VE–**1**–UR)–1–*JU*, in the other case (VE–**1**–UR)–1–(SA–**1**–NE). Together, these conjunctions represent the irresistible force of Oneness. The crowd was determined to get what it wanted, and nothing would stand in their way. The very close conjunction of Venus and Uranus, which occurs in both charts, suggests a clean break, a radical breakthrough, a thrilling beauty.

La Belle Dame Sans Merci
21 April 1819, 19.00 (+00.00)
London, England (51N30. 0W10).
Source: *John Keats* by Robert Gittings (see below).

((MO–**1**–SA–**1**–PL)–1–MA)–1–VE
                              –1–CH

We will end this chapter by looking at the chart for the time when John Keats was inspired to write his poem *La Belle Dame Sans Merci*. This is the poem which begins:

O what can ail thee, knight-at-arms,
Alone and palely loitering?
The sedge is withered from the lake
    And no birds sing.

The poem is a parable of men's fear that they will be bewitched, ensnared, enslaved and emasculated by the beautiful, wild, seductive, devouring female, and then finally cast out, a pale shadow of their former selves, into a world in which "no birds sing". This is an incredibly important theme. It is arguable that the whole history of men's subjugation of women, over the centuries and across the globe, is due to this fear. Men have done to women what they fear that women (if they were free) would do to men – except that men have enslaved women by sheer force and brutality, rather than by the use of the subtle arts which they fear in women.

In a letter to his brother George, Keats says that he felt a desire to "restrain the headlong impetuosity of his Muse"[12] while writing this poem. It is as though the poem 'came at him' like a bolt from the blue. Whereas most of his poems (such as *Ode to a Nightingale*) were slowly and meticulously worked out, this one was written at great speed and has an air of great simplicity and urgency. (Keats tried to revise the poem later, but the revised version is greatly inferior to the original.)

The chart is somewhat speculative, since Gittings[13] says only that Keats wrote the poem "on the evening" of 21st April, and I have chosen a chart for 7.00 p.m. However, conjunctions are longer-lasting than other aspects, and the sextuple conjunction is likely to have been operative for most of the evening.

The chart is remarkable not only for its sextuple conjunction of Moon, Saturn and Pluto (very close), Mars (close), and (more widely) Venus and Chiron, but also for its lack of any other strong harmonic aspects. It is as though the whole force of the chart is concentrated in the conjunction. The Sun is not involved, so Keats himself stands outside it, watching the "headlong impetuosity" of his Muse. We can see the Moon as representing the Muse which compelled him to write the poem, and also as representing the Belle Dame herself (Moon conjunct Saturn, Pluto and Mars as the image of the devouring female). The chart is a graphic illustration of the all-consuming power of Oneness.

Conclusion

We have now looked at a number of cases of people with exceptionally high levels of Oneness in their charts, and I think we can see that – at least when the Sun is involved in the conjunction – they are all people who pursued their goals with great single-mindedness and consistency, and who seem to have had a quality of inner certainty and stillness, a lack of self-doubt, which enabled them to stay true to themselves, or to their perception of themselves, throughout their lives. These are people who know what their lives are about. Whatever they do, they do it in original ways that owe little to precedent or convention. They are able to overcome tremendous *external* obstacles and difficulties because they have relatively few *internal* obstacles and difficulties with which to deal. Often they have great charisma, and are able to inspire great love and devotion among their followers and admirers. Some (but not all) of them have exceptional psychic gifts.

However, in those cases (Meurig Morris, Christine Keeler and George III) where the Sun is *not* involved in the conjunction, we have a different picture. In the absence of more cases it is hard to be sure about this, but it seems that, if the Sun represents one's view of one's own identity, then to have a powerful union of planets *apart from* the Sun may create a split in the personality (on the one hand I feel I am this, but on the other hand I feel impelled to be that) which can lead to unhappiness and even to madness.

We have been looking at these people in terms of their *actions*, because that is what is known about them. However, I feel that Oneness is essentially not about *doing* but about *being*. The more Oneness a person has in his or her make-up, the more he or she will be able to just *be* the inner stillness without having to *do* anything about it. Probably, for every person who feels impelled to act out their Oneness in the world, there are hundreds of others (also with high levels of Oneness in their charts) who live quiet and unassuming lives, just *being* the way they want to be, and so finding great happiness.

4

Twoness

Twoness is what happens when the One splits, or separates, into Two. This separation is the first action in the creation of the multiplicity of things out of the primordial Oneness. Twoness therefore stands for *separation*.

It also stands for *relationship* and *awareness*. Within Oneness there can be no relationship. However, as soon as there are two things, they are in relationship to each other and therefore, they are *aware* of each other. If two planets are opposite to each other in the chart, they are facing each other across the circle. They are intimately bound together in a relationship of Duality, or Twoness. Each is profoundly aware of the other, and is aware also of the other's awareness. "I am I and You are You. I am Self and You are Other."

Because they are aware of each other, they have a choice about how to relate to each other. Each may choose to see the other as the opponent, or the enemy, and so may act to try to diminish or destroy the opponent and establish its own superiority. Thus, Twoness is potentially about conflict. But also, each may be profoundly attracted to the other and may see the other as the missing half of itself, without which it feels incomplete, and so it may act to try to merge with the other and to re-establish the lost Oneness. Thus, Twoness is also potentially about attraction and about striving towards Oneness. And thirdly, the two may choose to have a relationship which is based not on enmity, nor on attraction, but on negotiation, in which they strive, not to destroy each other nor to merge with each other, but simply to find a way of co-existing.

No matter which of these paths is chosen, there is a tension or stressfulness which seems to be bound up with the very nature of Twoness. In all of these paths, there is a dissatisfaction with how things are, and a struggle to make things different. Two is a number within which it is hard to relax. There is no stable centre, there is always the tension between the two opposing forces, no matter whether they are striving to come together, striving to draw further apart, or striving to co-exist. This tension can lead to very great effort and expenditure of energy, and therefore to very great achievements. Twoness is about travelling towards a destination, or about goal-directed action, yet so long as one remains within Twoness, there is always the sense that the goal has not been reached and that more needs to be done.

It is no wonder that many mystics, and other thinkers, have seen Twoness, or Duality, as the evil force that needs to be overcome before one can enter into one's rightful heritage of Oneness. However Twoness is the most basic building block of the "ten thousand things" of which the world is made up. To be incarnated is to be obliged to come to terms with Twoness, and to work towards seeing it dispassionately, not as a force for evil, but as a necessary part of the way things are.

The geometrical figure representing Twoness is simply a line connecting two points. Because it is simply a line, it has nothing inside it: it has no *interiority*. Twoness is outward-facing, extrovert: each of the points defines itself simply in terms of the mirror image which it receives from the opposite point.

But 2 x 2 = 4, so Four also has the quality of pure Twoness, since it is made up of no numbers other than Two. The figure representing Four is a square, in which (if we join all the points together) there are two lines at right angles to each other. Now, if there are planets at each of the four points, each of them can say: "I am I and You are You: but we are united in our opposition to these other two planets whose line crosses our line". The tensions that were present in Twoness are still present in Fourness, but their nature is subtly different. Suppose we have just two planets with a 90° angle between them, so that their relationship has the quality of Fourness. These two planets are not facing each other across the circle; rather, each is aware that, in order to reach its goal (its opposite point), it must cross the line between the other planet and its goal. So now it is not a question of "I am opposed to you", but rather of "My goal is opposed to your goal".

Similarly, 4 x 2 = 8: so now (if we draw lines connecting all of the eight points) we have an eight-pointed figure with four lines crossing at the centre, in addition to numerous other lines. Now we have achieved great *interiority*. Yet each of these lines (or relationships between points) still has the quality of Twoness, since Eight is made up of no numbers other than Two. But once again, one can expect that there is a subtle change in meaning. If two planets have a 45° angle between them, so that their relationship has the quality of Eightness, the issue between them can perhaps be expressed as "My path towards my goal clashes with your path towards your goal". But these meanings become more difficult to express in words as one progresses into the higher levels of Twoness.

Similarly, 8 x 2 = 16, and 16 x 2 = 32. Thus, if we study all the harmonics up to 32, we are looking at five different levels of Twoness: 2, 4, 8, 16 and 32. But at the higher levels (beyond 8) we are looking at interplanetary links that have not been extensively studied by astrologers, and so we are venturing into unknown territory. We need to look at examples in order to discover whether Twoness has the same meaning at these higher levels as it has at the lower levels.

Twoness is also a component of all the other even numbers. For example, 3 x 2 = 6, and so Sixness is a combination of Threeness and Twoness. Likewise, 5 x 2 = 10, and so on. Thus, Two is a very dominant number. In the majority of charts (but not in all charts) Two is the strongest prime number: we can say that these charts contain more Twoness than Oneness, or Threeness, or Fiveness, or any other prime number. However, in this chapter we will confine ourselves to interplanetary links which are composed of *pure* Twoness (2, 4, 8, 16, 32), and we will look at composite numbers (6, 10, etc.) in later chapters. The assumption will be that, since Twoness is essentially about *striving*, Sixness is about *striving towards Threeness*, and Ten-ness is about *striving towards Fiveness*.

If we stay with the *pure* Twoness links, we find that the incidence of these links varies greatly between charts. Some charts contain a large number while in other charts they are almost entirely absent. In this chapter we will look at some examples of charts that contain unusually high concentrations of pure Twoness.

R.D. Laing

Born 7 October 1927, 17.15 (+00.00)
Glasgow, Scotland (55N53. 4W15).
Source: Birth certificate, via Paul Wright (and from Laing's autobiography
The Facts of Life). RR: AA.

(((MO–**2**–NE)–8/**8**–SO)–16/**16**/**16**–ME)–32/**32**/32/32–VE
ME–**2**–CH
MA–**4**–PL
MA–8–SA
JU–16–SA

One of the strongest Twoness charts that I have seen is that of the Scottish psychiatrist R.D. (Ronald) Laing, who wrote a book called *The Divided Self*.[1] (How appropriate this title is, as Twoness is all about division and separation.) Because Laing is such an outstanding example of Twoness, and because a great deal is known about his inner as well as his outer life, we will deal with his case in some detail.

From the brief biography by Stephen Ticktin published on the internet,[2] it is clear that Laing was an extremely complex person who led a very varied life (so different from the cases that we looked at in the chapter on Oneness!). It is also clear that he was emotionally highly charged and vulnerable, and also extremely self-aware (he claimed to remember his moment of birth). He had a drink problem, and he often fell out with his colleagues, on one occasion being forced to resign from a post because his behaviour had become "intolerable". At the height of his career he suddenly gave up everything to spend a year in Sri Lanka doing Buddhist meditation. He had ten children by four different women (three of whom were his wives). He died of a heart attack aged 61 while playing tennis. Ticktin describes him as "an extraordinarily spirited individual who saw through the sham, the love-lies, of so-called normal, conventional, existence and envisioned (and created) a way of living and being that was much more truthful (and sometimes the truth hurts!) and authentic".

Ticktin also says that Laing's "first 'existential crisis' came at the age of 5 when his parents revealed to him that Santa Claus was really them. This episode seems to resonate throughout the remainder of his life, culminating in the title of the last book he was working on shortly before he died, *The Lies of Love*". How was it that this revelation, which most children seem (at least on the surface) to recover from easily, was so traumatic for Laing?

Laing wrote: "We are all murderers and prostitutes … no matter how normal, moral, or mature, one takes oneself to be".[3] As a psychiatrist he set up what he called a "Rumpus Room" in which mental patients and doctors could relate to each other as equals. As a result of this he wrote his first and most famous book, *The Divided Self*,[1] in which he aimed to pull down the dividing wall between "madness" and "sanity" and to show that "madmen" (psychotics and schizophrenics) were acting and speaking in ways appropriate to their situation. If other people do not understand what the "madman" is saying, that is because they have failed to enter into his world and to understand that, from his point of view, his words make perfect sense. "Madness," wrote Laing, "is not necessarily a breakdown, but may represent, potentially, a breakthrough to a more authentic way of being".[2]

We can start by analysing Laing's main cluster of Twoness aspects: (((MO–**2**–NE)–**8**/**8**–SO)–16/**16**/**16**–ME)–32/**32**/32/32–VE.

MO–**2**–NE shows that there is a tense relationship between Laing's emotional and reactive nature (Moon) and his desire for closeness with others (Neptune). As we have said, planets that are opposite to each other may have a relationship of enmity, or of attraction, or of negotiation. In this case, it seems that the relationship is initially one of attraction: Laing longs to merge Moon with Neptune in order to regain a sense of Oneness and peace. That is to say, he longs for the closeness, the sense of being held and loved, which would enable him (in his Moon-nature) to be fully himself. He would do anything to achieve this, but (as a child) he cannot achieve it, because love has been withdrawn. (His relationship with his mother was cool and distant.)

We might say that very many children have this longing; but for Laing it was especially acute because of the awareness created by the opposition. Thus in MO–**2**–NE we can see the roots of Laing's anguish on finding that his parents had lied to him about Santa Claus. Here was the evidence that One had separated into Two, that there was no love to be found, and that Laing's efforts to achieve it were in vain. Neptune, in its role as the Deceiver, is projected out onto the parents, and a relationship of enmity between Moon and Neptune is set up. All his life Laing struggled with this issue about the withdrawal of love and about the deceits and obfuscations which prevent it from being regained. Because the Moon describes one's emotional and reactive nature, the feelings associated with this issue, and the desire to act out the feelings in extreme ways, must have been very strong. Thus Laing, observing his own nature, could see in this issue the seeds of his own potential madness.

But then we have MO/NE–8–SO. Since the Sun is about self-fulfilment and the sense of one's purpose in life, this shows that Laing felt driven to *make it his life's work* to deal with MO–2–NE. His sense of his own identity is bound up with this issue: it is as though he is saying, "This is who I am: in order to be myself, I have to struggle with my longing for love and closeness and with my pain about the withdrawal of this love".

But how is he to do this? The answer lies in the next link, which is SO/MO/NE–16–ME. We can sense that it was this Mercury link that enabled Laing to spend his life struggling to make sense of this whole SO/MO/NE pattern, and to tell the world about it. Thus we can see in this link the seeds of Laing's life work, and also of his success in overcoming his demons, not by suppressing them, but by being open and truthful about them. And in particular (since Mercury is about rationality) we can see here the roots of Laing's belief that the mentally ill are acting rationally in response to their situation. It would seem that this link was very beneficial for Laing. (It is important to stress this, because there may be a tendency among astrologers to see Two as a 'bad' number that can bring nothing but pain and stress. Two, like every other number, is morally neutral: its effects can be either 'good' or 'bad', depending on circumstances and the attitudes of the person involved.)

And then, at the next level of Twoness, we have SO/ME/NE–32–VE. Venus is about the need to make oneself (or one's work) attractive so as to gain the admiration and respect of others, and so as to create beauty and harmony in relationships. I believe that this link will have helped Laing to reach out to others and to help people whose issues were (in his view) similar to his own. Thus, Laing reaches out to others through communication (Mercury) that is idealistic and compassionate (Neptune), and also through the sheer force of his personality (Sun).

We can also look more briefly at Laing's other Twoness links. First, he has ME–2–CH. Chiron is, I believe, to do with the search for ways of being of service in the world, and so this link reinforces the importance for Laing of finding ways to serve others through communication and rationality.

MA–4–PL can be described as a 'workaholic' aspect, since it is about striving to push one's physical resources to the limit and to work relentlessly towards one's goals. The potency of this link is increased by the fact that Mars is One with the Sun (SO–1–MA). Also there is MA–8–SA, which indicates Laing's struggles against Saturnian authority.

Finally there is JU–16–SA, which is important because it is very close, and also because Jupiter is on the Ascendant. Twoness links between the outer planets are to do with moral dilemmas: thus, JU–16–SA shows that Laing struggles to reconcile the Jupiter principle of freedom with the Saturn principle of control and discipline. One can see Laing's whole life as a battle to find the right balance between these forces.

Thus, one can understand a great deal about Laing from studying the Twoness links in his chart. But of course this is not the whole story. Laing is also strong in Elevenness and Thirteenness (and he is unusually weak in Threeness). We will be looking at the significance of these numbers in later chapters.

Frida Kahlo
Born 6 July 1907, 08.30 (+06.37)
Mexico City, Mexico (19N24. 99W09).
Source: from birth certificate (photographed in *Frida* by Hayden Herreira) (ADB). RR: AA.

(SO–1–NE)–2/2/2/2–(MA–1–UR)
(SO–2–MA)–8–MO
            –16–ME
            –32–CH

The most basic level of Twoness is the opposition, where two or more planets face each other directly across the chart. At this level, the strongest pattern that I have found is in the chart of the Mexican painter Frida Kahlo, who has (SO–1–NE)–2–(MA–1–UR). (In addition she has (SO–2–MA)–8–MO, –16–ME, and –32–CH, with Chiron near the

Descendant.) The opposition of Sun and Mars is exact (Sun at 13° 23'
Cancer, Mars at 13° 23' Capricorn), which makes it extremely strong: it
is as though Sun and Mars have no escape from each other. In this case
SO–2–MA seems to stand for 'myself against my body'. Throughout her
life Kahlo was plagued by pain and injury and by the limitations of her
body. She had polio at age 6, and at age 18 she was involved in a bus
accident which left her with numerous injuries. At first she was forced to
stay flat on her back, encased in a plaster cast and enclosed in a boxlike
structure. Although she regained her ability to walk, she experienced
great pain and fatigue throughout her life, was often bedridden, and
underwent numerous operations. Eventually she had to have her right
leg amputated below the knee, due to a gangrene infection. Kahlo said,
"My painting carries with it the message of pain".

The pain of SO–2–MA is heightened by NE–2–UR. Sun is –1–NE,
showing Kahlo's great sensitivity and her desire to be close to others,
but Mars is –1–UR, causing her body to act (or be acted on) in sudden,
unpredictable, Uranian ways; and the opposition means that these two
forces work against each other, setting her apart from other people.

It seems that SO–2–MA represents not only Kahlo's relationship
with her body, but also her relationship with her frequently unfaithful
husband, Diego Rivera, who was the embodiment of Mars/Uranus.
Kahlo herself acknowledged this when she said: "I suffered two great
accidents in my life. One in which a streetcar knocked me down … The
other accident was Diego." Yet despite this, she and Diego were closely
bonded together: she could never escape from him, just as she could not
escape from her body.

Václav Havel
Born 5 October 1936, 15.00 (–01.00)
Prague, Czechoslovakia (50N05. 14E26).
Source: From birth records, via Jaroslav Mixa and David Fisher (ADB).
RR: AA.

(MO–1–CH)–2/2–JU
(MO–2–JU)–4/4/4/4–(SA–2–NE)
(VE–2–UR)–8/8–CH

The next level of Twoness is shown by 'Fourness' links, where the angle between the planets is one quarter of the circle. At this level of Twoness, the strongest chart that I have found is that of Václav Havel, the first President of the Czech Republic. Havel's pattern of (MO–2–JU)–4–(SA–2–NE) is a Grand Cross, with planets at all four points of a square, and with two oppositions at right angles to each other. (The orbs that I am using for the square aspect are very much narrower than those used by most astrologers; within these narrow orbs, Grand Crosses are very rare.) He also has Venus closely opposite Uranus.

Havel originally became known as a playwright and essayist, and also as a political activist campaigning against the Communist regime in Czechoslovakia. When the Communists were overthrown, Havel was invited to become President. As President, he has been very active, but he has also found time to write a number of very profound and inspirational political essays. He believes that "essayists, poets, dramatists, artists, musicians and philosophers carry responsibility for the well-being of the societies in which they live",[4] and he believes that politicians need to be responsive to the spiritual aspirations of the people whom they represent.

It is clear that moral issues are of tremendous importance to Havel, and it is therefore appropriate that he has a Grand Cross containing three of the outer planets, which, as I have said, are concerned with moral principles. Within the Grand Cross there are two oppositions: the first of these is MO–2–JU, which is about instinctively responding (Moon) to the idea of freedom (Jupiter), and therefore fighting to free his people from the tyranny of Communism; but cutting across this is SA–2–NE, which is about the struggle to reconcile duty and discipline (Saturn) with idealism and compassion (Neptune). (In Havel's own words, "The salvation of this human world lies nowhere else than in the human heart, in the human power to reflect, in human meekness and in human responsibility".[5]) Havel's life can be seen as a struggle to reconcile Moon/Jupiter with Saturn/Neptune, and in particular to resolve the conflict between Jupiter's longing for freedom and Saturn's acceptance of responsibility. In his later life it feels as though Saturn has gained the upper hand, although sometimes, as when he resigned from the Presidency, Jupiter (in the form of his longing for his own personal freedom) has re-asserted itself.

From this and other cases (including an examination of the oppositions and squares in my own chart) I have come to believe that Fourness links (squares) act in a rather different way from simple Twoness links (oppositions). Whereas with the opposition it is simply a case of two forces that are aware of each other, feel limited by each other, and may act to undermine each other, with the square there is more of an active search for reconciliation between the different forces. When the link is close (that is, when the angle between the planets is almost *exactly* one quarter of the circle), this search can become obsessive and can dominate the life, whether for good or ill.

Augustus John
Born 4 January 1878, 05.30 (+00.19)
Tenby, Wales (51N41. 4W43).
Source: *Augustus John* by Michael Holroyd (ADB). RR: B.

((SO–**1**–JU)–**4/4**–MA)–**8**/**8**/8/8/**8**/**8**–(VE–**2**–UR)

The next level of Twoness is Eightness, where the angle between the planets is one-eighth or three-eighths of the circle. (Astrologers call these links 'semi-squares' or 'sesquiquadrates'.) At this level, one of the strongest charts that I have found is that of the painter Augustus John, who has ((SO–**1**–JU)–**4/4**–MA)–**8**/**8**/8/8/**8**/**8**–(VE–**2**–UR). With (SO–**1**–JU)–**4/4**–MA, he is searching for ways of expressing his Martian energy that will bring him freedom (Jupiter) and self-fulfilment (Sun). He grew a beard, dressed as a Bohemian, drank heavily, and adopted a nomadic lifestyle, living for a time with gypsies. But also, Sun, Jupiter and Mars are –8– Venus and Uranus, which are opposite to each other, representing a tension between his love of beauty and his desire for originality of expression. It would seem that these Eightness links are the origin of John's determination to devote himself to painting. But his artistic inspiration burnt itself out early; according to one critic, "the painterly brilliance of his early work degenerated into flashiness and bombast, and the second half of his long career added little to his achievement". John is stronger on Twoness than any other painter whose chart I have seen, but he is comparatively weak on Fiveness and Sevenness, which are more commonly the source of artistic inspiration.

He is more famous for acting the part of a Bohemian painter than for the quality of his painting.

Françoise Sagan
Born 21 June 1935, 11.00 (–01.00) (name at birth: Marie Quoirez)
Cajarc, France (44N29. 1E50).
Source: Birth certificate, via Gauquelin (ADB). RR: AA.

(SO–**1**–ME)–**8**/**8**/**8**/**8**–(VE–**4**–JU)
(*SA*–2–*NE*)–4–CH
(*SA*–4–CH)–**8**/8–PL

The novelist Françoise Sagan has a close quartet of (SO–**1**–ME)–**8**–(VE–**4**–*JU*), as well as other Twoness links. She wrote her first novel *Bonjour Tristesse* in seven weeks at the age of 18, and it became an instant worldwide best-seller. Thereafter, though she continued to write novels, plays and other creative works, she became more famous for her reckless lifestyle (which mirrored that of many of the heroines of her books) than for her writings. She was a notoriously fast driver, and once she drove her car into a ditch and was in a coma for three days. She became increasingly dependent on drink and drugs, and was convicted for possession of cocaine; she was also convicted of tax fraud. She had two marriages and divorces within five years.

Here again, as with Augustus John, we can say that Sagan was more noted for acting the part of a rebellious author than for her actual works. And yet Sagan did have a real talent (as is indicated by her strong Fiveness and Sevenness links). It has been said that she is in a class of her own when writing about women's emotions and thoughts.[6] This is perhaps a sign of the self-awareness which is one of the characteristics of Twoness.

Steve Fossett
Born 22 April 1944, 01.58 (+05.00)
Jackson, TN, USA (35N37. 88W49).
Source: Birth certificate, via Pat Taglilatelo (ADB). RR: AA.

((*ME*–4–JU)–**8**/8–NE)–**16**/16/16/**16**/16/**16**–(MO–**8**–CH)
((MO–**8**–CH)–**16**/16/16/**16**)–(*ME*–**8**–NE))–**32**/32/32/32–MA

Steve Fossett was a billionaire and an unstoppable adventurer. Having made his millions by aggressive trading in the financial services industry, he embarked on a career of record-breaking in numerous sports. He was the first person to fly a solo non-stop flight around the world. He was the first solo balloonist to circumnavigate the world. He achieved the fastest speed ever for a non-supersonic plane. He has sailed across the Atlantic in a record-breaking time, and achieved the fastest circumnavigation of the world in a sailing boat. He has swum the English Channel, and climbed mountains in six continents. And so on, and so on. He planned to continue these adventures into his 80s, but at age 63 he was killed in a plane crash. He was an outstanding example of the characteristics of Twoness: restless activity, and constant striving to overcome obstacles, reach objectives, and notch up achievements.

We can perhaps best make sense of Fossett's complex pattern of Twoness by looking at the three planets which are linked by very close aspects: (JU–**8**–NE)–**16**–CH. (Chiron is in fact at the exact midpoint of Jupiter and Neptune.) JU–**8**–NE shows a striving towards visionary and expansive goals, and Chiron shows a determination to make this his life's work. These three planets are linked in with the more personal planets of Moon, Mercury and Mars to create a pattern of behaviour from which Fossett cannot escape.

We should note that much of Fossett's Twoness pattern is at the higher (or deeper) levels of Twoness: 16 and 32. I do not think that in practice it is always possible to separate the meaning of these numbers from the meaning of the 'lower' levels (2, 4 and 8). They are all manifestations of pure Twoness. But perhaps 16 and 32 tend to be more concerned with internal conflicts within the personality, and less concerned with conflicts between the individual and the outside world. Applying this to Fossett's case, we can say that he was not struggling against the world (he did not feel that the world was against him, or that his enemies had to be vanquished). His struggle was with himself: the struggle to prove to himself that he could do these things, and that his capacity for achievement was unlimited.

Cindy Sherman

Born 19 January 1954, 04.27 (+05.00)
Glen Ridge, NJ, USA (40N48. 74W12).
Source: Birth certificate, via Lois Rodden (ADB). RR: AA.

(SO–1–ME–1–VE)–2/**2**/2–MO
(SO–1–VE)–4/**4**–NE
((MO–**2**–ME)–**8**/8–_JU_)–16/**16**/16–PL)–32/_32_/32/_32_–UR

Cindy Sherman is a photographer who takes photographs of herself. As a
child she was preoccupied with mirrors, dressing up and applying make-
up, often fooling the neighbours by walking the streets dressed as a little
old lady. As a student she was notorious for appearing in public dressed as
Lucille Ball. In her early photographs she continued this theme, making
elaborate use of costumes, wigs and props to create images of herself as
a housewife, a slut, a film star, and so on. She has said, "I am trying to
make people recognize something of themselves rather than me". More
recently she has moved away from impersonating stereotypes, and has
taken photographs in which, in Els Barents' words, "the portraits seem
more refined, natural and closer to Cindy Sherman herself".[7] Looking
at these photographs, we feel we know exactly what it would feel like
to be this person – we can sense their emotions, and in particular their
fear and their vulnerability – and yet there is a mystery in all of these
portraits: is this Cindy Sherman who is being portrayed, or is it someone
else whom she is imagining?

Sherman has a strong Oneness pattern (SO–1–ME–1–VE–1–CH),
and she certainly has some of the inner stillness which is associated with
Oneness. But she also has a very strong Twoness pattern: (((MO–**2**–
ME)–**8**–JU)–16–PL)–32–UR, and also (SO–1–ME–1–VE)–2–MO and
(SO–1–VE)–4–NE). With Moon (the reflective planet) opposite to Sun,
Mercury and Venus, it is no wonder that Sherman has been obsessed with
mirrors and reflections – seeing herself reflected in others, and others
reflected in herself; herself as wielder of the external camera that shines
back on herself – and her career can be seen as an exploration of the
mystery of Twoness: the separation of the One into Self and Other, and
the longing of the Two to merge again into One. The strong Twoness
links between Moon/Mercury and Jupiter, Pluto and Uranus show the

adventurousness, dedication and originality with which she has pursued the task of communicating to the world the nature of this mystery.

Jürgen Bartsch
Born 6 November 1946, 10.50 (–01.00)
Essen-Rittenscheid, Germany (51N27. 7E00).
Source: "Time exact from his foster mother", via Hans-Jorg in *Astrological Quarterly* Autumn 1973 (ADB). RR: AA.

(SO–4–PL)–16–ME)–32–NE
(JU–4–SA)–16–VE

Alice Miller, in her book *For Your Own Good: The Roots of Violence in Child-Rearing*,[8] gives two examples of people whose addiction to violence was, she claims, fostered by the violence to which they were themselves subjected as children. These two examples are Adolf Hitler and the serial murderer Jürgen Bartsch. Both Hitler and Bartsch have strong patterns of Twoness in their charts; however, Hitler is strong in Fiveness and Sevenness as well in Twoness, and we will look at his chart as a whole in Chapter 18.

Jürgen Bartsch was abandoned by his mother immediately after his birth, and was left in hospital for nearly a year, with no one showing him any mother-love. He was then adopted by a woman (Frau Bartsch) who beat him mercilessly, cleaned him obsessively, forbade him to have contact with other children, and showed him no affection or understanding. Later he was sent to a convent school, where he endured constant beatings and deprivations. Also he was sexually abused by a cousin at the age of eight, and by a teacher at the age of thirteen. Between the ages of 15 and 19 he murdered four young boys in an extremely brutal and cruel way,[9] and he estimated that in addition he made more than a hundred unsuccessful murder attempts.

Bartsch's chart contains an unusual 'scissors' pattern. He has SO–1–JU and SA–1–PL, and also SO–4–PL (almost exact) and JU–4–SA. In effect, this amounts to a pattern of (SO–1–JU)–4–(SA–1–PL). It would seem that this pattern is the main indicator both of Bartsch's repression as a child and of his murderous drives. On the one hand we have SO–1–JU, showing that Bartsch naturally identifies with the Jupiterian values of freedom and expansion (everything that was denied to him as a child), but on the other hand we have SA–1–PL, signifying ruthless repression and denial of freedom. It would seem that as a child Bartsch *was* SO/JU, and that SA/PL was projected out onto and embodied by his external oppressors. However, Bartsch was driven (especially by the exact SO–4–PL) to 'turn the tables' and to become the ruthless oppressor himself, so that in his murderous acts he *became* SA/PL, depriving his victims of their freedom and indeed of their lives.

But Bartsch also has a very close pattern of ((SO–4–PL)–16–ME)-32–NE. I would suggest that this pattern describes, not Bartsch's murderous acts, but the way in which he subsequently dealt with them. Miller's book contains long extracts from letters written by Bartsch to his psychoanalyst Paul Moor. In these letters Bartsch shows that (in addition to remarkable literary ability) he has a compulsive desire to communicate, both about his experiences as a child and about his acts of murder. He strives both to understand himself and to be understood by others, and hopes to somehow redeem himself by doing so. All this is the acting out of (SO–4–PL)–16–ME. The influence of Neptune is less easy to pin down, but Neptune is to do with belonging, and we can perhaps sense that Bartsch strives, through his writing, to be allowed to belong once more to the human race. (But he did not achieve this goal: at the age of 29, he died in prison as a result of a botched castration operation.)

Could we have predicted the course of Bartsch's life simply from looking at his chart? My own belief is that we could not have done so. The chart shows, not what happens to a person, but how the person responds to what happens. Many children must have been born around the same time as Bartsch who did not become serial killers; and also, many children must have suffered childhoods as deprived as Bartsch's and yet did not become serial killers. What turned Bartsch into a murderer was the combination of, on the one hand, an extremely repressed childhood, and, on the other hand, a chart that contained the potential for murder. If Bartsch had had a different upbringing, these same planetary patterns would have worked themselves out in different ways.

(Other serial murderers with strong Twoness patterns include Nathaniel Bar-Jonah[10] [original name David Paul Brown], who killed and cannibalized young boys; Ted Bundy,[11] who killed women "for no other reason than his desire to kill"; Edward Gein,[12] who skinned his victims and made clothes and other objects from the skins; and Maria Swanenburg,[13] who poisoned 27 people, including her own parents, in order to get their money.)

Mahatma Gandhi

Born 2 October 1869, 07.11 (–04.38)
Porbandas, India (21N38. 69E37).
Source: Y.K. Prabhan in *Voice of India* 2/24 (ADB). RR: A.

(VE–**1**–MA)–2/**2**/**2**/**2**–(JU–1–PL)
((JU–1–PL)–2/**2**–MA)–**4**/4/4–MO)–8/8/**8**/8–CH
(MO–**4**–JU)–**16**/16–SA

No number has a monopoly of spirituality, and there are several spiritual leaders and teachers who have strong Twoness links in their charts. But I believe that their spirituality has a distinctive flavour, which we can call the *spirituality of action*. Twoness is essentially about action: it implies (as we said at the start of this chapter) a dissatisfaction with how things are, and a struggle to make things different: therefore it is concerned with action in the world, in order to achieve specific goals.

One of these spiritual leaders is Mohandas (known as Mahatma) Gandhi, who has the very strong cluster of Twoness aspects which is shown above. Rather than analysing this pattern in detail, I will simply note that Gandhi's whole emphasis was on non-violent action in order to achieve the goal of Indian independence. Rather than preaching to his followers, he invited them to follow the example of his actions.

We can also note that the Sun is not involved in Gandhi's Twoness pattern. Since the Sun indicates one's sense of one's purpose in life, we can say that any Twoness pattern involving the Sun is concerned with the *struggle for self-realization*. In Gandhi's case this is absent, and this is consistent with the impression that Gandhi created that his struggle was a *selfless* one: he sought nothing for himself, and his struggles were for the benefit of humanity as a whole.

Charles de Foucauld

Born 15 September 1858, 17.00 (–00.31)
Strasbourg, France (48N35. 7E45).
Source: from *Desert Calling* by Anne Freemantle (ADB). RR: B.

((SO–**1**–ME)–2–NE)–4/**4**/4–JU
　　　　　　　　　–**8**/8/8–PL
(SO–2–NE)–**8**/**8**/8/8/8/**8**–((VE–**2**–PL)–**4**/4–SA)
(MA–2–JU)–4/**4**–ME
(VE–**4**–SA)–**32**/32–CH

Charles de Foucauld, who has been beatified by the Catholic Church, has one of the strongest Twoness patterns that I have seen. The five clusters listed above can be brought together into a single pattern involving nine of the eleven planets:

(((((SO–**1**–ME)–2–NE)–4–(MA–2–JU))–8–((VE–**2**–PL)–**4**–SA))
　–32–CH

The key to de Foucauld's character can be found in the comment: "Charles de Foucauld was excessive in everything he did".[14] As a young Army officer he was known for consuming the best foie de gras and the best champagne, and he became almost obese. He insisted on bringing his mistress to all the gatherings of officers and their wives. When the Army objected to this, he resigned from the Army. Later he rejoined his division in order to fight the Arab tribes in the Sahara. However, he came to respect his adversaries, and he left the Army again to live among the Arab people. He learnt Arabic, and studied both the Quran and the Bible. Eventually he underwent a religious conversion (to Christianity, not Islam) and became a Trappist monk. As a monk he lived for 15 years among the Tuareg people of the southern Sahara, eating and sleeping as little as possible, and sharing the life of the local people, for whom he felt a deep love. He translated the Gospels into Tuareg, but made no attempt to convert the locals to Christianity. At the age of 58 he was killed by a band of robbers.

Foucauld's spirituality, like Gandhi's, was a spirituality of action. And Twoness always implies *choice* about what action should be taken. In Foucauld's case, his excess of Twoness implies action taken to extremes. In his youth he became obese through over-eating; in later years he contracted scurvy through under-eating. One feels that Foucauld's life could have gone in many different directions, but that he could never have been 'ordinary' or conventional.

Mary Baker Eddy
Born 16 July 1821, 17.38 (+04.46)
Bow, NH, USA (43N08. 71W52).
Source: from biography by Pakin, via Davidson in AQ vol.25/4 (ADB).
RR: B.

((UR–**1**–NE)–**4**/**4**–PL)–**8**/**8**/**8**/**8**/8/8–(MO–**2**–ME)
((MO–**2**–ME)–**8**–NE)–**16**/16/**16**–SO

Mary Baker Eddy, the founder of Christian Science, has a very strong
Twoness pattern, which can be brought together into a single cluster of
six planets:

   ((MO–**2**–ME)–8–((UR–**1**–NE)–**4**–PL))–16–SO

Eddy's message, that illnesses can be healed through faith rather than
through medication, is spelt out in this sextet of planets. We can see
the Moon as the significator of all the feelings (including physical pain)
to which the body is subject, and Mercury as the rational mind which
strives to understand these feelings and come to terms with them. The
very close opposition between Moon and Mercury shows Eddy's belief
that the feelings can be conquered by means of mental activity ("mind
over matter"). The three outermost planets, Uranus, Neptune and Pluto,
are collectively to do with spiritual values, and MO/ME–8–UR/NE/PL
shows the effort to employ these spiritual values in the struggle against
disease. Finally, –16–SO shows that the ultimate outcome of the struggle
is self-realization and fulfilment. Eddy's spirituality, like that of Gandhi
and Foucauld, is very much a spirituality of action. Throughout her long
life she was extremely active, not only in practising her methods but in
publicizing them and establishing the church of Christian Science.

Saint Thérèse of Lisieux
Born 2 January 1873, 23.30 (+00.00) (birth name: Marie Françoise
Thérèse Martin)
Alençon, France (48N26. 0E05).
Source: Mayoral register, via T. Pat Davis (ADB). RR: AA.

(MA–**2**–NE)–4/**4**–SA
((SO–**4**–CH)–**16**/16/**16**/16–(ME–**8**–UR))–32/32/**32**/**32**–NE

A different type of spirituality is displayed by Thérèse of Lisieux, who has been canonized by the Catholic Church. After a difficult childhood, she became a nun at the age of 15. She wrote an autobiography *History of a Soul*, and died of tuberculosis at the age of 24. She has been described as "a model of simplicity, sincerity, patience and devotion",[15] and her "way of confidence and love" has been an inspiration to many believers.

This may seem hard to reconcile with the fact that Thérèse's chart is extremely strong in Twoness. And yet Wikipedia says that "some authors suggest that Thérèse had a strongly neurotic aspect to her personality for most of her life". As a child, she was often sick and suffered from nervous tremors: her teeth were clenched, and she was unable to talk. A doctor pronounced that Thérèse "reacts to an emotional frustration with a neurotic attack".[16]

We can see Thérèse's stresses and tensions as indications of the internal struggle between SO–4–CH (the determination to devote herself to selfless service) and ME–8–UR (the desire to communicate with originality and brilliance). People with strong Twoness charts usually try to resolve their inner tensions by means of restless action, but, as a nun, Thérèse could not do this. She wrote:

> "Love proves itself by deeds, so how am I to show my love? Great deeds are forbidden me. The only way I can prove my love is by scattering flowers, and these flowers are every little sacrifice, every glance and word, and the doing of the least actions for love".[17]

Writing was the strongest form of action available to Thérèse, and as a writer she certainly expressed herself with Uranian brilliance and achieved her goal of serving the world. Thus we can see her career as an expression of the Twoness in her chart.

And yet it is also true that Thérèse won through to a profound peace and serenity. We should not forget that the essence of Twoness is a striving towards Oneness. Although there is almost no Oneness in her chart, Thérèse (like Ramana Maharshi, whom we will consider in Chapter 18) won through to Oneness by transcending her ego and so transcending the limitations of her birth chart.

My Lai massacre
16 March 1968, 08.10 (–07.00)
My Lai, Vietnam (15N11. 108E52).
Source: Wikipedia.

(UR–1–PL)–2/2–SO
(SO–1–CH)–2–UR
(ME–2–JU)–4/4–NE)–8/8/8/8/8/8–(MO–2–SA)

We will end this chapter with two mundane charts. The first of these
is the chart for the start of the My Lai massacre during the Vietnam
War, in which American soldiers went berserk and killed 504 unarmed
Vietnamese civilians, most of whom were women, children, and elderly
people. Many of the victims were sexually abused, beaten and tortured,
and some of the bodies were found mutilated. Although the killing of
civilians was not uncommon in this savage war, it seems to be agreed
that the My Lai massacre was a descent into barbarity unequalled on any
other occasion.

In the case of mundane charts, I am not sure how valuable it is to
analyse the chart in detail. What seems to count is the relative strength
of the different prime numbers. In the case of the My Lai massacre,
Twoness was very much stronger than any other prime number (though
Thirteenness was also strong). We can say that at the time of the massacre
there was a great deal of the stress and tension associated with Twoness
'in the air', and that this will have affected people's state of mind and
therefore their behaviour. It would seem that, when ordered to "go in
there aggressively, close with the enemy and wipe them out for good",[18]
the soldiers carried out this task with a great deal more thoroughness,
savagery and brutality than they would have done on a different day.

Nuneaton rail crash
6 June 1975, 01.55 (–01.00)
Nuneaton, England (52N32. 1W28).
Source: Wikipedia.

(MO–1–CH)–2–UR
((MO–2–UR)–4/4–VE)–8/8/8–SO
(VE–4–UR)–16/16–PL
(JU–4–SA)–32/32–UR

I have looked at the charts of many air, rail, road and sea crashes, and in general these charts have a surprising absence of strong patterns of Twoness: it would seem that crashes are more likely to result from the carelessness associated with Threeness than from the stress and tension associated with Twoness.

The Nuneaton crash, however, is an exception. The chart contains a very strong pattern of Twoness aspects (listed above), showing that this, like the time of the My Lai massacre, was a time when Twoness predominated over all the other prime numbers.

The London-Glasgow sleeper train left Euston station on time at 11.30 p.m., but after 28 minutes the engine failed, and, by the time it had been replaced, the train was badly behind schedule. Altogether it took 2 hours and 25 minutes to reach Nuneaton (a distance of less than 100 miles). By this time the driver was in a high state of stress and desperate to make up for lost time. A 20 m.p.h. speed restriction was in force through Nuneaton station due to a faulty track, but the driver (wrongly thinking that the restriction had been lifted) drove through at nearly 80 m.p.h. The train was derailed, crashing into the piers of a bridge, killing six people and injuring 38. Without analysing the chart in detail, we can clearly see from the Twoness patterns the high level of stress and tension that was in the air at the time.

Conclusion

In this chapter we have looked at charts with an unusually high level of pure Twoness, and we can see that, despite their huge differences, the people who own these charts have much in common. We can say that all of them are driven people. They are fighting to change the world, whether this is their own personal world or the world in general. They feel themselves to be faced by huge challenges which they struggle to overcome. The emphasis is on *action*, and their actions are carried out with great vigour and determination.

We could say that, just as Oneness signifies the state of being at peace, so Twoness signifies the state of being at war. Any Twoness link between planets suggests some kind of conflict between the forces represented by those planets, or, at the least, some kind of difficulty that the planets experience in working harmoniously with each other. There may (especially at the lower levels of Twoness, i.e. 2 and 4) be a tendency to project one of the planets (or groups of planets) onto the outside world, so that the Twoness link comes to signify, not a conflict *within* the person, but a conflict which he[19] perceives himself as having with the outside world.

This focus on conflict inevitably creates a high degree of restlessness, tension and dissatisfaction. Unless the Twoness is balanced by a large amount of Oneness (or perhaps Threeness), the person with a high concentration of Twoness will tend to be always 'on the go' and will find it hard to relax. 'Workaholism' is a common problem. We could say that Twoness represents the dominance of the Ego, which is defined by Eckhart Tolle[20] as the part of us that is always dissatisfied with the present moment, always seeking something more which will help it to feel more fully itself. No achievement is good enough for the ego, it always seeks more. There is the "rage for perfection" (the title of a biography of the tennis player John McEnroe,[21] who has some strong Twoness aspects), but perfection is never achieved. The ego is dependent on Duality (or Twoness): it needs to see the other as 'other', so that it can define itself by the nature of its difference from the other.

And yet, along with the awareness of conflict, there is usually a very strong desire to resolve the conflict and to find ways of achieving harmony between the opposing forces. Essentially, Twoness is about striving towards Oneness. Even if the Oneness is never achieved, the desire to achieve it becomes the motivating force in the person's life. Thus, Twoness is about success and failure. A person dominated by Twoness will be highly motivated to succeed in whatever task he has chosen. If he fails, he will be deeply affected by this, but this will spur him on to greater efforts in the future.

Often there is a strong desire to act out the resolution of the conflict between the opposing planets in *the work that he performs in the world*. Thus, up to a point, the Twoness pattern can be an indication of the area in which the person is most likely to succeed, or at least the area in which he is likely to make the greatest effort to succeed. And yet, as we have said, Twoness is more to do with effort than with talent. There is always the danger that, however hard he tries, the person may lack the ability to succeed in his chosen field. In such cases, the Twoness pattern may even drag the person *away* from the field in which his greatest gifts lie.

In this chapter we have looked at pure Twoness: that is, at numbers that contain no prime numbers other than Two. But Twoness is also present in all charts as an element within complex numbers that are the product of more than one prime number. Thus, when we look at Fiveness, we will be looking, not only at Five itself, but also at Ten (5 x 2) and Twenty (5 x 2 x 2). These numbers have the same relationship to Five as Two has to One: that is to say, just as Twoness is striving towards Oneness, so Ten-ness is striving towards Fiveness. We will be dealing with these complex numbers in later chapters of the book.

Most of us have less Twoness in our charts than the people whom we have discussed in this chapter, but we still have some Twoness links between planets. These links are an indication of areas where we feel ourselves to be faced by challenges and conflicts, or where there are tensions that need to be resolved through action. The positive side of Twoness is that it can spur us into action to resolve our problems. The negative side is that it can make us see problems where no problems really exist, and so make it hard for us to accept the message of the next number (Three) – which is that everything is OK as it is now.

5

Threeness

Three is the next number after Two, and also the next prime number. Because Two and Three are so obviously the most important prime numbers (after One), there is a tendency to contrast them with each other and to see them as opposites. There is an instinctive sense, when we move from Two to Three, that we have come through the pain, the struggle, and the darkness, and are moving into sunnier pastures. Two is dark whereas Three is light. Two is hard, whereas Three is soft. Two is about the avoidance of pain; Three is about the seeking of pleasure.

The geometrical figure associated with Three is the equilateral triangle – three points connected by three lines of equal length. Although the triangle (unlike the line) is a solid figure, there is nothing inside it. It is the simplest possible two-dimensional figure: three points connected by three lines. (Three is in fact the only number for which the number of points is equal to the number of lines connecting them. This is perhaps easier to understand if we think of the points as people. One person on his own has no relationships; two people have one relationship (A–B); four people have six relationships (A–B, A–C, A–D, B–C, B–D, C–D). But three people have just three relationships (A–B, A–C, B–C). There is something inherently satisfying about this equality between the number of people and the number of relationships.)

An equilateral triangle is, in my view, an innately pleasing figure. To contemplate it is to experience a sense of peace and harmony. We should remember also that, in an astrological context, the triangle that we are contemplating is a triangle within a circle (the circle of the zodiac). The triangle divides the circle into three arcs of equal length. An equilateral triangle within a circle is a potent symbol, used by witches in casting spells, and found also on ancient Celtic crosses as a representation of the Trinity. It symbolizes power, containment, and permanence. Robert L. Martin says, "The equilateral triangle is a symbol of stability in architecture and in nature ... [and also] is a Christian symbol for the body, mind, and spirit".[1]

Whereas Twoness is about goal-directed travel (getting from A to B), Threeness is about travel for its own sake, or standing still. To contemplate an equilateral triangle (especially one within a circle) is to realize that there is no ending point, no destination. The inclination is to keep travelling around the triangle (or the circle), just for the joy of travel, or else to stay still and contemplate the figure as a whole. The difference between Twoness and Threeness is the difference between a bicycle and a tricycle: a bicycle is an excellent device for getting from A to B, but, when it reaches its destination and stops, it falls over; a tricycle is less good at getting fast to one's destination, but it is stable and reliable even when stationary.

Since Threeness is about peace and harmony, it may seem that it is close in meaning to Oneness. And in fact there is a close connexion between Three and One, as is shown by the Christian concept of the Trinity (Three in One) and also by the Hindu Trimurti (Brahma the Creator, Vishnu the Maintainer, and Shiva the Destroyer). To divide the One into Two is to destroy Oneness; but to divide the One into Three (Father, Son, Holy Spirit; body, mind, spirit) is seen as compatible with maintaining Oneness, since the Three do not oppose one another but rather act to support and maintain one another. Thus we can say that Threeness is *compatible* with Oneness, in a way that Twoness is not.

And yet there is an essential difference between Threeness and Oneness. Oneness is about the absence of desire, whereas all the higher numbers are concerned with some kind of desire. Threeness is about the desire for pleasure, or (as the Declaration of Independence has it) the pursuit of happiness. One would expect a person who was strong on Threeness to be a hedonistic person, for whom the pursuit of pleasure took precedence over the pursuit of success (Twoness) and over other goals represented by prime numbers beyond Three.

We can also say that Three (in contrast to Two) is an essentially feminine number. It is to do with *yin* rather than *yang*, receptivity rather than proactivity, attraction rather than force.

The astrological aspect of pure Threeness is the trine (120°) representing one-third of the circle. If two planets are 120° apart, their relationship has the character of pure Threeness. But there is also the nonile (40°), representing one-ninth of the circle, and its multiples (80°, or two-ninths; 160°, or four-ninths). These are Nineness links. But 9 is 3 x 3, and so Nineness is a higher level of pure Threeness (just as Fourness is a higher level of pure Twoness). Also, we can have planetary links which have the character of Twenty-sevenness: but 27 is 3 x 3 x 3, so this again is a higher level of pure Threeness.

Traditionally, astrologers have looked at these Nineness and 27-ness links by drawing a separate chart, the 9th-harmonic chart, in which noniles (Nineness links) are shown as conjunctions and 27-ness links are shown as trines. The 9th-harmonic, or Navamsa, chart is important in Hindu astrology and is said in particular to describe the marriage partner.[2] There has been a tendency by writers on harmonics (including myself in my book *Harmonic Charts*) to treat the number Nine as if it was a prime number and as if it had a meaning entirely separate from Three. My later researches, however, have convinced me that Nineness is nothing more (or less) than a higher aspect of Threeness, and that noniles should be considered alongside trines as manifestations of the Threeness principle. Therefore, in this chapter we will look at all the levels of Threeness (3, 9 and 27).

In this chapter we will give examples of charts with a large number of Threeness links between planets. We will focus mainly on pure Threeness (3, 9 and 27), but we may also include some examples of Six (3 x 2) and Eighteen (3 x 3 x 2), in which an element of Twoness is combined with the Threeness.

Jerry Lewis
Born 16 March 1926, 12.15 (05.00)
Newark, NJ, USA (40N44. 74W10).
Source: Birth certificate, via Gene Lockhart (ADB). RR: AA.

((((SO–**1**–UR)–**3**–SA)–**6**/6/6–MA)–**9**/9/9/**9**/9/9/18/18–(VE–**1**–JU)
(JU–**9**–SA)–27/27/**27**/27–(NE–**9**–PL)

The strongest Threeness chart that I have seen is that of the comedian Jerry Lewis, which contains a massive configuration involving all of the planets except Moon and Mercury.

Jerry Lewis has been called the "King of Comedy". As a comedian, his personality is that of a clown, a person who is willing to make a complete fool of himself on stage or in film. According to one website, Lewis's skill is in "doing things just precisely at the wrong time. His body seems to flail about at random, triggering chain reactions of chaos in his surroundings".[3]

But Lewis is not only a comedian; he is also a filmmaker who, like Charlie Chaplin, produced, directed, wrote, and starred in his own films. As a filmmaker he has been called "a discoverer of beauty," and his cinema has been described as one of "pure pleasure, expressed through the control of colour, décor and camera movement … through dance, and through the indulgence of his love of big-band swing".[4] All this is very much in keeping with the spirit of Threeness.

Lewis is also known for his tireless fundraising for charitable causes, and especially for his 'telethons' on behalf of the Muscular Dystrophy Association. His efforts have helped raise approximately 2 billion dollars, and have caused him to be nominated for the Nobel Peace Prize. Yet he has also been criticized for certain remarks which have been seen as insensitive towards the disabled, characterizing them as helpless and homebound.[5]

We can also note that Lewis's ex-wife, Patti (by whom he had six sons), wrote a book, *I Laffed Til I Cried*, in which she complained of Jerry's "blistering temper, emotional absences, addiction to painkillers, profligate spending and philandering".[6]

And also, we can note that Lewis's account of his relationship with his one-time partner in comedy, Dean Martin, is entitled *Dean and Me, a Love Story*. Jerry was not gay, but he loved Dean deeply, as "my partner and my best friend, the man who made me who I am today" and as "a great and wonderful man"[7] (whereas Dean's attitude towards Jerry was much more hard-headed).

But perhaps the strongest clue to what makes Jerry Lewis 'tick' comes at the end of his official website, where it is stated:

"Jerry Lewis has a motto which reflects more than anything else his love affair with humanity: *'I shall pass through this world but once. Any good, therefore, that I can do or any kindness that I can show to any human being, let me do it now. Let me not defer or neglect it, for I shall not pass this way again!'*".[8]

From these notes a consistent theme emerges, which is that of *freedom*: freedom to make a fool of himself on stage; freedom to exercise his imagination unrestrainedly as a filmmaker; freedom to make careless remarks about the disabled; freedom to lose his temper, and to spend profligately; freedom to follow his impulses in being kind to others. The theme of seeking pleasure (for himself and for others) is specifically mentioned by Fujiwara[4] in his critique of Lewis as a filmmaker. It is clear also that Lewis is a very warm-hearted person, who could be described as having 'a love affair with humanity'. All these qualities are, I believe, related, to the predominance of Threeness in his chart.

Pat Rodegast

Born 17 March 1926, 13.00 (+05.00)
Stamford, CT, USA (41N03. 73W32).
Source: From her, via Linda Clark (ADB). RR: A.

(((SO–**1**–UR)–**3**–SA)–**6**/**6**/**6**–MA)–**9**/**9**/9/9/**9**/9/18/18–(VE–**1**–JU)
(SA–**3**–UR)–**9**/9–JU)–27/**27**/27/27/27/27–(NE–**9**–PL)

The second strongest Threeness chart that I have found is that of the medium Pat Rodegast, who for many years has channelled the words of an 'entity' named Emmanuel. She has also compiled a book of Emmanuel's sayings, *Emmanuel's Book*, which is subtitled *A manual for living comfortably in the cosmos.*[9] In the book she describes how, over the years, she has come to trust that Emmanuel will always be there when she opens to him, and how the experience of living with Emmanuel has been an opening up into a state of trust, fearlessness, and love.

In his introduction to *Emmanuel's Book*, Ram Dass raises the question of "whether Emmanuel is a separate being from Pat, or whether he is another part of Pat's personality with which she does not consciously identify". But, as he says, maybe in the end it doesn't matter, since the wisdom of his sayings remains the same. If Emmanuel is part of Pat, then his wisdom is Pat's wisdom. If he is a separate being, then he has chosen Pat as a suitable vehicle through whom to communicate.

What is clear is that Emmanuel's message is a message of pure Threeness. In the book, his opening words are:

> The gifts I wish to give you
> are my deepest love,
> the safety of truth,

the wisdom of the universe
and the reality of God.[10]

Emmanuel teaches that Love, Joy and Light are the only reality. "All darkness is a disturbance of light"; "What is evil but forgetfulness?"; "Pain can be dissolved into the reality of joy without denial". He invites us to *accept* ourselves, with all our imperfections. He tells us that we are "infinitely safe", and he invites us to "experience the loving, gentle kindness of the universe".

Pat Rodegast was born just one day after Jerry Lewis, and her Threeness pattern is almost identical to his. Once again there is a configuration of planets involving all the planets except Moon and Mercury, and the pattern of connections between them is the same (although there are differences in terms of which connections are closest to exactitude). How then can we explain the differences between them? Perhaps we can do so by looking at the angular planets. Jerry Lewis has Sun/Uranus culminating and Pluto rising, so he is motivated to display to the world the uniqueness of his personality in an uncompromising (Plutonian) way. In Pat Rodegast's case, however, the angular planets are Mercury culminating and Mars descending. Mercury shows that her destiny is to communicate; but Mercury is separate from the Threeness pattern, and this may explain why, in order to communicate her Threeness message, she had to attribute it to a separate (male) identity which is represented by Mars.

But the Threeness in the two charts is the same; and we can say, perhaps, that the message of love and light which was *implicit* in Jerry Lewis's life (his 'love affair with humanity') was made *explicit* by Pat Rodegast through her connection with Emmanuel.

Phyllis Diller and Benny Hill

Phyllis Diller
Born 17 July 1917, 01.00 (+06.00)
Lima, OH, USA (40N44. 84W08).
Source: Birth certificate, via Frank C. Clifford (ADB). RR: AA.

(MO–**1**–PL)–18/<u>18</u>–SO
(ME–**1**–SA)–**3**/3–CH
((MA–**3**–<u>UR</u>)–**9**–SA)–<u>27</u>–<u>VE</u>

Benny Hill
Born 21 January 1924, 08.15 (+00.00)
Southampton, England (50N55. 1W25).
Source: From him, via Russell Grant (FCC). RR: A.

(SO–6–MA)–9/**18**–PL
(VE–**3**–SA)–**9**–JU)–18/**18**/18–MO
(JU–**9**–SA)–27–UR

If Threeness is about seeking pleasure – and about giving pleasure
to others – then it is not surprising if comedians tend to be strong in
Threeness. Two comedians (in addition to Jerry Lewis) who have very
strong Threeness charts are Phyllis Diller and Benny Hill.

Phyllis Diller has been described as "one of the most beloved people in
show business".[11] She writes her own quickfire comedy routines, creating
"a stage persona of a wild-haired, eccentrically-dressed housewife who
makes jokes about a husband named 'Fang' while smoking from a long
cigarette holder",[12] and she has been a pioneer in women's stand-up
comedy. Like Jerry Lewis, she has been very active in charity work. Her
closest Threeness cluster is (MA–**3**–UR)–**9**–SA (with Uranus near the
Midheaven), which creates an image of controlled (Saturn) assertion
(Mars) of her originality (Uranus), all in the Threeness mode of carefree
light-heartedness.

Benny Hill was famous for his saucy slapstick comedy, which (despite
accusations of sexism) made him one of the most loved comedians
around the world. Like Jerry Lewis and Phyllis Diller, he wrote all his
own material.

All these comedians (including Jerry Lewis) can be described as
clowns, or light comedians, whose aim is solely to give pleasure, often
by inviting people to laugh at their antics. There is no element here
of 'dark' comedy, of malicious satire or of cutting wit at other people's
expense. Comedians whose humour includes this dark element tend to
have less strong Threeness charts. An example of this is John Cleese
,[13] the star and scriptwriter of *Fawlty Towers* and *Monty Python's Flying
Circus*, whose chart contains more Twoness than Threeness. Cleese has
said that, after he had undergone psychotherapy, he felt happier but
his comedic inspiration dried up: in other words, his inspiration was
dependent on the stress and tension induced by Twoness.

Michael Palin
Born 5 May 1943, 11.45 (–02.00)
Sheffield, England (53N23. 1W30).
Source: From him, via Eve Jackson (FCC). RR: A.

(ME–**1**–UR)–**9**–MA)–9/**9**/9–CH
(ME–**1**–UR)–18/6/18/6–(SO–9–PL)
(MA–**9**–UR)–**9**–CH)–18/18/**6**–VE
(MO–27–JU)–27/27–VE

Michael Palin is also known as a comedian; along with John Cleese, he was a member of the *Monty Python's Flying Circus* team, and he has also appeared in films such as *A Fish Called Wanda*, being (like the other comedians that we've mentioned) unafraid of making a complete fool of himself. Nowadays he is best known as the presenter of several series of travel documentaries on television, starting with *Around the World in 80 Days* and continuing with many others. In these documentaries he comes across as extremely laid-back, easy-going, relaxed, light-hearted, able to get on with everybody, always ready to laugh at his own misfortunes. He is a walking example of the essence of Threeness.

Cynthia Payne
Born 24 December 1932, 21.00 (+00.00)
Bognor Regis, England (50N47. 0W41).
Source: From her, via Frank C. Clifford (FCC). RR: A.

(SO–**9**–PL)–**18/6**–JU
(SO–**9**–PL)–27/27–MA)–27/**27**/27–UR
(MO–2–CH)–3/6–PL
(JU–3–CH)–**6**/6–PL

Cynthia Payne is Britain's best-known madam (or brothel owner), famous for throwing sex parties for middle-aged men. She herself wielded a whip for those clients who had masochistic tendencies. She was sent to prison for 18 months after police raided her home. Asked whether she had sex herself at the parties, she replied: "Not at the parties – I was too busy counting the lolly at the end of the afternoon". Asked whether she felt fine about what she was doing, she said, "Oh yeah, I felt like I was doing a real good service". She is now an after-dinner speaker, campaigning to liberalize Britain's sex laws. As a BBC reporter has written, she enjoys notoriety and loves to shock and to tease.

Payne's Threeness pattern, with SO–9–PL linked to MA, UR and JU, clearly shows her hedonistic approach to life: Sun (self-fulfilment) linked to Mars (sexuality), Uranus (originality and desire to shock), Pluto (dedication) and Jupiter (freedom and theatricality), all in a pattern of Threeness signifying pleasure-seeking and freedom from worry.

Linda McCartney

Born 24 September 1941, 10.00 (+04.00) (birth name: Linda Eastman)
New York, NY, USA (40N43. 74W00).
Source: From her, via Tom Hopke and David Goldstein (ADB) RR: A.

(SO–1–NE)–3/3/3/3–(SA–1–UR)
(((SO–3–UR)–9/9–VE)–9/9/9–MA)–18/18/18/6–JU
(ME–9–PL)–27–SA

Paul McCartney's first wife Linda, who died of cancer at the age of 56, has a very strong Threeness chart, with a close pattern of ((SO–9–VE)–9–MA)–18/18/6–JU, and several other Threeness links. Apart from her very close and loving marriage, Linda was best known as a photographer and also for her tireless campaigning for vegetarianism and for animal rights. I believe that she was motivated by a deep love for animals and a desire to relieve their suffering. (She said, "If slaughterhouses had glass walls, everyone would be vegetarian".) But her campaigning had none of the violence and malice which is indulged in by many animal rights activists; it was done in a spirit of Threeness. From the obituaries I have read of her, it is clear that Linda was a very warm-hearted person, who brought light into the lives of those who knew her.

Frank Farrelly

Born 26 August 1931, 02.15 (+06.00)
St Louis, MO, USA (38N38. 90W12).
Source: From him, via Neil Marbell (ADB). RR: A.

(SO–9–MO)–9–PL
          –27–UR
(ME–9–JU)–27/27/27/27–(MA–9–NE)
          –18–VE

Frank Farrelly was a maverick psychotherapist. He invented and practised a therapeutic approach which he called "Provocative Therapy", and he wrote a book with the same name.[14] In Provocative Therapy, the therapist behaves in ways which for most therapists would be absolutely taboo. For instance, if a client said "I feel I'm a hopeless case", the therapist might reply, "Yes, you're a hopeless case, I can't think of one good thing to say about you". This makes the client angry, and forces him out of his customary pattern of defending himself by defending his hopelessness.

Farrelly relates how a client told him that she wanted to commit suicide. He responded by picking up her purse and taking things from it, including her cigarettes and her money, saying "You won't be needing these any more," and commenting also on the shambolic organization of her purse. The client angrily tried to grab the purse, saying "It's not polite to go through a lady's purse", but Farrelly replied "Lady! Aw come on! Besides, why keep up these social niceties in your last hours?" When he took out the last three dollars, she said, "Come on, Frank, I need those three bucks to get home in the cab". He then gave her back the purse and the money, saying "I'm sorry, I forgot, you've got to get home to commit suicide. I sure as hell don't want you doing it here in my office". A month later, she sent him a cheque, with a note saying "You will notice that the bill is paid in full, less the cost of the carton of cigarettes you kept that night, Mr Omniscient". She no longer wanted to kill herself.[15]

We need to stress that, despite the apparent callousness of many of Farrelly's remarks to clients, he somehow made it clear to them that he was doing it with love. One of his clients described him as "the kindest, most understanding man I have ever met, wrapped up in the biggest son of a bitch I have ever met".[16]

It seems to me that Farrelly's aim was to introduce the lightness of Threeness into psychotherapy. He repeatedly stresses the importance of humour and laughter in therapy – the importance of helping clients to laugh at themselves, to laugh at the therapist, and to laugh *with* the therapist. Psychotherapy tends to be a rather grim business, and I guess there are not many therapists (and not many long-term therapy clients) who have strong Threeness charts. But Farrelly was trying (with considerable success) to help clients to heal themselves, by jerking them out of their "woundology"[17] and helping them to view themselves and their problems in a lighter, more humorous, more accepting and more loving way. In doing this, he was performing a service not unlike that performed by the comedians whom we considered earlier, who were also helping people to laugh at themselves. All this is to do with the healing power of Threeness.

Adi Da (Da Free John)

Born 3 November 1939, 11.21 (+05.00) (name at birth: Franklin Jones) Jamaica, NY, USA (40N41. 73W48).
Source: From his autobiography *The Knee of Listening* (ADB). RR: A.

(ME–1–VE)–3–(MO–**3**–JU)
((MO–1–PL)–3/**3**–ME)–**3**/3/3–JU
(ME–**3**–PL)–**27**–JU

Franklin Jones was a spiritual teacher who kept on changing his name. The name that he finally settled on was Adi Da, but he is probably best known as Da Free John, the name that he adopted during his most notorious period in the 1970s. ('Da' is a Sanskrit word meaning 'giver'.)

Adi Da was an extremely charismatic figure who inspired devotion among his followers. He stated that he was an avatar, an incarnation of God, and that "one needed only to meditate on his image or body in order to participate in enlightenment".[18] His essential teaching was that "seeing oneself as an individual separate from a divine unitive reality is an illusion and the cause of unhappiness".[18] However, his teaching methods (like his name) kept changing. For a time he directed his followers in 'sexual theatre', which involved public and group sex and the making of pornographic movies: this was part of his 'Crazy Wisdom' programme, to do with helping people to break free from habitual patterns and societal norms, so as to awaken their consciousness and enable them to surrender more completely to the guru and the community. Later, however, he abandoned all such practices, and spent his last years in solitary contemplation.

Adi Da's strong Threeness pattern has to be seen in the context of the Twoness that is also present in his chart. With Sun (near the Midheaven) –8–NE, –**16**–ME and –**32**–MO, he was compelled to spend his life restlessly thinking about his own purpose in the world and about how he could find self-fulfilment. Also, with MA–**4**–UR, there was a need to draw attention to himself by striking and dramatic actions. However, this Twoness was accompanied by a very strong pattern of Threeness, which is dominated by a ME–**3**–PL which is completely exact (Mercury at 2°55' Sagittarius, Pluto at 2°55' Leo). An exact trine like this is extremely powerful, and in this case it shows the communicative power of Mercury united with the ruthlessness and dedication of Pluto in the Threeness principle of pleasure: that is to say, it shows Adi Da rejoicing in his own ability to communicate powerfully and effectively and to influence others by the radicalism of his thought and the power of his oratory.

Adi Da can be compared with Ludwig Haeusser,[19] another spiritual leader with a strong Threeness pattern, who proclaimed himself to be the new Christ, and who encouraged his followers to shed their inhibitions and behave in ways that were unacceptable to society. These cases illustrate the power of Threeness to liberate people from society's expectations and to do whatever they please. Just as the comedians (whom we discussed earlier) were not afraid of making fools of themselves, so Abi Da and Haeusser were not afraid to proclaim their own divinity and to behave in ways that invited society's disapproval (and to encourage others to do so). Threeness is about the absence of fear. If one has no fear, there is no limit to what one can choose to do.

Caril Ann Fugate

Born 30 July 1943, 12.55 (+05.00)
Lincoln, NE, USA (40N48. 96W40).
Source: Birth certificate, via T. Pat Davis (ADB). RR: AA.

((SO–**1**–JU–**1**–PL)–**9**–VE)–**27**/27/**27**/**27**/27/27/27/27–(ME–**9**–NE)
     –6–UR
(VE–**3**–MA)–**9**/9–JU

In the previous chapter we listed several murderers with strong Twoness patterns. Murderers with strong Threeness patterns are less common; but one example of a murderer (or, at the least, an accomplice to murder) with a very strong Threeness pattern is Caril Ann Fugate, who at the age of 14, with her boyfriend Charles Starkweather, went on a killing spree which inspired the film *Natural Born Killers*.

The basic story is that Fugate came home to find that Starkweather (with whom she already had a relationship) had killed her mother, her stepfather, and her baby half-sister. The couple stayed in the house for a week with the bodies, after which they went out and killed seven more people before they were arrested. There was doubt about whether Fugate had carried out any of the killings herself. Starkweather was sentenced to death, and Fugate to life imprisonment. She was a model prisoner and was released after 18 years, since when she has refused to say a word about the killings.

Judging by her chart, it would seem that Fugate had none of the internal tension and rage which normally incites people to kill. She was clearly infatuated with Starkweather, and it seems that her Threeness caused her to feel that whatever he did was OK. We can assume that she enjoyed the killings, whether or not she carried any of them out herself. In the same way, she accepted life in prison, and never complained. The spirit of rebellion was absent from her nature.

George W. Bush

Born 6 July 1946, 07.26 (+04.00)
New Haven, CT, USA (41N18. 72W56).
Source: Hospital records, via Kim Castilla (ADB). RR: AA.

(MO–**9**–SA)–27/**27**–ME
(JU–3–UR)–9/**9**–MA
(MA–**9**–UR)–**27**/27–NE

Ex-President George W. Bush is not as strong in Threeness as the other people whom we have discussed in this chapter, nevertheless, Three is (by a considerable margin) the strongest prime number in his chart, and we can say that (despite several other important aspects) he is essentially a Threeness person. That is to say, he is a person with an easy-going, happy-go-lucky approach to life, whose primary motivation is to seek pleasure.

In view of Bush's well-known inadequacies as President, we can say that this highlights the negative side of Threeness. A Threeness person may be an excellent friend and companion, but he cannot always be trusted to respond adequately to challenging situations. He may be inattentive to detail, and prone (as Jerry Lewis was) to unintentional gaffes. In particular (just as Fugate fell under the spell of Starkweather) Bush's Threeness may have caused him to fall under the spell of people like Cheney and Rumsfeld who had the ruthlessness which he himself lacked.

Paddington and Selby rail crashes

Paddington (Ladbroke Grove) crash
5 October 1999, 08.09 (−01.00)
London, England (51N30. 0W10).
Source: Wikipedia.

(SO–3–UR)–9/9–JU
(MO–3–MA)–9–NE)–27/27/27–PL
(JU–9–UR)–27–SA

Selby crash
28 February 2001, 06.13 (+00.00)
Selby, England (53N48. 1W04).
Source: Wikipedia.

(MO–9–ME)–18/18/18/6–(SA–9–PL)
(VE–3–PL)–6–ME
        –9/9–SA

In the previous chapter we looked at the Nuneaton rail crash, which arose out of the stress and tension associated with an excess of Twoness. However, it seems to be more common for rail and air crashes to come from an excess of Threeness, which is associated, not with stress and tension, but with negligence and carelessness. The absence of fear, which is a feature of Threeness, may lead the driver or pilot to fail to notice, or to ignore, signs of approaching danger.

In the Paddington rail crash of 1999, two trains (an express train and a local train) collided, resulting in 31 deaths. The collision was caused by the driver of the local train failing to observe a series of red signals and continuing on when he should have stopped. The Threeness chart for this crash is very strong, and we can guess that the driver was in a kind of 'Threeness dream' when he passed the signals.

Another crash with a very strong Threeness chart is the Selby rail crash of 2001, which was caused by a car driver falling asleep at the wheel (surely a supreme example of carelessness). His car veered off the road, down an embankment, and onto a railway line, where it was hit by a train. The train was derailed and crashed into another train, causing 10 deaths.

Conclusion

We have seen that Threeness is connected to a light, easy-going, pleasure-seeking approach to life. If two planets in the chart have a Threeness link, the person will enjoy bringing these planets together and will find happiness by doing so. Especially when the outer planets (which are concerned with ideals and moral principles) are involved, he will seek happiness not only for himself but for others. He will try to increase the amount of happiness in the world.

Threeness people tend to accept the world as it is (rather than battling against it as Twoness people do). This includes accepting other people as they are, rather than seeing them as enemies. *Love* is a very real emotion for Threeness people: often they can be said to be in love with the world, or in love with humanity.

Humour is very important for Threeness people. They can laugh at themselves as well as at others. They aim to spread happiness through laughter.

Threeness people tend to have a spirit of optimism. They believe that things will work out all right, and so they are relatively free of worries about the future.

In some cases there is a deep spirituality, arising from a deep sense of joy at being part of the cosmos, but in other cases this spirituality is (or appears to be) lacking, and the search for happiness (for themselves and for others) is conducted entirely at a mundane level.

We have seen also that the downside of Threeness can take the form of carelessness or negligence. The spirit of optimism can lead Threeness people to ignore, or be unaware of, dangers. Fearlessness can slip into foolhardiness, and it may be that sometimes the spirit of pleasure-seeking can go 'over the top' and turn into a reckless hedonism which causes damage to others.

I think there is also a possibility that some Threeness people, because they are so much oriented towards seeking the light, may tend to be callous and lacking in understanding towards others (for instance, Twoness people) who are more aware of (or more at home in) the darkness. Threeness people may tend to ignore or suppress the shadow, both in themselves and in others. The focus on joy and happiness can lead to profound spirituality, but it can also lead to a shallowness and superficiality in which the person turns away from anything that is uncomfortable or disturbing.

How is it that the number Three has these meanings? I would like to suggest that, at a deeper level, Three is to do with the dawn of consciousness of Self. At the level of Oneness, everything is One, and so there is no consciousness of anything outside oneself. When we move from One to Two, Self becomes aware of Not-self, or of Other, and so there is the dawn of consciousness. But when we move from Two to Three, there is now a third point (the apex of the triangle), which is aware of both Self and Other, and can see the relationship between them. We can call this third point the *witness*. Thus, Three is the number within which consciousness becomes aware of itself.

Many spiritual teachers (such as Roberto Assagioli, the founder of Psychosynthesis, and also Eckhart Tolle) stress the importance of identifying with the witness, who is aware of the thoughts and feelings but does not believe he *is* the thoughts and feelings. In the words (greatly abbreviated) of Assagioli's Psychosynthesis Prayer: "I have a body, but I am not my body. I have emotions, but I am not my emotions. I have desires, but I am not my desires. I have an intellect, but I am not my intellect. I recognize and affirm that I am a centre of pure self-consciousness and of will".[20] According to Eckhart Tolle, when one completely identifies with the witness rather than with the thoughts and feelings that are being witnessed, one's normal state of anxiety and fearfulness gives way to "a sacred sense of Presence, a deep peace and serenity and complete freedom from fear".[21]

I believe that this is the root of the association of Three with happiness and pleasure. Ultimately, Three is about the profound peace and joy that comes when one disidentifies from the fearful thoughts and feelings of the ego and identifies oneself as a centre of pure consciousness. Within this state, one does not seek to deny or suppress the dark thoughts and feelings; one simply *accepts* that they are there, but one does not feel threatened by them. One accepts that things are as they are. In the language of Eckhart Tolle, one does not resist the present moment (the Now), no matter what it contains.

In this chapter, the nearest we have come to this profound peace and joy is in the writings of Emmanuel as channelled by Pat Rodegast. It is as though Rodegast, guided by Emmanuel, was able to separate the Threeness in her chart from all the other factors and to speak as the voice of pure unadulterated Threeness. For most people, however, their Threeness (even when it is very strong) is contaminated by the desires and anxieties associated with all the other prime numbers. They still seek peace, pleasure and happiness, but often at a more mundane level. They are a long way from incarnating the spirit of pure Threeness and yet, on occasions, they may still be touched by something of the quality of divine joy.

We have said that Threeness is about accepting that things are as they are. As the witness, one sees the relationship between Self and Other, and accepts that it is good. But the next question might be, "Yes, but what if I have the power to change myself or to change the world around me?" This is the question which is asked by the next prime number, which is Five.

6

Sixness

Before we move on to the next prime number which is Five, we need first to consider Six, which is 2 x 3 and so brings together the numbers Two and Three that we have already discussed. If Two means *striving* and Three means *pleasure*, then Six means *striving towards pleasure* or *pleasure in striving*.

In looking at Six, we will look not only at sextile aspects (pure Sixness), but also at aspects which involve twelfths (3 x 2 x 2) and twenty-fourths (3 x 2 x 2 x 2) of the circle. These aspects have the same meaning, except that the element of *striving* is stronger than in pure Sixness. (Eighteen (3 x 3 x 2) is also a multiple of Six, but it seems to me that in practice Eighteen is very close to pure Threeness, and so was considered in the previous chapter.)

Most charts contain a fair amount of Twoness and also a fair amount of Threeness, but there is a lot of variation between charts in how closely the Twoness and Threeness are linked to each other. There are some charts in which the Twoness and the Threeness are entirely (or almost entirely) separate: that is to say, there are clusters of planets linked by pure Twoness, and there are also clusters of planets linked by pure Threeness, but there is no connection between the two. These will tend to be the charts of people who have an area of their life in which they struggle to achieve, and a separate area of their life in which they relax and seek pleasure. To simplify, we could say that they are people who make a sharp distinction between work and play.

But on the other hand, there are people who have very little pure Twoness and very little pure Threeness. The Twoness and Threeness in their charts is contained entirely (or almost entirely) in Six or multiples of Six. These will tend to be people who find *pleasure in striving*. That is to say, for these people there is no distinction between work and play. Work brings pleasure, and relaxation and enjoyment are found in activities which involve effort and a struggle to achieve.

In this chapter we will look at a few examples of people who fall into this latter group.

Charles Harvey
Born 22 June 1940, 09.16 (–01.00)
Little Bookham, England (51N29. 0W13).
Source: From him. RR: A.

(MO–2–PL)–12–SO
((UR–3–NE)–6/6–MA)–8/24/24–VE
(VE–6–JU)–24/24/24/8–(MA–6–NE)

The astrologer Charles Harvey was an outstanding example of a person with a strong Sixness chart – a person for whom work was pleasure, and whose pleasure was in work. Charles lived and breathed astrology; his enthusiasm for it affected everything that he did, and infected everyone whom he met.

The central features of Charles's Sixness pattern are VE–6–JU (with Jupiter on the Midheaven) and MA–6–NE, linked together by '24' aspects. The Sun and Moon are not involved, so (within this pattern) Charles is seeking nothing for himself; his search is for an expansive beauty (VE–JU) attained through selfless action (MA–NE). But also, Sun and Moon (together with Pluto) are linked by '12' aspects, showing that the Sixness principle of *pleasure through action* was at the heart of Charles's personality and of his sense of his own identity.

Rolf Harris
Born 30 March 1930, 03.15 (–08.00)
Perth, Australia (31S57. 115E51).
Source: From him, via Sy Scholfield (ADB). RR: A.

(SA–3–CH)–18/6/18/6–(VE–9–MA)
(SA–3–CH)–6/12/6/12–(MA–4–JU)
(SA–3–CH)–12/4/12/12–(JU–6–UR)
(JU–6–UR)–9/18–NE

Rolf Harris is a multi-talented performer and entertainer, noted especially for the *facility* with which he does whatever he does. As an artist, he can easily mimic the styles of other artists, and he has the extraordinary ability to paint the first brushstrokes on an empty canvas knowing exactly what the final picture is going to look like (hence his catchphrase "Do you know what it is yet?"). As a singer he can invent songs like *Tie Me Kangaroo Down, Sport* and perform them with great dexterity and with a highly-developed sense of rhythm. He has also shown great skill as a television presenter on *Animal Hospital*, displaying great empathy with all the people (and animals) whom he meets.

In Harris's chart, five of the six outer planets (Jupiter, Saturn, Uranus, Neptune and Chiron) are linked by Sixness aspects. These aspects are built around an almost-exact SA–**3**–CH, showing Harris's joy in serving the world by tying himself down to particular activities. This focus on the outer planets shows, perhaps, that Sixness – the belief in striving to give pleasure, and the belief that by his actions he can give pleasure to others – is Harris's philosophy of life. He wants nothing for himself; the pleasure he gives to others is its own reward.

Luciano Pavarotti
Born 12 October 1935, 01.40 (–01.00)
Modena, Italy (44N40. 10E56).
Source: Birth certificate, via Bordoni (ADB). RR: AA.

(SO–**2**–MO)–**6**/3/3/**6**–(MA–**2**–CH)
(SO–**6**–MA)–**9**/18–PL
(MA–**2**–CH)–4/**4**–NE)–3/**6**/**12**–MO
(NE–**4**–CH)–**8**–ME)–**12**/**6**/**24**–MO
(ME–2–UR)–3/**6**–SA
(SA–**6**–UR)–**18**/**9**–JU

Pavarotti, gifted with one of the most beautiful tenor voices the world has ever known, was clearly another person (like Rolf Harris) whose aim was to bring pleasure to others (and to himself) by the performance of his craft. His chart contains more Twoness than Threeness, and he faced many struggles in his life, but his Sixness (centred on the Moon, that is, on instinctive reactions and feelings) ensured that he remained essentially a seeker after pleasure. It is said that he could not read music, and he relied on his natural 'ear': as with Rolf Harris, his musicality was a matter of facility, not of learning. His last album consisted, not of operatic arias, but of Italian pop music.

Amy Johnson

Born 1 July 1903, 01.30 (+00.00)
Hull, England (53N45. 0W20).
Source: From her secretary, via Wemyss (ADB). RR: A.

(SO–**8**–VE)–**24**/**24**/**12**/12/3/24–((JU–**4**–UR)–**8**–SA)

Amy Johnson was an aviator who set many long-distance records during the 1930s. In particular she was the first woman to fly solo from Britain to Australia. She died in a mysterious plane crash during the Second World War.

It would be easy to see Johnson as another relentless seeker after records (like Steve Fossett whom we considered in the chapter on Twoness): but one feels that in Johnson's case there was more of an element of pleasure-seeking, and that she was motivated by the sheer joy of flying as much as by the desire for personal achievement. The Sixness in her chart brings together the two Twoness patterns of SO–**8**–VE (an aspect which usually denotes a very strong need to be loved) and (JU–**4**–UR)–**8**–SA, which suggests a strong desire to break down barriers and find freedom by means of disciplined action. Certainly these Twoness patterns will have given Johnson a steely determination to succeed, but I feel that the Sixness uniting them will have enabled her to remain light-hearted and cheerful.

Meher Baba

Born 25 February 1894, 05.00 (–05.21)
Poona, India (18N32. 73E52).
Source: From his family, via Bob Mulligan (ADB). RR: A.

((SO–**3**–MO)–6/**6**–MA)–4/12/12–PL
(MO–**6**–MA)–**24**/**8**–VE
(ME–**6**–JU)–**12**/12–SA
(VE–**3**–SA)–**4**/12–JU
(SA–8–PL)–12/**24**–JU

Meher Baba was a spiritual master who became known as the 'Silent Guru,' since he was silent for the last 43 years of his life. However, he communicated by means of an alphabet board, and later by hand gestures which were interpreted by one of his followers. He travelled widely, and worked with lepers, the poor, and the mentally ill. He had no interest in rules, rites or rituals. On his website[1] he sets out a simple message of love expressed through actions: "To love God in the most practical way is to love our fellow beings ... They also serve who express their love in little things". The greatest good is to help and serve people in humble, loving, practical ways, without asking for anything in return. This is the essence of Sixness: joy in actions; actions that being joy.

Reginald and Ronald Kray

Born 24 October 1933, 20.00 (Reginald) and 20.10 (Ronald) (+00.00) London, England (51N30. 0W10).
Source: Birth certificates, via Ananda Bagley (ADB). RR: AA.

(Aspects given for Reginald; Ronald's are almost identical)
(ME–**3**–PL)–**8**/24/**24**/**24**–(JU–**3**–SA)
((ME–**3**–PL)–12/**4**–UR)–24/**24**/24–SA
((JU–**3**–SA)–6–MA)–**24**/**24**/8–PL

All numbers have their dark sides, and Six is no exception. The dark side of Sixness is illustrated by the Kray twins, Reginald ("Reggie") and Ronald ("Ronnie"), who dominated the London criminal scene in the 1950s and 1960s.

The twins first got into trouble when they were called up for National Service. In the Army they refused to submit to authority, caused all kinds of mayhem, and were dishonourably discharged. In the 1950s they became involved in protection rackets and in hijacking, armed robbery, and arson. Peter Rachman, the notorious landlord, then gave them control of a nightclub in the fashionable West End, and in the 1960s "they were widely seen as prosperous and charming nightclub owners and were part of the Swinging London scene ... [they] socialized with lords, MPs, socialites and show business characters such as the actors George Raft, Judy Garland, Diana Dors, Barbara Windsor and Frank Sinatra".[2] Ronnie, who was bisexual, is alleged to have had affairs with two male Members of Parliament, one Conservative and one Labour. This was the 'Swinging Sixties', and the Krays regarded them as the best years of their lives. Ronnie later wrote: "The Beatles and the Rolling Stones were rulers of pop music ... and me and my brother ruled London. We were fucking untouchable".[3]

In 1966-7 both the twins committed murders. Ronnie shot George Cornell who had called him a "fat poof". Reggie stabbed Jack "The Hat" McVitie because of an argument about money. They were both convicted and sentenced to life imprisonment, with a non-parole period of 30 years. Reggie died in prison. Ronnie was released on compassionate grounds shortly before he died of cancer, and was given an ostentatious funeral by people who still loved and admired him.

The twins have several important Twoness aspects (SO–8–VE, (MO–8–CH)–16/16–SA, (MA–4–NE)–8–UR, and (UR–4–PL)–8–MA), and also some important Threeness aspects (SO–9–MA, ME–3–PL, and JU–3–SA), which would take too long to analyse here. But the Twoness and the Threeness are linked together in a strong pattern of Sixness, showing that the twins would follow the Sixness philosophy of pleasure-seeking through action. Essentially they were hedonists, knowing no goal other than their own pleasure.

But I am not sure that there is anything in their charts that shows that they would direct this Sixness to criminal ends, rather than to benevolent ends like the other people discussed in this chapter. Clearly they were also influenced by their background (their father, Charlie Kray, was a scrap dealer who, when called up at the start of World War II, went into hiding and travelled the country avoiding the law). Also we can note that Ronnie, who seems to have been the dominant twin, suffered from paranoid schizophrenia. I am inclined to believe that such illnesses are not caused or affected by the astrological chart, so we must see the schizophrenia as an additional factor that would cause Ronnie (and, through him, his brother) to act out the chart in particular ways. As we noted in the case of Jürgen Bartsch in Chapter 4, the chart shows only *potential*.

Conclusion

These people with high levels of Sixness in their charts combine the drivenness of Twoness with the light-heartedness and pleasure-seeking of Threeness. They enjoy their work, and enjoy the process of striving to reach goals and notch up achievements. Often their enthusiasm is infectious, and they succeed not only in finding pleasure for themselves, but in giving pleasure to others. A key word is *facility*: they find it easy to achieve what for others would be a painful struggle.

The downside would seem to be that (as in the case of the Kray twins) the search for pleasure through achievement may sometimes be at the expense of other people, who may be carelessly trampled on or pushed out of the way. The competitiveness of Twoness together with the carelessness of Threeness can, in certain circumstances, be a lethal combination.

7

Fiveness

If Three is the number of God (the Trinity), then Five is the number of Man. Man has five fingers on each hand, and he has created the decimal system, which is a system of counting in fives. With the aid of the decimal system, he has changed the face of the Earth on which he lives. He has built scientific systems, technological systems, social systems, economic systems, religious systems, political systems, systems of thought – every possible kind of system – through which he has established mastery over his environment.

In speaking of 'Man', I do of course mean 'mankind', which includes women as well as men. Nevertheless, I feel that the number Five (to a greater extent even than Two) has inherent qualities which have traditionally been seen as masculine. It is to do with the *yang* principle of creativity, rather than the *yin* principle of receptivity. The system of counting in fives may have contributed to the dominance of patriarchal systems and the imbalance between the masculine and the feminine which have characterized human history, at least over the last few thousand years.

The basis of the decimal system is 10, which is 2 x 5. In choosing this system of counting, Man has bypassed 3 (the next prime number after 2), and has chosen to rely instead on the next prime number after 3, which is 5. It could be argued that, in bypassing 3, Man has bypassed God. Within the perspective of Threeness, Man accepts his place within God's creation. But within the perspective of Fiveness, Man himself becomes a creator, reshaping the world to suit his own needs.

We can perhaps speculate on how things might have been different if mankind had chosen a different system of counting. An obvious alternative to the decimal system is the duodecimal system, based on 12, which is 2 x 2 x 3. There are many signs that men and women once preferred to count in twelves rather than tens: twelve months in a year,

24 (12 x 2) hours in a day, 60 (12 x 5) minutes in an hour and seconds in a minute, 360 (12 x 2 x 3 x 5) degrees in a circle, twelve inches in a foot (and three feet in a yard, reinforcing the emphasis on Threeness), twelve old pence in a shilling, and (in astrology) twelve signs in the zodiac and twelve houses in the diurnal circle. But some of these systems have been or are being phased out, while others remain but are obliged to fit awkwardly into the decimal system. If Man had chosen a duodecimal system (in which the figure 10 would represent twelve, and two new digits would be introduced to represent ten and eleven), then we can guess that he might have done his counting in a different spirit, with a better balance between *yin* and *yang*, and with less of a desire to overturn the natural order and create his own new structures.

The geometrical figures associated with Five are the pentagon (a five-sided figure) and the pentagram (a five-pointed star). The pentagram in particular has been seen as the perfection of created beauty and symmetry. This perceived beauty is linked to the fact that the lines within a pentagram are related to each other in accordance with the Golden Section or Golden Ratio (*phi*), which is $(1+\sqrt{5})/2$, or 1.618.

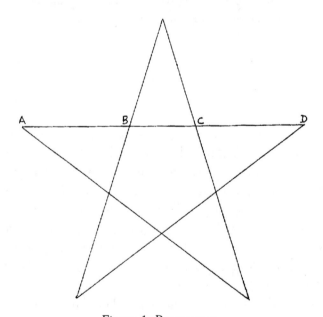

Figure 1: Pentagram

AD/AC=AC/AB=AB/BC=phi(1.618)

Thus, in the diagram (see Figure 1), AD/AC = AC/AB = AB/BC = 1.618. The Golden Section has always been used by artists, architects and others as a means of creating beauty and balance in design. Thus, the pentagram stands for *perfection in design*, or *designed perfection*.

A pentagram within a circle is known as a *pentacle*. Pentacles have been seen as a potent protection against evil, and have been hung outside houses to protect their occupants and inscribed on pots to protect their contents. Conversely, the inverted pentagram (with two upward points representing the horns of the devil) is a Satanic symbol, invoking the power of evil.

Pentagrams and pentacles have also been seen as representing the power of Man. The sixteenth-century occult philosopher Heinrich Cornelius Agrippa superimposed the figure of a man onto a pentacle, with the five points of the star coinciding with the head and with the outstretched hands and feet. This is said to represent "the golden symmetry of the human body",[1] and also to represent Man as a microcosm of the universe .[2] At the centre of the pentacle is the penis, symbolizing masculinity, and masculinity is also indicated by the planet Mars, whose sign is shown at the top of the pentacle above the head. The head is also associated with the fifth element of spirit (or consciousness), added to the four elements of fire, earth, air and water. The word *quintessence* means, originally, the 'fifth essence', or spiritual essence, of a thing (that which lies beyond its physical or material nature).

Fiveness is also related to the five human fingers and the five human senses. Thus, there are many ways in which Five is linked to the power of Man to shape his environment. It has been said that "the number 5 has always been regarded as mystical and magical, yet essentially 'human'".[2] Man is a microcosm of the universe, his nature is divine, and he can himself work magic and perform miracles. We can see from this how Fiveness – if it is not tempered by Threeness, which is about delighting in (or surrendering to) the world as it already is – can contribute vastly to the *hubris* which has characterized Man's actions. The spirit of Fiveness was expressed by Francis Bacon, who said that the most wholesome and noble ambition of Man was "to endeavour to establish and extend the power and dominion of the human race over the rest of the universe".[3]

We can expect, then, that the principle of Fiveness is concerned with the *creation and design* of *forms, structures and systems*.[4] It is the principle by which Man creates forms that were not present in nature. It is the process of creating order out of chaos (or what is seen to be chaos). It is therefore concerned with art, architecture, technology, and all the ways in which Man has imposed his stamp on the world. And it also applies to the process of systematic thinking, or the creation of *structures in the mind*: thus, as Harding and Harvey say, "Man's capacity for reflective self-consciousness, by which he is enabled to extract the underlying formal principles from matter, is very decidedly related to the function of Fiveness".[5] But also (just as the inverted pentagram can signify the opposite of the upright pentagram) Fiveness can be related to the *destruction* of systems and the creation of chaos out of order.

The aspects that have the quality of pure Fiveness are the quintile (72°) and the bi-quintile (144°): that is to say, if two planets are 72° or 144° apart from each other in the chart, their relationship will have the quality of Fiveness. But also, the angle between two planets may be one twenty-fifth (or two twenty-fifths, etc) of the circle, and this aspect will again have a quality of pure Fiveness, since 25 is 5 x 5. Also, there are several numbers below 32 in which Five is combined with other prime numbers: thus, 10 is 5 x 2 and 20 is 5 x 2 x 2 (striving towards Fiveness); 15 is 5 x 3 (pleasure in Fiveness); and 30 is 5 x 3 x 2 (striving towards pleasure in Fiveness).

In this chapter we will be concerned with all of these aspects which are Five or multiples of Five. The more of these aspects there are in a chart (and the closer they are to exactitude), the stronger will be the principle of Fiveness in the subject's personality. As in previous chapters, we will look at examples of charts that are exceptionally strong in Fiveness.

June and Jennifer Gibbons (the "Silent Twins")

Born 11 April 1963, 08.10 (June) and 08.20 (Jennifer) (–03.00)
Aden, Yemen (12N45. 45E12).
Source: *The Silent Twins* by Marjorie Wallace. RR: B.

(Aspects given are for June, but Jennifer's are almost identical)
((((MO–**1**–NE)–**3**–VE)–15/**15**/**5**–MA)–**15**/15/**15**/**15**/**15**/15/15/15–
     (ME–**5**–<u>SA</u>)–30/30/**10**/**10**/**30**/6–SO
((MO–**1**–NE)–**5**/5–UR)–<u>15</u>/15/3–ME
JU–<u>25</u>–PL

Of all the birth charts that I have seen, two of the strongest in terms of Fiveness are the charts of June and Jennifer Gibbons, who have become known as the 'Silent Twins'. The Silent Twins are a very special and unusual case, but they are worth studying in detail as they can tell us much about the nature of Fiveness.[6]

June and Jennifer, identical twins, were born ten minutes apart in Aden, Yemen, where their father was temporarily stationed in the British Royal Air Force. During their first year they moved to England, and at the age of eleven they moved to Haverfordwest, a small town in Wales, where for a time they (and their brother and sisters) were the only black children.

From an early age the twins made it a rule never to speak to any adults; in fact, they very rarely spoke to anyone except each other. They did not speak to their parents, nor to their older brother and sister, nor to their teachers, nor to other children at school. They spoke to each other very rapidly in a special language which no one else could understand. They were, however, able to talk to other people on the telephone. At home, "the twins took no part in family discussions but bowed their heads, eyes fixed on their plates, their faces without expression, tight and drawn in denial of the world around them".[7]

Up to the age of sixteen, the twins spent most of their time at home playing with dolls. But at that age (having left school) they suddenly entered on a period of frantic literary activity. They read voraciously. They wrote novels on themes of teenage violence and drug addiction. They recorded and interpreted all their dreams. They read books on astrology, witchcraft and hypnosis, and started practising all these skills. They kept diaries in which they recorded every detail of their thoughts and emotions, with remarkable psychological insight and literary skill. All these activities were carried out in the tiny bedroom where they now spent nearly all of their lives (food was brought up to them on trays). The relationship between them was one of intense love and also intense hatred: they could not live apart, but at the same time they deeply resented and feared each other. Jennifer was the dominant twin, and seemed to exercise a hypnotic power over her sister June.

At 18 they started to venture out of the house and to chase the local boys. Eventually one of these boys had sex with Jennifer in a church;

a week later, June also lost her virginity to him. But soon afterwards this boy (together with his brother, with whom the twins were in love) left the district. Heartbroken by this, the twins started on a two-month spree of theft and arson. They were caught, tried, classified as dangerous psychopaths, and sentenced for an indefinite period to Broadmoor, a high security psychiatric hospital, where they remained for twelve years.

In Broadmoor they continued to play games with their warders (as they had always done with social workers and others who had tried to help them), causing general frustration and bafflement. They refused to speak except through coded messages, and they took it in turns to 'eat for two' while the other twin starved. Also they continued their literary output. June in particular showed remarkable creative powers. Here is a sample of her writing:

> "My father, my mother, were they ever over the moon and proud to make two adorable twin daughters? Did they lie awake at night, thanking God for their beautiful gift? Did they wonder what young girls we would grow into? What kind of life was awaiting ahead for us? Did they even know our fate, the fate that entangled them? Did they know we were to be different from the rest of the family – that we were to be written into public papers for offences; that we would be law-breakers; that we would be condemned, sick – not fit to face society? Did they look into our cherubic baby faces and see the troubled, evil wickedness, the desire for destruction, which lay before us? How could they. We could not possibly have been born like that. It grew on us, as the years developed: self-consciousness, frustration, thwarted ambitions. Finally, it snapped".[8]

During their time in Broadmoor the twins became obsessed with death and with the belief that one of them must die in order that the other might live. On 9th March 1993 they were finally released, and were driven back to Wales in a minibus. During the journey June became aware that her sister was gravely ill. On arrival in Wales Jennifer was rushed to hospital, where she died on the same evening.[9] It was found that she had died of acute myocarditis (inflammation of the heart muscle). Since Jennifer's death, June has been trying to release herself from her identification with her sister and to live a more normal life. She talks now, but writes little.

The harmonic aspects between the planets are identical in both the twins' charts; however, June has Taurus rising whereas Jennifer has Gemini rising, and Jennifer's Saturn is almost exactly on the Midheaven, whereas June's Saturn is 2 degrees from the Midheaven. In both charts there is a massive Fiveness configuration involving six planets, which can be summarized as ((MO–**1**–NE)–3/15–(VE–**5**–MA)–15–(ME–**5**–SA)–10/30–SO. Also there is (MO–**1**–NE)–5–UR and JU–**25**–PL, so that all the planets except Chiron are involved in Fiveness aspects.

In my article *Harmonics and the Silent Twins*[10] I analysed the twins' Fiveness pattern in some detail. Here I will simply say that the twins' eccentric behaviour can be explained above all by the excess of Fiveness in their charts. We have said that Fiveness is about creating order out of chaos; but the negative side of this is that the person can become trapped in artificial and repetitive behaviour patterns. She is so determined to create her own world that she becomes trapped in the world that she has made; and she is so concerned with creating order out of chaos that she cannot allow any chaos to filter in from outside to disturb the orderliness of her behaviour. Another way of saying this is that life becomes a game in which one must obey the rules; the person has written the rules herself, and she allows the rules to bind her. People often complained that the twins were 'playing games' with them, and the twins clearly realized that they were trapped by their own games, and longed to step outside them and behave like 'normal' people, but were unable to do so. They were imprisoned by their Fiveness.

The creation of one's own system of order can also involve the destruction of external systems of order. This may help to explain the pleasure which the twins took in setting fire to buildings, and also the way in which they constantly tried to subvert the rules which governed an institution like Broadmoor. And yet in the end it is external chaos, rather than external order, that is most feared. Thus, it seems that Jennifer had to die rather than face the chaos of the outside world after twelve years in a rule-bound institution.

And she also had to die to save her sister. The twins had spent their lives reinforcing each other's Fiveness, playing games against each other, enabling each other to survive in the enclosed artificial world that they themselves had created. It seems that the twins knew that in the end they would have to break free and to find some accommodation with the outside world, but that, as long as they were together, this would be impossible. And Jennifer, as the one who had Saturn exactly on the Midheaven, knew that she was the one who had to die.

Bahá-u-lláh
Born 12 November 1817, 06.40 (–03.26)
Tehran, Iran (35N40. 51E26).
Source: From Baha'i literature ("sunrise"), via Rudhyar (ADB). RR: B.[11]

(<u>SO</u>–<u>5</u>–MA)–25/**25**/25/25–(MO–**5**–VE)
(MA–**4**–CH)–5/20–<u>SO</u>
((JU–**1**–UR)–**10**/10–ME)–20/**20**/20/20/20/**20**–(MO–**5**–VE)
(MO–<u>25</u>–MA)–25–<u>SA</u>
SA–**15**–PL

I have found several spiritual leaders and teachers who are very strong in Fiveness. Perhaps the most remarkable of them is Bahá-u-lláh, who was the founder of the Baha'i faith. Bahá-u-lláh has several close Fiveness configurations (see above), involving all the planets except Neptune and Pluto. (But he is also strong in Twoness and Sevenness.)

What strikes me most in reading about Bahá-u-lláh is his tremendous moral authority. He was clearly a charismatic leader who inspired great devotion among his followers, but his reputation and his lasting influence depend on his writings, most of which were written while he was in prison or house-bound as a result of his persecution by the authorities. According to the official website of the Baha'i faith:

> "Bahá-u-lláh presents a vision of life that insists upon a fundamental redefinition of all human relationships – relationships among human beings themselves, between human beings and the natural world, between the individual and society, and between the members of society and its institutions. Each of these relationships must be reassessed in the light of humanity's evolving understanding of God's will and purpose. New laws and concepts are enunciated by Bahá-u-lláh so that human consciousness can be freed from patterns of response set by tradition, and the foundations of a global civilization can be erected. 'A new life,' Bahá-u-lláh declares, 'is, in this age, stirring within all the peoples of the earth'".[12]

Later it is stated that, "in proclaiming the pivotal principle of the oneness of humankind, Bahá-u-lláh outlines a body of social precepts which he says must guide the future development of society". Prejudices of all kinds must be overcome: no racial or ethnic group is superior to another, and "women and men are fully equal in the sight of God". He stressed the importance of social justice, of universal education, and of consultative decision-making. He believed that it was necessary to work towards world government, so that conflicts between nations would cease. "The moral and spiritual transformation of society, the relief of the diverse peoples of the earth from conflict, injustice, and suffering, and the birth of a progressive and peaceful global civilization are not only possible, Bahá-u-lláh says, but inevitable".[12] In support of his beliefs, Bahá-u-lláh wrote letters to many of the world's rulers (including Pope Pius IX, Emperor Napoleon III of France, Czar Alexander II of Russia, and Queen Victoria) asking them to "accept his revelation, renounce their material possessions, work together to settle disputes, and [work] towards the betterment of the world and its peoples".[13]

It is clear that (although he also stressed the importance of devotion to God) Bahá-u-lláh was a very different kind of spiritual leader from the people (such as Padre Pio and Adi Da) whom we have considered in previous chapters. Bahá-u-lláh's vision was deeply imbued with the principles of Fiveness, which, as we have said, are to do with creating order out of chaos, and with a belief in the power of Man to create new structures and systems. He was campaigning for a new moral order. In Bahá-u-lláh's writings we can see Fiveness being manifested at its highest and most positive level, and his writings can teach us to value Fiveness as an essential part of God's plan.

Frank Buchman

Born 4 June 1878, 04.00 (+05.02)
Pennsburg, PA, USA (40N23. 75W30).
Source: From Zip Dobyns's file *Expanding Astrology's Universe* (ADB).
RR: A.

(SO–**5**–SA–**5**–UR)–10/<u>10</u>/10/<u>10</u>/10/**<u>10</u>**–(NE–**1**–CH)
    –10/10/**<u>10</u>**–CH)–<u>20</u>/20/**4**/20–PL
    –15/**<u>15</u>**/15–ME
    –**25**/**25**/25–VE

((SO–5–SA)–10–CH)–20/20/20/20/4/20–(JU–10–PL)

Frank Buchman, the founder of Moral Re-Armament (now known as Initiatives of Change), has an exceptionally strong Fiveness pattern involving all the planets except Moon and Mars. At the centre of the pattern is SO–5–SA–5–UR, showing that Buchman believes in himself as a person who can structure his world in disciplined and original ways.

Buchman was similar to Bahá-u-lláh in that he, too, was campaigning for a new moral order. His evangelical movement was "based on his concepts of God's guidance and the moral absolutes of piety, unselfishness, honesty and love".[14] He believed that "moral compromise was destructive of human character and relationships, and that moral strength was a prerequisite for building a just society".[15] He believed that "human nature could be changed and that change had to start in each individual, for one cannot change the world without first changing oneself".[16] The twelve-step programme of Alcoholics Anonymous is based on Buchman's teachings. It is clear that Buchman's vision was profoundly imbued with Fiveness. Like Bahá-u-lláh, he believed in the power of Man to change his world by creating new structures of thought and behaviour.

At the same time, we can see in Buchman something of the negative side of Fiveness. He was homophobic, and he praised Hitler (another Fiveness person) for having "built a front line of defence against the anti-Christ of Communism". One critic said that "Buchman oozed the oil of unctuous piety from every pore," and another said, "Buchman considered anyone who dared to criticize him to be obviously evil and working for the Devil".[17] The setting-up of new structures inevitably involves conflict with those who oppose these structures, and it is easy for Fiveness to lead to narrow-mindedness and intolerance.

Aurobindo
Born 15 August 1872, 05.00 (-05.53)
Calcutta, India (22N32. 88E22).
Source: From *Auroville: City of the Future*, via Marion March (ADB).
RR: B.

(ME–**3**–SA)–15/**5**–SO
(SA–**4**–CH)–**5**/20–SO
       –**20**/10–MO
((UR–**5**–PL)–**5**–MO)–15/15/**3**–NE
       –25–ME

Aurobindo, the Indian mystic and spiritual teacher, has a very complex Fiveness pattern which is shown above. In his youth, Aurobindo was a leader of a group of Indian nationalists known as the Extremists for their willingness to use violence and to advocate outright independence. He was jailed for a year, and while in prison he transformed himself from a nationalist leader into a spiritual seer as a result of meditating on the Bhagavad Gita, which caused him to "see compassion, honesty and charity [even] in the hearts of murderers".[18]

Aurobindo's "integral philosophy," which synthesized Western science with Eastern mysticism, centred around the concept of spiritual evolution. He believed that, just as physical life forms are evolving, so also spiritual awareness and realization have evolved and will continue to evolve, culminating in the final stage of 'supramentalization'. In order to help the spiritual seeker to progress as far as possible along this path, Aurobindo proposed a practical method which he called *integral yoga*. A person who successfully follows this path will be able to "station himself in the Supramental consciousness where he will rediscover the Oneness of Existence," and from that place will be able to "transform life on earth to that of heaven on earth – God in manifestation".[18]

Although Aurobindo's ultimate message of the "Oneness of Existence" is shared with all mystics across the globe, it seems to me that his particular approach to the task of attaining Oneness is suffused with the spirit of Fiveness. He is concerned with describing *systems* through which God's plan is evolving, and also with developing a systematic approach to the human task of transcending ordinary consciousness. In his writings he brings together numerous strands of Western and Eastern thought into a single integrated and orderly structure. Thus, it has been said that "Kant's sublime, Hegel's absolute, Schopenhauer's will, Kierkegaard's passion, Marx's matter, Darwin's evolution, Nietzsche's overman, Bergson's élan vital, all find their due representation in Sri Aurobindo's grand exposition. His thought successfully overarches cultural as well as religious chasms".[18] Charles Moore has said that Aurobindo has "arrived at a comprehensive and ... all-inclusive view of the universe and life, providing a world philosophy which ... brings together the East and the West".[19] All this is consistent with the essential nature of Fiveness, which is about building structures and creating order out of chaos.

Percy Bysshe Shelley

Born 4 August 1792, 22.00 (+00.01)
Horsham, England (51N04. 0W21).
Source: From statements by Shelley's father and grandfather, in biography (ADB). RR: A.

((SO–**1**–VE)–**5**–(MA–**1**–JU)–25/25/25/25–SA

I have found several *poets* who are strong in Fiveness. The writing of poetry is a Fiveness activity: the ideal poem is a created work of perfect beauty and symmetry, like a pentagram.

The poet Shelley has a configuration in which SO–**1**–VE is brought together with MA–**1**–JU (on the Descendant), and also with Saturn, by pure Fiveness aspects. This suggests that, whereas other people considered in this chapter were striving towards Fiveness (5 x 2) or taking pleasure in Fiveness (5 x 3), Shelley simply *was* Fiveness.

In Shelley's AstroDatabank biography it is stated: "Shelley regarded social reform as his life's work, believing that *man could aim for perfection* [my italics] and that love had the power to transform society". This is a very clear statement of a Fiveness outlook on life, putting Shelley alongside Bahá-u-lláh and Aurobindo as a person who believed that Man had the power to transform his world and introduce a new moral order. And yet Shelley, unlike Bahá-u-lláh and Aurobindo, did not believe in God. The perfection for which Man could aim was not God's perfection, but his own innate perfection (or rather, his perfectibility). Shelley's God was Beauty (SO–**1**–VE), and, like his contemporary Keats, he believed that Beauty was Truth.

Throughout his short life (he was drowned at sea at the age of 29), Shelley was true to his own radical beliefs. He hated all forms of tyranny and authority. Before he was 20 he wrote a pamphlet *The Necessity of Atheism* and a poem attacking the monarchy. He left his first wife, believing that the law against the divorce of loveless couples was an "intolerable tyranny," and eloped not only with the 16-year-old Mary Godwin but also with her stepsister. He practised vegetarianism, and wrote a poem in praise of incestuous love. He lived his life according to his own rules, not those of society. He was an outstanding example of Fiveness in action.

Sylvia Plath
Born 27 October 1932, 14.10 (+05.00)
Boston, MA, USA (42N22. 71W04).
Source: From her mother, via R.H. Oliver (ADB). RR: A.

(SO–**5**–MA)–**15**/15–JU
(ME–**4**–MA)–**5**/20–NE
(ME–**5**–NE)–**25**/**25**–MO)–**25**/25/25–VE
(MA–**3**–UR)–15/**15**–MO
              –15/**5**–JU
(UR–**10**–CH)–**15**/**30**–MO

Another poet with very strong Fiveness aspects is Sylvia Plath, who wrote about women's victimization, rage, and rebellion. Steven Axelrod says that her poems "enact loss and grief in such a devastating fashion that one wonders how the reader, let alone the author, can survive them".[20] In the end, Plath did not survive. Having made a suicide attempt when she was 20, she finally killed herself at the age of 30 after the break-up of her stormy marriage to fellow-poet Ted Hughes.

In order to understand Plath's Fiveness, we have to see it in the context of the Twoness, Threeness and Sevenness in her chart. With (ME–**4**–MA)–**16**/**16**–SA, MA–**3**–UR, and (VE–**6**–PL)–**24**/24–MO, Plath is marked out as a person liable to impulsive actions, with a strong tendency to introspection and despair, and with powerful and turbulent emotions. Also SO–**14**–MO and SO–**21**–ME show her as inspired by her own destiny (we will examine Sevenness in Chapter 8). But it was the Fiveness that made her a poet. The Fiveness aspects, centring on SO–5–MA and (ME–**5**–NE)–25–MO, enabled her to impose order onto her troubled emotional life and turn it into a thing of beauty. Her website says that she was "compelled towards perfection in everything she attempted",[21] and this is very much a Fiveness characteristic.

Graham Greene
Born 2 October 1904, 10.20 (+00.00)
Berkhamsted, England (51N46. 0W35).
Source: From mother's diary, quoted in Norman Sherry *The Life of Graham Greene* (ADB). RR: A.

$$((\underline{ME}\text{–}\underline{5}\text{–JU})\text{–}\underline{5/5}\text{–SA})\text{–}5/\underline{5}/5/\underline{5}/5/\underline{5}\text{–(MO–}\underline{1}\text{–NE))–}20/20/\underline{20}/4/\underline{4}\text{–SO}$$
$$-\underline{5}\text{–NE)–}15/\underline{3}/15/\underline{15}\text{–UR}$$
$$-\underline{20}/\underline{4}/20/20\text{–(SO–10–PL)}$$

The novelist Graham Greene has a massive Fiveness configuration, with Mercury (near the Midheaven) closely quintile to both Jupiter and Saturn, and linked also by Fiveness aspects to Sun, Moon, Uranus, Neptune and Pluto.

Greene is an extraordinarily difficult person to pin down. Michelle Orange said that he was:

"A stranger with no shortage of calling cards; devout Catholic, lifelong adulterer, pulpy hack, canonical novelist; self-destructive, meticulously disciplined, deliriously romantic, bitterly cynical, moral relativist, strict theologian, salon communist, closet monarchist, civilized to a stuffy fault and louche to drugged-out distraction, anti-imperialist and postcolonial parasite, self-excoriating and self-aggrandizing, to name just a few".[22]

I believe that this elusiveness is related to the nature of Fiveness. A person who is strong in Fiveness is good at creating structures, and this means that he is able to create a whole variety of structures: if he is dissatisfied with one structure, he can knock it down and build another. I am reminded of the Silent Twins, who were always playing games with people: sometimes they played one game and sometimes another, so that people never knew where they were with them. Graham Greene, similarly, was able to create a variety of different versions of himself, or else to create a single elaborate structure in which apparently irreconcilable elements were reconciled. What is harder to do (for the Fiveness person) is to stop playing the games and simply to be naturally oneself.

Some Fiveness people apply this structure-building to the structuring of themselves, and to the way in which they present themselves to the world; others apply it to the external things that they create and give to the world. Graham Greene did both. In his novels he created a variety of different worlds, and created them with such vividness and accuracy that many of them have easily been translated into films.

And yet there is a paradox here. Even though Fiveness people proceed through an artificial process of structure-building, in which they might seem to be moving away from authenticity, it seems that it is often possible for them, *within these structures*, to achieve an a remarkable degree of honesty, openness and self-disclosure. Thus, Sylvia Plath, within her carefully constructed and technically assured poems, was able to lay bare her emotional life with a candidness that has rarely been equalled; and Graham Greene did the same in his novels. Even though the feelings expressed in the novels are expressed through the mouths of invented characters, we can learn from them about the deepest secrets of Greene's inner life, and especially about how he was haunted by themes of suffering, sin, and doubt.

Fiveness, we must remember, is about creating order out of chaos. In this process, the things that were in chaos are not destroyed; rather, they are brought into an orderly structure, so that they can more easily be understood and communicated. Of course, it is true that some Fiveness people, having 'tidied up' their inner worlds, may then try to throw away, or to repress, the bits that are unpleasant, difficult, or embarrassing; but others, like Plath and Greene, may be able to accept these difficult elements and to communicate honestly to the world about them.

Thomas Hardy

Born 2 June 1840, 08.00 (+00.09)
Higher Bockhampton, England (50N47. 2W20).
Source: From biography by his wife *The Early Years of Thomas Hardy* (ADB). RR: B.

(((SA–**5**–CH)–**25**/25–SO)–**25**/25/**25**–VE)–25/25/**25**/25–MO
(MO–**3**–JU)–**10**/30–MA
(SA–**4**–UR)–20/**5**–ME
(SA–**3**–PL)–**5**/15–CH

Another novelist (and poet) with strong Fiveness is Thomas Hardy, who has a configuration of pure Fiveness linking Sun, Moon, Venus, Saturn and Chiron, as well as other Fiveness links. Hardy was a consummate master of structure-building, creating in his novels a world in which everything, from the landscape to the human characters, is closely observed and intricately interconnected, and in which his focus is on "elemental passion, deep instinct, and the human will struggling against fatal and ill-comprehended laws, a victim also of unforeseeable change".[23] In later life, however, Hardy chose to abandon fiction and (like Sylvia Plath) to focus instead on poems in which he laid bare the darkness of his own feelings.

Henri Matisse

Born 31 December 1869, 20.00 (–00.14)
Le Cateau, France (50N06. 3E33).
Source: Birth certificate, via Gauquelin (ADB). RR: AA.

(SO–3–_JU_)–15/15–NE
(SA–**5**–_PL_)–20/**20**–SO
(MO–6–_VE_)–15/**10**–CH
((ME–**2**–UR)–10/**5**–_VE_)–5/10/**10**–CH
(SA–**5**–_PL_)–**25**/25–ME
(ME–**5**–CH)–25–NE
(ME–**25**–SA)–25–NE

The painter Henri Matisse was a supreme stylist. He moved away from pure representation of the object painted, and towards an art in which what mattered was the *design* of the painting itself. In doing this, he has had an enormous influence over modern art and design (including advertising, corporate logos, and other things which we nowadays take for granted).

According to one website, the two outstanding qualities of Matisse's work are "geometric rightness" and "chromatic radiance".[24] Some quotes from Matisse himself will give more of the flavour of what he was trying to do:

> "Expression, for me, does not reside in passions glowing in a human face or as manifested by violent movement. The entire arrangement of my picture is expressive, the place occupied by the figures, the empty space around them, the proportions, everything has its share."

"I do not literally paint that table, but the emotion it produces upon me."

"Seek the strongest colour effect possible – the content is of no importance."

"What I dream of is an art of balance, of purity and serenity."

"A young painter who cannot liberate himself from the influence of past generations is digging his own grave".[25]

In all of this Matisse is expressing Fiveness. Rather than directly painting what he sees, he is re-ordering what he sees into new designs and structures, which give pleasure through their own inherent rightness, and through which also he can re-structure and present his own inner world ("the emotion it produces upon me"). Matisse's chart contains a complex pattern of Fiveness, of which perhaps the most important element is ((ME–**2**–UR)–10/**5**–VE)–5/10/**10**–CH: ME–**2**–UR showing a compulsion to communicate in original ways; VE–**5**–UR (with Venus on the Descendant) showing a search for an original, exciting and sharply-defined beauty; and Chiron showing his need to make this his life's work.

Laurence Olivier

Born 22 May 1907, 05.00 (+00.00)
Dorking, England (51N14. 0W20).
Source: From entry in baby book, reproduced in his autobiography *Confessions of an Actor* (ADB). RR: AA.

((JU–**1**–NE)–**2**–UR)–**5**/**5**/10–VE)–**5**/**5**/10/**5**–CH
　　　–25–(ME–**25**–MA)
　　　–**20**/20–PL

Talented actors are able to re-structure themselves so as to fit the personalities of the roles that they are playing, so it is not surprising that actors tend to be strong in Fiveness. An example is Laurence Olivier, who was regarded by many as the greatest actor of his generation. People like Olivier tend to seem nondescript and colourless when they are just being themselves, and only 'come to life' when they are playing a part. And yet, as with Graham Greene, we can see the paradox: that, within the parts that they play (or the structures that they create), these actors are able to probe the depths of human joy and suffering and to portray these feelings with great honesty and authenticity.

Barry Humphries
Born 17 February 1934, 06.30 (–10.00)
Camberwell, Australia (37S50.145E04).
Source: From him, via Dennis Sutton (FCC). RR: A.

(ME–5–CH)–5/5–JU
           –**10**/10–VE
(ME–**10**–VE)–**20**–SO
(JU–**4**–PL)–**20/10**–MO
(MO–**10**–PL)–30/15–NE

Comedians are not usually strong in Fiveness, but Barry Humphries is no ordinary comedian: he is a showman whose humour depends on his re-invention of himself as an outrageous larger-than-life character (the superstar Dame Edna Everage, or the appalling Sir Les Patterson). When he appears in public as himself, he seems uneasy; he only finds self-confidence behind a mask.

   Humphries has (in addition to other Fiveness links) two separate Fiveness clusters consisting entirely of very close aspects: (ME–**10**–VE)–**20**–SO, and (JU–**4**–PL)–**20/10**–MO. Hence his chart is very much about 5 x 2 x 2: striving towards Fiveness. The first of these clusters shows the depth of his need to find a structured way of communicating with people so as to win their love and admiration. The particular style which he has chosen to develop is shown by the second cluster (Dame Edna and Sir Les combine the characteristics of Jupiter and Pluto).

Richard Branson
Born 18 July 1950, 07.00 (–01.00)
Blackheath, England (51N28. 0E01).
Source: From his mother, via Frank C. Clifford (ADB). RR: A.

(MA–**1**–NE)–5/5–ME
((ME–5–NE)–25/**25**–PL)–25/25/25–MO
(SA–**25**–NE)–25/25–PL)–25–MO

The entrepreneur Richard Branson has a strong Fiveness pattern, which is mostly at the higher (or perhaps we should say deeper) level of Fiveness, which is 25. I would suggest this means that it operates at a deeper level within Branson's personality, and is less visible on the surface. On the surface he is more a Threeness person.

Branson is well known, not only for his enterprise in setting up the Virgin Group and becoming one of the ten richest men in Britain, but also for his informal style of dress and behaviour, and for his exploits in attempting to set records as an aviator and balloonist. He is an expert self-publicist, and has written an autobiography *Losing My Virginity* in which he describes his life (and especially his childhood) in very great detail; and yet his AstroDatabank biography can say: "Basically shy, his public persona is one of bravado, but the private man remains an enigma".

My suggestion is that Branson's strong 25-ness pattern is related to a compulsion to continually re-invent himself. In this he is similar to Graham Greene and to others whom we have considered in this chapter.

The stamp of Fiveness can also be seen in the following comment from Wikipedia: "Branson has been tagged as a 'transformational leader' by management lexicon, with his maverick strategies and his stress on the Virgin Group as an organization driven on informality and information, one that is bottom-heavy rather than strangled by top-level management".[26] Here again we see the experimentation with new structures, with the aim of bettering the lot of mankind, which is one of the marks of Fiveness.

Alexander Fleming

Born 6 August 1881, 02.00 (+00.17)
Darvel, Scotland (55N37. 4W18).
Source: Birth certificate, via Paul Wright. RR: AA.

(SO–**5**–MA)–25/**25**–<u>UR</u>
(SA–**3**–<u>UR</u>)–**5**/15–<u>ME</u>
            –15/**5**–VE
(JU–**1**–CH)–**10**/**10**/**10**/10–(VE–**5**–<u>UR</u>)
(VE–5–<u>UR</u>)–25/**25**–MA)–**25**/25/25–NE

Since Fiveness is (I believe) about re-shaping the physical world as well as the world of the mind, one might expect that scientists and engineers would be strong in Fiveness. I have the chart of one engineer (not famous, but known to me personally) with an extremely strong Fiveness pattern, whose only interests as a child were engineering, physics, and mathematics, and whose passion was to make things (engines, model aeroplanes, etc.).[27]

Among famous scientists and engineers, however, I have found only one person who is strong in Fiveness. This is Sir Alexander Fleming, the Nobel laureate and discoverer of penicillin.

As with many scientists, it is difficult to discover much about the kind of person he was. He has been described as a "quiet personality", and he was modest about his achievements: he once said "Nature makes penicillin, I only found it". However, one website states that "Alexander Fleming's scientific success lay in his open, enquiring mind, his strong technical intuition, and his penchant for naturalistic observation". On the same website, Henry Dale, another Nobel laureate, is quoted as saying about Fleming: "I can assure you that the elegance and beauty of his observations just as a naturalist observer of the phenomenon of lysozyme and penicillin, as he presented it, did make a great impression and everybody remembered these things".[28]

This comment on the elegance and beauty of his presentations seems to link Fleming to our other cases of people with strong Fiveness. Although much of the work on the development of penicillin was done by Fleming's colleagues Florey and Chain (with whom he shared the Nobel Prize), it was left to Fleming to act as the spokesman for the group and present the work to the public, and he did this very successfully. Thus we can say that Fleming, in common with most of our Fiveness cases, was good at analysing and describing new systems through the skilled use of words.

Sinking of the Titanic
14 April 1912, 23.40 (+03.30)[29]
Atlantic Ocean (41N46. 50W14).
Source: Wikipedia.

(SO–**1**–ME)–5–MA

((JU–**5**–NE)–**10**–VE)–**15**/**15**/**30**/15/**15**/**30**/**6**/**30**/**15**–((UR–**5**–_PL_)
    –**10**–CH)
((JU–**5**–NE)–**25**/25–_SO_)–25–MO

We will end this chapter with two mundane charts, both of which are exceptionally strong in Fiveness. The first is the chart for the sinking of the *Titanic* (or, rather, for the moment when the ship struck the iceberg).

At first I was puzzled as to why the chart for the *Titanic* sinking should be so very strong in Fiveness. But all became clear when I read a passage from Thomas Berry's book *The Dream of the Earth*.[30] Berry points out that there was plenty of evidence that icebergs were ahead, but the crew of the *Titanic* were reluctant to alter the ship's course. They were confident that the ship was unsinkable, and they had plenty of other things to occupy their minds: all the routines that had to be carried out correctly if the ship's maiden voyage was to be a success.

As we have said, mundane charts often describe the mindset of the people who caused the event; and this event was caused by the *Titanic*'s crew who failed to avoid the iceberg. Berry shows how the crew were wrapped up in the concerns of Fiveness. They were in charge of a sparkling new man-made system (the ship itself), and all of their attention was focused on serving this system and ensuring that it worked smoothly and effectively. But the iceberg came up at them from the natural world (the world outside Fiveness), and they were ill equipped to deal with it.

Ufton Nervet rail crash
6 November 2004, 18.12 (+00.00)
Ufton Nervet, England (51N41. 1W12).
Source: Wikipedia.

(MO–2–UR)–10/**5**–_PL_
((JU–**5**–UR–**5**–_PL_)–**5**–SA)–**1**/5/5/**5**–VE
             –10/**10**/10/10–SO)–20/20/**4**/20/20/
                              20/20/**4**–(ME–**10**–MA)

During the first half of November 2004, four of the outer planets – Jupiter, Saturn, Uranus and Pluto – came into a quintile relationship with one another. In the notation used in this book, there was a pattern of JU–5–

SA–5–UR–5–PL. This remarkable configuration lasted for several days, but it was at its strongest on 6th November.

The effects of this pattern on world events seem to have been mostly 'dark'. It was at this time that the US Army launched its attack on the town of Falluja, which was perhaps the bloodiest and most horrific event of the whole Iraq war. And it was also at this time that a macabre event occurred in the English countryside.

On 6th November, just as the Jupiter-Saturn-Uranus-Pluto quintile reached its peak, and at a moment also when these planets had several Fiveness links with other planets, a 48-year-old chef named Brian Drysdale, who had no previous history of deviant behaviour, drove his car onto an unmanned level crossing near the village of Ufton Nervet. He then turned his car to face the direction from which a train would come, turned off the engine, took off all his clothes, and waited. An off-duty policeman saw what was happening and tried to raise the alarm, but he was too late. The barriers came down, but Drysdale and his car were already inside the barriers. Then (just as Pluto crossed the Descendant) the train came, travelling at about 100 miles an hour. It crashed into the car, killing Drysdale, the train driver, and five passengers on the train. Luckily, the first-class carriages, which were almost empty, were at the front of the train; otherwise, far more people would have died.

We will never know what drove Drysdale into taking this action. But what is clear is the contrast between this rail crash and the rail crashes that we have looked at in previous chapters: the Twoness crash at Nuneaton, that was caused by stress and anxiety, and the Threeness crashes at Paddington and Selby, that were caused by carelessness and negligence. The Fiveness crash at Ufton Nervet was an act of deliberate destruction.

Conclusion

In this chapter we have seen how people who are very strong in Fiveness are always building new structures in their minds. Their desire is to re-invent the world: to create forms and systems that were not there before.

In some cases, this inventiveness is directed towards themselves: they wish to re-fashion themselves, to present themselves to the world in a way that they themselves have devised. Therefore they develop skills of self-presentation and of acting out roles. In extreme cases (as with the Silent Twins) this can lead to their seeming to inhabit an artificial world, with its own rules and constraints, and to be cut off from the world which other people inhabit.

In other cases, the inventiveness is directed more towards the external world. They may create physical objects that are ordered or structured in a new way; or they may (like Bahá-u-lláh and Aurobindo) create moral or philosophical systems which help them to make sense of the world, and which they may try to teach to others. The downside of this is that they may (like Frank Buchman) become very intolerant of people who do not see the world in the way that they see it. The danger of Fiveness is the danger of becoming trapped by the systems that one has created.

The central belief of Fiveness is the belief in the power of Man to re-shape his world. Clearly Fiveness can be a tremendous power for good, and can enormously help people to fulfil their potential and lead creative and constructive lives. But I believe myself that (partly as a result of the decimal system) one of the central problems of the modern world is that we have become too dependent on Fiveness. We have created a world which is dominated by man-made structures and systems, and we have become trapped within these systems.

How then can we escape from the trap of excessive Fiveness? One way might be to allow ourselves to *surrender* to forces which are not man-made, and over which we have no control because they cannot easily be re-structured and re-ordered. This is one of the themes of Sevenness, which we will consider in the next chapter.

Sevenness

It is quite a shock to move from the rational, ordered, man-made world of Fiveness into the magical, mystical, mysterious world of Sevenness. One feels that one has entered a world in which nothing quite makes sense, and nothing is quite as it seems on the surface.

The first thing to note about the number Seven is that it has no relation to the decimal system in which we do our counting. In the previous chapter I pointed out that the decimal system bypasses the number Three; and yet Three does have a relation to the decimal system, as is shown by the fact that 1/3 is 0.333333333. Similarly, 1/9 is 0.111111111, and 1/11 is 0.09090909. But 1/7 is 0.142857142: a seemingly random collection of numbers.[1] From this we can say that Seven is the first 'irrational' number, and in fact is the only such number before Thirteen. But, whereas Thirteen has a sinister reputation, Seven has generally been seen as benign.

Just as the number Five is represented by a pentagram, the number Seven is represented by a *heptagram* which is a seven-pointed star. But, whereas the pentagram has only one form, the heptagram has two forms: an *acute* heptagram and an *obtuse* heptagram, both of which are shown in Figure 2. If one meditates on these two figures, I feel that they give rise to quite different feelings from those that stem from the pentagram. The obtuse heptagram in particular has an unsettling effect: one feels that this is a figure which is fluid, constantly in motion, lacking in permanence.

In the previous chapter we said that Five was the number of Man, with the five points of the pentagram representing the head and the four limbs. From this, we can perhaps say that Seven is the number of the Angels and the Fairies, since angels and fairies have a head, four limbs, and also two wings, making a total of seven. But, the scientist will say, angels and fairies do not exist. Well, who knows? Many people believe that they have seen angels and fairies, and have communicated

Figure 2

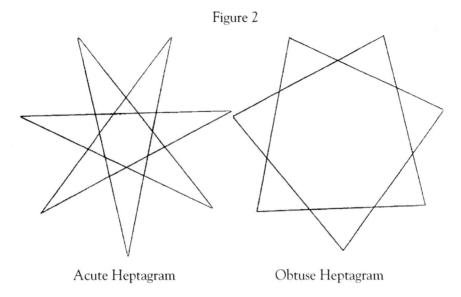

Acute Heptagram   Obtuse Heptagram

with them or been helped by them. Who are we to say that they were deluded? This kind of question, about whether something 'really exists' or whether it is a figment of the imagination, will crop up frequently in our discussion of Sevenness.

In Wicca, the acute heptagram (which Wiccans call a *septegram)* is known as the Elven Star or Fairy Star, and the heptagram is also important in other occult traditions. The obtuse heptagram is an important symbol in the Kabbalah. Seven is also an important number in alchemy: not only are there seven planetary metals (corresponding to the seven planets that were known to the ancients), but also there are seven stages of alchemical transformation (calcination, dissolution, separation, conjunction, fermentation, distillation and coagulation), which refer not only to the transformation of base metal into gold, but also (metaphorically) to the journey of the soul from base existence into enlightenment.[2]

People have always been prone to making lists of seven things: the seven deadly sins (and, less well-known, the seven virtues), the seven Wonders of the World, the seven Pillars of Wisdom, the seven continents, the seven seas, the seven chakras of the human body, the seven colours of the rainbow, and so on. With the exception of the Wonders of the World, none of these things are man-made: they are seen as divinely created and as part of the natural order of things, and it seems to be felt that God (unlike Man) works naturally in sevens and that we, by counting in sevens, can come closer to the heart of the Divine Mystery.

Above all, there are the seven days of the week (based on the seven days in which God is said to have made the world). I feel myself that this intrusion of Sevenness into the way in which we count time has been a saving grace for modern man. It has helped us to keep in touch with the divinity at the heart of things. If the French Revolutionaries had been successful in their attempt to introduce a ten-day week, we would be even more trapped within the decimal system than we are now.

Thus, Sevenness refers to the ways in which men and women try to rise above the baseness and humdrum-ness of their lives and to find their place in an order which is more profound and universal than the man-made order of Fiveness. Hence it has been said that the Sevenness aspects in a chart show what *inspires* one or *turns one on*. James Elroy Flecker writes:

> "For lust of knowing what should not be known
> We take the Golden Road to Samarkand."

This "lust of knowing what should not be known" (and, one should add, of feeling what should not be felt) is the driving force of Sevenness, and the Sevenness aspects in our charts can teach us about the nature of our own personal Samarkand, the magical city where our dreams will come true. (The rural equivalent of Samarkand is Arcadia. Both Samarkand and Arcadia are real places, but in real life they have none of the magic which is ascribed to them in legend. Their true identity is as places of the mind, places that can inspire the weary traveller to continue on his journey towards the Promised Land of the imagination.)

In this chapter, we will look at the charts of people who are unusually strong in Sevenness aspects, in order to discover more about the nature of Sevenness.

"Walk-in from Sirius"

Born 19 June 1948, 02.00 (+04.00)
Montreal, Canada (45N31. 73W34).
Source: From him, via Aya Mothership (ADB). RR: A.

(((SO–**1**–UR)–7/**7**–MO)–**7**/7/7–SA)–**7**/7/**7**/**7**–NE
((SO–**7**–SA)–**7**/**7**–NE)–**14**/**14**/**14**–MA

AstroDatabank does not give this person's name, but calls him "Walk-in from Sirius". His AstroDatabank biography reads as follows:

> "Canadian walk-in. The original entity born on this date and time left his body because he was not having any fun. He was world-travelled and spoke four languages. The entity from Sirius took over this entity's body and is now enjoying himself as well as helping in any way he can to heal people going through this present Earth crisis. He is a healer and a shaman, living with his girlfriend Sakina."

"Walk-in from Sirius" has one of the strongest Sevenness charts that I have seen, with Sun and Uranus septile to Moon, Saturn and Neptune, and with Sun, Saturn and Neptune also –**14**– Mars. So we can presume that he is exceptionally open to the 'trans-human' forces of Sevenness. The question, of course, is: Is it possible for an "entity from Sirius" to take over a human body? Whatever one's answer is to this question, the important thing is that the person himself believes that this has happened, and believes himself to have arrived at his personal Samarkand.

Alice Bailey

Born 16 June 1880, 07.32 (+00.00)
Manchester, England (53N30. 2W15).
Source: Dane Rudhyar in *American Astrology*, Sept. 1937. RR: C.[3]

((MO–**7**–VE)–**7**/**7**–SA)–**7**/**7**/**7**–MA)–**21**/**21**/21/21–NE
                    –**14**/**14**/**14**–UR

In previous chapters we have looked at the charts of spiritual teachers who were strong in particular numbers. Thus, Padre Pio, Josemaria Escriva and Teilhard de Chardin were strong in Oneness; Mahatma Gandhi and Charles de Foucauld in Twoness; Adi Da and Pat Rodegast in Threeness; and Bahá-u-lláh, Aurobindo and Frank Buchman in Fiveness.

When it comes to Sevenness, the spiritual teacher with the strongest Sevenness pattern is Alice Bailey. She has Moon, Venus, Mars and Saturn conjoined by pure Sevenness aspects, and with Sevenness links also to Neptune and Uranus.

Alice Bailey was unhappy as a child, and attempted suicide three times. However, at the age of 15 she had a vision of a stranger (whom she later identified as one of the Ascended Masters) who told her to discipline herself in preparation for the work which was planned for her. Despite this, she led an 'ordinary' life, with an unhappy marriage and three children, until the age of 35, when she broke from her husband and also from Christianity, and joined the Theosophical Society. When she was 39, she was contacted by a discarnate being whom she called 'the Tibetan,' and over the next 30 years she published 24 books which 'the Tibetan' had channelled to her.

It would be impossible here to summarize the vast range and complexity of Alice Bailey's message to the world. However, two aspects can be mentioned. First, she believed that "behind all human evolution stands a brotherhood of enlightened souls who have guided and aided humanity throughout history":[4] these were the Ascended Masters, or Masters of Wisdom. Secondly, she taught that there are seven Rays (note the emphasis on the number seven) emanating from the ultimate Source (the One Life). "On a cosmic level these seven rays of energy are the creative forces of planets and stars. On a microcosmic level they are the creative forces conditioning the physical, psychic, and spiritual constitution of man."[4] The seven rays are respectively concerned with: Power or Will; Love-Wisdom; Active Intelligence; Harmony, Beauty and Art; Concrete Knowledge and Science; Devotion and Idealism; and the Ceremonial Order of Magic.

It is plain that Alice Bailey was a very different kind of spiritual teacher from the ones we have discussed in previous chapters. Bailey herself used the words 'esoteric', 'occult' and 'arcane' to describe her work: these words are all concerned with the imparting of hidden or mysterious knowledge, which, as we have said, is a central theme of Sevenness. Bailey's aim was to transmit to mankind cosmic knowledge which had hitherto been hidden, but which had been vouchsafed to her by 'the Tibetan'. We can note also that Bailey's Sevenness is centred on the Moon, not the Sun, and so is concerned with the *receptive* side of her personality. Bailey was the receiver of the Sevenness knowledge, and she was able to pass it on while still (in her Sun-nature) living in the world as an 'ordinary' person.

George Van Tassel and Jean Miguères

George Van Tassel
Born 12 March 1910, 08.30 (+06.00)
Jefferson, OH, USA (41N44. 80W48).
Source: Birth certificate, via Frank C. Clifford (ADB). RR: AA.

SO–28–NE
(ME–1–CH)–7/7–SA
(VE–7–MA)–7–MO
(VE–7–MA)–14/14–PL)–28/4/28–CH)
(JU–21–CH)–21/21–NE

Jean Miguères
Born 11 May 1940, 23.00 (–01.00)
Algiers, Algeria (36N47. 3E03).
Source: Birth certificate, via Petitallot (ADB). RR: AA.

(SO–1–UR)–7/7–MO
(MO–7–UR)–21–MA)–21–PL

Both George Van Tassel and Jean Miguères claimed to have had contact with extra-terrestrial beings who gave them a mission, and both of them spent the rest of their lives trying to fulfil that mission.

Van Tassel claimed to have been transported astrally to an alien spaceship where he met the all-wise 'Council of Seven Lights'. (Seven again!) Later he was visited by aliens from Venus who gave him the design for the Integratron, a machine that would prolong life by rejuvenating living cell tissues. Van Tassel spent the next 25 years trying to build this machine. The structure that he built still stands; there is no evidence that it has prolonged anyone's life, but many people have felt rejuvenated by visiting it.

Jean Miguères, an ambulance driver, was involved in a crash in which a car travelling at very high speed struck his ambulance, causing both vehicles to disintegrate.[5] Miguères was trapped in his vehicle with multiple injuries for three hours, and was pronounced to be brain dead.

Nevertheless, after 18 operations, he was restored to health; doctors said his recovery was 'miraculous'. Miguères claimed that at the time of the accident he was visited by an alien who gave him the option of surviving if he agreed to devote his life to spreading a message. The message was that extra-terrestrial civilizations were concerned about Man having landed on the moon, and feared that he might go further. The alien warned that we must not bring our illnesses and our lethal weapons to civilizations that "are less developed than ours and are unable to protect themselves".[6] Miguères spread this message for 23 years until his death in 1992.

Van Tassel has an exceptionally strong and complex Sevenness configuration which is shown above. Miguères' Sevenness pattern is less complex, but SO–7–MO (linked also to UR, MA and PL) shows that Sevenness was at the heart of his personality.

AstroDatabank has the birthtimes of several other UFO abductees and other people who claim to have made extra-terrestrial contacts, and most of them do not have strong Sevenness patterns. But the distinguishing fact about Van Tassel and Miguères is that (like Alice Bailey) they devoted their lives to the dissemination of hidden knowledge.

Anita McKeown

Born 5 July 1961, 00.15 (+07.00)
Van Nuys, CA, USA (34N11.118W27).
Source: From her, via Linda Clark (ADB). RR: A.

(MA–1–PL)–7/7–SO
(VE–3–SA)–21/7–UR
((ME–7–SA–7–UR)–28/28/28/28/28/28–(PL–2–CH))–14/14/14/
    28/28–MO

Anita McKeown (known to her colleagues as "Calamity Jane") is described by AstroDatabank as an "accident-prone policewoman". During the three years after she joined the Santa Monica police force in August 1984, she was "stabbed, shot at, hit by speeding cars both as a pedestrian and as a driver, and she slipped on a wax floor. She also has broken her ankle, finger, sternum and wrenched her back, and been bitten by a rattlesnake. She also dislocated a shoulder during training at the Police Academy." Most of these accidents occurred during 1984-85;

but then, in 1987, she "was involved in an auto accident which required two weeks of recuperation; on her first day back to work following the accident, a motorist backed into her police car".[7]

Anita McKeown has the strongest Sevenness cluster that I have seen, with nine of the planets (all the planets except Jupiter and Neptune) linked by Sevenness aspects. In particular, Mercury, Saturn, Uranus, Pluto, Chiron and the Moon are tied together in a very tight cluster which combines the qualities of Sevenness and Twoness.

So how is accident-proneness connected to Sevenness?

We have seen how Sevenness is linked to the hearing of 'voices' which impart hidden information – no matter whether these 'voices' are seen as coming from an alien being, or whether they are coming purely from the person's intuition or imagination. In McKeown's case, it seems that her accidents started only when she joined the police force (after obtaining a degree in psychology), so it appears that her 'voices' were telling her very strongly that this was the wrong career for her. McKeown, however, chose to ignore the voices (PL–2–CH suggests an obstinate determination to persist in a career path), so the voices persisted until they finally got what they wanted (when the police force decided that they could no longer employ her because of her accident-proneness).

We can note that McKeown's Sevenness is tied up with Twoness (14 = 7 x 2; 28 = 7 x 2 x 2), so that her relationship with her 'voices' is inherently difficult and stressful. She is a Sevenness person, and yet she does not have an easy relationship with Sevenness.

But why should McKeown's 'voices' take the form of external events (people shooting at her and stabbing her, cars crashing into her, rattlesnakes biting her)? I cannot say. Everything about the number Seven is hidden, mysterious, and inexplicable to the rational mind. But it seems possible that McKeown unconsciously *caused* the accidents, in the same way that people who are the centre of poltergeist activity cause strange things to happen around them.

Roger Federer
Born 8 August 1981, 08.40 (–02.00)
Basel, Switzerland (47N33. 7E35).
Source: From his website (www.rogerfederer.com), via David Hamblin.[8]
RR: A.

(JU–**1**–SA)–**7**/**7**–SO
(ME–**7**–UR)–7–SA
    –**14**/14–NE
    –**21**/21–**VE**)–21/21/**21**–PL

If Anita McKeown displays the 'dark' side of Sevenness, then the 'light' side is shown by Roger Federer, the six-times Wimbledon champion who is regarded by many as the greatest tennis player of all time. Federer's special talent is to make it all seem easy. Whereas his great rival Rafael Nadal[9] bounds around the court with superhuman energy, Federer always seems able, with great economy of effort, to find the perfect shot and the perfect angle, delivered with perfect grace and elegance.

    Federer's tennis fluency is, in its way, just as magical and mysterious as the other cases of Sevenness that we have seen. But we can note that, whereas McKeown's Sevenness was bound up with Twoness, Federer's is bound up with Threeness (21 = 7 x 3). His strongest Sevenness cluster is (ME–**7**–UR)–**21**–VE–**21**–PL, with these planets forming a Grand Trine in his seventh-harmonic chart. Sevenness combined with Threeness means inspiration combined with ease and fluency, and this is a perfect description of Federer's tennis style.

Bruce Chatwin
Born 13 May 1940, 20.30 (–01.00)
Dronfield, England (53N19. 1W27).
Source: From biography by Nicholas Shakespeare, via Filipe Ferreira (ADB). RR: B.

(_SO_–**1**–_UR_)–14/**14**–MO
(_ME_–**7**–VE)–**21**–MO
(_ME_–**7**–VE)–14/14/14/**14**–(NE–7–PL)
(UR–**3**–NE)–**21**/**7**–PL

Among famous writers, the strongest Sevenness chart that I have found is that of Bruce Chatwin. Chatwin was a very unusual and charismatic person. He was very beautiful, and is said to have been infatuated by his own beauty.[10] He was "possessed of a gargantuan ego, and talked so incessantly that, as one friend memorably put it, he 'murdered people with talk'".[10] He wrote a book called *Anatomy of Restlessness*, and indeed throughout his life he was obsessively restless, always travelling in search of new insights and experiences, oblivious of his own safety. He was bisexual, and died of AIDS aged 48, although he had done his best to hide the fact that he had AIDS, claiming that he suffered from "a rare Chinese disease".

Among his best-known books are *The Songlines* (set among Aboriginals in the Australian outback) and *In Patagonia*. It has been said that "if *In Patagonia* is a novel thinly disguised as a travel book, then *Songlines* is … a travel diary that claims to be a novel".[10] There is a blurring of the boundary between fact and fiction in Chatwin's work, and I feel that this is because he is engaged on a Sevenness quest: he is trying, not to describe the facts about the places he has visited and the people he has met, but to uncover the hidden meaning behind his experiences. He was reporting on his own inner voices, which, although they were inspired by his travels, had their origin in his own imagination. He was turning Patagonia or outback Australia into his own Samarkand, a mythical place with only a thin resemblance to the actual location on the Earth's surface.

Thus, there are people in Patagonia who are still furious with Chatwin for having misreported or misrepresented them; and, in the case of *Songlines*, it has been said that Chatwin "never gleaned anything but the most superficial understanding" of the Aboriginal culture that he claimed to be describing.[10] Yet in the end this does not matter, because of the brilliance and originality of Chatwin's vision. He was "in search of the miraculous",[11] and he was able to find it and convey it to the reader.

Chatwin's chart is weak in both Twoness and Fiveness. With SO–**3**–NE he was to some extent a Threeness person, a carefree seeker after pleasure. But above all he was a Sevenness person, a seeker of hidden meaning. (SO–**1**–UR)–14/**14**–MO shows how Sevenness was at the heart of his personality and of his sense of his own uniqueness, and ME–

<u>7</u>–VE, linked by Sevenness aspects to MO, NE and PL, shows how he was inspired by ideals of beauty and was receptive to the deeper spiritual insights that are represented by Neptune and Pluto.

Herman Melville
Born 1 August 1819, 23.30 (+04.56)
New York, NY, USA (40N43. 74W00).
Source: From family bible, as recorded in biography by J. Keyda (ADB).
RR: AA.

(ME-<u>7</u>-SA)–<u>14</u>–SO
   –7–MO
SO–<u>21</u>–NE
MO–<u>21</u>–MA
MA–<u>28</u>–UR

Another writer with a strong Sevenness chart is Herman Melville, the author of *Moby Dick* and *Billy Budd*. The most important configuration in Melville's chart is the very close pattern of (ME–<u>7</u>–SA)–<u>14</u>–SO, showing that Melville was moved to communicate inspirationally on Saturnian themes, and that this was closely bound in with his sense of his identity and his purpose in life.

Melville's greatest novel, *Moby Dick,* is certainly full of the 'search for hidden meaning' which we have identified as a primary theme of Sevenness. The story of the hunt for the giant sperm whale is told, not for its own sake, but for its allegorical and symbolical significance. It has been said, "In *Moby Dick*, Melville employs stylized language, symbolism and metaphor to explore numerous complex themes. Through the main character's journey, the concepts of class and social status, good and evil, and the existence of gods are all examined as Ishmael speculates upon his personal beliefs and his place in the universe".[12] And throughout the book there is an atmosphere of doom and fatalism which we can identify as being Saturnian.

Hector Berlioz
Born 11 December 1803, 17.00 (–00.25)
La-Côte-Saint-André, France (45N23. 5E15).
Source: Birth certificate, via Gauquelin (ADB). RR: AA.

(SA–7–NE)–7–PL
        –14/14–JU)–4/28/28–VE
        –4/28/28/28–(VE–14–UR)
SO–21–CH
ME–28–CH

Hector Berlioz is a composer with a strong Sevenness chart. The main Sevenness pattern consists of 'difficult' Sevenness links (14 and 28) between Venus (which is further emphasized by being on the Descendant) and five of the outer planets: Jupiter, Saturn, Uranus, Neptune and Pluto. Chiron is also involved by its Sevenness links with Sun and Mercury.

Berlioz has been described as "innately romantic," as is shown by "his love affairs, his adoration of great romantic literature, and his weeping at passages by Virgil, Shakespeare and Beethoven".[13] (In relation to the first of these, he was prone to falling overwhelmingly in love with women on first seeing them – notably with the actress Harriet Smithson, whom he first saw on stage performing Shakespeare and with whom he embarked on a disastrous marriage.) This extreme sensitivity to romantic beauty is well shown by the Sevenness links between Venus and all of the outer planets. As a composer, Berlioz is noted for his development of 'programme music': that is to say, music designed to tell a story and to arouse in the listener emotions appropriate to that story. Here we can see again the 'search for hidden meaning' which is characteristic of Sevenness.

James Ensor
Born 13 April 1860, 04.30 (–00.10)
Ostend, Belgium (51N53. 2E55).
Source: Birth certificate, via Gauquelin. RR: AA.

(SO–7–MA)–14/14–NE)–28/28/28–SA
        –7/7–CH
(MO–7–PL)–7–SA
(SO–4–MO)–28/7–SA

James Ensor (who, despite his English name, was a Belgian who lived all his life in Ostend) was a painter with a very strong pattern of Sevenness. According to one website, "he took his subject matter principally from

Ostend's holiday crowds, which filled him with revulsion and disgust".[14] He painted people as clowns or skeletons, or replaced their faces with carnival masks. His most famous painting is *The Entry of Christ into Brussels*, in which "a vast carnival mob in grotesque masks advances towards the viewer. Identifiable within the crowd are Belgian politicians, historical figures, and members of Ensor's family. Nearly lost amid the teeming throng is Christ on his donkey: although Ensor was an atheist, he identified with Christ as a victim of mockery".[15]

Ensor is very strong in Fiveness as well as Sevenness, and the Fiveness may be related to his meticulousness in preparing his paintings and to his obsessiveness in following established routines. However, it is the Sevenness aspects that involve the Sun (and are therefore concerned with Ensor's view of himself and his purpose in life) and also Neptune which is exactly on the Ascendant. Thus, the most important single aspect in Ensor's chart is SO–**14**–NE, which is almost exact, and is linked by close Sevenness aspects to Saturn and Mars. In this pattern, we see Ensor reaching out towards transcendence ("he identified with Christ") and feeling thwarted and persecuted, and in the Sevenness links between Moon, Saturn and Pluto we can see the grimness and ruthlessness of the fantasies which he converted into paint.[16]

Martin Heidegger
Born 26 September 1889, 11.30 (–00.36)
Messkirch, Germany (47N59. 9E07).
Source: Birth records, via Steinbrecher (ADB). RR: AA.

((MO–**1**–UR)–**7**/**7**/**7**/7–(VE–**1**–SA)–21/21/**21**/21–SO
(JU–**7**–NE)–21/21–UR

The philosopher Martin Heidegger has a strong pattern of Sevenness. I will not attempt here to summarize his philosophy, which is notoriously difficult and complex, but will simply say that throughout his working life he was concerned with the essential nature of Being (his major work is entitled *Being and Time*) and with the attempt to go beyond the study of Beings to the study of Being itself. What does it mean to 'be' a being existing in time? Iain McGilchrist says:

> "Philosophy does not answer our questions but shakes our belief
> that there are answers to be had; and in so doing it forces us to look

beyond its own system to another way of understanding. One of the reasons why reading Heidegger is at the same time so riveting and such a painful experience is that he never ceases to struggle to transcend the Cartesian divisions which analytic language entails, in order to demonstrate that there is a path, a way through the forest, the travelling of which is in itself the goal of human thinking …. Perhaps inevitably, Heidegger's last writings are in the form of poems".[17]

We can see that, with the '21' (7 x 3) links between the Sun and four other planets, Heidegger was happy to live in the world of Sevenness which is concerned with the hidden meaning of Being itself, rather than in the 'real' world in which one has to relate to particular Beings. He was happiest when staying in a country retreat where he could be alone with his thoughts. In the 'real' world his behaviour could seem naïve and self-contradictory; thus, he remained a member of the Nazi party throughout the Nazi period, and opened his lectures with "Heil Hitler", despite the fact that he befriended Jews and helped a Jewish family to escape from Germany. After the end of the war, he experienced a nervous breakdown. But this 'real world' was not where he belonged; he belonged in the world of Sevenness, where he found his Samarkand.

Ira Einhorn, Charles Starkweather, and Ian Brady

Ira Einhorn
Born 15 May 1940, 15.33 (+04.00)
Philadelphia, PA, USA (39N57. 75W10)
Source: From him, via M.J. Makransky (ADB). RR: A.

((SO-**7**-CH)-**7/7**-MO)-21/**21**/21-MA
(MO-**7**-CH)-21/**3**/**21**/21-(MA-7-SA)
(UR-**3**-NE)-**21**/**7**-PL

Charles Starkweather
Born 24 November 1938, 20.10 (+06.00)
Lincoln, NE, USA (40N48. 96W40).
Source: Birth certificate, via Victoria Shaw (ADB). RR: AA.

(NE–**7**–PL)–**7**/7–MO
((MO–**7**–NE)–**14**/**14**/14/14–(MA–**7**–UR)–**28**/4/**28**/**28**–ME

Ian Brady

Born 2 January 1938, 12.40 (+00.00)
Glasgow, Scotland (55N53. 4W15).
Source: Birth certificate, via Victoria Shaw (ADB). RR: AA.

(((ME–**1**–VE)–**7**–PL)–**7/7/7**–NE)–**21/21/3**/21–SA

A large number of murderers have strong Sevenness clusters in their charts. We will look at three examples.

Ira Einhorn was a flamboyant character, a well-known hippie and leader of the counter-culture (as well as being a competent astrologer) in the 60s and 70s. His relationships with women were often violent, and he wrote in his diary "Violence often marks the end of a relationship". In 1977 he bludgeoned to death a girlfriend (Holly Maddux) who had threatened to leave him; her decomposing body was later found in his flat. Einhorn fled bail, saying that "after a lifetime of not answering for his actions he had no intention of starting now",[18] and spent the next sixteen years in Europe, living the good life with a rich Swedish woman whom he had married. Finally he was extradited to the USA and sentenced to life imprisonment.

Charles Starkweather was the boyfriend of Caril Ann Fugate, whom we considered in the chapter on Threeness. Starkweather was teased and bullied at school because of his misshapen legs and slight speech impediment, and developed an intense hatred of bullies and of authority in general. He killed his first victim (a petrol station attendant) at the age of 18, and claimed that after this murder "he believed that he had transcended his former self to reach a new place of existence, in which he was above and outside the law".[19] He then killed Fugate's parents after an argument, and he and Fugate then went on a two-month spree in which they killed eight more people, some by shooting, some by stabbing. He was put to death in the electric chair at the age of 20.

Ian Brady was the infamous 'Moors murderer' who, with his accomplice Myra Hindley,[20] sadistically killed at least five children and buried them on Saddleworth Moor. He was born to a single mother in the Glasgow slums, and did not know his father's identity. As a child he tortured and killed animals, and he obtained inspiration from the writings of the Marquis de Sade and from reading about Nazi atrocities. Before their first killing (of Pauline Reade in 1963) he told Hindley that he wanted to commit "the perfect murder". He obtained pleasure from watching his victims suffer. He and Hindley became increasingly reckless, allowing Hindley's brother to witness the last killing, and not suspecting that he would go to the police (which in fact he did). It was as though Brady, like Einhorn and Starkweather, felt himself to be above the law. After he was convicted and sentenced to life imprisonment, he collapsed into mental illness.

It is clear that, despite their differences, these three killers were the same kind of killer: the kind of killer who revels in the act of killing, and for whom it is an assertion of their personal power and their independence from society's expectations. Einhorn killed only once, because he was able to find many other ways of asserting himself; Starkweather and Brady killed repeatedly, because they knew of no other way to assert their 'specialness' and rebelliousness.

For these murderers, the search for their own personal Samarkand took a particularly unpleasant form: they created a world in which they were free to kill, and free also from the laws and conventions by which other people were bound. The nature of this world was different in each of the three cases. Brady (whose Sevenness was mingled with Threeness, and especially with SA–<u>3</u>–PL) experienced an intense pleasure in the act of killing, and for him killing was its own reward. For Starkweather (whose Sevenness was mingled with Twoness) killing was a way of getting his revenge on society ("dead people are all on the same level," he said). For Einhorn, killing in itself was not important; the important thing was that he had created a world in which he was free to do whatever he wished, and was not accountable for his actions.

Conclusion

If we look back at our examples of people strong in Sevenness, we can see that all of them were (in one way or another) standing outside the world in which they found themselves. Within the previous prime numbers, we accept the world as it is and work with it: thus, in Twoness, the world presents us with challenges which we strive to overcome; in Threeness, we take pleasure from living in the world; and in Fiveness, we try to re-shape the world to satisfy our needs. But in Sevenness, re-shaping the world is no longer sufficient; we are in search of a different world, a magical world, a Samarkand that we have created out of our imagination and our inner resources. We are searching for the hidden meaning that lies below the surface of the tangible world.

It was said of Bruce Chatwin that he was "in search of the miraculous," but in fact this can be said, in one way or another, of all of these people who are strong in Sevenness. All of them are seeking (and in some cases finding) a way of being in which the miraculous happens and the normal rules of our mundane existence no longer apply. Some of them simply 'live' the miracle; others see themselves as messengers of the miraculous; others create works of art in which the miracle becomes a reality. For some, the miraculous world that they create is beautiful and uplifting, while for others (as for our three murderers) it appears to outsiders as evil and distorted. Sevenness, like all the other numbers, is in itself neither good not bad: it can be made either good or bad by the ways in which it is applied.

The case of Anita McKeown suggests that, if the Sevenness person tries to ignore the search for the miraculous and to live a 'normal' life (as McKeown did in becoming a policewoman, an upholder of the established order), then the miraculous will keep intruding on their lives and forcing them to attend to it.

The people whom we have considered in this chapter are people with an exceptional amount of Sevenness in their charts. But all of us have *some* Sevenness in our charts, and I believe that this can be highly beneficial. At the start of this chapter I said that the division of the week into seven days has helped us to keep in touch with the divinity at the heart of things, and I feel that the same is true of the Sevenness in our charts. What I have called "the search for the miraculous" is also the search for the divine, the numinous, the transcendent. Sevenness puts us in touch with a sense of wonder and of mystery. It helps us to realize that we are not the masters of the universe and cannot understand everything, and so can help us to achieve humility.

It has rightly been said that the Sevenness aspects in our charts are a key to what inspires us or "turns us on".[21] Sevenness is to do with intuition and inspiration. When two planets are linked by Sevenness aspects, their relationship takes on a more magical and mystical quality. To take one example: Aspects between Sun and Saturn are normally to do with awareness of limitations surrounding the Self, and awareness of the need for discipline and self-control, but when Sun and Saturn are linked by Sevenness aspects, their relationship takes on the quality of tragedy. The person will tend to see his or her life in a tragic light, and this awareness will inspire him and will impart to his life a deeper meaning.

Another key word for Sevenness is *wildness*. Sevenness can be seen as a rebellion against the ordered, rational, technological world of Fiveness, and a breakthrough into a wilder, less controlled, more innovative world, in which the person is more able to set his own rules rather than abiding by the rules of society.

We have said that, if Five is the number of Man, then Seven is perhaps the number of the angels. But angels are like human beings with wings. So perhaps we can say that Seven is also a number of Man: but, since I see Seven as a more feminine number than Five, I need to translate this into the feminine. So Seven is a number of Woman. It represents, not her rational mind or her earthbound intelligence, but her ability to fly into the realms of imagination, intuition, fantasy, mysticism and magic, her ability to probe deeply into the mysteries of this strange universe in which we find ourselves. So long as we accept that the insights of Sevenness are not certainties but are simply attempts to shed light on that which can never be full known, then Sevenness can illuminate and enrich our lives. Without it, our lives would be very much more humdrum, colourless and uninspiring.

9

Introduction to the Higher Prime Numbers

We have now looked at the first five prime numbers, One, Two, Three, Five and Seven, and it may feel as though we have come to the end of the road. We have seen how, in the beginning, everything is united in Oneness; and then we have seen how, in Twoness, the One becomes aware that there is Another standing outside him, and comes into a relationship with this Other; and how, in Threeness, the person becomes able to stand outside this relationship and to take pleasure in all the forms and relationships of this complex world; how, in Fiveness, he becomes able to re-shape the world in accordance with his own desires and needs; and finally, how, in Sevenness, he learns how to contact the hidden and mysterious meanings that lie beneath the surface of the apparent world.

It may seem that there is nowhere else to go from here. Yet Seven is, of course, not the last prime number. After Seven there is, for the first time, a gap (because the next three numbers, Eight, Nine and Ten, are not primes), and then there is another prime number, Eleven, followed quickly by another, Thirteen; then there is another gap, and then the prime numbers continue in an infinite series. Obviously we cannot continue down this series for ever, we have to stop somewhere, and we have already decided that we will stop at 32. So before 32 there are seven new prime numbers to consider: 11, 13, 17, 19, 23, 29 and 31.

What astrological significance (if any) do these numbers have? Here we are entering into uncharted territory. We need to venture into this territory with an open mind, ready to record whatever we may find there. My intention is to devote a chapter to each of the prime numbers from 11 to 31, to look at some examples of charts that are particularly strong in each of the numbers, and to make some proposals about the astrological significance of each number. However, I wish to stress that these proposals will be tentative. I do not wish to lay down the law and to say "This is definitely what Elevenness (or Thirteenness, or

Seventeenness) means". Rather, I will be providing pointers, which may or may not be helpful to other astrologers who venture into this area.

Although, as I have said, it is important to enter this territory with an open mind, it is worthwhile at this point to make a few comments about what I might expect to find, and to say something also about the difficulties of working in this area.

Firstly, we can surely expect that these numbers will have *some* astrological significance. Since the prime numbers as far as Seven are so very important and meaningful, it would be surprising if the prime numbers beyond Seven were completely without importance and meaning. Surely we can expect that the basic law of harmonic astrology – that each prime number introduces a new quality, which is different from the quality of all other prime numbers – will continue to operate beyond Seven.

On the other hand, we can also expect that, as we move further and further down the list of prime numbers, the importance and significance of each number will gradually become less and less. One reason for this is that is rare to find a chart in which a number higher than Seven is the strongest of all the prime numbers. Thus, in the following chapters we will be looking at charts which contain strong clusters of Elevenness, Thirteenness and so on, but in nearly every case these charts also contain even stronger clusters of Oneness, Twoness, Threeness, Fiveness or Sevenness. So we can say that the quality of Elevenness (or Thirteenness) is strong in the personalities of the people who own these charts, but it is rarely the strongest factor.

In fact, there are many charts that contain no important clusters of planets involving these higher numbers, and, for these charts, the interpretation of the higher numbers can safely be ignored. But there are also many charts that do contain such clusters, and in these cases it does seem to be important to attempt to interpret the higher numbers, since they may contain clues to the interpretation of some facets of the person's behaviour for which there is no explanation elsewhere in the chart.

One difficulty in interpreting the higher numbers is that they may refer to factors which are hidden deeply within a person's internal world, and which may not always manifest in his or her external behaviour. In my book *Harmonic Charts* I suggested that "as we proceed further along the sequence of prime numbers, we are proceeding further towards *internality:* that is, towards desires, thoughts and feelings which have their origins within the person's mind and are also increasingly introspective (concerned with the contemplation of the person himself), so that they bear no relation to the person's objective situation within his environment".[1] If this is the case, it follows that unless we know the person very well (in the way that one knows an intimate friend, or in the way that a therapist knows a client), we may be unable to detect the ways in which the higher numbers affect his personality. But in this book we are looking mainly at the charts of famous people, who are known by virtue of the external behaviour which made them famous, and (unless these famous people have been very self-disclosive) we may be unable to interpret the higher numbers because we do not know enough about the person's inner world.

However, one principle that may help us to interpret the higher numbers is that *each prime number seems to be a response to, or a reaction against, the previous prime number.* Thus, if we take the prime numbers from One to Seven, we can say:

Two says to One: I wish to reject the idea that all is Oneness, since I am aware of a separation between Self and Other, and I am aware of conflicts that have to be dealt with and challenges that have to be met.

Three says to Two: I am tired of dealing with conflicts and challenges, and I wish to accept the world as it is and to rejoice in its beauty.

Five says to Three: I am tired of accepting the world as it is, I wish to re-shape it to suit my own needs.

Seven says to Five: I am tired of trying to re-shape the world, I wish to probe its deeper meaning and of be aware of things that are beyond my control.

If this pattern continues beyond Seven, we can expect that Elevenness is a reaction against Sevenness, Thirteenness is a reaction against Elevenness, and so on, and this may provide clues to the meaning of the higher numbers.

Bearing these ideas in mind, let us now delve into the attempt to probe the mysteries of the higher numbers.

10

Elevenness

The first prime number beyond Seven is Eleven, and in this chapter we will investigate the astrological meaning of Elevenness by looking at charts that contain a large number of Elevenness links between planets. It is important that we do this with an open mind. Much has been written about the significance of the number Eleven,[1] but it is all based on the special position of Eleven in the decimal system, in which Eleven is written '11', or One-One. But in this book we are not operating within the decimal system: we are looking at the cosmic significance of the prime numbers, as they existed before Man imposed the decimal system upon them. So, rather than summarizing what has been said before about Eleven, I will go straight into giving examples of birth charts that are strong in Elevenness, and will then ask: What do these people have in common, and how does this help us to identify the special quality of Elevenness?

Fred Astaire
Born 10 May 1899, 21.16 (+06.00)
Omaha, NE, USA (41N16. 95W56).
Source: Birth certificate, via Ed Helin (ADB). RR: AA.

(((SO–**11**–<u>UR</u>)–<u>11</u>/**11**–NE)–<u>11/11</u>/11–JU)–11/11/11/<u>11</u>–VE)–
–22/22/**2**/**22**/<u>22</u>–SA
–22/22/**2**/22/<u>22</u>/22–(<u>MO</u>–11–SA)
(VE–<u>11</u>–JU)–<u>22</u>/22/22/**22**–(MA–<u>11</u>–SA)

Fred Astaire has the strongest cluster of Elevenness that I have seen, with eight of his planets linked by Elevenness aspects. We should note that tied up in this Elevenness pattern are two close oppositions, MO–**2**–UR and SA–**2**–NE, which we can regard as the main driving forces in Astaire's personality. These oppositions (which in themselves are pure Twoness) are brought together with each other, and with four other planets including the Sun, in this complex pattern of Elevenness.

Astaire is of course known for his scintillating ability as a dancer, but apart from this it is difficult to find out what kind of person he was. He was put onto the stage at the age of 5, and his stage and film career lasted for 76 years. It would seem that he lived entirely for his work, and outside it was a somewhat colourless character. But one characteristic that stands out is his legendary perfectionism. He relentlessly insisted on rehearsals and retakes, agonizing during the whole process, frequently asking colleagues for acceptance for his work; as Vincente Minnelli stated, "He lacks confidence to the most enormous degree of all the people in the world. .... He always thinks he is no good".[2] As Astaire himself observed, "I've never got anything 100% right. Still, it's never as bad as I think it is".

Again, Astaire's AstroDatabank biography says:

> "Astaire had a passion for perfection and was a hard taskmaster for himself, as well as for his partner. He would rehearse a number until it became second nature and he could do it in his sleep. To make his performance look effortless, he would rehearse up to 18 hours a day for six to eight weeks".

Since Astaire is so exceptionally strong in Elevenness, we can expect to find that this perfectionism is an expression of the spirit of the number Eleven. If we look at Astaire's Elevenness cluster, we see that Sun is united by Elevenness aspects with Venus, Jupiter, Uranus and Neptune. So the way in which Astaire seeks love and beauty (Venus), freedom and growth (Jupiter), originality and distinctiveness (Uranus), and idealism and transcendence (Neptune) is an 'Elevenness' kind of way: and then we see also that all these planets are linked by 'Twenty-twoness' aspects (22 = 11 x 2) to Saturn, showing that Astaire strives to find an 'Elevenness' way of disciplining himself so as to achieve all these goals. It seems reasonable to suppose that this Elevenness is related to the dogged persistence and search for perfection that was so marked a feature of his character.

Richard Pryor

Born 1 December 1940, 13.02 (+06.00)
Peoria, IL, USA (40N42. 89W35).
Source: Birth Certificate, via Gauquelin Book of American Charts (ADB). RR: AA.

((VE–**1**–MA)–**2**–JU)–11/**11**/**22**–UR)–**11**/11/22/**11**–SO
              –**11**/11–MO)–11/**11**/11–UR)–**11**/11/**11**/11–SO

Richard Pryor has been voted the greatest stand-up comedian of all time. His Elevenness pattern is nearly as strong as Astaire's, with (VE–**1**–MA)–**2**–JU linked by Elevenness aspects with Sun, Moon and Uranus.

Pryor is described by AstroDatabank as "a sharp, brash star of night clubs, TV and films who thrived on chaos". His childhood was marred by poverty and sexual abuse. He loved to shock, using words like "fuck" and "nigger" (one of his albums was called *That Nigger's Crazy*). Once he walked onto the stage, looked at the sold-out crowd, exclaimed over the microphone "What the fuck am I doing here?", and walked out. He had a reputation for being difficult and unprofessional on film sets, and for making unreasonable demands: Gene Wilder (quoted in Wikipedia) said that Pryor was frequently late to the set during filming of *Stir Crazy* and that he demanded, among other things, a helicopter to fly him to and from set. He was married seven times, and most of his marriages were marked by violence, mainly in connection with his use of drugs.

However, Pryor was also a deeply compassionate man, who used comedy to campaign for the rights, not only of black people, but also of animals, for whom he cared very deeply. Bill Cosby (quoted in Wikipedia) said, "Richard Pryor drew the line between comedy and tragedy as thin as one could possibly paint it". Pryor himself said, "I love each person I play; I have to be that person. I have to do him true".[3]

Pryor clearly has some of Astaire's passion for perfection, but in Pryor's case the Elevenness links to Sun, Moon and Uranus are attached to the cluster of (VE–**1**–MA)–**2**–JU which is the most powerful pattern in Pryor's chart. Thus, Pryor strives to find expansive (Jupiterian) ways of expressing his personal charisma and magnetism (VE–**1**–MA): but also, he seeks 'Elevenness' ways of making this behaviour self-fulfilling (Sun), expressive of his feelings (Moon), and original and striking (Uranus). If Elevenness is to do with dogged persistence, I feel that this well expresses what we might call Pryor's obstinate awkwardness – his tendency to persist in 'unreasonable' behaviour in order to demonstrate his refusal to follow the rules. More positively, it demonstrates his determination to be true to other people's individuality ("I have to do him true").

Donald Trump
Born 14 June 1946, 10.54 (+04.00)
Queens, NY, USA (40N41. 73W52).
Source: From birth certificate, as posted by him on the internet (ADB).
RR: AA.

(SO–**11**–VE)–22/**22**/22/**22**–(ME–**11**–JU)
((PL–**11**–CH)–**11**–MO)–**22**–SA

Donald Trump is an American billionaire, business magnate, socialite, and television personality. He has two clusters of Elevenness in his chart: a 'Sun cluster' and a 'Moon cluster'. The Sun cluster brings the Sun together with Venus (Sun-Venus aspects are always to do with self-love and the need for love) and also Mercury and Jupiter. The Moon cluster also involves Jupiter, together with Pluto and Chiron.

Donald Trump's extravagant lifestyle and outspoken manner have made him a celebrity for many years. In business he has always taken huge risks, which in the past have brought him to business bankruptcy and close to personal bankruptcy, but he has recovered from this and in recent years has been hugely successful. He has also been in the news for his extra-marital affair and subsequent divorce. His philosophy of life can be gauged from the following quotes:

"The point is that you can't be too greedy."

"Without passion you don't have energy, without energy you have nothing."

"You have to think anyway, so why not think big?"

"Money was never a big motivation for me, except as a way to keep score. The real excitement is playing the game."

(speaking of himself in the third person) "Love him or hate him, Trump is a man who is certain about what he wants and sets out to get it, no holds barred. Women find his power almost as much of a turn-on as his money."[4]

Trump's most important Elevenness aspect is SO–**11**–VE. Sun-Venus aspects reflect the way in which the person seeks to make himself attractive, and so in Trump's case this search has an Elevenness quality; and this is linked to ME–**11**–JU, showing that Trump also has an Elevenness way of 'talking big' (which I feel is demonstrated by the above quotes). Also there is (PL–**11**–CH)–**11**–MO, showing that Trump is instinctively drawn towards a fanatical obstinacy in sticking to his chosen path, no matter what setbacks may occur. "Women find his power a turn-on": there could hardly be a clearer demonstration of Trump's desire to make himself attractive to others by his 'no-holds-barred' behaviour.

Humphrey Lyttelton

Born 23 May 1921, 07.00 (–01.00)
Windsor, England (51N29. 0W38).
Source: As stated by him on television, via David Hamblin.[5] RR: A.

((SO–**11**–MO)–**11**–JU)–22/22/22/22/**2**/22–(UR–**11**–CH)

Humphrey Lyttelton (known to everyone as 'Humph') was educated at Eton College, the 'posh' boys' boarding school, but he turned his back on this elitist background and became a jazz trumpeter and band leader. He was a friend of Louis Armstrong, who praised him as the best British trumpeter. Lyttelton was also known as a cartoonist, and as the chairman of the radio panel game *I'm Sorry I Haven't a Clue*, in which his role was to give the panellists "silly things to do," such as "singing one song to the tune of another". He continued in this last role until well into his eighties, and was known and loved for his dry humour, his brilliant sense of comic timing, and his ability to tell extremely risqué jokes which no one else could have got away with. However, he kept his family life entirely private; not even his close friends knew his home telephone number, and, if anyone found out what the number was, he would change it.

Lyttelton's Elevenness cluster brings together the Sun, the Moon, and three other planets, and is also built around a close opposition between Jupiter and Uranus. We can see how Lyttelton doggedly pursued a free and independent lifestyle ((SO–**11**–MO)–**11**–JU) combined with an original and startling choice of career (UR–**11**–CH).

Princess Grace of Monaco (Grace Kelly)

Born 12 November 1929, 05.31 (+05.00)
Philadelphia, PA, USA (39N57. 75W10).
Source: Birth certificate, via Steinbrecher (ADB). RR: AA.

(MO–**11**–ME)–22/**22**/22/**2**–(UR–**11**–CH)
((UR–**11**–CH)–11/**11**–JU)–22/**22**/22–MO

Grace Kelly was born into a rich and well-connected family. AstroDatabank says that she "never gained attention or approval from her father, thus setting the pattern in her adult life to seek older, important men who were father substitutes". She became a film star, starred in eleven films, but gave an impression of aloofness: Alfred Hitchcock said that she was a "volcano covered by snow, but the public sees only the snow". She then married Prince Rainier, moved to Monaco, and became Princess Grace. This was the end of her acting career: Rainier had no interest in the arts, and imposed a strict protocol governing visits to the palace. In later years Grace felt trapped within a loveless marriage, but felt that escape was impossible.

All the Elevenness people whom we have looked at have been totally dedicated to their work. This is true also of Grace Kelly, but for most of her adult life her 'work' was fulfilling her duties as the Princess of Monaco. However, because Sun is not involved in the Elevenness cluster, this was in the end unfulfilling for her, and there was a sense of frustration and dissatisfaction.

Vincent Van Gogh, Paul Gauguin and Paul Cézanne

Vincent Van Gogh
Born 30 March 1853, 11.00 (–00.19)
Zundert, Netherlands (51N28. 4E40).
Source: Birth certificate, via Gauquelin (ADB). RR: AA.

((MO–**11**–CH)–11–(VE–**11**–PL))–22–NE

Paul Gauguin
Born 7 June 1848, 10.00 (–00.09)
Paris, France (48N52. 2E20).
Source: Birth certificate, via Françoise Gauquelin (ADB). RR: AA.

(SO–**11**–CH)–22/22/22/**22**–(SA–**11**–PL)
(MA–11–UR)–22–NE
(MO–**2**–NE)–11/22–UR

Paul Cézanne
Born 19 January 1839, 01.00 (–00.22)
Aix-en-Provence, France (43N32. 5E26).
Source: Birth certificate, via Gauquelin (ADB). RR: AA.

(MO–**11**–MA)–11–NE)–11/11/11–PL
JU–**22**–SA

All three of these artists have strong clusters of Elevenness, in every case involving the Moon, Neptune and Pluto. I will not attempt here to summarize their complex and fascinating lives, but will simply say that all three of them were loners and innovators who doggedly pursued their artistic vision throughout their lives with very little support from outside. All of them suffered from depression; Van Gogh committed suicide, and Gauguin also tried to do so. Cézanne has been described as "the ultimate outsider",[6] and lived much of his life as a hermit. Gauguin fled to Tahiti in order to escape from "everything that is artificial and conventional".[7]

These three painters also had much in common in the nature of their artistic vision, and I will say more about this when I summarize the meaning of Elevenness at the end of this chapter.

David Carpenter and Dennis Nilsen

David Carpenter
Born 6 May 1930, 21.16 (+08.00)
San Francisco, CA, USA (37N46. 122W25).
Source: Birth certificate, via Vic Shaw (ADB). RR: AA.

(SO–**11**–_JU_–**11**–UR)–<u>22</u>–ME
MA–**11**–PL
SA–**11**–NE

Dennis Nilsen
Born 23 November 1945, 04.00 (+00.00)
Peterhead, Scotland (57N20. 1W49).
Source: Birth certificate, via Paul Wright. RR: AA.

(MO–**11**–UR)–11–SO)–<u>22</u>/22/22–VE
(ME–11–<u>CH</u>)–11/<u>11</u>–PL
        –<u>22</u>/22–<u>SA</u>

Two murderers with strong Elevenness patterns are David Carpenter and Dennis Nilsen. Carpenter stabbed seven young women to death in remote parks; before killing them, he psychologically tortured them, but did not sexually abuse them. Nilsen lured fifteen young men into his flat, where he strangled them, masturbated over their bodies, then dismembered them and attempted to flush the remains down the toilet. (It was said that he had been greatly affected by the death of his beloved grandfather when he was a child; he had grieved over his grandfather's body, and, unloved by his parents, he had come to feel that the only loving body was a dead one.) Of course the Elevenness is not the whole story about why Carpenter and Nilsen turned to murder, but they were both loners who doggedly pursued their chosen paths, repeating the same pattern of behaviour over and over again until they were caught.

Winston Churchill
Born 30 November 1874, 01.30 (+00.00)
Woodstock, England (51N52. 1W21).
Source: From letter by father, via John Addey; also from _Jennie_ (a biography of Churchill's mother) by R.G. Martin (ADB). RR: B.

SO–**11**–MO–**11**–PL
VE–**11**–MA
ME–<u>22</u>–SA

Our last example of a person with a strong Elevenness pattern is Winston Churchill, who has almost-exact Elevenness aspects linking Sun, Moon, and Pluto, and also Venus and Mars. Churchill's career as a politician, a war leader, and a brilliant and inspirational orator (and also as a writer and painter) is well-known, but we should also remember that for much of his life he was regarded as a loner and an outsider, and that he suffered from repeated bouts of severe depression, which he called the "black dog". With SO–**11**–MO–**11**–PL (and it seems to me that the essential qualities of Pluto have much in common with the qualities of Elevenness – perhaps we could say that Elevenness is 'ruled' by Pluto), Churchill could be regarded as the archetypal Elevenness person, and it was these Elevenness qualities that made him an outstanding war leader.

Conclusion

So what do these people with strong Elevenness patterns have in common, and what can they tell us about the meaning of Elevenness?

It seems to me that they all share a kind of dogged persistence and resilience. They knew what was important in their lives, and they stuck to it resolutely and unswervingly. This goes with a certain 'apartness' from the rest of society, a tendency to be aloof and demanding in one's dealings with other people, and a tendency to be seen as a loner and an outsider. There is a tendency also towards depression, which is manifest in many of these cases and may well be present (though hidden) in others.

Thus, Fred Astaire stuck to his dancing career for 76 years, and strove towards perfection in his work, making great demands on his partners and colleagues. Richard Pryor also was difficult and demanding in his relationships (both at work and in marriage), and his outburst ("What the fuck am I doing here?") is an indication of the 'apartness' of Elevenness.

Donald Trump sees himself as "a man who is certain about what he wants and sets out to get it, no holds barred," and as a man who likes to exercise power over others; not even the experience of bankruptcy could deflect him from the pursuit of wealth and power. His tendency towards bravado and self-glamorization may well be a cover-up for inner feelings of loneliness and depression.

Humphrey Lyttelton rebelled against his elitist background, and stuck resolutely to his chosen path; like Fred Astaire, he continued working into his 80s. Although he developed an affable persona, he kept his family life entirely hidden; and also, on *I'm Sorry I Haven't a Clue*, he cultivated the image of a person who stands apart from the fray, a rock of sanity in the midst of chaos, which seems to be in keeping with the spirit of Elevenness.

Grace Kelly, as an actress, seemed aloof and apart from her colleagues; and then she went voluntarily into a life of almost total 'apartness' as Princess Grace, and stuck to it for the rest of her life, even when it brought her great unhappiness.

The three painters, Van Gogh, Gauguin and Cézanne, were all loners who stuck resolutely to their chosen path in the face of the disapproval or indifference of the outside world. (Van Gogh and Gauguin shared a house for a while, but they quarrelled terribly; it would seem that, when two Elevenness people come together, there is bound to be trouble.) And the two murderers, Carpenter and Nilsen, are textbook examples of the murderer as loner.

Finally, Winston Churchill was sidelined for much of his life by his colleagues, who saw him as too aloof, too self-willed, not a good team player. He came into his own during the war, when the qualities of Elevenness were needed on a national scale. In Churchill's speeches ("I have nothing to offer you but blood, toil, tears and sweat"; "We shall fight them on the beaches .... we shall never surrender") we can hear the voice of Elevenness speaking: the voice that says, "We must stick resolutely to our chosen path; we must endure hardship in the pursuit of our goals; we must allow nothing and nobody to deflect us".

Thus, we can hypothesize that, when two or more planets are linked by Elevenness aspects, their relationship will have this quality of determination, defiance, resilience and 'stickability'.

In Chapter 9 we suggested that each prime number is a reaction against the previous prime number, so that we can expect Elevenness to be a reaction against Sevenness. Sevenness is about the 'search for the miraculous', the search for the hidden meaning that lies beneath the surface of things. But in Elevenness there are no miracles, no probing beneath the surface; rather, one has to take life as one finds it, and to accept the surface as the true reality.

Thus, Churchill made it plain that the war would be won, not by miracles or by the hand of God, but only by hard graft. But this message is clearest in the work of the three painters, Van Gogh, Gauguin and

Cézanne, all of whom made it their life's work to come into a deeper relationship with the surface world of Forms, and to reflect this understanding of Forms in their paintings. All of them believed in painting directly from nature. Van Gogh said: "It is not the language of painters but the language of nature that one should listen to …. The feeling for the things themselves, for reality, is more important than the feeling for pictures";[8] and Cézanne saw Mont St-Victoire (which he painted repeatedly) as "the essence of all that he had felt had eluded the Impressionists – firmness, solidity, permanence".[6]

And Gauguin's most famous painting is entitled: "Where do we come from? What are we? Where are we going?" These are the kinds of questions to which a Sevenness person would try to find answers; but Gauguin offers no answers, and his painting seems to be telling us that there are no answers. All he shows us is the people standing there in their natural environment, in their beauty, their stability, and their perplexity, asking the questions but receiving no guidance. There are no miracles; the reality is the world as we see it around us.

Thirteenness

The next prime number after Eleven is Thirteen. Thirteen has gained a reputation as an unlucky number, due to its association with the traitor Judas Iscariot who was the thirteenth person present at the Last Supper, and also to the Death card which is the thirteenth card in the Major Arcana of the Tarot pack; and there is even a word, *triskaidekaphobia*, which means fear of the number Thirteen. However, in this chart we will look at Thirteen with an open mind, focusing on charts that are strong in Thirteenness; but we will also be asking the question: Is there anything inherent in the nature of Thirteenness that might cause people to be afraid of it?

Catherine the Great
Born 2 May 1729, 02.30 (–00.58)
Stettin, Germany (53N24. 14E32).
Source: From biography by Anthony, via Mark Johnson (ADB). RR: B.

((SO–*1*–CH)–**13**–UR–**13**–NE)–**26**–MO
MA–**13**–JU

Catherine the Great was Empress of Russia from 1762 to 1796. She was the daughter of a minor German prince, and at the age of 16 she married Peter, the heir to the Russian throne. When Peter succeeded to the throne, he proved to be totally incompetent, and was eventually deposed and murdered (but it seems likely that Catherine was not a party to the murder). At the age of 33, Catherine became absolute monarch of Russia, and was one of its most enlightened and popular rulers, pushing through many far-reaching reforms. (Her greatest regret was that she was unable to end the system of serfdom.) She was highly intelligent and well read, and even found time to write a number of stories and even operas; she was also famous for the number of her young lovers (at least 22). It is extraordinary how this woman (who is described by AstroDatabank as "ambitious, cruel, egotistical and domineering" but also as "cultured, intelligent, studious and charming"), having no Russian blood and no knowledge of the Russian language until after her wedding, was able to establish such complete dominance over a society that was alien to her.

Catherine has an exact Sun-Chiron conjunction (signifying her total identification with her role as 'saviour of the nation'), and this conjunction forms many aspects with other planets. But the strongest configuration is the cluster of Thirteenness, in which Sun-Chiron forms very close Thirteenness links with Uranus and Neptune, and also (if the birth time is accurate) with the Moon; and, in addition, Mars has a very close Thirteenness link with Jupiter.

What does this Thirteenness mean? We will have to look at some more examples before we can be sure about this, but it must surely have some relevance to Catherine's success in establishing herself as an all-powerful monarch in an alien country.

Antoine de Saint-Exupéry and Amelia Earhart

Antoine de Saint-Exupéry
Born 29 June 1900, 09.15 (–00.09)
Lyon, France (45N45. 4E51).
Source: Birth certificate, via Françoise Gauquelin (ADB). RR: AA.

(SO–13–MO)–**26/26**/26/26–(VE–**13**–UR)
ME–13–CH

Amelia Earhart
Born 24 July 1897, 23.30 (+06.00)
Atchison, KS, USA (39N34. 95W07).
Source: From her to Mrs Yerington; also from biography by Lovell *The Sound of Wings* (ADB). RR: A.

((MA–**1**–JU)–13/**13**–ME)–13/13/**13**–VE

Antoine de Saint-Exupéry and Amelia Earhart were both pioneer aviators. Saint-Exupéry was born into an impoverished aristocratic family; as a child he was extremely unruly and wilful. He obtained his pilot's licence at the age of 21, and he became one of the pioneers of international postal flight in the days when aircraft had few instruments and pilots flew by instinct. Later he complained that those who flew the more advanced aircraft were more like accountants than pilots. Saint-Exupéry was also a writer (his most famous book is *The Little Prince*), and he wrote with great sensitivity and originality. The following quote gives us a sense of his outlook on life:

"A single event can awaken within us a stranger totally unknown to us. To live is to be slowly born".[1]

Amelia Earhart had an unhappy childhood, being brought up by strict grandparents (her father was alcoholic and her mother was 'repressed'). As a child she was a tomboy, and she kept a scrapbook of clippings about successful women in male-dominated fields. At the age of 20 she became enamoured of flying, and she became the first woman to obtain a pilot's licence and the first to fly solo across the Atlantic; she also reached a world-record altitude of 14,000 feet. Among her sayings are the following:

"The lure of flying is the lure of beauty."

"The fears are paper tigers. You can do anything you decide to do. You can act to change and control your life, and the procedure, the process is its own reward."

"Women, like men, should try to do the impossible. And when they fail, their failure should be a challenge to others."

"Adventure is worthwhile in itself."[2]

Both Saint-Exupéry and Earhart died in mysterious flying accidents. Saint-Exupéry's plane disappeared while he was making a reconnaissance flight during the Second World War. Earhart's plane also disappeared over the Pacific while she was attempting a solo round-the-world flight; no trace of it was ever found.

Saint-Exupéry's chart is dominated by a very close opposition between Mars and Jupiter, with Mars on the Midheaven and Jupiter on the I.C., which forms links with many other planets. But the strongest configuration is the cluster of Thirteenness, which brings together Sun, Moon, Venus and Uranus.

Earhart's chart is dominated by an almost-exact conjunction between the same two planets, Mars and Jupiter. This again forms many aspects, but the most striking link is the Thirteenness cluster which brings Mars and Jupiter together with Mercury and Venus.

Both Saint-Exupéry and Earhart believed in risk-taking and in testing themselves to the limit: "trying to do the impossible", as Earhart said. We can suggest that this risk-taking may be related to the spirit of Thirteenness.

Basel, Bahrain and Dalian air crashes

Basel air crash
10 April 1973, 10.17 (–01.00)
Basel, Switzerland (47N33. 7E35).
Source: Wikipedia.

((SO–**1**–VE)–**13**–ME)–13/13/**13**–SA

Bahrain air crash
23 August 2000, 19.20 (–03.00)
Manama, Bahrain (26N13. 50E35).
Source: Wikipedia.

((JU–**13**–UR)–13–ME)–**26**/**26**/26–NE

Dalian air crash
7 May 2002, 21.40 (–08.00)
Dalian, China (38N50. 121E40).
Source: Wikipedia.

((VE–**1**–SA)–**13**–JU)–**13**/13/13–SO
MO–13–MA
MO–26–NE

Since both Saint-Exupéry and Earhart died in air crashes, this is a good point at which to mention that I have also found several air crashes with strong Thirteenness in their charts. Three examples of this are given here. In all of these cases, the plane crashed into a mountain (Basel) or into the sea (Bahrain, Dalian) shortly before it was due to land. In two cases (Basel, Bahrain) the crashes were blamed on pilot errors. The Dalian crash, however, was caused by a passenger (who had taken out extensive insurance policies before the flight) lighting a fire inside the plane.

All these crashes resulted in terrible loss of life, but my belief (as always with mundane charts) is that the chart describes the causes of the incident, not its effects. Here the causes would seem to be to do with risk-taking, or foolhardiness, on the part of the pilots (or, in one case, of the passenger). In Chapter 5 we pointed out that some crashes are caused by carelessness, which is connected with Threeness; but foolhardiness is different from carelessness, and is perhaps connected with Thirteenness.

Peter Sellers

Born 8 September 1925, 06.00 (−01.00)
Portsmouth, England (50N48. 1W05).
Source: From him, via Ed Steinbrecher (FCC). RR: A.

((SO–**13**–MO)–**13**/**13**–SA)–13–CH
UR–**13**–PL

The comic actor Peter Sellers was known for his part in the *Goon Show* as well as for his roles in numerous films. His strength lay, not in cultivating and exaggerating a part of his own personality, but rather in taking on the personalities of other people and *becoming* them in a totally convincing but also humorous way. His skill in doing this, and the range of personalities he was able to assume, was extraordinary. Indeed, Sellers took this so far that he did not know who he really was. Robert Parrish, the film director, said of him, "He walked this strange tightrope of not being a real person at all," and his friend Peter O'Toole said, "Pete had an extraordinary sense of not being there. He genuinely felt that when he went into a room no one could see him".[3] Because of this, Sellers always felt the need to appear as somebody else (as, for instance, when he appeared on Michael Parkinson's chat show dressed, not as himself, but as a Nazi officer).

Sellers's Sun and Moon are linked by a close Thirteenness aspect, and they have Thirteenness links also with Saturn and with Chiron. The Sun-Moon-Saturn link is very strong, and suggests that Sellers felt in some way weighed down by his Thirteenness. Certainly he took great risks in trying himself out in different roles, but underneath there was this sense of his own non-existence. Maybe this helps to explain why Thirteenness people devote their lives to adventure and risk-taking: they are *in search of themselves*, trying to find out who they really are. But in Sellers' case this search was doomed to failure, as the Saturnian sense of restriction and limitation was too strong.

Truman Capote
Born 30 September 1924, 15.00 (+06.00)
New Orleans, LA, USA (29N57. 90W05).
Source: From Capote by Gerald Clarke (ADB). RR: B.

(SO–_13_–MA)–13–(MO–_13_–PL)
(VE–_1_–NE)–_13_/13–ME
(ME–_13_–VE)–_26_–SA

Truman Capote, the author of *Breakfast at Tiffany's*, had (like many other Thirteenness people) an unhappy childhood. His father disappeared when Truman was 4, and he was then grossly neglected by his mother (who later committed suicide) and his stepfather. He longed for the attention which his parents had denied him, and he coped with this by constructing an elaborately flamboyant and provocative persona. He paraded his homosexuality and his problems with drugs and alcohol; he threw extravagant parties and mixed with famous people, claiming to know (and sometimes to have had sexual relations with) people whom he could not possibly have known; he had himself photographed in 'suggestive poses'; he claimed that everyone (men and women) found him irresistible. Once he asked a conjuror to turn him into a woman. He died of an overdose of drugs and alcohol at the age of 59.

In his writings, Capote often explored themes from his own lonely childhood. His story *Other Voices, Other Rooms* is about a 13-year-old boy, Joel, who has lost his mother, and who goes in search of the father who had abandoned him at birth. Eventually he finds his father, who is paralysed and almost speechless. He leaves his father, and after further adventures comes to "accept his destiny, which is to be homosexual, to always hear other voices and live in other rooms".[4] He has made peace with his own identity. Capote himself described the story as "a poetic explosion in highly suppressed emotion" and as an attempt to exorcise his demons.

Capote was also interested in exploring human darkness: his "non-fiction novel" *In Cold Blood* was based on a detailed study of the mysterious murder of a family of four in rural Kansas. Here again one feels that Capote is really exploring the darkness inside himself.

Capote's chart is dominated by a very close conjunction of Venus and Neptune. Venus and Neptune are joined to Mercury and Saturn by

Thirteenness aspects, and there is also a separate Thirteenness cluster of Sun, Moon, Mars and Pluto. We can certainly see how Capote, like Peter Sellers, felt the need to try himself out in various extravagant roles in order to overcome his sense of non-existence and find his true identity. But in Capote's case (although Saturn in involved in the Thirteenness) the dominant link is SO–**13**–MA, so his risk-taking has a more flamboyant, aggressive quality.

Rainer Werner Fassbinder
Born 31 May 1945, 01.55 (–02.00)
Bad Wörishofen, Germany (48N00. 10E36).
Source: Birth certificate, via Steinbrecher (ADB). RR: AA.

(UR–**13**–NE–**13**–PL)–13–MO
(NE–**13**–PL)–13–SA

The German film writer and director Rainer Werner Fassbinder is similar to Capote in many ways. He too was openly gay; he too cultivated an outrageously flamboyant persona; he too explored the depths of human darkness; and he too died of a drugs and alcohol overdose. Joe Ruffell writes that Fassbinder's "self-awareness of his own tortuous personality is also the source of his undeniable genius".[5] Because he was so aware of the darkness in himself, he was able to portray it openly in his films. He was able to be compassionate both to the victims and to the victimizers, because he reocognized both of them in himself.

Fassbinder has a very close Thirteenness cluster bringing together Moon, Uranus, Neptune and Pluto. In his case I have a sense that, more than for Sellers or Capote, his search for himself had been successful; he had found out who he really was, and this knowledge inspired his films.

Hermann Hesse
Born 2 July 1877, 18.30 (–00.35)
Calw, Germany (48N43. 8E44).
Source: From mother's diary, via Zeller *Portrait of Hesse* (ADB).
RR: AA.

((SO–**13**–JU)–13/**13**–SA)–**26/26**/26–UR
ME–**13**–PL
MA–**13**–NE

Hermann Hesse, winner of the Nobel Prize for Literature, has a profusion of Thirteenness links, as shown above. He was brought up in a family of pious missionaries. He was a child prodigy, and his parents felt unable to cope with such a brilliant son. He attempted suicide at 15, and throughout his life struggled with manic depression, alcohol addiction, hypochondria and severe headaches. His three marriages all ended in divorce. And yet Hesse achieved a degree of happiness and serenity by withdrawing into what Wikipedia calls "a private life of self-exploration through journeys and wanderings". He wrote:

> "My intention [in writing *Peter Camenzind*] was to familiarize modern man with the overflowing and silent life of nature. I wanted to teach him to listen to the earth's heartbeat, to participate in the life of nature, and not to overlook in the press of his own little destiny that we are not gods, not creatures of our own making, but children, parts of the earth and of the cosmic whole." [6]

He also wrote:

> "A man is not at his best as a member of an association, a participant in a conspiracy, or a voice in a choir. Instead of community, camaraderie and classification, he seeks the opposite; he does not want to run with the pack and adapt himself, but to reflect nature and world in his own soul, experiencing them in fresh images. He is not made for life in the collective but is a solitary king in a dream world of his own creation." [6]

Many would disagree with this as a manifesto for the whole of humanity, since they would see human fulfilment as being bound up with the person's relationships with his fellow men and women. But perhaps it makes sense as a manifesto for the Thirteenness person, whose task is to seek himself through solitary exploration. We will return to this theme at the end of this chapter.

Janis Joplin

Born 19 January 1943, 09.45 (+05.00)
Port Arthur, TX, USA (29N54. 93W56).
Source: Birth certificate, via Ruth Hale Oliver (ADB). RR: AA.

((MO–**13**–MA)–**13**/13–NE)–13/**13**/13–PL

The singer and rock star Janis Joplin has a very strong cluster of Thirteenness. To quote her AstroDatabank biography, she was "an overweight, unhappy kid [who] expressed her resentment and hunger in heavy-duty parties and indiscriminate sex with both men and women, generally living on what she called 'the outer limits of probability' until her death at 27 of a heroin/ morphine overdose in a Hollywood motel room". She cultivated flamboyant dresses and hairstyles, and painted her car in psychedelic colours. She said, "I was always outrageous"; and she also said, "On stage I make love to twenty-five thousand people; and then I go home alone".[7]

Che Guevara
Born 14 May 1928, 03.05 (+04.00)
Rosario, Argentina (32S57. 60W40).
Source: From biography by Jon Lee Anderson (ADB). RR: B[8]

(SO–**13**–JU)–**13**–MA
((MO–**13**–CH)–**13**–SA)–13/13/**13**–NE
–26/**26**/**26**–PL

Che Guevara is described by Wikipedia as a "Marxist revolutionary, physician, author, intellectual, guerrilla leader, military theorist, and a major figure of the Cuban revolution". Very early in life he developed an "affinity for the poor". At the age of 21 he started to travel by motorbike round the whole of Latin America, staying with the poorest people and being deeply moved by their plight. This led to his developing a strong hostility to American-dominated capitalism in all its forms, and he developed his military expertise and helped to precipitate revolution in several countries, not only in Latin America but also in the Congo. His friend Fidel Castro saw him as a brilliant and charismatic leader, but also as taking too many risks, even having a "tendency towards foolhardiness". Guevara said, "The true revolutionary is guided by a great feeling of love", and he wrote a "last letter" (to be read by his children after his death) of which the final passage was: "Always, always be capable of feeling deeply any injustice committed against anyone, anywhere in the world. That is the most beautiful quality in a revolutionary".[9]

Guevara has one of the strongest Thirteenness charts. There are two Thirteenness clusters, one involving the Sun, the other involving the

Moon, so that both the proactive and the receptive sides of Guevara's personality are suffused with Thirteenness. We can note also that Guevara's chart has a remarkable and surprising absence of Twoness, so that it seems that all of his revolutionary zeal derives not from the quality of Twoness (struggle, conflict, fighting against the enemy) but from the quality of Thirteenness, whose nature we will discuss at the end of this chapter.

Roberta Cowell
Born 8 April 1918, 02.00 (–01.00)
Croydon, England (51N23. 0W06).
Source: From her, in *Astrological Quarterly* Winter 1954 (ADB). RR: A.

(MO–**1**–VE)–13/**13**–MA)–13/**13**/13–CH
((VE–**13**–MA)–13–CH)–**26**/26/**26**/26/26/26–(JU–**13**–NE)

Roberta Cowell was the first person in Britain to undergo a successful sex change from man to woman. (It is not clear whether she was the first in the world, but she was two years ahead of Christine Jorgensen in the US). As Robert Cowell, he was a racing motorist, became a fighter pilot in the Second World War, and was married and had children; but he had felt himself to be female from the age of ten, and in his thirties went through a long programme of surgery, facelifts and hormone treatments which finally enabled him/her to live as a woman. To go through such a process when it had never been done before must have required enormous courage and an intense commitment to becoming the person that she inwardly felt herself to be.

Cowell's chart is dominated by a very close conjunction of Moon and Venus (surely a classic indication of feeling oneself to be female), and these planets have Thirteenness links with four other planets.

Black Wednesday
16 September 1992, 08.00 (–01.00)
London, England (51N30. 0W10).
Source: See note.[10]

(SO–**1**–ME–**1**–JU)–**13**/13/13–SA
(ME–**1**–JU)–13–(*MA*–**13**–*NE*–**13**–PL)
(SO–**13**–SA)–**13**/13–*UR*

Finally in this chapter, we will look at the chart for 'Black Wednesday', the day on which frantic selling of pounds on the currency markets forced the British government to withdraw from the Exchange Rate Mechanism. George Soros, the best-known of the currency market investors, made over US$1 billion profit on this one day by selling sterling. The events of Black Wednesday destroyed the reputation of the Conservative government for sound economic management.

The chart is dominated by a very close conjunction of Sun, Mercury and Jupiter, with ME–**1**–JU almost exact. These planets are linked by Thirteenness aspects to five other planets, and in particular to a very close Thirteenness cluster of Mars, Neptune and Pluto. Certainly Black Wednesday was a day on which investors seemed to lose their inhibitions and to test to the limit their ability to destroy the status quo and establish a new reality.

Conclusion

So what do these Thirteenness charts have in common, and what can we deduce about the meaning of Thirteenness?

I feel that a central question for Thirteenness people is "Who am I?" They tend to start with an uncertainty about their own identity, and they cope with this in varying ways. Often this uncertainty arises from a feeling of *rootlessness*, a feeling of not being rooted in the family, the place, or the nation into which they were born. The family itself may be rootless (as in the case of Peter Sellers, whose parents were always on the move), or the family may have been disturbed by the absence of the father or the mental instability of one of the parents. Or else the family is rooted, but the child feels neglected, misunderstood, or unloved, or feels that the family is trying to force him into a mould which is alien to his true nature.

So the child feels a need to break away, and often does so at an early age, sometimes travelling great distances to be as far away from the parents as possible, and setting up a lifestyle which is far removed from that of the parents. This sets up the Thirteenness person's love of travel, adventure and risk-taking. The typical Thirteenness person seems to be always on the move, reluctant to settle down, and willing to take great risks with his or her personal safety. Travel is often loved for its own sake, as there is often a very great appreciation of the beauty of the natural world and of foreign cultures.[11] But it can also be a means of constantly running away from the central question of "Who am I?"

Thirteenness people are similar to Elevenness people in that they often feel themselves to be outsiders, but their response to this is different. Whereas the response of the Elevenness person is combative and aggressive, the Thirteenness person typically responds in a more subtle way. He may, as we have seen, respond by running away, but he may also choose to stay in society and try to make himself acceptable. He cares very much about his public image, and very much wants to be accepted by society. It is as though he is saying, "Since I don't know who I am, I will put on a mask and make people believe that the mask is who I am". Hence the preoccupation with acting and with playing parts. Some Thirteenness people may develop a whole variety of masks and become skilled actors or impersonators,[12] while others may put all their energy into developing and perfecting a single mask. This mask can be enormously effective, as in the case of Catherine the Great.

In particular, some Thirteenness people (Capote, Fassbinder, Joplin) may construct a mask through which they present themselves as flamboyant, outrageous, larger-than-life personalities, opening parading their eccentricities and especially their sexuality. Others (Saint-Exupéry, Earhart) may focus on constantly taking risks and exposing themselves to danger, presenting themselves to the world as courageous and fearless. (This tendency towards risk-taking and foolhardiness is also evident in the case of the air crashes with strong Thirteenness links, and also perhaps in the case of Black Wednesday.)

Yet this mask-building can itself be seen as a running away from the question "Who am I?" Thus, some Thirteenness people succeed in going beyond the mask-building and conducting a deep exploration of their own darkness, their own hidden depths, in an attempt to live according to their own true natures. In cases such as Saint-Exupéry, Hesse, Fassbinder and Guevara, this can lead to a great empathy with the whole human condition, and to a passionate commitment to improve the lot of mankind.

In all of this, the themes of restlessness and solitariness are apparent. Men with strong Thirteenness links tend either not to marry, or else to go through a series of short-lived and unsuccessful marriages. Women with strong Thirteenness links may marry a husband who is very rich, powerful, famous or talented, but these marriages tend to be short-lived and fraught with difficulties. (Examples of this include Jacqueline Kennedy Onassis,[13] who had two such marriages; Vivien Leigh,[14] who married Laurence Olivier; and Mary Shelley,[15] who eloped to marry the poet Shelley.) For both men and women, the commitment to personal development is too strong to be easily compatible with stable family life.

Thirteenness can be seen as a reaction against Elevenness, in that the Thirteenness person is rejecting the stoicism, obstinacy and single-minded determination of Elevenness in favour of a much more adventurous and risk-taking approach to life. Miracles are once again possible; life is whatever we make of it; our task (as Hermann Hesse said) is to explore the world, and through doing so to find ourselves.

At the start of this chapter I asked whether there was anything inherent in the number Thirteen that might cause people to be afraid of it. And the answer is: Yes, perhaps there is. Thirteen is associated with rootlessness, restlessness and risk-taking, and, for cautious people who are afraid of change – that is, for superstitious people who avoid walking under ladders and who avoid the number Thirteen – there is plenty to fear here. And also, even though many Thirteenness people have lived to a great age, there are also several who met an early death, whether as a result of suicide, murder, plane crashes, over-indulgence in drink and drugs, or a variety of illnesses, suggesting that the traditional association of Thirteen with death is not entirely fanciful.

And yet we must not forget the immense positive potential of Thirteenness. In this chapter we have looked at the people with the strongest Thirteenness charts – that is, it might be said, at the people who have too much Thirteenness. But I believe that a modicum of Thirteenness in the personality is desirable, in helping to shake people out of complacency and enabling them to live more adventurous, authentic and self-fulfilling lives.

12

Seventeenness

After Thirteen there is a gap (as the next odd number, Fifteen, is not a prime), and then we come to Seventeen.

From now onwards, we are looking at numbers about which we have less information and fewer examples. This is because we are not looking at divisions of the circle beyond 32. In the case of Thirteen, we were able to study examples, not only of 'Thirteenness' aspects, but also of 'Twenty-Sixness' aspects (since 13 x 2 is 26). But in the case of Seventeen, we can look only at 'Seventeenness' aspects, since 17 x 2 is 34, which is a higher number than 32.

Once again, we will look at examples of people who have strong clusters of Seventeenness in their charts, in order to make deductions about the essential nature of Seventeenness.

Madalyn Murray O'Hair
Born 13 April 1919, 09.00 (+04.00)
Pittsburgh, PA, USA (40N26. 79W59).
Source: Birth certificate, via *Contemporary American Horoscopes* (ADB).
RR: AA.

((MO–**17**–VE)–17–ME)–7/17/17–JU
  –17/17/17–UR

Madalyn Murray O'Hair was a militant atheist, who devoted her whole life to writing and campaigning against religion in all its forms and trying to prove the non-existence of God. She said, "Religion has caused more misery to all of mankind in every stage of human history than any other single idea".[1] AstroDatabank says that she became "the most hated woman in America" and that "her life was repeatedly threatened, her children beaten, her property and finances systematically destroyed". Her son William turned against her, and said: "She was just evil. She stole huge amounts of money. She misused the trust of people. She cheated children out of their parents' inheritance".[2] O'Hair, together with her son Jon and her adopted granddaughter, were brutally murdered by a criminal who had stolen from O'Hair's organization, and whose crimes O'Hair had tried to expose.

The dominant aspect in O'Hair's chart is MO–2–CH, but Moon is also joined by Seventeenness aspects to Mercury, Venus, Jupiter and Uranus. We should note that O'Hair is also strong in Nineteenness, which we will consider in the next chapter. However, Seventeen is her strongest number, so we need to find out whether her militancy is typical of people with high Seventeenness.

L. Ron Hubbard
Born 13 March 1911, 02.01 (+06.00)
Tilden, NE, USA (42N03. 97W50).
Source: From him, via Doris Chase Doane (ADB). RR: A.

(JU–**17**–SA)–**17**–SO
(MO–**17**–NE)–**17**/**17**–MA

L. Ron Hubbard, the founder of Scientology, started adult life as a writer of science fiction and adventure stories. Between 1933 and 1938 he wrote 138 novels, writing at what a friend called "incredible speed". He was also a hypnotist, and followed the black magic practices of Aleister Crowley. In 1938, in a letter to his wife, he wrote: "I have high hopes of smashing my name into history so violently that it will take a legendary form".[3]

In 1950 he published his book *Dianetics, the Modern Science of Mental Health*, setting out the principles of what he later called Scientology. He claimed that his discoveries were "a milestone for Man comparable to his discovery of fire and superior to his inventions of the wheel and the watch".[3] The book was an instant bestseller, and Hubbard founded the Church of Scientology which now has at least two million members and has been said to be a "highly coercive dictatorship". Hubbard's followers regarded him as sincere and altruistic, but he has also been called "a pathological liar".

Hubbard's chart has two clusters of Seventenness, one involving the Sun and the other involving the Moon. The chart is also notable for the large number of aspects involving Mars, which is very closely conjunct to Uranus. Hubbard, like O'Hair, was certainly a militant campaigner, although his campaigning was not on behalf of a recognized 'cause' such as atheism, but on behalf of the dissemination of his own ideas. We can note that Sun is linked by Seventeenness aspects to both Jupiter and Saturn, suggesting both the grandeur and extravagance of Hubbard's ideas and the steadfast discipline with which he promoted them.

Nicolae Ceauşescu

Born 5 February 1918, 12.00 (–01.44)
Scornicesti, Romania (44N34. 24E33).
Source: Birth certificate, via Mihaela Dicu (ADB). RR: AA.

(SO–**17**–JU)–17–NE
(VE–**1**–UR)–17/**17**–MO

Nicolae Ceauşescu was the Communist dictator of Romania from 1965 to 1989. He was seen at first as an enlightened ruler, but as time passed he showed increasing signs of extreme paranoia and indeed of madness (making his dog a colonel in the Romanian army) as he tried to emulate the Cultural Revolution of China and the personality cult of Kim Il-Sung in North Korea. He passed laws making abortion illegal and divorce almost impossible, and rewarding mothers of large families, with the result that the population exploded and thousands of children were abandoned by their parents and housed in abject conditions in orphanages. Wikipedia says: "By 1989, Ceauşescu was showing signs of complete denial of reality. While the country was going through extremely difficult times with long bread queues in front of empty food shops, he was often shown on state TV entering stores filled with food supplies, visiting large food and arts festivals, while praising the 'high living standard' achieved under his rule. Special contingents of food deliveries would fill stores before his visits, and even well-fed cows would be transported across country in anticipation of his visits to farms".

In the end, Ceauşescu was overthrown in a popular uprising, and he and his wife were put to death on Christmas Day 1989.

Ceauşescu's chart (like Hubbard's) contains two clusters of Seventeenness, one involving the Sun and the other the Moon. The cluster of (SO–**17**–JU)–17–NE is especially notable, since Sun is close to the Midheaven, Jupiter close to the Ascendant, and Neptune (together with Saturn) close to the I.C. Ceauşescu was an instigator of reforms which were both grand and optimistic (Jupiter) and idealistic (Neptune), but which (as can happen with Neptune) became more and more unrealistic. Also we can recall that Scientology (led by Hubbard) has been called a "coercive dictatorship": Ceauşescu was certainly a coercive dictator, so maybe dictatorial behaviour is linked to the spirit of Seventeenness.

Roger Vadim
Born 26 January 1928, 21.30 (+00.00)
Paris, France (48N52. 2E20).
Source: Birth certificate via Didier Geslain states 22.00, but Vadim in his autobiography *Memoirs of the Devil* states 21.00 (ADB). I have chosen the midpoint between these two times. RR: B.

(((JU–**1**–UR)–17/**17**–MA)–17/17/17–NE)–17/17/**17**/**17**–ME
(((MA–**17**–UR)–**17**–NE)–17/17/**17**–ME)–17/17/17/**17**–PL

Roger Vadim was the film director who launched Brigitte Bardot's career with the film *And God Created Woman*. He was known both for his sensuous films and for his sensuous lifestyle, and AstroDatabank says that he "pursued beauty on and off-screen". He was married five times to beautiful women, including Brigitte Bardot and Jane Fonda, and he also had a child by Catherine Deneuve. He said, "You wouldn't ask Rodin to make an ugly sculpture, or me to make a film with an ugly woman".[4]

In Vadim's chart, Jupiter and Uranus (which are together on the Descendant, close to the Moon) are linked by Seventeenness aspects to Mars (which, together with Venus, is close to the I.C.) and also to Mercury, Neptune, Pluto and Chiron. (He also has a very close Moon-Venus square, which would seem to be the main indicator of his pursuit of beauty.)

It might seem that Vadim was simply a playboy, cheerfully pursuing his hedonistic lifestyle in defiance of the rest of society. But the fact that he called his autobiography *Memoirs of the Devil* suggests that he saw himself as aiming not just to defy society, but to change it and subvert it. In this he was similar to the other Seventeenness people that we have considered.

Harold Pinter
Born 10 October 1930, 14.00 (+00.00)
London, England (51N30. 0W10).
Source: From him, via David Fisher (ADB). RR: A.

(SO–**17**–VE)–17–(MO–**17**–NE)
PL–**17**–CH

The playwright Harold Pinter, winner of the Nobel Prize for Literature, was born in the East End of London and experienced the Blitz as a child. As an adult he first became an actor, specializing (as he said himself) in "sinister" parts. But then he wrote the first of his 29 plays, which, despite an initially hostile reception, made him in many people's eyes the greatest playwright of the second half of the twentieth century. Pinter's early plays have been described as "comedies of menace". They deal mainly with the lives of downtrodden people, and show a profound empathy with the predicaments in which their characters are placed, as well as a deep sensitivity to the rhythms of everyday speech. The final line of his play *The Caretaker* (as the character Stan is carried away to be dealt with by the authorities) is "Stan, don't let them tell you what to do!", and Pinter once said that this was the theme of his life. In his citation for the Nobel Prize it was said that "in his plays [he] uncovers the precipice under everyday prattle and forces entry into oppression's closed rooms".[5]

In his later plays Pinter turned more and more to political themes, and he became known as a holder of extreme left-wing views and a campaigner on behalf of various left-wing causes. He called Tony Blair a "blithering idiot" and compared George W. Bush's administration to Nazi Germany.

Pinter's chart contains a very large number of harmonic aspects, and he was plainly a very complex character. But Seventeen is one of his strongest numbers, as it is the number where his Sun comes together with his Moon and also with Venus and Neptune. So it would seem that his Seventeenness is linked to his militant campaigning, though in his case this is linked to the search for beauty (Venus) and idealistic visions of the future of humanity (Neptune).

(We can note also that the Irish playwright Samuel Beckett,[6] whom Pinter greatly admired and who, like Pinter, wrote dark comedies about downtrodden people, has (SO–_17_–SA)–17–JU and also MO–_17_–NE.)

Vanessa Redgrave
Born 30 January 1937, 18.00 (+00.00)
Blackheath, England (51N28. 0E01).
Source: From *Life among the Redgraves* by Rachel Kempson (Vanessa's mother), also from Vanessa's autobiography (ADB + FCC). RR: B.

(SO–_17_–CH)–17–UR
((MA–_17_–SA)–_17_–ME–_17_–PL

Vanessa Redgrave is another person who has combined a life in the theatre with extreme left-wing views. As an actress it has been said that she has "a luminous transparency that makes audiences feel they can see right through a character's skin".[7] As a political activist she has worked tirelessly for the Workers Revolutionary Party, and once stood for Parliament as their representative. The two sides of her life are both expressions of the same revolutionary fervour. Michael McWilliams has said of her:

> "Redgrave's antagonistic defence of belief in her life and work directly reflects that of her foes, both political and aesthetic. Her willingness to appear ugly or naked or unappealing onscreen is a conscious political statement. She's drawn to characters who are outsiders, emotionally and socially. The more ostracized or persecuted her characters are, the freer Redgrave becomes – she seems in touch with another world".[8]

As shown above, Redgrave has two strong clusters of Seventeenness in her chart, one uniting Sun, Uranus and Chiron, and the other bringing together Mercury, Mars, Saturn and Pluto.

Diane Keaton
Born 5 January 1946, 02.49 (+08.00)
Los Angeles, CA, USA (34N04. 118W15).
Source: Birth certificate, via the Wilsons (ADB). RR: AA.

((MA–_17_–UR)–_17_–MO)–17/17/17/17/17/_17_–(ME–_17_–CH)

Another actress with a strong Seventeenness pattern is Diane Keaton, who starred in several Woody Allen films, of which the best-known is *Annie Hall*, for which she won an Oscar. As is often the case with versatile actors (especially when, like Keaton, they are strong in Fiveness and are therefore good at creating new roles for themselves), it is hard to tell what kind of person she really was. However, it does seem that in *Annie Hall* she was, to a large extent, playing herself. Wikipedia says:

> "Allen based the character of Annie Hall loosely on Keaton ('Annie' is a nickname of hers, and 'Hall' is her original surname). Many of Keaton's mannerisms and her self-deprecating sense of humour were added into the role by Allen. (Director Nancy Meyers has claimed 'Diane's the most self-deprecating person alive'.) Keaton has also said that Allen wrote the character as an 'idealized version' of herself ... Her acting was later summed up by CNN as "awkward, self-deprecating, speaking in endearing little whirlwinds of semi-logic," and by Allen as "a nervous breakdown in slow motion".[9]

Keaton herself supplied most of the clothing for the character, which consisted mainly of vintage men's clothing (she had been dressing in a tomboyish style for years). AstroDatabank says: "Her rebellion has always been discreet, dressing in asexual layers, looking like Annie Hall long after the movie, quietly breaking the rules, hanging out like a recluse".

In Keaton's chart the Moon is conjoined by Seventeenness aspects with Mercury, Mars, Uranus and Chiron. She displays the rebelliousness (which seems to be associated with Seventeenness) in a more restrained and subtle form than the other Seventeenness people we have considered.

Oscar Wilde and Dorothy Parker

Oscar Wilde
Born 16 October 1854, 03.00 (+00.25)
Dublin, Ireland (53N20. 6W15).
Source: Baptismal certificate, via Fagan (ADB). RR: AA.

((SO–**17**–PL)–17–ME)–17/17/17–SA

Dorothy Parker

Born 22 August 1893, 21.50 (+05.00)
West End, NJ, USA (39N50. 75W09).
Source: From *The Late Mrs Dorothy Parker* by Leslie Previn ("shortly before 10.00 p.m.") (ADB). RR: B.

((MO–**17**–ME)–**17**/**17**–UR)–17–MA

Oscar Wilde (who, on arrival at the customs desk in New York, said "I have nothing to declare but my genius"[10]) has – as might be expected of such a complex and colourful character – strength in several harmonic numbers. But Seventeen is one of his strongest numbers, as his Sun, Mercury, Saturn and Pluto are linked by Seventeenness aspects.

Oscar Wilde is remembered above all for his sparkling wit: his plays, such as *The Importance of Being Earnest*, are filled with scintillating epigrams on every page. So it is interesting to note that another famous wit, Dorothy Parker,[11] has a Seventeenness cluster of Moon, Mercury, Mars and Uranus. (Note that Mercury is involved in both cases.) So could this ability to coin clever witticisms be related to Seventeenness?

Bertrand Russell

Born 18 May 1872, 17.45 (+00.00)
Trelleck, Wales (51N45. 2W43).
Source: From *The Life of Bertrand Russell* by Ronald W. Clark, via F.C. Clifford (ADB). RR: B.

((SO–**1**–MA)–**17**/**17**–SA)–**17**/**17**/**17**–CH

The philosopher Bertrand Russell (who, like Harold Pinter, won the Nobel Prize for Literature) wrote ponderous works such as *Principia Mathematica* (a treatise on mathematical logic), but he also wrote more popular works on various subjects, in which he often displays a caustic wit. For instance, in an essay entitled *In Praise of Idleness*, he wrote: "Work is of two kinds: first, altering the position at or near the earth's surface relatively to other such matter; second, telling other people to do so. The first kind is unpleasant and ill paid; the second is pleasant and highly paid".[12]

Russell campaigned actively on behalf of various causes, including atheism (he said "No one can sit at the bedside of a dying child and still believe in God"), free love (he advocated free love in *Marriage and Morals*, and both he and his wife had sexual relationships outside marriage), and pacifism (though he accepted the need to fight Hitler). In 1958, at the age of 86, he became founding president of the Campaign for Nuclear Disarmament, and at the age of 89 he was imprisoned for a week in connection with anti-nuclear protests.

Russell's chart is dominated by a very close conjunction of Sun and Mars, and Sun and Mars are joined to Saturn and Chiron by very close Seventeenness aspects. This seems to be a good recipe for the very active and determined form of campaigning which he practised.

Neville Heath and Randall Woodfield

Neville Heath
Born 6 June 1917, 09.30 (–01.00)
Ilford, England (51N32. 0E05).
Source: From him via Fagan ("between 9.00 and 10.00 a.m.") (ADB).
RR: A.[13]

(SO–**17**–MO–**17**–MA)–17–SA

Randall Woodfield
Born 26 December 1950, 00.58 (+08.00)
Salem, OR, USA (44N57. 123W02).
Source: Birth certificate, via Victoria Shaw (ADB). RR: A.

((ME–**17**–MA)–17/17–SA)–17/17/17–PL
                –17/17–CH
SA–17–UR–17–PL

Neville Heath and Randall Woodfield are two serial murderers with very strong clusters of Seventeenness. In Heath's case the cluster is notable because it brings together the Sun and the Moon, along with Mars and Saturn. In Woodfield's case the cluster is notable because of the absence of other strong harmonic links, so that Seventeen is the strongest number in his chart. (Note that the cluster involves Mars and Saturn in both cases.)

No number has a monopoly of murder, and we have already seen cases of murderers who were strong in other numbers. But the distinctive thing about Heath and Woodfield seems to be a kind of exhibitionism,

and also of anger. Both of them were handsome men: Woodfield
was 6 feet 1 inch tall and a "star athlete," and Heath is described by
AstroDatabank as "exceptionally handsome and charming" and as a
"debonair playboy". Woodfield is also described by AstroDatabank as
being driven by "deep hostility". Heath brutally killed two women in
hotels. Woodfield was compulsively addicted to indecent exposure and
also to stealing; eventually he moved on to murder, and brutally killed
nearly 50 women of all ages, forcing them to expose themselves and to
perform oral sex before he killed them.

Conclusion

So what can we deduce from these cases about the essential nature of
Seventeenness?

It seems to me that the spirit of *rebelliousness* is very strong in all of
the cases that we have considered. Seventeenness people feel themselves
to be apart from the rest of society, and feel a need to rebel against it. We
have noted this 'apartness' in both Elevenness and Thirteenness, but in
the case of Seventeenness the flavour is different. Whereas Elevenness
people cope with their apartness by resolutely sticking to their chosen
path, and Thirteenness people cope with it by defiant risk-taking in
search of their own true nature, Seventeenness people are more likely
to feel that their mission is to *change society* to fit in with their own view
about how it should be. They are often filled with anger about the way
that things are, and feel that this anger must find an outlet.

Thus, the spirit of *revolutionary fervour* is strong in many of these cases
of strong Seventeenness.[14] Seventeenness people are likely to feel that
they are right and that society is wrong, and that they must do what they
can to change society.[15] Thus, they may campaign on behalf of left-wing
causes, or causes such as atheism, free love, or pacifism. In extreme cases
they may, like L. Ron Hubbard, set up an organization whose purpose
is to radically change people's beliefs and lifestyles. Or, like Ceausescu,
they may be so carried away by the task of changing society that they
lose contact with reality.

However, many Seventeenness people may feel that, much as they
would like to change society, they cannot do so. Hence, they may resort
to making clever, sarcastic and humorous comments about it, destroying
society with words rather than actions. Many of these Seventeenness

people are very clever with their use of words. Or, like Diane Keaton, they may resort to a much milder and more subtle form of rebellion, "quietly breaking the rules," making clear their disapproval of society's norms without actively trying to change them.

Like every other number, Seventeen is in itself neither good nor bad, and can be used in either 'good' or 'bad' ways. Thus, on the one hand, the revolutionary fervour of many of these Seventeenness people can be seen as a force for good, shattering other people's complacency and forcing them to questions beliefs which they had taken for granted. But, on the other hand, Seventeenness can be used in 'evil' ways, as in the cases of Neville Heath and Randall Woodfield, whose anger against society led them to rape and murder.

Seventeenness can be seen as a reaction against Thirteenness, in that the Seventeenness person is rejecting the Thirteenness person's need to explore the world in order to find their true nature. Seventeenness people know who they are, and so do not need to go in search of themselves. It is not they themselves, but society, that needs to be changed.

In this chapter we have looked at some of the people who have the strongest clusters of Seventeenness. But there are many more people whose charts contain at least one close Seventeenness aspect between two planets. For these people, we can expect that the relationship between these two planets contains something of the rebellious spirit of Seventeenness, even though this may be hidden beneath the surface and may not manifest itself strongly in the person's external behaviour.

13

Nineteenness

The next prime number after Seventeen is Nineteen, and we will go straight into looking at charts that are exceptionally strong in Nineteenness.

Jean Sibelius

Born 8 December 1865, 00.30 (–01.38)
Tavastehus, Finland (61N00. 24E27).
Source: From biography by Santeri Levas, via Markko Manninen (ADB).
RR: B.

((SO–**19**–JU–**19**–SA)–**19**–MO)–19/19/19/19–VE

The composer Jean Sibelius has the strongest Nineteenness cluster that I have found, with Sun and Moon closely linked by Nineteenness aspects to Venus, Jupiter and Saturn, so we can expect that he can give us some important clues about the nature of the quality of Nineteenness.

Sibelius played the piano from the age of five, and intended (until he discovered his gifts as a composer) to pursue a career as a solo violinist. Wikipedia says that "as a child, he was often in a world of his own". When he started composing, he quickly established his reputation, and became a national hero for the people of Finland. However, he made it clear that, rather than revelling in this fame, he wished to live the life of a recluse. At the age of 38 he retired into the country, saying "In Helsinki the song died within me," and found peace in the solitude of the countryside, where he could obtain inspiration from nature. His biographer Santeri Levas says, "Very few men have such an intimate relationship with nature as he had, and all his life it was a source of inspiration and joy".[1] His later music (culminating in the beautiful tone poem *Tapiola*) is essentially about the rhythms of nature, and has nothing to do with human society; it has a quality of clarity and purity. He said:

"Music for me is like a beautiful mosaic which God has put together. He takes all the pieces in his hand, throws them into the world, and we have to recreate the picture from the pieces."[2]

Also he said:

"Whereas other modern composers are engaged in manufacturing cocktails of every hue and description, I offer the public pure cold water."[3]

Tapiola, composed when he was 60, was his last published composition, and he last appeared in public on the occasion of his 70th birthday. After this, although he lived on, in good health and of sound mind, to the age of 91, he became a total recluse. In music, in spite of his fame and originality, he established no schools and had no important followers. His biographer Santeri Levas describes him as "an independent figure, a lone wolf, who trod his own paths in the broad woodlands".[4]

Since Nineteenness is so very strong in Sibelius's chart, we will start with the hypothesis that this quality of independence and reclusiveness is related to the spirit of Nineteenness.

Jane Austen

Born 16 December 1775, 23.45 (+00.05)
Steventon, England (51N05. 1W20).
Source: From letter by father ("before midnight"), via Elisabeth Pagan (ADB). RR: A.

(SO–**19**–JU)–19–ME
(MO–**19**–MA)–19/19–CH
VE–**19**–PL

Jane Austen has three separate patterns of Nineteenness, which between them involve Sun, Moon, the three inner planets Mercury, Venus and Mars, and also Jupiter, Pluto and Chiron, so we can say that Nineteenness pervades the whole of her character.

It might seem that (apart from the fact that they were both creative geniuses) Jane Austen was almost the opposite of Sibelius. Sibelius withdrew from society, whereas Jane Austen was totally involved with society, and her genius is based on her profound understanding of how people interact with one another and of the way in which society works.

Nevertheless, it seems to me that there is a similarity. Both Sibelius and Austen were dispassionate observers, whose goal was to create works of art which would reflect the beauty and complexity of that which they were meticulously observing. Neither of them was remotely concerned with self-promotion, or with being agents of change; they wished only to record how it really is. Sibelius chose to focus on the world of nature, and to re-create it in music; Austen chose to focus on the world of human relationships and to re-create it in words; and yet their aims were similar. One feels that Sibelius's comment about music ("Music for me is like a beautiful mosaic…") could, if one substitutes 'society' for 'music', have been spoken by Austen.

Gerry Rafferty
Born 16 April 1947, 10.55 (–02.00)
Glasgow, Scotland (55N53. 4W15).
Source: Birth certificate, via Paul Wright. RR: AA.

(VE–**19**–JU–**19**–CH)–**19**/19/19–SA

Gerry Rafferty was a singer-songwriter who was uncomfortable with fame. His best-known song *Baker Street* was an expression of this discomfort, and yet it brought him the very fame and success which he did not seek. His manager, Michael Gray, said that Rafferty "disliked being recognized", and that his own job as manager was "mostly to say 'no' to people".[5] Rafferty at one point discharged himself from hospital and disappeared; he later issued a statement saying he was living in Tuscany, when in fact he was living in Dorset. In the end he succumbed to alcoholism, and died of liver disease aged 63.

We should note that Rafferty's Nineteenness pattern, unlike those of Sibelius and Austen, does not involve his Sun or Moon; rather, it consists of a Nineteenness connection between Venus and three of the outer planets. This suggests that Rafferty was 'in love with' Nineteenness, rather than naturally 'being' Nineteenness as were Sibelius and Austen. So if Nineteenness is to do with being a detached observer, then Rafferty was in love with this quality. He said: "There have been periods in my life when I have experienced depression … It has been through some of my darkest moments that I have written some of my best songs. For me, singing and writing is very therapeutic … My main ambition is to continue to write music, which helps me to evolve in a spiritual sense and hopefully to inspire others".[6]

Gavin Maxwell
Born 15 July 1914, 15.55 (+00.00)
Elrig, Scotland (54N49. 4W29).
Source: Birth certificate, via Paul Wright. RR: AA.

(SO–**19**–VE)–19–JU
MO–**19**–UR–**19**–CH

Gavin Maxwell was an adventurer and naturalist who wrote many books, of which the most famous is *Ring of Bright Water*, the story of a sick otter which he found in Iraq, nursed to health, and took home with him to Scotland. Maxwell was a complex, restless, gregarious, impetuous man, and cannot be described as a recluse, but nevertheless he spent most of his adult life in remote locations in Scotland, and displayed a love of nature similar to that of Sibelius. As a university student he was "easily distracted … content to roam the local countryside collecting insects and birds' eggs, wildfowling and looking after animal waifs and strays".[7] One sentence which I feel is particularly relevant to his Nineteenness is the following: "He was hypersensitive to beauty in many forms and had a rare gift of expressing in words what he saw and felt".[8]

Fred Kimball
Born 12 November 1904, 15.45 (+05.00)
Providence, RI, USA (41N49. 71W25).
Source: From him, via Lois Rodden (ADB). RR: A.

(SO–**19**–UR)–19–(JU–**19**–NE)
(MO–**1**–CH)–**19**/19–SA

Fred Kimball was a "pet psychic," which means "a clairvoyant whose speciality is telepathic communication with animals". According to one website, he was "the first pet psychic who attained a high level of renown," and "displayed an uncanny level of accuracy when communicating with cats, dogs and horses about their families, their homes, and their communities".[9] Daphne Negus[10] describes a session in which Kimball communicated with her cat and her dog, and answered her questions about the animals' attitudes and feelings.

Kimball's chart is dominated by a very close conjunction of Moon and Chiron close to the Midheaven (an excellent indication of psychic abilities used for healing). This conjunction is linked to Saturn by Nineteenness aspects, and there are also Nineteenness links between Sun, Jupiter, Uranus and Neptune.

Frank Skinner
Born 28 January 1957, 17.15 (+00.00)
West Bromwich, England (52N31. 1W56).
Source: From his autobiography, via Frank C. Clifford (FCC). RR: B.

(VE–**19**–SA)–19–<u>SO</u>
<u>MA</u>–**19**–JU–**19**–UR

The comedian Frank Skinner has two strong trios of Nineteenness aspects. It might seem that he is different from the other cases considered in this chapter, in that he has actively sought fame and appears to revel in it. To explain this, we have to consider some other features of his chart: firstly, that he has a very close SO–**17**–JU, so that his Nineteenness is tempered by the rebellious spirit of Seventeenness; and secondly, that his chart is dominated by a very close conjunction of Moon and Mercury, which has links to other planets in several harmonic numbers, and in particular has a close Fiveness link with Sun and Neptune, so that he feels compelled to find creative ways of communicating to others about his inner thoughts and feelings.

In spite of this, it seems to me that his particular style of comedy is suffused by the spirit of Nineteenness. According to one reviewer, "it would be hard to dislike Frank Skinner. He is easy-going, self-deprecating, and incapable of keeping a straight face".[11] This self-deprecation is a central part of Skinner's humour. It is as though he was saying to his audiences, "I'm no different from you, I'm just an ordinary bloke, I have just the same faults and sillinesses as you have". (His choice of the very ordinary-sounding name 'Frank Skinner' – his birth name was Christopher Collins – supports this.) At the same time, Skinner is (like Jane Austen) an extremely acute observer of the workings of society and of the foibles of individuals. He is able to involve members of the audience in his acts and to laugh at their eccentricities, and yet he does so in such a caring and empathic way that they do not feel threatened.

Norman Lamont
Born 8 May 1942, 17.55 (–02.00)
Lerwick, Shetland, Scotland (60N09. 1W09).
Source: Birth certificate, via Paul Wright. RR: AA.

(SO–19–MO)–19–ME
　　　　　　　–19/19–PL
((SA–1–UR)–19/19–MA)–19/19/19–VE

Norman Lamont was the Chancellor of the Exchequer in John Major's Conservative government in the UK, until he was forced to resign after the events of Black Wednesday (which we discussed in Chapter 11).

Lamont has an extremely strong pattern of Nineteenness, coupled with an unusual lack of other strong harmonic aspects. However, it is very difficult to find out what kind of person he really is, and I have the impression that, even more than most politicians, he has been successful in hiding his private life from the public eye. Occasional glimpses emerge: thus, one website says:

> "Until he was named chancellor of the exchequer last week, 48-year-old Norman Lamont was better known to readers of Britain's tabloid press as 'the man with the black eye'. That unwanted sobriquet came in 1985 when a jealous suitor punched the married Lamont as he left the apartment of heiress Olga Polizzi, daughter of millionaire hotelier Lord Forte. For days, Lamont wore dark glasses as he carried out his duties as a junior minister in Margaret Thatcher's government. And he denied deeper ramifications of the story – first declaring that he had 'walked into a wall', then explaining that the incident was 'innocent but complicated'".[12]

There is also the story of how Lamont hired a security firm to evict a lady who called herself "Miss Whiplash" from the basement flat of his property.

Lamont was also prone to political gaffes: for instance, he said, "Rising unemployment and the recession have been the price we have had to pay to bring inflation down. That is a price well worth paying" – a remark which caused great anger among the unemployed. After Black Wednesday he was asked why he looked so happy, and he said, "My wife heard me singing in the bath this morning".

My impression is that Lamont, even as he carried out his governmental duties, was somehow detached from them, keeping his real nature and his thoughts and feelings hidden. If so, this seems to be in the spirit of Nineteenness. But it is also a reminder that all of the higher harmonic numbers are concerned with a person's inner thoughts and feelings, and we cannot always rely on their showing on the surface. The first prime numbers (Two, Three and Five) are to do with the person's dealings with the outside world, but, as we proceed further down the sequence of prime numbers, we are diving deeper and deeper into the *interiority* of the person's life.

Conclusion

We have looked at fewer cases of Nineteenness than of the other numbers that we have considered, and this is because there seem to be fewer famous people who are strong in Nineteenness. I believe that this fact is significant. It may be that people who are strong in Nineteenness are less motivated to seek fame than people who are strong in other numbers. If they find fame, they may tend (like Sibelius and Gerry Rafferty) to run away from it, and to try to live in places where they will not have to suffer the embarrassment of being recognized and of having to perform in public. Or, like Norman Lamont, they may hide behind a mask, and try to ensure that nothing is really known about them; or, like Frank Skinner, they may feel the need to apologize for their fame, and to assure people that they are 'ordinary'.

Nineteenness, I believe, is about humble acceptance of, and empathy with, the world in which one finds oneself. It is a reaction against Seventeenness, in that the rebellious spirit of Seventeenness is no longer present. The Seventeenness person wants to change the world, but the Nineteenness person accepts the world as it is and tries to find his place in it. He or she is an acute observer of the world, and may develop an acute sensitivity to its rhythms and its beauty, and an ability to interpret this through creative expression. This observation may be focused on the workings of human society (Jane Austen) or on the workings of nature and the lives of animals (Sibelius, Maxwell, Kimball). In all this there is an absence of the desire for self-promotion. The individual seeks to surrender to the world that surrounds him and to become a channel for the expression of forces that are greater than himself.

As I have repeatedly said, no number is in itself good or bad, and every number can be expressed in both functional and dysfunctional ways. I believe that the 'dark' side of Nineteenness may well take the form of an opting-out: a refusal to accept one's responsibilities as a proactive person and as an agent of change in the world. The Nineteenness person may become a passive dreamer, who simply accepts everything as it is and is reluctant ever to lift a finger to help themselves or to help others. This passivity can be a problem, especially if the person is in a position of responsibility for others, for instance as a parent or as an employer. To counteract this, the Nineteenness person may need to be helped to develop their huge capacity for empathy, and to find ways of expressing this.

14

Twenty-threeness

The next prime number after Nineteen is Twenty-three. Once again, we will look at charts that are strong in this number, in order to discover the nature of the quality of Twenty-threeness.

Dylan Thomas
Born 27 October 1914, 23.00 (+00.00)
Swansea, Wales (51N38. 3W57).
Source: From him in a letter, via Sy Scholfield (ADB). RR: A.

(SO–23–UR)–23/23–MA
VE–23–JU–23–CH
((SA–1–PL)–23/23–ME)–23–MO

The poet Dylan Thomas has three separate clusters of Twenty-threeness, which together involve ten of his eleven planets. Thomas was in love with life, and also in love with words: in love with the sheer energy and vitality of being alive, and in love also with the energy and vitality of words. His love of living is expressed in the refrain of his most famous poem:

> Do not go gentle into that good night,
> Rage, rage, against the dying of the light

And his love of words is evident if one goes to his cottage on the seashore at Laugharne and listens to the tapes that are played there of the poet reading his own poems: the way in which he savours each word, rejoicing in its sheer sound, and rejoicing in the way in which the words pile up on one another and create a multi-coloured cascade of sound. The meaning of the words is less important than their music, and less important than the fleeting images that they conjure up as they sail past.

In Thomas's radio play *Under Milk Wood*, the narrator invites us to listen to the dreams and innermost thoughts of the inhabitants of a small Welsh village. The characters in the play are both comical and tragical, and are very starkly eccentric and individual; none of them is in any way 'ordinary'. Thomas portrays them with great vivacity: once again he is creating a tapestry full of vivid and contrasting colours. Thomas said that *Under Milk Wood* was "developed in response to the atomic bombing of Hiroshima, as a way of reasserting the evidence of beauty in the world".[1]

Dylan Thomas believed in living life to the full. As AstroDatabank says, "he and his wife were known for their drinking and brawling. Attractive, even lovable when sober, he became crude and unmanageable when drunk, using offensive language and making lewd advances towards strange women". In the end, his drinking killed him.

Marie Duplessis
Born 15 January 1824, 20.00 (–00.01)
Nonant le Pin, France (48N42. 0E13).
Source: Birth certificate, via Petitallot (ADB). RR: AA.

SO–23–MO
((ME–**23**–SA)–23–PL)–23/23/23–JU
((MA–**23**–CH)–23/**23**–UR)–23–PL

Marie Duplessis was born in Normandy in abject poverty. Her mother had abandoned her, her father was vicious and debauched, and her grandmother had been a prostitute. At the age of 14 Marie arrived in Paris, dirty, starving and in rags, and started to work as a dressmaker. Her beauty caught the eye of a rich young nobleman, and after this she was kept in luxury by a number of rich lovers. Her bills were paid by an 80-year-old retired Russian diplomat. AstroDatabank says, "She had a natural refinement, distinction and good taste, both in appearance and behaviour. When she arrived in Paris she could only sign her name, but she soon learned to write correctly, to ride, to dance and play the piano, to behave like a great lady". At 22 she married a Viscount, though they never lived together. At 23 she died of consumption. Her life inspired Dumas's novel *La Dame aux Camélias*, which in turn inspired Verdi's opera *La Traviata*.

Duplessis has three clusters of Twenty-threeness, involving eight of her planets, and she is one of the very few people for whom Twenty-three is stronger than any other prime number. We can see how she, like Dylan Thomas, believed in living life to the full, recklessly making the most of every opportunity. She achieved more in her very short lifetime than most of us do in a far greater span of years.

O. Henry

Born 11 September 1862, 21.00 (+05.19)
Greensboro, NC, USA (36N04. 79W48).
Source: From family bible, via American Federation of Astrologers (ADB). RR: AA.

MO–**23**–MA–**23**–SA–**23**–NE
(MO–**23**–SA–**23**–NE)–23–UR

O. Henry was the pen name of William Sydney Porter, who achieved fame as a writer of short stories. Porter, whose mother had died when he was three, led a very opportunistic life, working in various jobs, performing in singing and drama groups, and playing the guitar and mandolin. But all the time he was writing stories. While he was working in a bank, he was accused of embezzlement, a charge which he denied. To escape the courts he fled to Honduras, but had to return when his wife became ill with tuberculosis. He came back to face the death of his wife, and was found guilty of embezzlement and sentenced to five years in jail. In prison he continued writing, and it was at this time that his stories were first published and he became famous. But after his release his health deteriorated, and he died at the age of 47 from cirrhosis of the liver, brought on by excessive drinking.

O. Henry's stories are known for their witty narration, their optimism, and their surprise endings. Many of them involve a kind of reversal of the expected situation: for instance, there is the story of two men who kidnap a boy of ten, hoping for a ransom, but the boy turns out to be so obnoxious that the men pay the boy's father $250 to take him back. O. Henry clearly loved human eccentricity in all its forms, and his stories (just like Dylan Thomas's *Under Milk Wood*) are a hymn to human variety and individuality as it flourishes even in the most humdrum environments.

O. Henry's Twenty-threeness is centred on his Moon, so we can expect it to refer to the way in which he instinctively *responds* to the world about him. Clearly his responses were very warm and open. He loved New York City, which he called "Baghdad-on-the-Subway", and he believed that every one of its four million inhabitants was worthy of his attention.

Salvador Dali
Born 11 May 1904, 08.45 (+00.00)
Figueras, Spain (42N16. 2E58).
Source: Birth certificate, via Juan Trigo (ADB). RR: AA.

SO–**23**–VE–**23**–UR
MO–23–CH
JU–**23**–PL

The painter Salvador Dali has strength in several harmonics, including Five, Seven, and (surprisingly) Nineteen, but his Twenty-threeness connections are very strong, including a very close link between Sun, Venus and Uranus, and a close link between Moon on the Midheaven and Chiron close to the Descendant.

In Dali's case the pursuit of eccentricity and startling individuality was carried to extremes. AstroDatabank says that, when he was a child, "although his teachers found him impossible to deal with, his parents encouraged his attention-getting behaviour and approved his narcissism. By the time he was in junior school he was as bizarre in his dress and manner as he was in his behaviour". As an adult he was racked by shyness, but overcame it by hiding behind an outlandish mask, loving to shock and offend people. His flamboyant waxed moustache became his trademark. AstroDatabank says that he "reportedly once told a woman that he enjoyed eating dates for dessert because his then-sticky fingers could wax his moustache, enabling it to stand erect. When she inquired whether the practice attracted flies, he replied, 'My most paradisiac moment is when I am lying naked in the sun covered with flies like a piece of carrion'."

As a painter he was extremely gifted. His paintings are full of vivid colours, and he was able to paint so realistically as to achieve a *trompe l'oeil* effect. However the paintings contain surreal images which are often disturbing. Perhaps the most famous of these are the melting watches in the painting *The Persistence of Memory*, which are said to be "a rejection of the assumption that time is rigid or deterministic".[2]

It would of course be wrong to attribute all of Dali's eccentricities to his Twenty-threeness. (Probably the starting-point for a full interpretation would be SO–**4**–SA, but see also the full list of his harmonic aspects in Appendix III.) However, I do believe that the Twenty-threeness is an important factor. SO–**23**–VE–**23**–UR tells us that his attitude to his own lovability (Sun-Venus) and to his own individuality and originality (Sun-Uranus) was suffused by the quality of Twenty-threeness. If this quality (as suggested by the cases of Thomas, Duplessis and others) is about living life to the full and rejoicing in variety and contrast, then we can see how this will have influenced Dali's behaviour and also his painting style. Dali himself spoke of his "love of everything that is gilded and excessive, my passion for luxury and my love of oriental clothes".[2] This seems to be in keeping with the spirit of Twenty-threeness.

Edward Gorey

Born 22 February 1925, 19.25 (+06.00)
Chicago, IL, USA (41N51. 87W39).
Source: From birth certificate, via the Wilsons (ADB). RR: AA.

(SO–**1**–MO)–**23**/**23**/23/23–(SA–**23**–CH)

Edward St John Gorey was a writer and illustrator of whimsically macabre books. He produced more than 100 small volumes, one of which was an Alphabet containing twenty-six drawings of children undergoing a gruesome fate, each one accompanied by a caption such as:

> E is for ERNEST who choked on a peach
> F is for FANNY, sucked dry by a leech
> M is for MAUD who was swept out to sea
> N is for NEVILLE who died of ennui

His books are popular with children, but it is said that Gorey did not like children much and had little association with them. He also saw himself as asexual, neither straight nor gay. As a painter, Gorey had a style remarkably similar to Dali's, with vivid colours, realistic representations, and surrealist themes.

Gorey's chart is dominated by a close conjunction of Sun and Moon. This conjunction has Twenty-three links with Saturn (very closely) and with Chiron (less closely). We can see that Gorey had something of the same extravagant eccentricity that is present in our other Twenty-three cases, but, because it is Saturn that is linked to Sun and Moon, the mood is darker and the originality is expressed in a more disciplined and limited form. We could say that, just as Dylan Thomas and O. Henry humorously celebrated the richness and variety of human life, so Edward Gorey humorously celebrated the richness and variety of human death.

Hans Christian Andersen
Born 2 April 1805, 01.00 (–00.42)
Odense, Denmark (55N24. 10E23).
Source: From parish records, via De Marre (ADB). RR: AA.

(JU–**23**–UR–**23**–PL)–23–SO
(VE–**23**–MA)–23–ME

Another children's writer with strong Twenty-threeness is Hans Christian Andersen, the author of fairytales including *The Ugly Duckling* and *The Emperor's New Clothes*. Andersen, like Gorey, had no children of his own and is said to have been not very fond of children. Like Gorey, he never married and remained a virgin all his life, though unlike Gorey he had strong sexual feelings.

Andersen regarded himself as ugly and unattractive. He was desperately keen to obtain recognition and approval, and AstroDatabank says that "his fame was compensation for his poor looks, poverty, and deep sense of inferiority".

Many of Andersen's characteristics can be explained by other features of his chart (such as ((SO–**1**–ME)–**2/2**–SA)–8/**8**/**8**–NE). My feeling is that the Twenty-threeness is relevant mainly to the content of his fairytales. I feel that Andersen's stories, with their simple messages (the Ugly Duckling is really a swan; the Emperor really has no clothes), have something in common with Gorey's pictures of Ernest choking on a peach, and with Dali's melting watches, and with O. Henry's story of the men paying a ransom instead of receiving it, and with Dylan Thomas's creations in *Under Milk Wood* (such as Mrs Ogmore-Pritchard, who keeps a guesthouse but won't let anyone stay in it in case they make it dirty), and even with the real-life rags-to-riches story of Marie Duplessis. All of these stories have qualities of simplicity and also of subversiveness. There is no attempt at deep characterization, and yet there is a message: surprising things can happen; things may be the opposite of what they seem; people are odd and quirky and fascinating. This kind of message occurs so often in people with strong Twenty-threeness in their charts that one feels it must be related to the essence of Twenty-threeness.

Karl Marx

Born 5 May 1818, 02.00 (–00.27)
Trier, Germany (49N45. 6E38).
Source: From "official records", via Lyndoe (ADB). RR: AA.

(MA–**23**–JU)–**23**–ME)–**23**/**23**/23–SA)–**23**/**23**/23/**23**–CH

Karl Marx was a complex character, but here we are concerned only with his Twenty-threeness. If we look at the quintet of planets that are linked by Twenty-threeness aspects in Marx's chart, we see that they are centred, not on Sun and Moon, but on Mercury and Mars. This suggests that this Twenty-Threeness cluster is concerned less with Marx's personality, and more with his thoughts, his writings, and his calls to action.

The *Communist Manifesto* (written jointly by Marx and by Friedrich Engels,[3] who himself has SO–**23**–ME) ends with the famous rallying cry which (loosely translated) reads:

> "Workers of the world, unite! You have nothing to lose but your chains, and a world to win."

Elsewhere in Marx's writings is the equally famous statement: "From each according to his abilities, to each according to his needs". This is the goal of communism: a society in which each person would do the work for which he was best suited, and in which goods would be distributed to those who most needed them. This is based on the belief that in a communist society there would be no shortages; there would be enough to meet everyone's needs, as there would no longer be a rapacious ruling class creaming off more than their fair share. Eventually, Marx believed, the state would wither away; people would selflessly pursue the interests of society as a whole.

This is a long way from the reality of totalitarian communism as it has now been practised in many countries, and we can see now that it is a fantasy, albeit an uplifting and inspiring one. In fact, it has the flavour of an Andersen fairytale. The Emperor will be seen to have no clothes; the Ugly Duckling will become a swan; the downtrodden workers will cast off their chains and become masters of the universe. Thus, we can see that Marx's theories are in keeping with the spirit of Twenty-threeness.

Timothy McVeigh
Born 23 April 1968, 08.19 (+05.00)
Lockport, NY, USA (43N10. 78W41).
Source: From his baby book, via Michael Johnson (ADB). RR: AA.

((VE–**1**–SA)–23–SO)–**23**/23/23–MA

Several murderers have strong Twenty-threeness links in their charts. One of these is Timothy McVeigh, who planted the bomb which exploded at 9.02 a.m. CDT on 19 April 1995 in the Alfred P. Murrah Building in Oklahoma City, killing 186 people (including 19 small children and babies in a day care centre in the building) and injuring 450.

McVeigh expressed no remorse for his actions, referring to the deaths as "collateral damage," although he did say that if he had known that the day care centre was open he might have chosen a different target. It turned out that he was consumed by anger against the federal government, saying, "The government is continually growing more and more powerful and the people need to prepare to defend themselves against government control".[4] He had served in the Army in Iraq in the first Gulf War, and believed that US policy towards Iraq was totally hypocritical. Also he had been particularly angered by the government's actions during the Waco Siege, and said that his bomb was "revenge for what the government did at Waco". He was put to death by lethal injection on 11 June 2001.

McVeigh's chart is dominated by a very close conjunction of Venus and Saturn, and these planets are joined by close Twenty-threeness aspects to Sun and Mars. (Fans of midpoints may like to note that Sun is at the midpoint of Mars and Venus/Saturn; the distance from Sun to Mars and also from Sun to Venus/Saturn is one twenty-third of the circle.)

It may seem surprising that McVeigh should be so strong in Twenty-threeness, since his anger against society appears to be more typical of Seventeenness (which is absent from his chart apart from PL-_17_-CH). However, I feel that McVeigh's anger has a different flavour from that of the people whom we discussed in the chapter on Seventeenness. It is more visceral, less rational, more focussed on violent action than on long-term campaigning. Twenty-threeness people, as we have seen, like to live life to the full, and often are impelled towards dramatic actions whose purpose is to shock or disturb other people and assert their own uniqueness and individuality. Or, if they do not actually take such actions, they fantasize about them.

The origins of McVeigh's anger, I believe, lie mainly in his strong pattern of Twoness (see Appendix III), but the Twenty-threeness pattern will have helped him to find this dramatic and shocking way of expressing the anger. Wikipedia says that "McVeigh claimed to have been a target of bullying at school and that he took refuge in a fantasy world where he retaliated against those bullies. At the end of his life he would state his belief that the United States government is the ultimate bully". By detonating his bomb, McVeigh turned his fantasy into grim reality.

Charles Sobhraj
Born 6 April 1944, 22.00 (−07.00)
Saigon, Vietnam (10N45. 106E40).
Source: From *Life and Crimes of Charles Sobhraj* by Richard Neville and Julie Clarke (ADB). RR: B.

((MO–**23**–PL)–23–SO)–23/23/23–MA
((ME–**23**–SA)–23–UR)–23–CH

Another murderer with a very strong Twenty-threeness pattern is Charles Sobhraj, whose has two Twenty-threeness clusters involving eight of his planets including Sun and Moon.

Sobhraj, otherwise known as the 'Serpent', is Asia's best-known serial killer, and is thought to be responsible for at least 20 killings (mostly by poisoning) in India, Thailand, Afghanistan, Turkey, Nepal, Iran and Hong Kong. However, it has been said that "while Sobhraj is widely believed to be a psychopath, his motives for killing differed from those of most serial killers. Sobhraj was not driven to murder by deep-seated violent impulses, but as a means to sustain his lifestyle of adventure".[5] His victims were mostly rich tourists, whom he would rob of their money, passports and possessions; sometimes they were people who had threatened to expose him.

The story of his life, as recounted by both AstroDatabank and Wikipedia, is incredibly colourful and complex, and would take far too long to recount here. I will just say that Sobhraj has demonstrated extraordinary cunning and ingenuity, and seems also to have had a remarkable ability to charm people and win their loyalty. One of his tricks was to poison people so as to cause them to be ill, and then nurse them back to health, thus gaining their allegiance. When he was in prison in India, he threw a birthday party for himself and invited all the guards and prisoners, whom he plied with grapes. Surreptitiously, he injected sleeping pills into the grapes, knocking out all the guests except himself and four other inmates, who then walked out into the streets of New Delhi. However, his motive in doing this was not to escape but to prolong his stay in prison, since if he had been released he would have been deported to Thailand, where he faced a death sentence. He was duly caught and sentenced to another ten years in prison. When he was finally released, the warrant for his deportation to Thailand had expired, and he was able to escape to France.

In France he lived the life of a millionaire celebrity, charging huge sums for interviews. He is said to have charged over $15 million for the rights to a film based on his life. However, in 2003 he visited Nepal, where he was arrested and sentenced to life imprisonment.

Sobhraj is clearly an outstanding example of Twenty-threeness expressed in negative and antisocial ways. He lived life to the full, and his life can be seen as one long fairytale with himself in the role of evil and cunning monster. He could be said to have been 'living the dream'.

John Perkins
Born 28 January 1945, 18.55 (+04.00)
Hanover, NH, USA (43N42. 72W17).
Source: From him, via John Cook and Shelley Ackerman (ADB). RR: A.

((SO–**23**–MO)–23–VE–23–CH

Having looked at Charles Sobhraj as an example of the 'dark' side of Twenty-threeness, I will end this chapter with a case which shows how Twenty-threeness can be used in positive and beneficial ways.

In 1971 John Perkins was employed by a shadowy firm of consultants to work as an "economic hit man" (EHM for short). His role was to persuade the governments of poorer countries to accept enormous development loans, and to use the money to set up infrastructure projects which would be contracted out to US companies. In this way, these countries would become saddled with huge debts and would become economically totally dependent on the United States. Perkins remained in this role for nine years, but then left, overwhelmed with guilt about how his work was destroying the cultures of the indigenous peoples in the countries which he visited. He then created a company which was committed to producing environmentally friendly electricity. Later he founded an organization called Dream Change, whose aim is to help indigenous people to preserve their culture and environment. In 2004 (despite numerous efforts by 'people in high places' to persuade him to remain silent) he published his best-selling book *Confessions of an Economic Hit Man*,[6] which has perhaps done more than any other book to reveal the hidden truth about "the greed and power that is corrupting our world"[7] and about the ways in which the United States builds and maintains what Perkins calls its "global empire".

Perkins's organization Dream Change is described as a "worldwide grass roots movement of people from diverse cultures and backgrounds, dedicated to shifting consciousness and promoting sustainable lifestyles".[8] The name Dream Change is based on Perkins's belief that "the world is as you dream it" (which is the title of one of his books). By changing people's dreams (their visions about how they want the world to be), you can change their reality. I believe that this is a very 'Twenty-threeness' statement, since Twenty-threeness is about dreaming and about the effort to live the dream. With his Sun and Moon linked by Twenty-threeness aspects to Venus (his search for love and beauty) and to Chiron (his sense of his role in the world), Perkins is a born 'dreamer', and he is doing the world a huge service by helping people to be conscious of their dreams and to translate them into reality.

Conclusion

The Twenty-threeness person is a dreamer, a spinner of tales and fantasies. He or she dreams of living life to the full, playing a part in the fairytale, becoming the embodiment of the dream. Twenty-threeness is a reaction against Nineteenness, in that, whereas the Nineteenness person seeks to accept the world as it is, surrender to it, and become a passive observer of it, the Twenty-threeness person seeks to play an active part in the world and to shape the world in accordance with the dream. The dream tends to be painted in bright primary colours; there is a love of brilliance and excess, of recklessness and of magical transformations.

The people whom we have described in this chapter are mostly people who succeeded, at least to some extent, in translating the dream into reality, and in so doing they found a degree of happiness and fulfilment. Perhaps the unhappiest of these people was Hans Christian Andersen, who, although he was a spinner of fairytales, did not succeed in living the dream in his own life; in his own view he remained an Ugly Duckling rather than a swan. Probably, for every happy and fulfilled Twenty-threeness person, there are hundreds of others who remain dissatisfied dreamers, unhappy with the frustrations and the humdrumness of ordinary life, and dreaming of a different life which they are unable to translate into reality. They may try to express the dream in writing, painting or music, and Twenty-three is probably the most creative number that we have found apart from Five and Seven.

The dream itself can take many forms, and we have seen from the case of Charles Sobhraj that it can sometimes be a very dark dream indeed. Thus, one of the dangers of Twenty-threeness is that the person may try to impose his personal dream onto others, for whom it may be inappropriate and damaging. We will return to this point in Chapter 18, where we will consider the case of Tony Blair, who has a strong pattern of Twenty-threeness.

15

Twenty-nineness

After Twenty-three there is a gap (because the next two odd numbers, 25 and 27, are not primes), and then we come to the last two prime numbers that we will discuss in this book, which are Twenty-nine and Thirty-one.

First, we will look at the charts of people who are strong in Twenty-nineness, starting with four remarkable women.

Margaret Mead
Born 16 December 1901, 09.00 (+05.00)
Philadelphia, PA, USA (39N57. 75W10).
Source: From her, via Helen Weaver (ADB). RR: A.

((MO–**29**–NE)–29–(PL–**29**–CH))–29/29/29/29–SO
VE–**29**–SA

Margaret Mead was the most famous anthropologist of the twentieth century. She went to university in defiance of her father's wishes (even though he was himself a university teacher). As a student her dress and outlook were unconventional, and the other students shunned her. However, she switched from psychology to anthropology, and developed a lesbian relationship with her teacher, Ruth Benedict, which lasted for most of her life. At the age of 23 she boarded a boat to Samoa to study the culture of Samoan adolescents. The resulting book, *Coming of Age in Samoa*, was a bestseller and made her name. Later she researched many other societies, developing her thesis that personality was shaped more by culture than by heredity. She was an advocate of liberal social reform, and her views on child-rearing were revolutionary for their time.

She married three times, divorcing all of her husbands, but claiming that she had benefited from all of her marriages. She also had a number of other close relationships, with both male and female partners.

Margaret Mead's chart is dominated by a very close conjunction of Mars, Jupiter and Saturn on the Ascendant, which forms links with several other planets. She is also strong in Thirty-oneness as well as Twenty-nineness. But Twenty-nine is her strongest number, as it connects the Sun with the Moon and also with Neptune, Pluto and Chiron, and also links Venus to Saturn.

Gertrude Stein
Born 3 February 1874, 08.00 (+05.20)
Allegheny, PA, USA (40N28. 80W01).
Source: From her (from her father), quoted in *Charmed Circle* by James R. Mellow (ADB). RR: B.

((SO–**1**–ME)–**29**–CH)–29–UR
MA–29–SA

Gertrude Stein was an American writer who spent most of her adult life in Paris, where she was at the centre of a circle of famous writers and artists. She was painted by Picasso, and had her own private art gallery. She had a mannish appearance and was openly lesbian, developing a life-long 'marriage' with Alice B. Toklas. Her best-known book is *The Autobiography of Alice B. Toklas*, which is her attempt to get inside Alice's mind and to write from Alice's perspective.

She had studied at two universities, but flunked out of both in the turmoil of a lesbian affair. (She wrote at the top of one of her examination papers, "Dear Professor James, I am sorry but really I do not feel a bit like an examination in philosophy today".) Her most famous quotation is "A rose is a rose is a rose" (she also wrote "To write is to write is to write is to write"), and I believe that this is related to the quality of Twenty-nineness: everything is, quite simply, just what it is. Her chart is dominated by an almost exact conjunction of Sun and Mercury, and this is conjoined by Twenty-nineness aspects to Chiron and Uranus, with Mars also –29– Saturn.

Edith Sitwell

Born 7 September 1887, 13.30 (+00.00)
Scarborough, England (54N17. 0W24).
Source: From her through a mutual friend, via Martin Harvey (ADB).
RR: A.

((MO–**29**–_PL_)–**29**–MA)–29/29/29–SO

The poet Edith Sitwell was, like Gertrude Stein, a champion of
modernism, and befriended and helped many writers and musicians.
Her poem *Façade* was set to music by William Walton, and there is a
recording of her reciting the poem accompanied by the music; it has an
aggressive, spiky, rebellious quality. Nothing seems to be known about
her sexuality, but she never married, was six feet tall, and had a mannish
appearance. Her manner of dress was extravagant and flamboyant. She
said: "I am not eccentric. It's just that I am more alive than most people.
I am an unpopular electric eel set in a pond of goldfish".[1]

Twenty-nine is the number that brings her Sun and Moon together,
and they are linked also by Twenty-nine aspects to Mars and Pluto.

Elizabeth Taylor

Born 27 February 1932, 02.15 (+00.00)
London, England (51N30. 0W10).
Source: Taylor's mother, in an article in *Good Housekeeping* magazine,
says "about 2.00 a.m.", but the biography by Alexander Walker says
02.30. AstroDatabank has chosen a time midway between these two
times. RR: A.

((SO–**1**–ME)–**29**/29–MO)–29/29/29–SA
(JU–29–PL)–29–CH

The film star Elizabeth Taylor (who, like Edith Sitwell, has been
made a Dame of the British Empire) is known for her eight marriages
(including two to Richard Burton), her beauty, and the sultriness of
her performances, and also for her dedication to the fight against HIV/
AIDS. It has been said that, unlike other movie stars, she "really was
a sex goddess – she adored sex, she loved inspiring lust and satisfying
it".[2] Films such as *Who's Afraid of Virginia Woolf?* (for which she won an

Oscar) have shown that she had great acting talent and the ability to display powerful and destructive emotions.

Taylor's chart has two very close conjunctions (Sun-Mercury and Venus-Uranus), and these two conjunctions are brought together by Nineness (3 x 3) aspects, showing that the Threeness principle of the pursuit of pleasure is very strong for Taylor. But Twenty-nine is the number that brings Sun-Mercury together with Moon and also with Saturn.

I feel that these four women (Mead, Stein, Sitwell, Taylor) share a quality which I would call "being proud to be different". In their different ways, all of them have been willing to show themselves to the world, warts and all, and to publicly display their departures from society's norms. This applies especially to their sexuality. Mead was bisexual, Stein was lesbian, Sitwell was either lesbian or asexual, and Taylor, though rampantly heterosexual, has shown herself sympathetic to deviant sexuality through her close friendship with Rock Hudson and Michael Jackson and her fight against AIDS. Maybe this quality is related to the core quality of Twenty-nineness.

Lord Byron

Born 22 January 1788, 14.00 (+00.01)
London, England (51N30. 0W10).
Source: From family records in British Museum, via *Notable Nativities* (ADB). RR: AA.

(MA–**29**–JU)–29–VE–29–NE
MO–29–ME
SA–29–PL

The poet Byron was certainly proud to be different, especially in matters of sex. Primarily homosexual, he fled to Venice in order to be able to satisfy his sexual appetite more freely, and even his friend Shelley (whose attitude was very liberal) was shocked by Byron's insatiable indulgence in orgies and sordid sexual encounters. But he also had sexual relationships with various servant girls as well as with members of his own class, and also (allegedly) with his own half-sister. For a short time he was married, but he found the restraints of marriage intolerable.

Byron's main cluster of Twenty-nineness is centred on Venus (which is close to the Midheaven) and Mars (which is close to the Ascendant), and is therefore especially concerned with his sexuality. We would have to look to other numbers to explain other features of his personality, including his gifts as a poet.

Michael Hutchence
Born 22 January 1960, 05.00 (–10.00)
Sydney, Australia (33S52. 151E15).
Source: From interview in *Juice* magazine (ADB). RR: B.

(((VE–**1**–JU)–29/**29**–CH)–**29**/29/**29**–SO)–29/**29**/29/29–MA

Michael Hutchence was a charismatic Australian pop star. On a visit to London he was interviewed on television by Bob Geldof's wife Paula Yates, and the sexual attraction between them was obvious to the viewer. Soon after this Yates left Geldof and joined up with Hutchence, saying that, when he took her to bed, "he did six things within the first hour that I was sure were illegal". Hutchence and Yates were planning to marry, and they had a daughter, Tiger Lily; but then Hutchence was found dead in a hotel room. It was pronounced to be suicide, but Yates insisted that Hutchence had died of accidental asphyxiation during an auto-erotic experiment. (Three years later Yates killed herself; Tiger Lily, who had lost both of her parents, was brought up by her mother's ex-husband Bob Geldof.)

Hutchence, like Byron, has a Twenty-nineness cluster that involves Venus, Mars and Jupiter, but in Hutchence's case it also involves Sun and Chiron. His case would seem to confirm the connection between Twenty-nineness and unusual forms of sexual expression.

Allen Ginsberg
Born 3 June 1926, 02.00 (+04.00)
Newark, NJ, USA (40N44. 74W10).
Source: From his assistant, via McKay-Clements; also from biography by Barry Miles (ADB). RR: A.

(VE–**29**–NE)–29–MO
(MA–**29**–JU)–29/**29**–PL

The theme of exuberant sexuality comes up again in the case of the poet Allen Ginsberg, since Ginsberg was openly bisexual, fought tirelessly against sexual repression, and claimed to have had a mystical vision while masturbating. However, there was far more to Ginsberg than this. He vigorously opposed materialism, militarism, and anything which stood in the way of the freedom of the individual. His best-known poem *Howl* starts with the words: "I saw the best minds of my generation destroyed by madness". Asked to define his political and social views, he said simply: "Absolute defiance".

Ginsberg's revolutionary fervour has something of the flavour of both Seventeenness and Twenty-threeness, and indeed he has strength in both of these numbers: he has (VE–**1**–CH)–**17**/17–JU, and he has SO–23–PL, ME–**23**–MA, and VE–**23**–UR. But his strongest number (apart from Three) is Twenty-nine, where he has the two clusters listed above, involving Moon, Venus, Mars, Jupiter, Neptune and Pluto.

Perhaps the key to the meaning of Ginsberg's Twenty-nineness lies in Michael Schumacher's statement: "The foundation of Ginsberg's work was the notion that one individual's thoughts and experiences resonated among the masses".[3] Ginsberg said "It occurs to me that I am America". His writings are essentially about himself, but he believed that by writing about his own "different-ness" he could awaken and illuminate the different-ness of others. This was how he reconciled the individualism of Twenty-nineness with the revolutionary fervour of Seventeenness and with the dream of a better society which is characteristic of Twenty-threeness.

Luc Jouret
Born 18 October 1947, 10.04 (–01.00)
Kikwit, Belgian Congo (5S02. 18E49).
Source: From him, via Petitallot (ADB). RR: A.

(SO–**29**–MA)–**29**–MO
(ME–**29**–VE)–**29**–NE
                    –29–MO

Every number has its dark side, and something of the dark side of Twenty-nineness is shown by the case of Luc Jouret, who was the co-founder of the Order of the Solar Temple, 53 of whose members (including Jouret himself) were found dead in Switzerland and Canada on the night of 5th October 1994, the victims of either murder or suicide. Members of the Order (following Jouret's teachings) believed that the Earth was about to be destroyed by fire, and that followers would be reborn on another planet revolving around the star Sirius.

The Order had two leaders, Jouret and Joseph Di Mambro,[4] who was known as the 'dictator' and was in charge of finances. However, Jouret was the charismatic leader who inspired people by his talks and was responsible for recruiting people to the Order. He allegedly believed that he was the third reincarnation of Jesus Christ. Before the group's rituals he would have sex with one of the women present, in order to give himself "spiritual strength".[5]

The simultaneous deaths of so many of the Order's members were widely assumed to be the result of a suicide pact, but in fact there were many indications that some of the victims had shown signs of struggle, and that others had been given sleeping pills before being shot to death. But, if they were murdered, it is not clear who was responsible.

Jouret has close Twenty-nineness aspects linking Sun, Moon and Mars, as well as another cluster involving Mercury, Venus and Neptune (which may be connected with his inspirational powers as a speaker). Clearly he was a person who, like others whom we have considered in this chapter, felt himself to be different from 'ordinary' mortals and free from the restraints by which other people are bound.

However, I feel I need to express a caution. Other cult leaders who were in many ways similar to Jouret (such as Jim Jones,[6] the leader of the People's Temple, who led his followers to mass suicide, and David Koresh,[7] the leader of the Dravidian Sect, who with his followers was gunned down by the FBI in Waco, Texas), do not have strong patterns of Twenty-nineness, and we would have to look elsewhere in their charts to find explanations for their behaviour. So we cannot make a simple connection between cult leadership and Twenty-nineness: we can say only that, in Jouret's case, his Twenty-nineness may have helped to push him in this direction, by helping him to feel 'special', separate and apart from other people.

Steven Spielberg
Born 18 December 1946, 18.16 (+05.00)
Cincinnati, OH, USA (39N10. 84W27).
Source: Birth certificate, via Joan Negus (ADB). RR: AA.

SO–**29**–MO–**29**–VE
JU–**29**–NE–**29**–CH

The film director Steven Spielberg has one of the strongest Twenty-nineness charts, with very close Twenty-nineness aspects linking Sun, Moon and Venus and also Jupiter, Neptune and Chiron, so that one would expect the qualities of Twenty-nineness to be especially evident in his life.

In fact, however, Spielberg has displayed none of the flamboyant eccentricity that characterizes such people as Lord Byron, Edith Sitwell or Allen Ginsberg. He lives quietly with his wife and his seven children, and gives money unostentatiously to charity. In public he is unfailingly affable and courteous. As a child he suffered from racial prejudice caused by his Jewishness, but it would seem that, since the overwhelming success of *Jaws* in 1975, he has had no worries – except for worries about his health, which he has been anxious not to publicize. We can note that, in addition to his strong Twenty-nineness, he also has strength in Nineteenness – (SO–**19**–NE)–**19**/19–ME – so perhaps the reclusive tendencies of Nineteenness have taken precedence for him over the exhibitionist tendencies of Twenty-nineness.

However, we can perhaps find some clues to Spielberg's Twenty-nineness in the content of his films. Wikipedia notes three themes that recur throughout Spielberg's work: firstly, "ordinary characters searching for or coming into contact with extraordinary beings or finding themselves in extraordinary circumstances"; secondly, "a childlike, even naïve, sense of wonder and faith"; and thirdly, "tension in parent-child relationships, [with] parents (often fathers) reluctant, absent or ignorant". The first of these themes especially seems to be relevant to the 'pride in being different' which we have identified as inherent in Twenty-nineness. An "extraordinary being" such as ET (in the film of that name) is clearly very very different, and the film is about how ordinary people learn to respect his differentness and to love him just as he is. Again, the theme of "ignorant parents" is about parents' failure to understand and respect the differentness of the child.

Despite this, Spielberg's case is a reminder that the higher harmonic numbers may not always show up in a person's external behaviour. If Spielberg had not made his films, we would not know that these themes were important for him.

Suicide of Donald Crowhurst
1 July 1969, 11.20.40 (–01.00)[8]
Atlantic Ocean (approx. 33N00. 40W00).
Source: Nicholas Tomalin & Ron Hall, *The Strange Last Voyage of Donald Crowhurst,*[9] p.274.

((ME–**29**JU)–29–VE)–29/29/29–MO
(UR–29–CH)–29–MA
SO–29–NE

I will end this chapter, not with a birth chart, but with a death chart: the chart for the time when Donald Crowhurst jumped into the Atlantic Ocean, leaving his unmanned boat, the *Teignmouth Electron*, to drift until it was discovered nine days later.

Crowhurst was born in India in 1932 (there seems to be no record of his date of birth, let alone of the time). He became an engineer and an amateur sailor. In 1968 he decided to take part in the Golden Globe Race, a single-handed round-the-world yacht race sponsored by the *Sunday Times*. He entered the race at the last minute and after inadequate preparations. Halfway down the Atlantic it became clear to him that his boat was not seaworthy enough to complete the round-the-world voyage; but if he had given up and returned home, he would have faced bankruptcy as well as humiliation. So he decided to fake the voyage. He hung around for several months in the South Atlantic, all the time keeping two logbooks: a false one detailing his pretended journey around the Southern Ocean, and a true one detailing his actual movements. Then, after a suitable time had elapsed, he re-established radio contact and informed his sponsors that he had rounded the Horn and was heading back up the Atlantic.

By this time all the other competitors had dropped out of the race, with the exception of Nigel Tetley, who was on course to win the race. But then Tetley's boat disintegrated, and he too withdrew from the race. Crowhurst now realized that, if he continued, he could not avoid being the winner. If he came home as the winner, he would be given a hero's welcome, but then his logbooks would be scrutinized and his fakery would be revealed. (Of course, he could have destroyed the 'true' logbook, but he seems to have been very reluctant to do that.)

Crowhurst decided that his only option was suicide. During his final days, he wrote feverishly in his notebooks (which were found on the boat). His writings are incoherent, but it is clear that he was undergoing a spiritual transformation brought on by his awareness of his approaching death. He saw himself as a "cosmic being," or as the son of God. He saw himself as playing a game whose rules had been set by God. He wrote, "There can only be one perfect beauty, that is the great beauty of truth". (This is surely related to his decision to leave the 'true' logbook on board, thus revealing to the world how he had broken the rules of the game.)

All the time he was watching the clock, and noting the time in his notebook. At 11.17.00 on July 1st his final words were: "At 11.20.40 I shall resign the game. There is no reason for harmful…"

Why did Crowhurst choose this moment to die? He could not have known that this was the *exact* moment when Saturn crossed the Midheaven, or that Saturn at that moment had an exact Twenty-threeness link with the Sun (dream of the subjugation of Self). Nor could he have known that the chart for that moment contained a very strong pattern of Twenty-nineness, linking Moon with Mercury, Venus and Jupiter, and Mars with Uranus and Chiron.

And yet this Twenty-nineness pattern seems to be very descriptive of Crowhurst's state of mind. It depicts a lonely individual, deeply aware of his separateness from the rest of humanity, coming to terms with his fate. Twenty-nine, like every other prime number, is divisible only by itself and One. Crowhurst was reaching out from the Twenty-nineness towards the Oneness into which we will all be drawn when we die.

Conclusion

My suggestion is that people who are strong in Twenty-nineness tend to be very conscious of their own separateness and uniqueness. They feel themselves to be different from other people, having different abilities, different desires, different needs. In some cases the feeling is that other people are all the same and that they themselves are the exception, while in other cases there is an awareness of the distinct individuality of *every* person, themselves included.

Most of the famous people whom we have looked at in this chapter have been proud of their uniqueness, and may sometimes have felt that their uniqueness makes them superior to other people. But there may well be many others who are, to a greater or lesser degree, ashamed of their uniqueness, feeling that it makes them inferior. Or the person may switch between these two poles: sometimes he may feel that he 'sticks out like a sore thumb', while at other times he may feel that he can be a beacon and an inspiration for others. (Edith Sitwell's remark "I am an unpopular electric eel in a pond of goldfish" is a good expression of the negative side of this.)

The feeling of uniqueness may go with a feeling of being free from the rules that guide other people's behaviour, and free to set one's own rules or to live without rules. It seems that (especially when Venus and/or Mars are involved in the Twenty-nineness) this is especially evident in the field of sexuality. Thus, the person may be openly gay or bisexual, even in societies where this is frowned on. They may display an extravagant sexual appetite, or may sometimes (as in the case of Edith Sitwell) go the other way and choose to be asexual.

The feeling of one's own uniqueness goes with an awareness of the separateness and distinctiveness of all things. In Gertrude Stein's words, "a rose is a rose is a rose". Each thing is simply what it is, and needs to be valued for its distinctive qualities.

Twenty-nineness is a reaction against Twenty-threeness in the sense that the dream of a better society (or of a society into which the person can fit more easily) is no longer present. The Twenty-nineness person accepts himself as he is, and other people as they are. (Allen Ginsberg may seem to be an exception to this, but, as we have said, this is probably due to his strength in other numbers.) In so far as they are trying to help others, they are helping them to be more truly themselves.

And yet this is probably an over-positive interpretation of the meaning of Twenty-nineness. Twenty-nineness can also lead to loneliness (a feeling that "nobody understands me"). Perhaps it can also sometimes lead to an excessive self-regard and an excessive preoccupation with self, and to an indifference to others' needs; or to a belief that "I am right and everyone else is wrong". There is likely to be an absence of the spirit of compromise, which helps people to resolve their differences and to live amicably together.

16

Thirty-oneness

Thirty-one is the last prime number that we will consider in this book. As before, we will look at some examples of people whose charts contain strong clusters of Thirty-oneness, in order to clarify the essential qualities of this number.

Sigmund Freud and Carl Gustav Jung

Sigmund Freud
Born 6 May 1856, 18.30 (–01.13)
Freiburg, Austria (now Pribor, Czech Republic) (49N38. 18E10).
Source: From father's diary, via Philip Lucas (ADB). RR: A.[1]

((JU–**31**–_PL_)–**31**/31–_CH_)–**31**–ME)–31/31/31/31–SO

Carl Gustav Jung
Born 26 July 1875, 19.32 (–00.37)
Kesswil, Switzerland (47N36. 9E20).
Source: From his daughter Gret Baumann, in her biography of Jung (ADB). RR: A.[2]

(UR–**31**–_PL_)–31–_SO_
(MO–**31**–SA)–31–ME

Both Sigmund Freud, the founder of psychoanalysis, and Carl Gustav Jung, the founder of analytical psychology, have strong patterns of Thirty-oneness, involving in both cases Sun, Mercury and Pluto. Jung was originally a follower of Freud, but then broke away to develop his own theories and found his own school.

This is not the place to attempt to summarize the complex theories of Freud and Jung. It is enough to say that both of them, in their different ways, were concerned with investigating the workings of the unconscious mind and with the ways in which conscious thoughts, feelings and behaviour are affected by the unconscious. Freud wrote *The Interpretations of Dreams*, believing that people express their repressed sexual desires in dreams, and that dreams are "the royal road to the unconscious". He also developed the concept of the "id", which he described as "the dark, inaccessible part of our personality ... a chaos, full of seething excitations".[3] The id is governed by the "pleasure principle," whereas the ego (the conscious mind) is governed by the "reality principle".

Jung wrote an autobiography *Memories, Dreams, Reflections*, in which he wrote that all his creative work came from his internal visions, fantasies and dreams. He developed the concept of the "collective unconscious", which is common to all human beings, and is built up of "archetypes" which are "the conceptual matrices or patterns behind all our religious and mythological concepts, and, indeed, our thinking in general".[4]

Our hypothesis, then, is that this delving into the unconscious mind may be related to the essential quality of Thirty-oneness.

Marquis de Sade

Born 2 June 1740, 17.00 (–00.09)
Paris, France (48N52. 2E20).
Source: Birth records, via Richard Rongier and Ed Steinbrecher (ADB).
RR: AA.

((MO–**31**–VE)–**31**–NE)–31/31/**31**–MA
(JU–**31**–SA)–**31**–PL

The original 'sadist', the Marquis de Sade, has a strong pattern of Thirty-oneness involving the Moon and five other planets including Venus and Mars (which together indicate sexuality). He has strong clusters in other numbers, especially Three and Five (see the list in Appendix III), but Thirty-one is by far the strongest of the higher prime numbers.

Both in his life and in his writings, de Sade pursued unrestrained and often violent and cruel sexual expression. He described his own novel *The 120 Days of Sodom* as "the most impure tale ever to spring from the mind of man".[5] Also he said: "In order to know virtue, we must acquaint ourselves with vice. Only then can we know the true measure of a man".[6] In Freudian terms, it is almost as though de Sade had resolved to live his life in accordance with the dictates of the id rather than the ego, and to bring into the open all of the id's hidden desires. And in fact Simone de

Beauvoir saw de Sade as a forerunner of Freud, in that he saw eroticism as the mainspring of human behaviour.[7]

Jack Smith
Born 14 November 1932, 11.05 (+05.00)
Columbus, OH, USA (39N58. 83W00).
Source: Birth certificate, via Lois Rodden (ADB). RR: AA.

((MO–**31**–PL)–31–(VE–**31**–CH))–**31**–NE
        –**31**/31–UR
((VE–**31**–CH)–**31**–NE)–**31**/**31**/31–SA

Jack Smith was an underground artist, film-maker, writer and photographer who can be seen as a modern version of de Sade (although without the cruelty), in that he too aimed, both in his life and in his art, to bring out into the open the desires and fantasies which for most people remain hidden in the unconscious. He was gay, though he also loved women platonically. He has been called "a magical trickster manically involved in all kinds of projects at all times".[8] His masterpiece is a short film called *Flaming Creatures*, in which a cast of male transvestites play orgiastic games, expose their genitals, and stage a mock-rape of a woman who appears out of a coffin. It has been called obscene (it is still banned in New York, where it was made), but it has also been called (by Susan Sontag) a "film about joy and innocence".

Like de Sade, Jack Smith has a massive cluster of Thirty-oneness, involving the Moon and six other planets. (Moon, Venus, Saturn, Neptune and Pluto are linked by Thirty-oneness in the charts of both Smith and de Sade.)

Federico García Lorca
Born 5 June 1898, 00.00 (–00.15)
Fuente Vaqueros, Spain (37N13. 3E47)
Source: Birth certificate, via Felipe Ferreira (ADB). RR: AA.

(((SO–**1**–PL)–31/**31**–MO)–**31**/31/31–SA)–31/31/31/**31**–ME
((SO–**31**–SA)–31/**31**–ME)–31–MA

The Spanish poet and playwright Federico García Lorca has an extremely strong Thirty-oneness cluster, with Sun and Moon linked to four other planets. Lorca was gay, and had an affair with Salvador Dali. During the Spanish Civil War he was put to death by right-wing extremists, who saw him as a "subversive writer, a Russian spy, and a homosexual".

Lorca's poems have been described as "disquieting in their projection of a part-primitive, part-private world of myth moved by dark and not precisely identifiable forces",[9] and his plays deal with "unspecified dark forces (associated with earth, blood, sex, water, fertility/infertility, death and the moon").[9] Clearly this is related to Jung's theme of the archetypes in the collective unconscious.

Robert Mapplethorpe
Born 4 November 1946, 05.45 (+05.00)
New York, NY, USA (40N43. 74W00).
Source: From him, via Gar Osten (ADB). RR: A.

((MO–**31**–<u>SA</u>)–31–(ME–**31**–CH)–31–SO

The photographer Robert Mapplethorpe has a cluster of Thirty-oneness involving Sun, Moon, Mercury, Saturn and Chiron. Mapplethorpe was gay and was deeply into sadomasochism; his early photographs are a documentation of the New York S & M scene, and were widely regarded as shocking and obscene, although they were also greatly admired for their beauty and technical mastery. He said, "Whenever you make love to someone, there should be three people involved – you, the other person, and the devil".[10] He died of AIDS.

Marcel Marceau
Born 22 March 1923, 08.00 (+00.00)
Strasbourg, France (48N35. 7E45).
Source: Birth certificate, via Steinbrecher (ADB). RR: AA.

(((ME–**1**–UR)–**31**/31–MA)–31/<u>31/31</u>–JU)–<u>31</u>/31/**31**/<u>31</u>–NE

The theme of uninhibited sexuality has been present for most of these cases of strong Thirty-oneness, but this is not the case for Marcel Marceau, who is regarded as the greatest mime of the twentieth century. From an early age Marceau started to imitate everything around him, and as an adult he perfected the art of conveying, by the subtlest movements and gestures, complex stories about a person's inner thoughts and feelings.

He believed in the communicative power of silence; words, he thought, interfered with the ability to communicate a person's inner truth. He said, "I have tried to shed some light on the shadow of man startled by his anguish".[11]

We can note that Marceau's Thirty-oneness cluster (unlike those of our other Thirty-oneness cases) does not involve the Sun or the Moon, but is centred around Mercury and Mars. This makes it less personal: less concerned with Marceau's view of himself, and more concerned with how he interprets the world outside him and communicates with it through his actions.

Marc Dutroux

Born 6 November 1956, 07.35 (–01.00)
Ixelles, Belgium (50N50. 4E22).
Source: Birth certificate, via Michael Mandl and Grazia Bordoni (ADB).
RR: AA.

((((ME–**31**–MA)–**31**/31–UR)–31/31/31–SA)–**31**/31/31/31–PL)–
    31/31/31/**31**/31–MO

I have found several murderers with strong patterns of Thirty-oneness. Perhaps the most notorious of them is the Belgian paedophile murderer Marc Dutroux, who has the strongest single cluster of Thirty-oneness that I have seen, with the Moon linked to five other planets.

Dutroux was convicted of having kidnapped, tortured and sexually abused six girls between the ages of 8 and 19, four of whom he murdered. It is likely that the actual number of his victims was far higher than this. He was unemployed but had money from drug-dealing and probably from the sale of pornographic videos, and he owned six dilapidated houses in which he hid the girls. One of his victims was Sabine Dardenne, whose chart we looked at in Chapter 3: she was discovered, drugged, in the basement of one of his houses. His trial caused enormous revulsion in Belgium, and one-third of all the Belgians who were named Dutroux changed their name after the trial.

We can note that both Dutroux and the Marquis de Sade have Thirty-oneness links involving Moon, Mars, Saturn and Pluto (with Pluto angular in both cases). It would seem that this combination may be indicative of sexual cruelty.

Robert Black
Born 21 April 1947, 20.35 (–02.00)
Falkirk, Scotland (56N00. 3W48).
Source: Birth certificate, via Paul Wright. RR: AA.

SO–**31**–VE–**31**–MA–**31**–CH
JU–31–NE–31–PL

Another paedophile murderer is Robert Black, who was convicted of abducting, raping and murdering three young girls (though he may have killed far more). Black's Thirty-oneness pattern is exceptionally strong, with Sun, Venus, Mars and Chiron all linked by very close Thirty-oneness aspects.

Jeffrey Dahmer
Born 21 May 1960, 16.34 (+05.00)
Milwaukee, WI, USA (43N02. 87W54).
Source: Birth certificate, via Stephen Przybylowski (ADB). RR: AA.

SO–31–PL
((ME–**31**–MA)–31/**31**–NE)–31/31/**31**–MO

Jeffrey Dahmer confessed to between 11 and 17 gruesome murders as a necrophiliac cannibal. A large number of body parts were found in his apartment. He said that eating his victims was "a way of making me feel that they were a part of me … A compulsive obsession with what I was doing overpowered any feelings of repulsion. It was the only thing that gave me satisfaction in life".[12]

Probably the main driving force in Dahmer's chart is a very powerful cluster of Fiveness and Threeness – (JU–**6**–CH)–**10/15**–MO)–**15/10**/30–MA – which will tend to lead to obsessive and repetitive behaviour patterns. But the cluster of Thirty-oneness will also have played a part, helping Dahmer to overcome his egoic inhibitions and to surrender to what Freud would call the impulses of the "id". (We can note that Moon-Mars – outward action in response to inner feelings – is common to both of these clusters.)

Gavrilo Princip

Born 13 July 1894, 16.40 (–01.00)
Gornji Oblajaj, Yugoslavia (44N11. 16E23).
Source: From his mother, quoted in biography by V. Bogicevic (ADB).
RR: B.

(ME–__31__–_VE_–__31__–CH)–__31__–SO
(JU–__31__–SA)–__31__/__31__–_PL_

Gavrilo Princip was the assassin who on 28 June 1914, at the age of 19, shot Archduke Franz Ferdinand of Austria in Sarajevo, triggering the First World War.[13] He has an extremely strong Thirty-oneness pattern, but he was plainly a very different type of killer from Dutroux, Black and Dahmer.

How then can we explain his Thirty-oneness? Perhaps a clue can be found in the fact that he was initially rejected by the Black Hand guerrilla organization because he was "too small and too weak," and Vladimir Dedijer suggests that this rejection was "one of the primary personal motives which pushed him to do something exceptionally brave in order to prove to others that he was their equal".[14] This suggests that Princip, rather than killing for purely political reasons, was acting in response to deep-seated personal needs, and in this he was true to the spirit of Thirty-oneness.

Carol Burnett

Born 26 April 1933, 04.00 (+06.00)
San Antonio, TX, USA (29N25. 98W30).
Source: Birth certificate, via Gauquelin Book of American Charts (ADB). RR: AA.

(SO–__31__–UR)–__31__–(MA–__31__–JU)

After all this darkness it is a relief to turn to the comedian Carol Burnett, who wears her Thirty-oneness much more lightly. Carol Burnett is portrayed by AstroDatabank and on various websites as a brilliant actress and a hilarious performer, loved by everyone for her kindness, her generosity, and her ability to bring laughter and happiness into people's lives. So how then are we to explain her cluster of Thirty-oneness, in which Sun comes closely together with Mars, Jupiter and Uranus?

We need first to say that there are other aspects in Burnett's chart which help to explain her bright and cheery personality. In particular she has (SO–_1_–VE)–_3/3_–NE, which suggests a confidence in her own attractiveness and a joy in reaching out to people and connecting with their hopes and dreams.

My feeling is that the Thirty-oneness is connected with a certain wackiness, or craziness, in Burnett's stage personality. It seems that a large part of her humour lay in portraying characters (such as the downtrodden charwoman who was one of her favourites) "with the lid off": that is to say, she portrayed them, not as they would behave in real life, but as they would behave if they were able to cast off their egoic inhibitions and follow their subconscious desires. In this she was not too different from some of the other people considered in this chapter, such as Jack Smith and Marcel Marceau.

Carol Burnett was also famous for her 'Tarzan yell' which she would sometimes let out for no apparent reason. This again suggests a kind of controlled surrender to the irrational forces beneath the surface.

It is interesting that Carol Burnett is the only famous woman that I have found with a strong cluster of Thirty-oneness.[15] Maybe women are better than men at keeping Thirty-oneness in check, using it but not being overwhelmed by it, and so are not subject to the extremes of antisocial behaviour indulged in by some of our male Thirty-oneness people. Or (to put it another way), maybe Thirty-oneness plus testosterone is a dangerous combination.

Conclusion

It seems that, under the influence of Thirty-oneness, the boundary between the conscious and unconscious minds (or between the ego and the id) becomes more blurred. People become conscious of needs, desires and fantasies which for other people are buried in the unconscious mind.

This awareness can be either beneficial or harmful. On the one hand, it can help the person to gain a deeper understanding of himself or herself, and so to be more fully in charge of their own lives. That which has been brought into consciousness can be managed and controlled, whereas if it remains unconscious it will exercise a hidden control over the person's thoughts, feelings and actions. Jung describes how, for an extended period, he devoted his life to a detailed examination of his own dreams, fantasies and inner drives, taking copious notes on everything that he found. During this period it was difficult for him to function in the world, but, when he emerged from it, he had a far deeper understanding of himself and of humanity in general. And this heightened self-awareness can help the person to help others as well as himself. One imagines that, if one studied the charts of a large number of psychotherapists (and of others in the helping professions), one would find a greater-than-average amount of Thirty-oneness. And maybe this would be true, not only of the helpers, but also of the helped: that is to say, of people who benefit from psychotherapy and find it a worthwhile pursuit.

On the other hand, if a person becomes conscious of hidden desires and drives, and lacks the ability or the willingness to try to understand and control them, they may overwhelm him and take over his life. This is well expressed by Jeffrey Dahmer's comment: "A compulsive obsession with what I was doing overpowered any feelings of repulsion. It was the only thing that gave me satisfaction in life". That is to say, Dahmer felt compelled to follow the drives of the id, even though in his egoic mind he knew that his actions were repulsive or, at least, were unacceptable to society.

Both of these tendencies are evident in a person like the Marquis de Sade. On the one hand, de Sade's statement that "in order to know virtue, we must acquaint ourselves with vice: only then can we know the true measure of a man" would be highly acceptable to Freud and to most modern psychotherapists; but on the other hand, de Sade showed (by the way in which he lived his life, and also by the way in which, in his writings, he seemed to be revelling in 'vice' for its own sake) that he was in the grip of these 'vicious' forces, and was not really intent on controlling them so as to attain 'virtue'.

Thirty-oneness is a reaction against Twenty-nineness, in that the theme of being 'proud to be different', and of revelling in one's individuality (which we identified as a dominant theme of Twenty-nineness), is not so much present for the Thirty-oneness person. The Thirty-oneness person is not so much interested in whether he is different from other people; in fact, he may well believe that other people are the same as him, and that his own behaviour is more authentic than other people's behaviour because he is expressing things which for other people remain repressed. This, again, can be either good or bad. It can lead to an apparent callousness towards other people, and a refusal to entertain the idea that they may be different and may have needs of their own; or (as in the cases of Jack Smith, Marcel Marceau and Carol Burnett) it can cause the person to devote his or her life to illuminating the lives of others, by showing them (often in a light-hearted way) things about themselves of which they were unaware.

Thirty-one is the last of the prime numbers that we will consider in this book. But Thirty-one is, of course, not the end of the road. Beyond Thirty-one there are other prime numbers (37, 41, 43...), which can be expected to have some significance, at least in cases where they bring together three or more planets.

But we have travelled far enough. Let us rest now.

17

Progression of the Prime Numbers

We have now looked at all the prime numbers from One to Thirty-one, and have found that each prime number represents a distinctive quality. We will now summarize these findings, by taking a journey through the prime numbers, noting how the quality of each number differs from the quality of the number that precedes it. We will call this the "progression of the prime numbers," since "progression" is defined by Chambers Concise Dictionary as "a sequence of numbers, each of which bears a specific relationship to the preceding term".

I will, however, take the numbers in the reverse order, starting with Thirty-one and ending with One. Conventionally this would be seen not as a progression but as a retrogression, a movement in a backwards direction. But I believe that, for mankind, this is truly the 'forwards' direction. We are all striving towards Oneness: unity, peace, wholeness. All the numbers are striving towards Oneness, but Thirty-one is further from the Oneness than any of our other numbers. By moving from Thirty-one towards One, we are moving in the direction of our ultimate goal.

In describing this journey through the numbers, I will use the first person plural: "we", "us", "ourselves". This is because this is a journey in which we are all involved. We may have a stronger connection with some numbers than with others, but we all have some connection with all of the numbers. Each number represents a different way of being, a different way of living our lives and of relating to other people and the outside world. We have choices about where we sojourn along this journey.

Thirty-one
Within Thirty-oneness, we are very much wrapped up in ourselves, and feeling very separate from the rest of humanity. We are aware that within

us there is a seething cauldron of desires and drives, which, although they may remain mostly in the unconscious mind (except when manifested in dreams), may burst out into consciousness and threaten to take over our lives. We may choose to surrender to these desires and let them rule our lives, or we may choose to try to understand them and master them so that we have them under control. Our relationships with other people are very much bound up with these inner drives. We may use other people thoughtlessly in pursuit of our personal needs; or we may seek their help in trying to come to terms with our inner demons; or we may set ourselves up as helpers, offering assistance to people who (we realize) are struggling with the same inner conflicts that we too have struggled with.

Twenty-nine

Moving from Thirty-oneness to Twenty-nineness, the preoccupation with unconscious drives recedes, and we become more conscious of ourselves as whole people trying to live our lives to the full. However, we still feel very separate from the rest of humanity, and the sense of differentness and isolation is perhaps stronger for this number than for any other. There is a sense of being a misfit, a person who does not fit into society and to whom society's rules do not apply. We may be proud of being different, and may choose to ostentatiously parade our individuality and to break all the rules; or we may be ashamed of being different, and may spend our lives feeling lonely and misunderstood. However, we may also be able to recognize and appreciate the individuality of other people, and to form relationships in which the individuality of both partners is fully expressed. If we try to help other people, it will be in the direction of helping them to be more fully themselves.

Twenty-three

Moving from Twenty-nineness to Twenty-threeness, we become dissatisfied with being unable to fit into society, and we long for a better society in which we would have a sense of true belonging. We become spinners of stories, dreams and fantasies, in which we imagine the world as we would wish it to be. We may live out our lives as dissatisfied dreamers, or we may have some success in 'living the dream,' translating it into reality, so that the world of our immediate environment becomes the world of our dreams. Our best relationships will be with people who share our dream: but we may also try to impose our dream on others to whom it is not acceptable. If we try to help others, it will be in the direction of helping them to realize their dreams.

Nineteen

Moving from Twenty-threeness to Nineteenness, we cease to dream of a better world, and we resolve to accept the world as it is and our own place in it. We become acute observers of the ways of the world (the world of human society, or the world of nature), and, if we are creative, we will try to mirror the world as we see it and to express its essence. We will tend to avoid situations which put us in the spotlight and make people feel that we are 'special'; we do not want to be special, we want to be ordinary. We may become reclusive, avoiding other people's company, or we may be happy living unobtrusively with others. We have a capacity for empathy and for putting people at ease; but we may be lacking in the capacity for purposeful action, preferring to passively accept situations rather than look for solutions.

Seventeen

Moving from Nineteenness to Seventeenness, we are no longer willing to passively accept our situation. We develop a spirit of rebelliousness, a desire to fight for what we believe to be right. We are still acute observers of the ways of the world, but now we focus on how it needs to be changed. Often we are filled with anger about how things are. We develop strong opinions, and may campaign on behalf of causes. If we feel that we cannot change the world, we may become sarcastic observers of it, making comments which make clear our non-acceptance of the status quo. Our best relationships will be with people who share our views and who can collaborate with us in working to change the world.

Thirteen

Moving from Seventeenness to Thirteenness, we come to feel that it is not the world, but we ourselves, that need to change. We therefore embark on a journey in search of ourselves. We are rootless and restless, and do not know where we truly belong. We travel widely, and take great risks, in search of experiences which will give us a greater insight into our own true nature. We experiment with masks, or false personalities, which may be eccentric and flamboyant, and we may feel very uncomfortable when we are not wearing a mask. We may be very creative, and able to shock and surprise people by the freshness and originality of our creations. We tend to be solitary; we are not good at stable long-term relationships, and those we do have tend to be short-lived.

Eleven

Moving from Thirteenness to Elevenness, we abandon this restless search, and adopt an attitude towards the world of dogged persistence and defiance. We feel now that we know who we are, and our task is to stay true to ourselves in spite of all the world's attempts to change us or to force us to behave according to its rules. We seek permanence and stability; we seek to be rooted in a particular place, and among people whom we can trust. If we are creative, we will create things that embody this permanence. We are preoccupied with the outward Form of things. We tend to be perfectionists in what we do, paying great attention to detail. We can be difficult and demanding in relationships, since we expect of other people the same high standards that we have set for ourselves.

Seven

Moving from Elevenness to Sevenness, we become dissatisfied with this preoccupation with outward Form, and we seek the hidden meaning that lies beneath the surface of things. We are intuitive, imaginative, inspirational and emotional. We long to escape from the humdrumness of everyday existence and to find our own personal Samarkand or Arcadia where there is a heightened sense of aliveness and where everything is pervaded with meaning. We believe in miracles, and we are scornful of rational materialism. We may be intensely creative, creating works of art which arouse strong feelings in the reader or the observer. We easily fall in love, and become involved in romantic relationships. We are governed by the heart rather than the head.

Five

Moving from Sevenness to Fiveness, we turn away from the imaginative world of Sevenness. For us, that is an unreal world, and we want to live in the real world; we realize that we have the ability to shape the real world to suit our needs. Hence we become builders of structures and systems. We may build physical things in the outside world, or create technological systems; we may create works of art in which great attention is paid to structure and style, or we may create systems of thought, and rules governing our own and other people's behaviour. Since we are good at structuring our own behaviour, we may become consummate actors or performers. We believe in the capacity of Man to better himself and to create a better world, and we believe in the ability of the human brain to find a solution to every problem. We are governed by the head rather than the heart.

Three

Moving from Fiveness to Threeness, we turn away from the effort to change the world and to better ourselves. We accept the world as it is, and rejoice in its beauty and complexity; we accept ourselves as we are. We can see how other people are consumed by stress and suffering, and our response is to laugh. Our goal in life is simply to enjoy ourselves and be happy; we follow the pleasure principle. We can bring great joy to other people by our light-heartedness, our humour, and our optimism. The downside is that we may seem indifferent to other people's suffering, and also that we may be careless and slapdash in performing tasks that require attention to detail.

Two

Moving from Threeness to Twoness, we lose our detached awareness of the world, and become wholly caught up in the struggle: the struggle to survive, the struggle to achieve, the struggle for happiness. Life is a continual series of battles and challenges. The myriad complexity of the world is now reduced to just Two: Self, and Other; me, and the enemy I am fighting right now. There is right, and there is wrong; there is good, and there is evil; there is success, and there is failure. And yet the paradox of Two is that, even though it is so caught up in the separation, it is the closest number to Oneness. We are striving towards a reconciliation between Self and Other; striving towards a union of opposites. We are aware of the possibility of Oneness.

One

Moving from Twoness to Oneness, the boundary between Self and Other dissolves. All is unity, peace, and wholeness. We realize the truth of the saying: *You are already that which you seek.* There is no need for action. We are able to simply Be.

18

Interpreting the Whole Chart

Now that we have studied the harmonic numbers and gained some understanding of their meaning, we are able to use them in chart interpretation.

In this chapter I will analyse ten charts using the harmonic numbers. As well as listing the harmonic aspects, I will present the chart itself. House cusps will not be shown, so readers will be free to insert the cusps according to the house system of their choice.

In the interpretations I will refrain from mentioning signs and houses, since the aim of this book is to demonstrate that harmonic aspects *on their own* can yield valid insights. However, readers are welcome to add their own insights based on signs and houses to the insights offered here, and so to reach a more complete interpretation of the chart as a whole.

It may be worthwhile at this point to repeat the description given in Chapter 1 of the way in which harmonic aspects are presented.

<u>*Bold underlined italics*</u> show aspects that are very close to exactitude. For instance, Margaret Thatcher has Jupiter very closely opposite to Pluto.

<u>Underlining</u> shows aspects that are close (but not very close). For instance, Margaret Thatcher has Sun closely conjunct Mercury.

Aspects presented without underlining are wide (not close). The permitted orbs for each of these degrees of closeness are described in Chapter 1.

Clusters of three or more aspects are shown using brackets. For instance, in Margaret Thatcher's chart, (JU–**2**–PL)–16/<u>16</u>–UR shows that:

    Jupiter is very closely –2– Pluto
    Jupiter is widely –16– Uranus
    Pluto is closely –16– Uranus.

When the letters for a planet are shown in _underlined italics_, this means that the planet is within 8 degrees of one of the Angles. For instance, Margaret Thatcher has Saturn close to the Ascendant and Moon close to the Midheaven.

I will mostly be using the charts of people who are very well-known and need no introduction, and whose charts may already be familiar to astrologers. I will start with three people who have recently held the office of Prime Minister of the United Kingdom.

Margaret Thatcher
Born 13 October 1925, 09.00 (+00.00)
Grantham, England (52N55. 0W39).
Source: From her private secretary, via Charles Harvey (ADB). RR: A.

1:    SO–1–ME
      MO–1–NE

2:    (JU–2–PL)–8–MO
                –16/16–UR
                –32/32–CH
      ME–2–CH

3:    (ME–2–CH)–6/3–NE
      (SA–3–NE)–9–PL
      (ME–6–NE)–9/18/18/9–(JU–6–SA)

5:    SO–15–SA
      ME–25–MA
      (VE–5–CH)–20/20–SA

7:    SO–7–MO
      VE–21–PL
      MA–21–SA
      SA–14–UR

11:   (MA–11–CH)–11/11–UR
      VE–11–NE

13:   SO–13–NE
      MO–13–ME
      VE–13–UR

17:    (VE–<u>17</u>–JU)–<u>17</u>–SO

19:    SO–<u>19</u>–PL
       MA–<u>19</u>–JU
       UR–<u>19</u>–NE

29:    SO–<u>29</u>–CH

I have listed all of Margaret Thatcher's harmonic aspects (except for 'wide' aspects that are unconnected to 'close' ones), and readers may find the list long and somewhat daunting. However, with practice it becomes easy to sort out the really important aspects from the less important ones. If we were doing a full and detailed analysis we might need to look at all of these aspects, but here we can focus on the most significant ones. We should always bear in mind that 'very close' aspects are more significant than less close aspects, and that clusters of aspects are more significant

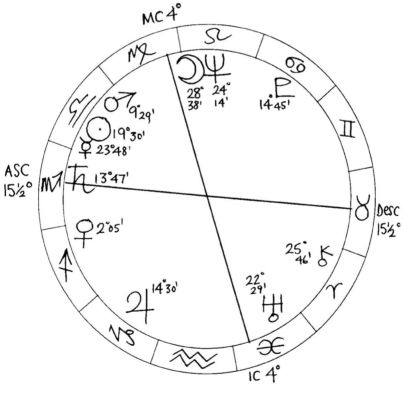

Margaret Thatcher

than single aspects. Also, special attention should be paid to aspects involving the Sun. (If the birth time was accurately known, this would apply also to aspects involving the Moon, but if, as in Thatcher's case, the birth time is 'on the hour' and so is likely to be somewhat inaccurate, we have to be cautious about these aspects, especially when they involve the higher harmonic numbers.)

Margaret Thatcher's chart is dominated by a very close opposition between Jupiter and Pluto (JU–**2**–PL), which suggests a struggle between the expansive, freedom-loving drives of Jupiter and the single-minded determination of Pluto. Jupiter sees Pluto as fanatical and narrow-minded, while Pluto sees Jupiter as lax and irresponsible. With the opposition, there is always a tendency to see oneself as embodying one of the planets and to project the other planet out onto other people. I suggest that there is a contrast here between how Margaret Thatcher saw herself and how other people saw her. She probably saw herself (mostly) as Jupiter, fighting for freedom against the narrow-minded bigotry of people like General Galtieri (from whom she seized back the Falkland Islands) and Arthur Scargill of the miners' union. But other people have tended to see her (mostly) as Pluto, intent on destroying people's freedoms by her own single-minded intransigence.

In any case, I see this aspect as the main astrological cause of Thatcher's confrontational approach to politics, in which, if you are not 'one of us', you are the enemy. And we can note also that this is an aspect of undiluted Twoness. In many charts, the Twoness of close oppositions is diluted by aspects involving other harmonic numbers (3, 5, 7, 11, 13) which involve both of the planets in the opposition (as would be the case, for instance, if Mars – or any other planet – was –3– Jupiter and –6– Pluto). But in Thatcher's case the only aspects involving both Jupiter and Pluto are other aspects of pure Twoness: –8–MO, –16–UR, and –32–CH. So, for Thatcher, the Jupiter-Pluto struggle is a deadly serious matter: a struggle for survival, unmitigated by any factors indicating pleasure or creativity. No wonder she was called the 'Iron Lady'.

However, there is some Threeness in Thatcher's chart. The clusters of Threeness in her chart are complex and would take a long time to analyse in full, but we can note that by far the strongest Threeness aspect is ME–**18**–SA. This aspect is within 1 minute of exactitude and so is extremely strong, and it gains still further strength from the fact that Saturn is close to the Ascendant. 18 is 3 x 3 x 2, and so is mainly Threeness (ease and pleasure) but with a dash of Twoness (struggle and effort). ME–**18**–SA shows that, for Thatcher, the main source of pleasure in life was Saturnian thinking and communication: this is what she most enjoyed doing. We can see in this the roots of her workaholism and her fierce self-discipline, working far into the night and giving herself very little sleep, and the origins also of the strict way in which she controlled her subordinates, expecting them to work as hard as she did, and requiring them to explain their decisions to her in detail. Perhaps also her commitment to Saturnian thinking helps to explain her lack of a sense of humour (speechwriters would insert jokes into her speeches, but they had to explain the jokes to her as she couldn't see them). Humour inevitably involves 'thinking outside the box', but Saturn kept Thatcher's thinking firmly inside the box.

Turning to Fiveness, one of Thatcher's most important clusters is (VE–**5**–CH)–20/**20**–SA. Fiveness is about creating things in the outside world, but it can also be about structuring one's own behaviour, creating a *style* through which one presents oneself to the world. VE–**5**–CH shows how Thatcher was able to use her femininity (Venus) in the furtherance of her career (Chiron), and –20/**20**–SA shows how this was linked in with her rising Saturn, and how her femininity helped her to maintain control over people. Her colleagues (almost all of whom were men) treated her differently because she was a woman, and it seems that, because of her femininity, they often felt unable to argue with her or answer her back. (She was much less successful in dealing with other women.) This links in with SO–15–SA, which shows that Thatcher was easily able to display her Saturnian authority without in any way being untrue to herself.

Also, ME–**25**–MA shows how Thatcher was able to develop a style of forceful communication. When she started as a politician her voice was quite shrill, but she deliberately cultivated a deeper, slower, more powerful way of speaking, which gave her more authority. Her statements, like "The lady's not for turning," show ME–**25**–MA in action. (However, she could go over the top and seem to be parodying herself, as when, on the birth of her first grandchild, she publicly announced "We are a grandmother".)

It's important that Thatcher has SO–_7_–MO. Aspects between the Sun and the Moon show how the person feels about himself or herself, and SO–_7_–MO shows that Thatcher's feelings about herself were invested with the quality of Sevenness. That is to say, she saw herself as an inspirational person, able to inspire others. This aspect is backed up by several other close Sevenness aspects involving Venus, Mars, Saturn, Uranus and Pluto. The effects of these Sevenness links were shown when, on becoming Prime Minister, she quoted the inspirational words of St Francis; and, despite the hostility which she aroused in many people, there is no doubt that for many other people she was an inspiration; they felt that she had liberated British politics from the straitjacket in which it had previously been bound.

(MA–_11_–CH)–11/_11_–UR shows that for Thatcher (as for her idol Winston Churchill) the Elevenness qualities of sticking resolutely to one's guns were very important.

Thatcher also has a remarkable number of close aspects involving the Sun in the higher prime numbers: SO–_13_–NE; SO–_17_–VE and –_17_–JU; SO–_19_–PL; and SO–_29_–CH. Rather than analysing these aspects one by one, I will simply say that all of the higher prime numbers (in different ways) are about feeling oneself to be *apart* from other people, a unique and separate individual. There is no doubt that Thatcher was a 'one off', very different from the people around her, and therefore having difficulties in forming close and 'normal' relationships with other people; and these aspects seem to show that she was aware of this and coped with it in various complex ways.

However, one number which is definitely *not* emphasized in Thatcher's chart is Thirty-one, since the chart contains absolutely no Thirty-oneness (not even any 'wide' aspects). This total absence of a particular number is quite rare, and shows that Thatcher was certainly *not* prone to investigating the contents of her own unconscious mind. One cannot imagine her going into psychotherapy.

Tony Blair

Born 6 May 1953, 06.10 (–01.00)
Edinburgh, Scotland (55N57. 3W13).
Source: Birth certificate, via Caroline Gerard (ADB), also via Paul Wright. RR: AA.

1:    <u>MA</u>–1–<u>JU</u>
      SA–<u>1</u>–NE

2:    (SA–<u>1</u>–NE)–2–ME
                    –4–<u>CH</u>
      (VE–<u>4</u>–UR)–8–<u>JU</u>
                    –<u>32</u>–ME

3:    (VE–<u>4</u>–UR)–<u>12</u>/<u>6</u>–SO
      MO–<u>24</u>–ME
      MO–<u>18</u>–<u>CH</u>
      VE–<u>27</u>–NE
      PL–<u>12</u>–<u>CH</u>

5:    SO–<u>20</u>–<u>MA</u>
      (SA–<u>1</u>–NE)–<u>5</u>/5–<u>JU</u>
                    –<u>25</u>/25–VE
      (<u>JU</u>–<u>5</u>–SA)–<u>10</u>/10–MO
      (VE–<u>4</u>–UR)–<u>20</u>/10–PL
      (VE–15–<u>MA</u>)–<u>30</u>/30–<u>CH</u>

7:    MO–<u>7</u>–UR
      <u>MA</u>–14–PL

11:   (ME–<u>11</u>–<u>JU</u>)–<u>22</u>–PL

13:   SO–<u>26</u>–<u>JU</u>
      ((SA–<u>1</u>–NE)–<u>13</u>/<u>13</u>–<u>MA</u>)–<u>26</u>/26/26–UR

17:   MO–<u>17</u>–VE

19:   (SO–<u>19</u>–ME)–19–<u>CH</u>
      MO–<u>19</u>–PL

23:   (SA–<u>1</u>–NE)–23/23/<u>23</u>/<u>23</u>–(SO–<u>23</u>–MO)

29:   ME–<u>29</u>–<u>MA</u>

31:   (UR–<u>31</u>–<u>CH</u>)–31–<u>JU</u>

Whereas Margaret Thatcher's chart was dominated by a single opposition, Tony Blair's is dominated by two conjunctions: <u>MA</u>–1–<u>JU</u> and SA–<u>1</u>–NE. <u>MA</u>–1–<u>JU</u> is powerful because Mars and Jupiter are close to the Ascendant, and SA–1–NE is powerful because it is very close to exactitude.

MA–1–JU shows how Tony Blair projects himself as a person of superabundant, free-flowing, optimistic energy. This was certainly how he projected himself when he first became Prime Minister. What a relief, people felt, after the lethargy and dullness of the John Major years. Now we have someone who will really open things up, and really get things done.

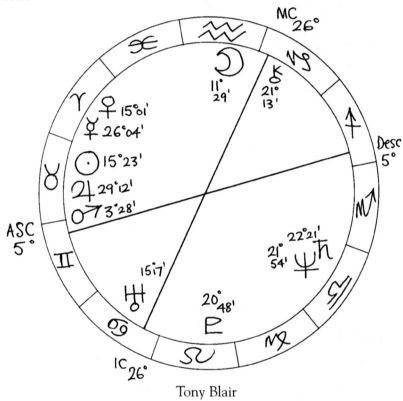

Tony Blair

SA–1–NE denotes a merging into One of the Saturnian principle of control and limitation and the Neptunian principle of universality and idealism. It therefore indicates a kind of controlled idealism, a belief that by Saturnian discipline and self-control one can achieve the Neptunian goal of bettering the lot of mankind. It indicates the kind of beliefs that brought Tony Blair into politics, but it also helps to explain why, despite all his Mars-Jupiter energy, he was more cautious about introducing reforms than one might have expected. Neptunian idealism must always be tempered by Saturnian caution.

This SA–**1**–NE conjunction has links with several other planets in various harmonic numbers. In particular:

– It is –**4**–_CH_ (with Chiron close to the Midheaven), showing that Blair is engaged in a struggle to bring this Saturn-Neptune idealism into fruition in his career, and in his role as a 'healer' (putting right what was wrong in the world). The Twoness of this aspect suggests that Blair did not find this easy. There were always practical difficulties blocking the achievement of his goals.

– It is –5/5–_JU_, showing that, despite these difficulties, Blair maintained his optimism and was able to project an image of himself as someone who was open-mindedly seeking solutions to problems.

– It is involved in a cluster of Thirteenness aspects: ((SA–**1**–NE)–13/**13**–_MA_)–26/26/26–UR. This cluster (together with SO–**26**–_JU_) shows that Blair has many of the characteristics of a Thirteenness person – someone who seeks adventure, breaks the rules, takes risks, in the process of trying to discover who he really is. The adventurousness of this cluster is tempered by the cautiousness of Saturn, but it is Neptune, not Saturn, that has a very close Thirteenness link to rising Mars, and we can see how this cluster will sometimes have caused Blair to abandon caution and to take risky and (some would say) ill-advised action, most notably in deciding to invade Iraq.

– Most importantly, it is involved in a tight cluster of Twenty-threeness aspects which unites it with the Sun and Moon: (SA–**1**–NE)–23/23/**23**/**23**–(SO–**23**–MO). Sun-Moon aspects, as we have said, describe how the person feels about himself or herself, and SO–**23**–MO shows that Blair sees himself as a 'dreamer of dreams'; and the 'dreaminess' of this cluster is further intensified by the fact it is Neptune, not Saturn, that has the very close Twenty-threeness links with both Sun and Moon. Twenty-threeness people create fairytales and fantasies, and do their best to translate the fantasy into reality. They tend to see the world in bright primary colours, with an absence of subtle distinctions, and a sharp contrast between light and dark or between good and evil. They are, at least to some extent, out of touch with reality. All this can be very beautiful and admirable in some contexts, but there are clearly dangers in putting a Twenty-threeness person in charge of a country, and I feel that the United Kingdom is lucky to have emerged relatively unscathed from ten years of being led by a Twenty-threeness person like Tony Blair.

We can now turn to other aspects that are not connected to the Saturn-Neptune conjunction. The most important of these is the tight cluster of (VE–4–UR)–12/6–SO. SO–6–UR shows how Blair obtains pleasure through striving (6 = 3 x 2) to act in original, unpredictable, Uranian ways, and SO–12–VE emphasizes his need to be loved, and the pain he experiences when he is rejected. VE–4–UR is a very dynamic aspect that can be summed up as 'the search for a thrilling beauty'. As I wrote in another article:[1] "Observers of Tony Blair have always commented on his palpable need to be loved, and I think it is true that he has wanted to be loved for his Uranian qualities of originality, vivacity and uniqueness. He has wanted to be seen as a bright light, a shining star, a brilliant contrast to the drabness and dullness of his political rivals. His famous comment on the death of Princess Diana ('She was the people's princess…'), which caused his popularity rating to rise above 90%, was a Uranian comment: sharp, incisive and memorable. But it is also true that, since it became clear that most people did not accept his judgment about the invasion of Iraq, he has built a wall of defensiveness around himself, and has seemed not to care any more whether people loved him or hated him. It is as though he was saying, 'You *ought* still to love me, because I have been true to my Uranian principles. If you don't love me, that must be because you are so dull, so boring, so un-Uranian, that you can't see me for who I am. So I don't care whether you love me'."

VE–4–UR is also involved in a cluster of (VE–4–UR)–20/10–PL, showing that Blair is motivated to support his 'search for a thrilling beauty' by creating Plutonian structures and systems; and, in addition, there are a number of other Fiveness patterns which show that Fiveness is very important in Blair's personality – especially SO–20–MA, which shows that Blair strives to find forceful (Martian) ways of expressing himself in the world and of imposing his will upon others. Many people have commented that Blair is essentially an *actor*, greatly concerned with self-presentation, and having many skills that enable him to present himself in a favourable light. These are very much the skills of Fiveness.

And I feel that these aspects are related to Blair's addiction to 'spin' (the weaving of stories around events which deflect people's attention from the true nature of those events), and in particular to the way in which he misled Parliament into believing that there was firm evidence of Saddam Hussein's "weapons of mass destruction".

Finally, I will mention <u>MA</u>-14-PL, which gains strength from Mars's position on the Ascendant, and is very nearly close enough to be regarded as 'very close': thus, it is the strongest Sevenness aspect in Blair's chart. This aspect suggests that Blair is inspired by programmes of action that are ruthless, hard and uncompromising: or, to put it more bluntly, that he is inspired by the idea of war.

The invasion of Iraq was the climactic event in Tony Blair's career, and was very much his personal responsibility. Whereas in the USA, for Bush, Cheney, Rumsfeld and others, the invasion was the culmination of a policy which they had collectively developed over many years, in Britain it was Tony Blair who, single-handedly and impulsively, drew his country into the war, in spite of the two million people who had demonstrated against it. I believe that Blair's harmonic aspects give many indications of why Blair was motivated to do this, and of how he was able to carry it out successfully.

Gordon Brown

Born 20 February 1951, 08.40 (+00.00)
Giffnock, Scotland (55N48. 4W20).
Source: Birth certificate, via Pulsar collection (ADB). RR: AA.[2]

1:    MO–<u>1</u>–PL
      (VE–<u>1</u>–MA)–1–JU

2:    ME–<u>2</u>–PL
      (SA–<u>4</u>–<u>CH</u>)–<u>8</u>–ME
      VE–<u>32</u>–<u>UR</u>
      JU–<u>32</u>–<u>NE</u>

3:    ((SA–<u>4</u>–<u>CH</u>)–<u>8</u>–ME)–<u>12</u>/<u>6</u>/24–SO
      ((ME–<u>8</u>–SA)–24/<u>12</u>–SO)–12/24/<u>24</u>–JU
      MO–<u>18</u>–JU
      VE–<u>27</u>–JU
      <u>NE</u>–<u>6</u>–PL

5:    (SO–**12**–SA)–**20**/15–MO
      SO–25–ME
      ME–10–MA
      VE–**5**–PL
      (SA–**4**–CH)–20/**5**–NE

7:    ((VE–**1**–MA)–7/**7**–UR)–**7**/7/**7**–NE
      (MA–**7**–UR)–**21**/21–SA

11:   MO–22–JU

13:   SO–**26**–UR
      MO–**13**–VE–**13**–CH

17:   SA–17–PL

19:   ME–19–VE
      PL–19–CH

29:   MO–**29**–UR
      JU–29–CH

31:   SO–31–VE
      ME–**31**–UR
      MA–**31**–CH

Gordon Brown was Tony Blair's Chancellor of the Exchequer for ten years, and then succeeded him as Prime Minister. Brown is famous for his violent temper; for his difficulty in communicating effectively with the public, especially on television; and for his long-running feud with Tony Blair, who, he believed, had repeatedly promised him that he would stand down as Prime Minister and let Brown take over, and repeatedly broken his promise. On the positive side, he is generally reckoned to have acted decisively and effectively during the economic crisis of 2008, and to have played a major part in saving the world from a much more severe recession.

Rather surprisingly, Brown has Venus very closely conjunct Mars. One would expect this to signify great personal magnetism and charm, and indeed it is said that Brown can convey these qualities in private, though it does not fit in with his public persona. The only links which VE–**1**–MA has with other planets are Sevenness links: ((VE–**1**–MA)–

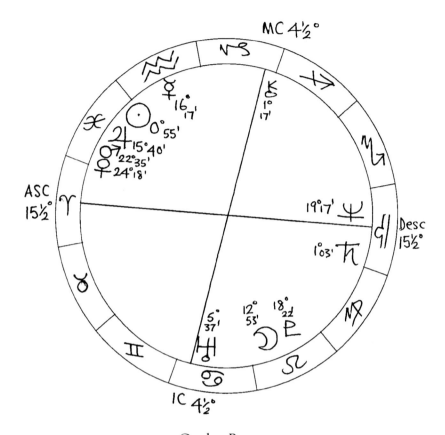

Gordon Brown

7/**7**–U**R**)–**7**/7/**7**–NE, showing that it is linked to Uranus on the I.C. and Neptune on the Descendant. Also Mars has Sevenness links with Saturn: (MA–**7**–U**R**)–**21**/21–SA. These Sevenness links show Brown as an idealist. He is inspired by a vision of a better future for mankind (Neptune descending); he believes that his own background gives him unique qualities which help him to implement his vision (Uranus on the I.C.); he can work towards these goals in a way which is disciplined but not repressive (because the Sevenness links to Saturn contain Threeness, not Twoness); and he is able to inspire others by his vision (VE–**1**–MA). These links say a great deal about how Brown was able to rise to the top in politics, and to be widely regarded as a politician of exceptional ability.

So why is it that Brown is generally thought to have been a failure as Prime Minister, and to have lost an election mainly because of his own personal inadequacies? To understand this, we must look at other aspects. These aspects tell a complex story, which we will try to unravel.

Firstly, there is a very tight cluster of Twoness: (SA–4–CH)–8–ME, with Chiron close to the Midheaven, and with Mercury also –2–Pluto. SA–4–CH shows that Brown feels that Saturnian obstacles are continually being put in the way of his goal of becoming a 'healer' for mankind, and (SA–4–CH)–8–ME shows that he thinks about this obsessively, believing that there must be a rational way of getting rid of the obstacles. ME–2–PL increases the single-mindedness of this obsession; but also, because it is an opposition, Brown will tend to project Pluto onto other people and to believe that they are 'out to get him'. Thus, these aspects contain the seeds of paranoia. There is a huge amount of tension wrapped up in this pattern, and I feel that it is the main indicator of Brown's tendency to lose his temper with anyone who he feels is getting in his way.

(SA–4–CH)–8–ME is also linked in with the Sun: ((SA–4–CH)–8–ME)–12/6/24–SO. This greatly increases Brown's personal involvement with these issues and makes it hard for him to view them objectively. We saw earlier that Tony Blair has SO–12–VE, showing that he greatly desires to be loved. Gordon Brown, on the other hand, has SO–12–SA. What Brown desires is not love but respect. Just as Blair feels pain when he is not loved, Brown feels pain when he is not respected.

SO–12–SA also has Fiveness links with the Moon: (SO–12–SA)–20/15–MO. This is a difficult cluster to interpret as it spreads across three prime numbers (Two, Three and Five). However, it contains the aspect SO–20–MO, and Sun-Moon aspects are important in describing the core of a person's personality, his basic way of being in the world and of relating to other people. The number Twenty (5 x 2 x 2) is about struggling to find a style. Thus, SO–20–MO shows that Brown finds it hard to relate to people easily and naturally. In an unfamiliar situation, he will struggle to find an appropriate way of behaving, and sometimes he may get it wrong. This helps to explain the awkwardness of Brown's behaviour during public performances, smiling at the wrong times or in the wrong way, and generally giving an impression of insincerity and of lack of warmth. And the links to Saturn show that this is very much bound up with his search for respect. He tries so hard to win people's respect, and he keeps on getting it wrong.

Brown also has other important Fiveness aspects. VE–_5_–PL is almost exact, and gives Brown a love of the Plutonian qualities of dedication and single-mindedness; and ME–_10_–MA helps him to convey his thoughts in an aggressive, forthright style. These, I believe, are positive aspects, which will have helped Brown to be a decisive and innovative Chancellor and to 'hold his own' against Tony Blair despite the latter's greater power and superior people-skills.

But also, Brown has an _exact_ NE–_5_–CH (with Neptune on the Descendant and Chiron on the Midheaven), which is tied in with the SA–_4_–CH that we have already discussed: (SA–_4_–CH)–20/_5_–NE. NE–_5_–CH shows the intensity of Brown's idealism: he really believes that he has the capacity to 'heal' the world, and that it is his destiny to do so: but he is continually thwarted by the machinations of Saturn.

Like Tony Blair, Brown also has a strong Thirteenness pattern: SO–_26_–UR (whereas Blair had SO–_26_–JU) and also MO–_13_–VE–_13_–CH. I believe this helps to explain the difficult relationship between Blair and Brown. Thirteenness people tend not to be good at stable relationships: they are too much wrapped up in themselves, too preoccupied with their own personal journey. (Blair called his autobiography A Journey, which is in keeping with the spirit of Thirteenness.) Probably, when two Thirteenness people meet each other, they find it particularly difficult to maintain an amicable relationship, since each resents the other's self-absorption.

Finally, Gordon Brown (like both Margaret Thatcher and Tony Blair) has a large number of close links in the higher prime numbers (Seventeen, Nineteen, Twenty-nine, Thirty-one). All three of these Prime Ministers were highly unusual characters, with characteristics that set them apart from other people and caused them, in their different ways, to tread a lonely path.

Adolf Hitler

Born 20 April 1889, 18.30 (–00.52)
Braunau am Inn, Austria (48N15. 13E02).
Source: From church records, via Heinz Noesselt (ADB). RR: AA.

1:    <u>SO</u>–1–<u>ME</u>
      MO–**1**–JU
      VE–**1**–MA
      NE–1–PL

2:    (MO–**1**–JU)–2/**2**–CH
      (<u>UR</u>–**8**–PL)–<u>32</u>/**32**/32/32–(<u>SO</u>–**16**–JU)

3:    <u>SO</u>–**12**–NE

5:    ((((MO–**1**–JU)–2/**2**–CH)–**5**/5/10–NE)–**5**/5/10/5–SA)–
      10/<u>10</u>/**5**/10/<u>10</u>–<u>ME</u>
      (VE–**1**–MA)–25/<u>25</u>/**25**/<u>25</u>–(MO–**5**–NE)
      (MO–**5**–NE)–**5**–SA)–25/<u>25</u>/25–VE
      (VE–**1**–MA)–**20**/20–PL

7:    (<u>SO</u>–**7**–SA)–21/<u>21</u>–PL
      MO–**14**–<u>UR</u>
      ((VE–**1**–MA)–**7**/7–CH)–7–<u>UR</u>
      (VE–**1**–MA)–**14**/<u>7</u>/14/**7**–(JU–**2**–CH)

11:   PL–<u>11</u>–CH

13:   <u>UR</u>–13–NE

17:   MO–<u>17</u>–PL
      <u>ME</u>–<u>17</u>–VE

23:   (VE–**1**–MA)–<u>23</u>/**23**–SO

29:   <u>ME</u>–**29**–<u>UR</u>
      (VE–**1**–MA)–<u>29</u>–SA

Adolf Hitler's chart is remarkable for its strength in Twoness, Fiveness and Sevenness, and also for its almost total lack of Threeness. Hitler was definitely *not* someone whose aim in life was to relax and follow the pleasure principle.

He has two very close conjunctions, VE–**1**–MA and MO–**1**–JU. We saw VE–**1**–MA also in the chart of Gordon Brown, but in Hitler's case it is even closer to exactitude and indicates the very great personal magnetism which Hitler had (in spite of his unprepossessing appearance). MO–**1**–JU (if we interpret it negatively, as we must in the case of Hitler)

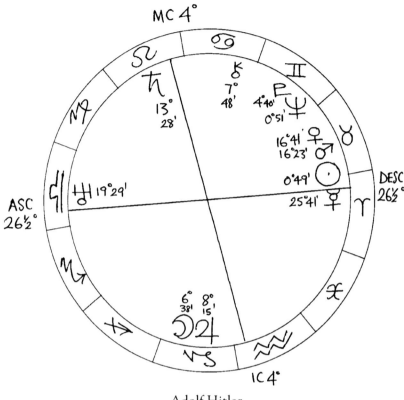

Adolf Hitler

indicates a tendency to respond to events in an overblown way, with exaggerated displays of emotion.

When we turn to Twoness, we see that MO–**1**–JU is closely opposite Chiron: (MO–**1**–JU)–2/2–CH. If Hitler projects Chiron onto other people (as usually happens with the opposition), then he becomes the person who is responding strongly against other people's attempts to 'heal' him – or, in other words, against the 'establishment' which thinks it knows what is best for people. This is a template for right-wing extremism, and we can see in it the roots of Hitler's personal philosophy as expressed in his book *Mein Kampf* ('My Struggle'). It would seem that Hitler projected Chiron especially onto the Jews, of whom he developed a passionate hatred.

At the Twoness level there is also a complex pattern: (UR–**8**–PL)–32/**32**/32/32–(SO–**16**–JU). This configuration at the higher (or deeper) levels of Twoness shows a struggle that is going on deep within Hitler's psyche. He needs to find ways of expressing himself that involve Jupiter, Uranus and Pluto. This particular combination of planets (lacking in the restraining influence of Saturn and the softening effect of Neptune) contains the seeds of violence and of ultra-dramatic, flamboyant behaviour. And it is a characteristic of Twoness that satisfaction is never achieved: no matter how much success is gained, one still needs more.

Alice Miller portrays Hitler as permanently damaged by the brutal treatment he had received from his father as a child. He had been beaten every day, and had lived "in a hell of continual fear and severe trauma".[3] As an adult he would wake in the night with "convulsive shrieks," shaking with fear, and with sweat streaming down his face.[4] All this was the expression of the unresolved Twoness within Hitler's psyche, at the heart of which is UR–8–PL: the feeling that, the more he expresses his own individuality (Uranus rising), the more he will be ruthlessly punished. This is the hidden side of Hitler, of which the public was unaware: but it clearly had its effect on the brutal nature of the Nazi regime.

The only Threeness aspect in Hitler's chart is SO–12–NE, but it contains more Twoness than Threeness, since 12 is 3 x 2 x 2. We saw that Tony Blair had SO–12–VE, and longed to be loved, and that Gordon Brown had SO–12–SA, and longed to be respected. Hitler had SO–12–NE, so perhaps we can say that he longed to be revered.

The pattern of Fiveness in Hitler's chart is one of the strongest that I have seen. Although, in the list of Hitler's harmonic aspects, it appears as four separate clusters, it is in reality one single complex cluster, which brings the two conjunctions of VE–1–MA and MO–1–JU together with each other, and involves also Mercury, Saturn, Neptune, Pluto and Chiron. Thus, Sun and Uranus are the only two planets that are not involved in this massive configuration of Fiveness. Fiveness is about creating and building, and this pattern shows Hitler as the chief creator and architect of the Nazi regime, which was one of the most tightly-controlled and all-embracing regimes in history, determining the ways in which people were expected to think and behave. The nature of the regime is perhaps most clearly shown by the planets that are not involved. Sun and Uranus are about expressing one's individuality and being free to behave in eccentric and unpredictable ways; but such behaviour was stamped on by the regime, which expected everyone to act as loyal servants of the Führer.

Hitler's Fiveness will also have enabled him to build up his own public image, and especially his skill as an orator. We can note especially ME–**5**–CH (with Mercury on the Descendant). However, Hitler would not have been able to exercise such a hold over the German people if he had not also been strong in Sevenness, which introduces the element of *inspiration*. The chart contains three strong Sevenness links:

Firstly, (SO–**7**–SA)–21/21–PL. SO–**7**–SA shows that Hitler felt himself to be marked out by destiny, fated to subordinate his own personal welfare to that of his people; and –21/21–PL reinforces this by introducing the Plutonian quality of single-minded devotion to duty. These aspects will have helped Hitler to inspire the German people and to persuade them to accept him as a leader who was worthy of their devotion because of his own devotion to their welfare.

Secondly, MO–**14**–UR is perhaps the strongest indicator of Hitler's skill as an orator, able to whip up strong emotions by the passionate and electrifying delivery of his speeches.

Thirdly, the complex pattern of Sevenness aspects linking VE–**1**–MA to Jupiter, Uranus and Chiron greatly reinforces Hitler's personal magnetism and his ability to inspire others. We must remember that Sevenness is about the search for hidden meanings and the desire to escape from the humdrumness and meaninglessness of everyday life. Hitler was devoted to the music of Wagner, which for him symbolized the greater glory to which the German people could aspire. He was able to inspire others by this vision, and so dispel the sense of gloom and cynicism which had descended on the nation as a result of defeat in the First World War and severe economic hardship. In other circumstances this visionary quality could have been a force for good; but in Hitler's case it was tainted by the negative factors that we have already mentioned, and led to the ruthless suppression of all those who were deemed to be 'outside the dream' – not only the Jews, but other dissident minorities, and also the inhabitants of the other countries which Hitler invaded and subjugated.

There are other aspects in the higher harmonic numbers which help to complete the picture, but essentially it is Hitler's strength in Twoness,

Fiveness and Sevenness which made him an exceptional person who was able to change the course of history.

Fred West
Born 29 September 1941, 08.30 (–01.00)
Much Marcle, England (52N02. 2W25).
Source: From *Fred and Rose* by Howard Sounes, p.13, via F.C. Clifford (ADB). RR: B.

1:    SA–<u>1</u>–UR
      PL–<u>1</u>–CH

2:    (<u>MO</u>–<u>16</u>–VE)–<u>32</u>/32/32/<u>32</u>–(SA–<u>16</u>–PL)
      (JU–8–PL)–16/<u>16</u>–SA

3:    SO–<u>6</u>–PL
      <u>MO</u>–<u>27</u>–JU
      (SA–<u>1</u>–UR)–<u>3</u>/3–NE
      (SA–<u>3</u>–NE)–3–<u>MO</u>
      ME–<u>18</u>–CH
      <u>MA</u>–<u>9</u>–UR
      <u>MA</u>–24–PL

5:    (SA–<u>1</u>–UR)–<u>5</u>–CH
      ME–<u>25</u>–JU

7:    SO–<u>14</u>–ME
      <u>MO</u>–<u>21</u>–<u>MA</u>
      ME–<u>21</u>–PL
      VE–<u>7</u>–<u>MA</u>
      UR–<u>7</u>–PL

11:   <u>MO</u>–11–CH
      VE–<u>22</u>–NE
      UR–<u>11</u>–PL

13:   <u>MO</u>–13–ME
      VE–<u>13</u>–UR
      <u>MA</u>–13–CH

17:   ME–<u>17</u>–<u>MA</u>
      JU–<u>17</u>–UR

19:   MA–19–SA

23:   ME–**23**–VE

31:   (SO–**31**–JU)–31–SA
           ME–**31**–UR
           NE–31–CH

Fred West was charged with the murders of eleven women, including his first wife Rena, his daughter Heather, and his stepdaughter Charmaine. In nine of the murders his second wife Rosemary (whose birthtime is unknown) was an accomplice. Fred and Rosemary together would lure women into their car and take them to their house in Gloucester, where the women were sexually abused, tortured and butchered. Rosemary also worked as a prostitute, and Fred would listen in through the intercom that he had wired into her room. Their secret was discovered when workers who were clearing blocked drains found pieces of human bodies. In prison awaiting trial, Fred hanged himself on 1st January 1995, leaving Rosemary to face trial on her own.

Rather than analysing Fred West's chart as a whole, I will focus on the question: What clues can we find in the harmonic aspects that helps to explain his appalling behaviour?

Perhaps the strongest clue lies in the fact that the only two very close aspects to West's Sun are SO–**31**–JU and SO–**6**–PL. Very close aspects to the Sun are always important, since the Sun is about self-fulfilment, and so these aspects show what the person most strongly feels that he needs to do in order to fulfil his potential. (It could be argued that an analysis of harmonic aspects should always start by listing these very close aspects to the Sun.)

SO–**31**–JU is an exact aspect, and so is very powerful. We have seen that Thirty-oneness is about bringing to the surface, and giving expression to, the deeper and darker desires of what Freud calls the "id". Fred West seems to have been totally in thrall to these desires, and to have devoted his life to expressing them in an uninhibited, extravagant, Jupiterian way. This is reinforced by ME–**31**–UR, showing how he was also disposed to thinking about (and perhaps glorying in) the shockingness of his own actions.

SO–**6**–PL shows that West sought pleasure through ruthless

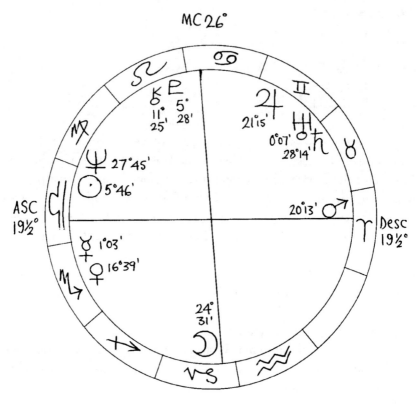

Fred West

uncompromising Plutonian actions. We can see in this aspect why West felt compelled to carry his obsessions through to their ultimate conclusion. Sixness is about seeking pleasure, and West (who in photographs always has a cheery smile on his face) seems to have had no motive for torturing and killing other than personal enjoyment.

Another clue lies in MO–21–MA (linked also to VE–7–MA). Moon and Mars are the only two angular planets in West's chart (with Moon very close to the I.C. and Mars very close to the Descendant). Moon-Mars links are about impulsive action in response to feelings, and MO–21–MA shows that West found inspiration and enjoyment (21 = 7 x 3) from acting out his feelings in an aggressive Martian way. Coupled with the other aspects that we have mentioned, this helps to explain why West was even able to kill his own daughter Heather when she offended him by showing signs of rebelliousness.

Finally, we can mention the complex pattern of Twoness in West's chart – <u>MO</u>–<u>16</u>–VE)–**32**/32/32/**32**–(SA–<u>16</u>–PL) – which is similar to the pattern of Twoness that we found in the chart of Adolf Hitler. It seems that this kind of configuration, bringing together several planets at the deeper levels of Twoness (16 and 32), is indicative of a complex and unresolved struggle deep within the psyche. <u>MO</u>–<u>16</u>–VE is about the struggle to respond to people tenderly and lovingly, and SA–<u>16</u>–PL is about the struggle to control and discipline the fanaticism of Pluto; but the –32– aspects show that these two struggles are themselves in conflict with each other, perhaps leading West to kill that which he loved, and to love that which he killed.

We can speculate that this pattern of deep inner Twoness is related to West's inability to empathize with the suffering of his victims: for him they were just objects to be used for his pleasure. Twoness is about drawing a sharp boundary between Self and Other: people who are classified as Other become non-persons, as the Jews were for Hitler and as his victims were for West. Also we can note that both Hitler and West killed themselves when they realized that they would have to face trial: they could not bear the thought of the tables being turned, and of being used and condemned by others as they themselves had used and condemned.

All these aspects taken together help to explain West's actions, but we need to remind ourselves that astrology is not the only factor influencing people's behaviour. West himself was sexually abused as a child, and it seems that he had never known an environment in which people behaved caringly to one another and were able to control their violent impulses. If West had been born with the same chart but in a different environment, he probably would not have become a serial killer. The tendencies shown in the chart would still have been there, but he would have found less harmful ways of expressing them.

Prince Charles
Born 14 November 1948, 21.14 (+00.00)
London, England (51N30. 0W10).
Source: From news reports, via Judith Gee (ADB). RR: A.

1:    _VE_–1–_NE_

2:    JU–**2**–UR
       (ME–8–MA)–16/16/16/16–(_NE_–**8**–CH)

3:    (JU–**2**–UR)–**3**/**6**–MO
       (MO–**3**–JU)–27/27–ME
       (_VE_–**6**–PL)–18/**9**–ME
       _VE_–27–UR
       MA–27–_NE_
       JU–**27**–PL

5:    (_VE_–**6**–PL)–**10**/**15**–SO
       (MO–25–MA)–25–SO
       _NE_–**25**–PL

7:    (SO–**14**–SA)–28–_NE_
       PL–**7**–CH

11:   MO–**11**–_NE_
       (JU–**2**–UR)–**22**/**11**–SA

13:   (MO–13–_VE_)–**26**/26–SA
       MA–26–PL
       SA–13–CH

17:   MO–17–PL
       (ME–**17**–UR)–17–(_VE_–**17**–CH)

19:   (JU–**19**–_NE_)–19–SO
       MO–**19**–CH
       SA–19–PL

23:   SO–23–ME
       JU–**23**–CH

29:   UR–29–CH

31:   UR–31–PL

Prince Charles has _VE_–**1**–_NE_ close to the I.C., showing that he is a person of very great sensitivity, artistic rather than practical, seeking an idealized beauty. However, the strongest aspects to his Sun are SO–**10**–

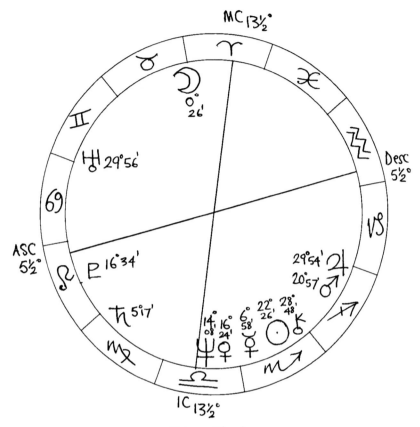

Prince Charles

<u>VE</u>, SO–**15**–PL, and SO–**14**–ME. The first two of these are conjoined in the cluster (<u>VE</u>–**6**–PL)–**10/15**–SO.

SO–**10**–<u>VE</u> is an aspect that I can easily relate to, as I have it also in my own chart. I see it as being about the need to find self-fulfilment by creating an ordered beauty. In my own case I realize that I am acting out this aspect by writing this book, and in particular by finding ways of presenting the complexities of the chart in a structured, orderly and (I hope) attractive way. In Charles's case, he acts it out by the intense care he puts into managing his garden at Highgrove, creating an ordered and manageable beauty out of the chaos of nature, and also into the building of his 'ideal community' at Poundbury, creating an environment in which he hopes that people will live ordered and peaceful lives. But, for

Charles, this aspect is linked to SO–**15**–PL, showing that he also enjoys finding orderly ways of expressing himself with Plutonian force and ruthlessness. We can see this in his fulminations against 'bad' architecture – that is, architecture which, in his view, destroys the ordered beauty of its surroundings. And in fact he has become famous for what his critics regard as 'meddling', writing angry letters to Government ministers demanding action on one topic or another. All this is an expression of SO–**15**–PL.

In this connection we can note also Charles's strong pattern of Seventeenness: (ME–**17**–UR)–17–(VE–**17**–CH), in addition to MO–17–PL. We have seen that people who are strong in Seventeenness tend to be campaigners on behalf of causes, trying to put the world to rights. Charles's commitment to the green movement, and his work on behalf of unemployed people through the Prince's Trust, are very much in the spirit of Seventeenness.

However, SO–**10**–VE and SO–**15**–PL will not have served Charles well in his relationship with his first wife Diana. With VE–1–NE he will initially have been naïve and gullible, seeing Diana through rosy spectacles and not seeing her for who she really was. He will have hoped and expected that she would meekly fit in to his own ordered world – an order partly created by himself, and partly consisting of all the rules and customs that govern the behaviour of the royal family. When he found out that she was unable or unwilling to do this, that she needed to break the rules or to make her own rules, and that she needed his help and support in ways that were entirely unfamiliar to him, Charles had no idea how to cope.

The other very close Sun-aspect in Charles's chart is SO–**14**–SA. In the royal family, Saturn appears to signify the burden of royalty: Charles' mother the Queen has Saturn on the Midheaven, signifying her commitment to carrying out her duties in the role which has been assigned to her. Charles does not have Saturn in such an exalted position, but SO–**14**–SA shows that the burden of being royal is nevertheless an inspiration to him. Sevenness aspects between Sun and Saturn seem to mean that the person sees himself as a tragic figure, and I believe that secretly this is how Charles sees himself. He feels weighed down by the expectations that are placed upon him as a king-in-waiting and his inability to break free of his role, and yet he feels inspired by the magnitude of his responsibilities. He has probably steeped himself in the (often tragic) stories of his royal predecessors, and strives to be a worthy recipient of their inheritance. During the period when his own popularity was eclipsed by that of Diana and he was widely hated for his treatment of her, this sense of the tragedy of his own life was probably at its most intense.

Charles's chart also contains an almost exact Jupiter-Uranus opposition (JU–**2**–UR). Twoness links between Jupiter and Uranus seem to be common in the royal family: Charles's father Philip also has JU–2–UR, and his brother Edward has JU–**8**–UR. I feel that Jupiter (like Saturn but in a different way) is an indicator of royalty. Royalty brings duties and obligations, but it also brings immense wealth and fame and the opportunity to live life on a grand scale: but this opportunity to be flamboyantly royal can easily conflict with the Uranian desire to be true to oneself, to be original and experimental and unpredictable. I feel that Charles is constantly trying to find the right balance between these two directions. On the one hand he wants to make the most of his opportunity to live opulently as a royal prince, but on the other hand he wants to break all the rules and just be himself.

However, there are two clusters which reduce the tension of this opposition and make it more bearable for him: (JU–**2**–UR)–**3/6**–MO, and (JU–**2**–UR)–**22/11**–SA. The Threeness links to the Moon show that Charles actually enjoys dealing with the challenges which the opposition presents for him, choosing sometimes to follow the impulses of Jupiter and sometimes those of Uranus, but able to be flexible around this. And the Elevenness links to Saturn (coupled also with MO–**11**–NE) show that Charles also has within him an Elevenness quality of doggedness: the ability to stick resolutely to his chosen path, in spite of all the pain and unpopularity that this may bring him. (These two clusters, suggesting on the one hand flexibility and on the other hand inflexibility, may seem to conflict with each other: but life is full of these contradictions.)

We can also mention Charles's strength in Nineteenness – (JU–**19**–NE)–19–SO, and also MO–**19**–CH and SA–**19**–PL – which shows that there is a side of Charles that would like to retire from the world and live a solitary life in communion with nature; and finally, we can mention

SO–23–ME, which shows Charles as a dreamer of dreams and a spinner of fantasies (he has written a storybook for children).

Princess Diana
Born 1 July 1961, 19.45 (–01.00)
Sandringham, England (52N50. 0E30).
Source: From her mother, via Charles Harvey (ADB). RR: A.

1:   MA–1–PL

2:   ((MO–2–UR)–4–VE)–8/8/8–SO
        (PL–2–CH)–32/32/32/32–(SO–8–MO)
        MA–32–SA

3:   (SO–3–NE)–3–CH
        (MO–27–MA)–27–NE
        MO–18–JU

5:   SO–20–SA
        JU–20–UR
        JU–25–NE

7:   (SO–7–JU)–7/7–MA
        (MO–4–VE)–14/28–ME
        (SA–7–UR)–7–ME
        (PL–2–CH)–28/28/28/28–(SA–7–UR)

17:   ME–17–JU

23:   (NE–23–PL)–23–ME
        VE–23–JU–23–CH

29:   (JU–29–PL)–29–UR

I will not go into great detail about Princess Diana's chart, which has already been very extensively discussed by astrologers. My aim here is simply to show that the harmonic aspects can yield some additional and valuable insights.

The most important cluster in Diana's chart is ((MO–2–UR)–4–VE)–8/8/8–SO. This shows that Diana was engaged in a lifelong struggle to find herself (SO–8–MO), to find love (SO–8–VE and MO–4–VE), and to find her own uniqueness and originality (SO–8–UR, MO–2–UR,

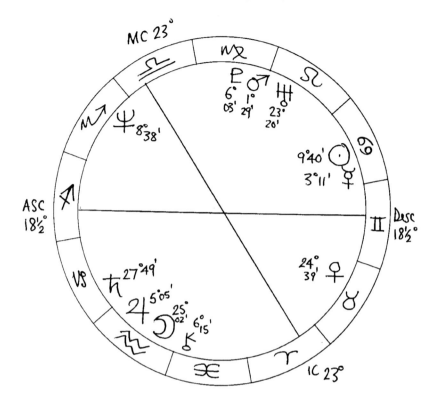

Princess Diana

and VE–4–UR). Central to this pattern is MO–2–UR, showing that at the instinctive emotional level Diana felt that other people were always trying to obstruct or deny her individuality. And central to it also is the need to be loved – and not only to be loved, but to find beauty and harmony in her life. The pure Twoness of this pattern suggests that the struggle could never be completely resolved: despite the huge adulation that she received from the public, Diana was still unsure about her lovability, and the pain of feeling unloved by her husband never left her.

Also there is PL–2–CH: a struggle between Pluto as the fighter (note also MA–1–PL) and Chiron as the healer. This represents a dilemma in Diana's public life: is she the one who fights resolutely against the system, not flinching from hurting people when necessary, or is she the one who reaches out to heal wounds and to give consolation to people in their suffering? Well, she was both (sometimes both at the same time), but PL–2–CH suggests that this was always a dilemma for her. And PL–2–CH has Thirty-twoness links to SO–8–MO, suggesting that this dilemma was linked to the central question "Who am I?", and to Diana's efforts to find herself by finding a role in the world.

Nevertheless, at another level Diana did deeply believe in herself, as is shown by her strong pattern of Sevenness. (SO–7–JU)–7/7–MA shows that, at the inspirational level she believed in herself as a bringer of Jupiterian hope, optimism and freedom, and also in her ability to change the world by charismatic Martian action. (There is a strong contrast between Diana's SO–7–JU and Charles's SO–14–SA, and I would suggest that this was a major cause of their incompatibility.)

(MO–4–VE)–14/28–ME shows that Diana was prone to thinking and communicating in an inspirational way about her own search for love. We can see the effects of this in the famous photograph of Diana sitting alone in front of the Taj Mahal, and also in the televised interview with Martin Bashir in which she inspired the nation by the story of her suffering in her marriage.

And then also there is SA–7–UR, which is linked by –28– aspects to PL–2–CH which we have already mentioned. SA–7–UR suggests that Diana saw herself as a unique and tragic figure: and this is how she is now perceived by the public, partly as a result of her untimely death, of which she may have had some presentiment.

At the Fiveness level Diana's strongest aspect is SO–20–SA, which indicates her unsuccessful struggle to fit into the rules and customs of the family into which she married (Saturn as the indicator of the burden of royalty, as we discussed in the case of Prince Charles).

Finally I would like to mention Diana's strength in Twenty-threeness, which shows her as a spinner of stories and fantasies. At this level Diana has two separate clusters: (NE–23–PL)–23–ME and VE–23–JU–23–CH, linked respectively to the two poles of the Pluto-Chiron opposition. This suggests that Diana's own story has given rise to two separate fairytales, both of which have exercised a hold on the public imagination. One is a Mercury-Neptune-Pluto story, about the brave woman who by ruthless communication was able to destroy the mystique of royalty and create her own mystique. And the other is a Venus-Jupiter-Chiron story, about the fairytale princess who, through her beauty and her openness and optimism, was able to heal people's wounds and alleviate their suffering.

Alain Vareille

Born 3 May 1956, 07.45 (–01.00)
Versailles, France (48N48. 2E08).
Source: Birth certificate, via Petitallot (ADB). RR: AA.

1:    (MA–**1**–CH)–1–<u>MO</u>
      <u>JU</u>–1–<u>PL</u>

2:    ((MA–**1**–CH)–4–SO)–**8/8**/8–<u>VE</u>
      ((MA–**1**–CH)–**8**–<u>VE</u>)–16–ME
      ME–2–SA
      UR–**4**–NE

3:    <u>VE</u>–6–<u>PL</u>
      <u>JU</u>–27–NE

5:    ((MA–**1**–CH)–4–SO)–5/**5**/**20**–SA
      ME–**5**–NE

7:    SO–7–<u>PL</u>
      <u>VE</u>–**7**–SA
      ((MA–**1**–CH)–**7**–NE)–<u>28</u>/28/**4**–UR

11:   (<u>MO</u>–11–UR)–11–<u>VE</u>

13:   SO–13–NE
      (ME–13–UR)–13/<u>13</u>–<u>PL</u>

17:   <u>MO</u>–**17**–NE
      (MA–**1**–CH)–<u>17</u>/17–<u>JU</u>

19:   SO–**19**–UR
      SA–**19**–<u>PL</u>

23:   ME–**23**–JU
      NE–**23**–<u>PL</u>

31:   <u>JU</u>–**31**–UR

I am including Alain Vareille among these case-studies because I feel that an astrologer with knowledge of harmonic aspects might have been

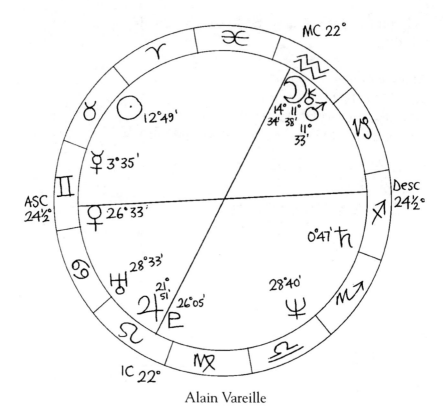

Alain Vareille

able to help him, and might even have helped to avert the tragic actions for which he was responsible.

I know nothing about Alain Vareille except what is stated in his AstroDatabank biography, which reads as follows:

> "French engineer and head of a firm founded by his dad. On the morning of 12 September 1987 he shot and killed his two kids on an Atlantic beach. He drove to his home at Bougival where he shot his pregnant wife Carole in her sleep and put her corpse in the trunk of his car where he had the children. He was sentenced on 24 November 1989 to 20 years prison. After many attempts to commit suicide, he escaped on 16 July 1995. He went to the graves of his family where he shot himself through the head, 20 July 1995, 2.30 p.m. MEDT, La Teste de Buch, France."

This account contains no mention of why Vareille felt compelled to kill his family. However, in the notes below this account, AstroDatabank does give a clue. Next to "shot his two kids" there is a note: "Hardship – Little money". From this we can perhaps deduce that the business which Vareille had inherited from his father had failed, and that Vareille had no idea how he could continue to provide financially for his wife and two (shortly to be three) children. Also he was perhaps overwhelmed with guilt about his failure to sustain the business which his father had successfully founded.

Looking at Vareille's chart, we can note, first of all, that the chart (like Adolf Hitler's) is deficient in Threeness. The light-hearted, pleasure-seeking approach to life, which is typified by Threeness, does not come easily to Vareille. He is a person who takes life very seriously.

Perhaps the most important aspect is MA–1–CH, which is almost exact (orb 00° 05'). Chiron is about the urge to help and heal people, but for Vareille it is united with Mars, which is about taking aggressive and forceful action. So Vareille knows no way to help people except by forceful action; and (MA–1–CH)–1–MO (with Moon close to the Midheaven) shows that he is easily spurred into such action in response to events that affect him emotionally.

MA–1–CH has a number of harmonic links with other planets. First, at the Twoness level, we have (MA–1–CH)–4–SO, showing that for Vareille the ability to act out MA–1–CH is bound up with his sense of his self-worth. SO–4–MA is (for men) about the need to prove to the world one's manliness and virility. If Vareille fails to solve problems by means of aggressive action, he feels that he has failed as a man.

And, even more strongly, we have (MA–1–CH)–8–VE. (Venus is on the Ascendant, so Vareille must have come across as a loving and caring person, and it seems likely that he loved his wife and children dearly.) VE–8–MA is completely exact (orb 00° 00') and so is extremely powerful. It shows a deep-seated struggle between the Venus desire for love and tenderness and the Mars desire for virility and power. Because it is a Twoness aspect, Vareille is always struggling to find *actions* which will reconcile Venus with Mars (and also with Chiron). There could scarcely be a stronger indication of the impulse to kill those whom he loved in the belief that this was the only way to 'rescue' them from extreme financial hardship.

Next, we can look at the Sevenness aspects, where we see that MA–1–CH has a very close Sevenness link to Neptune: (MA–1–CH)–7–NE.

The downside of Sevenness is that it can cause one to lose touch with reality and to get lost in a world of fantasies and delusions, and this is perhaps especially true when Neptune is involved. Thus, (MA–**1**–CH)–**7**–NE will further increase Vareille's tendency to take wild impulsive actions in the false belief that by doing so he is working towards some higher goal. And Uranus too is involved in the Sevenness pattern: ((MA–**1**–CH)–**7**–NE)–28/28/**4**–UR. So Vareille's Mars-Chiron actions will tend also to have Uranian qualities: sharp, decisive, original and shocking.

There are also two other Sevenness links: SO–**7**–PL, which (I believe) shows that Vareille was inspired by the idea of self-punishment, almost as though he felt that by killing his family he was punishing himself for his own failings; and VE–**7**–SA, which seems to show that he was somehow drawn towards grief and loss, needing to kill his loved ones so that he could grieve for them. Taken together with (MA–**1**–CH)–**7**–NE, this adds up to a large amount of Sevenness, showing that Vareille was very much a Sevenness person, ruled by the heart rather than the head.

We can also (though I think this is less important) mention (MA–**1**–CH)–**17**/17–JU. Jupiter (together with Pluto) is on the I.C., and may represent the qualities which Vareille feels he has inherited (or should have inherited) from his father. Seventeenness is to do with rebellious anger, and so it seems that Vareille's Mars-Chiron actions are also infused with this rebellious spirit. Is this rebellion against the father, or is it Vareille trying to emulate the father's own rebellious spirit? We cannot know, but we could question Vareille about this if we were talking to him.

Thus we can see that, simply by looking at MA–**1**–CH and the harmonic aspects linked to it, we can gain an understanding of why Vareille felt impelled to kill his family. Of course there are other aspects which would give us a more rounded picture of Vareille's personality: among them ME–**2**–SA, VE–**6**–PL, ME–**5**–NE, SO–**13**–NE, SO–**19**–UR, and ME–**23**–JU. But I feel it is the Mars-Chiron links which are most relevant to the murders.

However, there is also a counter-indication. (MA–**1**–CH)–**4**–SO is linked to Saturn by Fiveness aspects: ((MA–**1**–CH)–**4**–SO)–5/**5**/**20**–SA. Here the strongest aspect is SO–**20**–SA, showing that Vareille struggles to find creative ways (20 = 5 x 2 x 2) of controlling and disciplining his urge for self-fulfilment. Also (MA–**1**–CH)–5/**5**–SA shows that he is capable of controlling his Mars-Chiron impulses. I feel that, if we as astrologers were counselling Vareille, this might be the key to how we might try to help him. In counselling him we would need to show great compassion for his plight, and great understanding of why he felt the desire to kill, and yet we would be helping him to find other (Saturnian) ways of coping that did not involve the destruction of his loved ones and ultimately of himself.

I feel that such an attempt might well have succeeded. Although Vareille was, like Fred West, a killer of his own children, he was very far from being a brutal, heartless, pleasure-seeking killer like West. Clearly, after the killings, he felt great remorse for his actions. I believe that he would have benefited from greater self-understanding, and from the opportunity to stand back from his own behaviour and view it more dispassionately. Harmonic astrology could well have provided him with such an opportunity, helping him to have a better understanding of his own desires and drives and to find more positive ways of expressing them.

Murder of James Bulger
12 February 1993, 15.39 (+00.00)
Liverpool, England (53N25. 2W58).
Source: Wikipedia.

1:   SO–1–SA
     UR–**1**–NE

2:   ((VE–**4**–MA)–8/**8**–SO)–32/**32**/32–NE
     (UR–**1**–NE)–**32**/32/32/**32**–(SO–**8**–MA)
     SA–2–CH

3:   ((VE–**4**–MA)–8/**8**–SO)–12/3/24–ME
     (UR–**1**–NE)–**12**/12–CH
     MO–**27**–VE

5:   ((ME–**3**–MA)–**5**/15–JU)–15/15/15/15/**15**/15–(UR–**1**–NE)
     (ME–**5**–JU)–25/**25**–SO

7:   (SO–**7**–MO)–21/**21**/21/21–(UR–**1**–NE)
     (ME–**3**–MA)–**7**/21–PL)–**21**/21/**21**–SA

11:   MO–<u>22</u>–CH

13:   (MO–**<u>13</u>**–<u>JU</u>)–<u>26</u>/26–PL

17:   <u>JU</u>–<u>17</u>–SA

19:   <u>VE</u>–<u>19</u>–PL

23:   ((UR–<u>1</u>–NE)–**<u>23</u>**/<u>23</u>–<u>VE</u>)–<u>23</u>/**<u>23</u>**/<u>23</u>–SA

29:   MO–<u>29</u>–SA
         ME–<u>29</u>–CH

31:   <u>VE</u>–<u>31</u>–<u>JU</u>

My belief about mundane charts (charts for events other than births) is that they very often reflect the mindset of the person or people who caused the event to happen. Thus, if there is a creative act (as in the case of the poem *La Belle Dame sans Merci*, that we looked at in Chapter 3), the chart describes the mindset of the creator. If there is a rail or air crash caused by driver or pilot error (as in the several cases that we have mentioned), the chart describes the mindset of the driver or pilot.

One consequence of this is that, if the act is *premeditated*, the nature of the act may not show up so strongly in the chart. For instance, when Thomas Hamilton burst into the school at Dunblane and killed sixteen children and their teacher, we can assume that his action was premeditated: he came into the school fully armed, and had clearly planned his action in advance. Thus, it is probable that the chart that would most clearly describe his action would be the chart for the time when he *decided* on it: and we cannot know what that time was. The same could be said for a large number of murders and other crimes.

However, the murder of James Bulger is, I think, an example of a crime that was not premeditated, but was carried out spontaneously without prior thought. Therefore we can expect that the chart will contain clear indications of the mindset of the killers.

Two-year-old James Bulger somehow became separated from his mother in a shopping mall. He was spotted by two ten-year-old boys, Robert Thompson and Jon Venables, who led him away through the streets, and eventually took him to waste land near a railway line, where they subjected him to appalling tortures (apparently including sexual abuse), and struck him with an iron bar, which killed him. They then

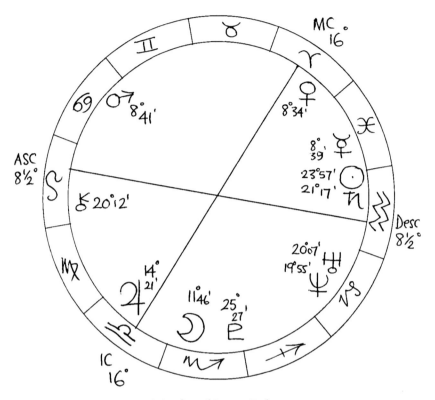

Murder of James Bulger

left his body lying across the railway track, so that it would appear that he had been hit by a train.

Strictly speaking, the chart is for the time of the abduction, not the killing, as this was the time when Thompson and Venables were caught on CCTV leading James Bulger through the shopping mall.

The chart contains a very strong pattern of Twoness, at the centre of which is (VE–**4**–MA)–8/8–SO. SO–8–VE (with Venus close to the Midheaven) is about the need to be loved, but SO–8–MA is stronger because it is closer to exactitude, and is about the need to be seen as strong, manly and virile. We can see how, for impressionable young boys from a disturbed background, this pattern would give rise to a very strong desire to do something powerful, and perhaps violent, in order to gain approval and loyalty. (I imagine that Thompson and Venables were very much motivated by the desire to *impress each other* by the ruthlessness and violence of their actions.)

Next, if we look at the Threeness clusters, we see that this pattern of (VE–*4*–MA)–8/8–SO is linked by Threeness aspects to Mercury: ((VE–*4*–MA)–8/8–SO)–12/3/24–ME. This includes an almost-exact Mercury-Mars trine (ME–*3*–MA), which suggests that the boys were able to obtain great pleasure from thinking and communicating about their violent actions. We must remember that the negative side of Threeness is carelessness: doing what one feels like doing, without regard to the consequences. And then, if we look at the Fiveness links, we see that this ME–*3*–MA is joined by close Fiveness aspects to Jupiter (on the I.C.) – (ME–*3*–MA)–*5*/15–JU – suggesting a kind of Jupiterian extravagance in thinking of ways to convert their violent impulses into action. All this suggests that the boys were 'carried away' by what they were doing – they were on a 'high', with one reckless action leading to another.

If we then move on to the Sevenness clusters, we see that ME–*3*–MA is linked by Sevenness aspects to Saturn and Pluto – (ME–*3*–MA)–7/21–PL)–21/21/**21**–SA – with an almost-exact SA–**21**–PL. Saturn and Pluto taken together (especially when we are dealing with Sevenness which is to do with hidden meanings) have an association with death, so here we have an indication of the sinister form which the boys' actions took: they felt *inspired* by the idea of combining Saturn with Pluto, or of ruthless action with destructive consequences. This is coupled with SO–7–MO, which shows, I believe, that at this time there was an all-pervading atmosphere of Sevenness, causing people to follow the dictates of their imagination rather than of reason and commonsense.

None of this has anything to do with poor James Bulger, who was the innocent and helpless victim of the boys' actions. The chart describes the mindset of the perpetrators, not of the victim.

There are other close harmonic aspects in the chart, but I feel that the ones that I have discussed are the important ones for this purpose. We must remember that a mundane chart will have only a transitory and fleeting effect on people's consciousness – as opposed to a birth chart, which imprints itself onto a person's consciousness for the whole of a lifetime, and so is able to influence him or her in more complex and subtle ways.

Ramana Maharshi

Born 30 December 1879, 01.00 (–05.12)

Madurai, India (9N56. 78E07).

Source: From *Astrology Magazine*, 6/1950, source not stated (ADB). RR: C.

1:   (NE–**1**–CH)–1–MA

2:   (SO–**8**–VE)–**16**–ME
     SO–4–SA
     MO–32–SA
     JU–**2**–UR

3:   ((((NE–**1**–CH)–**3**/3–UR)–3–SO)–**6**/6/**2**/6–JU)–**12**/12/12/4/
                 12–SA
     MO–27–JU
     ME–9–PL

5:   ((NE–**1**–CH)–**5**/5–ME)–5–MO
     (MO–5–NE)–15/15–UR
     (JU–**2**–UR)–30/15–MO

7:   SO–**28**–MO
     (VE–**21**–MA)–21–SA
     (NE–**1**–CH)–28/28–VE
     (JU–**2**–UR)–**14**/7–PL

11: (JU–**2**–UR)–**11**/22–MA
     (NE–**1**–CH)–**22**/22–PL

13: ME–13–JU

17: VE–**17**–JU

19: ME–19–SA

29: ME–29–MA
     VE–**29**–JU

31: VE–**31**–SA–**31**–CH

In the case of Ramana Maharshi I have broken my own rule, which is to only use charts with a Rodden Rating of AA, A or B. Ramana's chart has a rating of C ('caution'), because the original source of the data is not known. However, in Ramana's case I want to say: Let us trust that this is the right chart, and see what it has to tell us.

At the age of 16 Ramana had a profound spiritual experience. He seemed to experience the death of his own body, and yet realized that, though the body was dead, his consciousness (the awareness of 'I') was still present. He later wrote, "So I am the Spirit transcending the body. The body dies but the Spirit that transcends it cannot be touched by death".[5]

Thereafter, Ramana moved to the holy mountain of Arunachala and never left it until his death at the age of 70. His spiritual awareness never left him, and people experienced a profound stillness in his presence. He was mostly silent, but would sometimes reply to people making spiritual enquiries. He showed no concern for his own physical welfare, but was immensely caring towards other people and towards animals. When

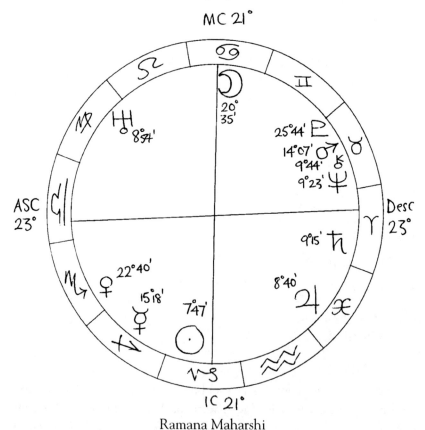

Ramana Maharshi

in his sixties he developed a very painful form of cancer, he accepted it with total equanimity. He taught a spiritual path which in English is called 'self enquiry', and he has had a profound influence on many modern spiritual teachers. Paula Marvelly says that his life exemplified "immaculate humility and benevolence".[6]

It seems to me that, by transcending his identification with the body and also with the thinking mind, and realizing his true identity as the still consciousness that cannot be touched by death, Ramana had also transcended his own birth chart. The birth chart describes all the complex workings of the thinking mind, which combine the qualities of Twoness, Threeness, and all the other numbers, but Ramana had moved into the Oneness. For him, Twoness and Threeness no longer had meaning. For him, all was unity, all was peace, all was stillness.

Therefore, we cannot find indications in the birth chart of how Ramana lived his life. But we can perhaps find indications of what enabled him to break through into the Oneness. How was it that Ramana was able, spontaneously at the age of 16, to attain a state of enlightenment which for most people is beyond their reach?

We can note, first of all, that there is not very much Oneness actually present in Ramana's chart. But there is NE–**1**–CH, showing that Ramana's sense of his purpose, his role in the world, is infused with idealism and lofty goals; and (NE–**1**–CH)–**1**–MA shows that he will tend to work towards this with energy and determination.

However, at the Twoness level there is a very important cluster: (SO–**8**–VE)–**16**–ME. SO–**8**–VE usually indicates a very strong need to be loved; the person feels himself to be unlovable, and needs constant assurances from the outside world that he is indeed loved. But, for Ramana, both Sun and Venus are very closely –**16**– Mercury, and this shows that he is determined to make the effort to resolve the Sun-Venus dilemma through thought. We can see here the roots of Ramana's teaching of self-enquiry. Ramana says that one should constantly be asking the question "Who am I?" One needs to go on doing this until the thinking dissolves, and one knows for certain that 'I' am nothing but pure awareness.

In Chapter 17 I said: "The paradox of Two is that, even though it is so caught up in the separation, it is the closest number to Oneness. We are striving towards a reconciliation between Self and Other; striving

towards a union of opposites. We are aware of the possibility of Oneness."
Thus I believe that it was this very strong cluster of Twoness – (SO–**8**–
VE)–**16**–ME, together with SO–**4**–SA – which, above all else, made it
possible for Ramana to break through into the realization of Oneness
and, by so doing, to cast aside Twoness and all the other numbers which
indicate plurality.

This, I believe, is the most important factor. We do not need to look
at the other harmonic aspects, since they describe, not the person that
Ramana was, but the person he would have been if he had not attained
enlightenment.

However, we should perhaps mention the great cluster of Threeness
– ((((NE–**1**–CH)–**3**/3–UR)–3–SO)–6/6/**2**/6–JU)–**12**/12/12/**4**/12–SA –
in which the Sun is brought together with five of the outer planets,
Jupiter, Saturn, Uranus, Neptune and Chiron. Normally this kind of
cluster (which contains elements of both Threeness and Twoness, and so
has the characteristics of Sixness that we discussed in Chapter 6) would
denote a person who was very active in the world, and was able to relate
to people with a great deal of confidence and self-assurance. I believe
that we can relate this to the fact that Ramana possessed a high degree
of personal magnetism and charisma. He did not seek this, and in his
view it was irrelevant to who he really was; but it contributed to the fact
that so many people were drawn to him, and that he has exercised such
a powerful influence over the development of modern spirituality.

19

Conclusion: The Spirit of Numbers

This book will have two conclusions. In Chapter 20 I will make some comments about the practice of astrology. In the present chapter, however, I will comment on the meaning of numbers for their own sake, since I believe that the concept of the 'spirit of numbers' is relevant, not just to astrology, but to the whole way in which we live our lives.

There is a tendency for spiritual teachers to believe that the only alternative to Oneness is Duality (or Twoness). In this view, if we do not feel ourselves to be One with the universe, we are caught up in the *polarities* which are the essence of Duality. We perceive the world as hostile, since we feel a sharp dichotomy between Self and Other. We feel ourselves to be in a conflict situation. We see sharp contrasts between good and evil, right and wrong, success and failure. We are fearful of failure, fearful of pain, fearful of death. All our activities tend to be goal-directed: we do things, not because the doing of them brings us satisfaction in the present moment, but because we are working towards a future goal in which we will have vanquished whatever we perceive as the 'enemy'. The only escape from this all-pervading Twoness is to transcend the Ego and to find pure Oneness, in which all the conflicts disappear.

But in fact, the true alternative to Oneness is not Duality but Plurality; and Plurality includes not only Twoness, but also Threeness, Fiveness, and all the other numbers. Twoness may be more predominant than any other single number, but, taken collectively, the other numbers are at least as important as Two. We can perhaps say that, just as the physical world is made up out of the 92 chemical elements, so the world of consciousness is made up of the essences of all of the numbers. And the preoccupation with *polarities* is a characteristic only of Twoness. The other numbers have other concerns.

So, if you are performing an activity – *any* activity, whether it is eating, washing, talking to friends, doing housework, reading, writing, having sex, climbing a mountain, or even just thinking – it is worthwhile to ask yourself the question: *In what spirit am I doing this?*

You may be doing it in the spirit of Twoness. If so, you are indeed caught up in the polarities. You see the activity as a battle, from which you have to emerge as the winner. The activity itself is less important to you than the intended outcome. You are preoccupied with 'getting it right'. You may hate doing this thing, but you feel that you have to do it because otherwise disaster would befall you, in the form of punishment, humiliation, rejection or pain. Or else you are hoping that, if you succeed, you will be praised and rewarded.

Or you may be doing it in the spirit of Threeness. If so, you are doing this thing because you enjoy doing it. The pleasure is in the doing, rather than in the intended outcome. And yet there is still the ego involvement, in the sense that you feel more fulfilled doing this thing than if you were not doing it. The performance of this activity brings you something which helps you to feel more fully yourself.

Or maybe you are doing it in the spirit of Fiveness. If so, you are preoccupied with creating order out of chaos. You are trying to reshape the world. Maybe you are reshaping your inner world, by making sense of your own thoughts and putting them into order; or maybe you are creating or assembling something in the outside world, creating a new Form out of the existing Forms. This involves some ego commitment both to the activity itself (wanting to do it well) and to the desired outcome (wanting to create Forms which satisfy your criteria of beauty or rightness).

Or perhaps you are doing it in the spirit of Sevenness. If so, you are doing it because in some way it *inspires* you. Your commitment is less to the activity itself than to the inner meaning that it has for you. Maybe the doing of this activity helps you to see yourself in a different light – as a nobler person, or a more compassionate person, or a more daring person, or a wiser person, or a person with more charisma. Or it may help you to find inspiration in the world around you, and to see in it a beauty and profundity which it did not have before.

It is possible also that you are doing it in the spirit of one of the higher prime numbers. If you are doing it in the spirit of Elevenness, it will be an activity which helps you to feel rooted in the world, tied to its solidity and permanence. If you are doing it in the spirit of Thirteenness, it will be an activity which helps you to feel that you are taking risks, testing yourself to the limits of your capacity, in order to find something new about your true nature.

If we look in this way at the spirit in which we do things, we may often find that we are combining two or more prime numbers. Twoness combined with Threeness is common, and is essentially about *enjoying the battle*: this is the essence of Sixness. In the same way, Fiveness can be combined with either Twoness or Threeness, giving rise to activities which have the qualities of Ten or of Fifteen.

It is also possible that we are doing things in the spirit of Oneness. This is less likely, not because we have no Oneness in our natures, but because Oneness is more associated with Being than with Doing. If we are in a state of Oneness, the greatest desire is to be still, and simply to *experience* the Oneness which we share with the whole universe. Even the internal activity of thinking may fall away. Ramana Maharshi, who lived in the Oneness, was for a time reluctant even to feed himself, since the goal of keeping himself alive had ceased to be important for him. Nevertheless, it may be possible to perform activities while remaining in the Oneness; if so, there is no attachment either to the activity itself or to its outcome. Pleasure and pain, success and failure, acceptance and rejection, are all experienced with the same equanimity.

Looking in this way at the spirit in which we do things can, I believe, be beneficial, since it can give us the opportunity to change. We might choose, for instance, to bring more Sevenness into our lives. We are all capable of entering into the spirit of all of the numbers. It is true that people whose birth charts are dominated by a particular number may be more prone than others to act in the spirit of that number: thus, people whose charts contain many Sevenness aspects may spend more time than others acting in a Sevenness way. But we have free will, and we can choose to change our behaviour. We do not need to be bound by our birth charts. It has been said that the Ego needs to be our servant, not our master; in the same way, the birth chart (which, as I said in Chapter 2, can be seen as a map of the Ego) needs to serve us, not to control us.

Thus, I believe that the study of the spirit of numbers can help us greatly in our lives. Even if we do not practise astrology, and know nothing about our birth charts, we can still familiarize ourselves with the essence of the spirit of each of the numbers, and use this to obtain a better understanding of how we are living our lives, and so to live with greater self-awareness and greater freedom of choice.

And on a wider scale, the concept of the 'spirit of numbers' can help us to obtain a more profound understanding of the workings of the universe, and of our own place in it. As I said at the start of this chapter, the alternative to Oneness is not Duality but Plurality, or 'many-ness'. Instinctively we understand this. In English as in most other languages, nouns and verbs have two forms, the singular and the plural. 'I' am one person; 'we' are more than one person, no matter whether we are two, or three, or any other number. 'It' is one thing; 'they' are many things. The One can divide itself into two, or into three, or into any other number.

Thus the multiplicity of Forms in the world comes into existence. In Zen Buddhism they are referred to as the 'ten thousand things'. The creation and dissolution of the 'ten thousand things' is a cyclical process. The Forms arise out of the Oneness, shine in all their diversity, and then sink back into the Oneness. On Earth, we can see this in the cycle of the seasons, and in the cycle of day and night; and we can see it also in the cycle of our own lives. To be incarnated is to take one's place in the world as one of the ten thousand things. We arise out of the Oneness, we grow, we shine, and then when we die we sink back into the Oneness.

The infinite diversity of the 'ten thousand things' is possible only because of the different spiritual essences of the different numbers. If the world of Form was composed only of Duality or Twoness, it would be a world in which there was nothing but polarity, nothing but struggle and conflict between opposing forces. But, in the real world, the struggle of Twoness is tempered by the joy of Threeness, the creativity of Fiveness, the wildness of Sevenness, and all the other numbers, and all these elements combine and interact with one another in an infinite variety of different ways. We have seen this in the birth chart, and we can see it also in the diversity of the 'ten thousand things' that make up our world. We can see and love this diversity of Forms, and we can see and love also the Oneness that unites them all in a single grand design.

20

Conclusion: Astrology

In the previous chapter we looked at the 'spirit of numbers' in a wider context. We can now come back to astrology, and look at how harmonic astrology (based on an understanding of the spirit of numbers) can affect the way in which astrology is practised.

My own belief is that harmonics can make a very valuable contribution to astrology, and that, if it is ignored, the interpretation of the chart will always to some extent be incomplete. This is not to deny the importance of signs and houses (or of other aspects of astrology, such as the Moon's Nodes,[1] which I have not included in this book), nor is it to belittle the immense skill and insight which astrologers have displayed using traditional methods. But I feel that (for instance) an attempt to analyse Adolf Hitler's chart without taking into account his strength in Fiveness, Sevenness, and the higher levels of Twoness (and also his lack of strength in Threeness) would be bound to be incomplete, since it would omit some of the most important factors which explain the nature of Hitler's individuality.

To a greater or lesser extent, the same is true of all other charts. In the great majority of cases, the most important prime numbers are One, Two, Three, Five and Seven, and we can obtain a fairly complete picture by looking at these numbers alone. But there are also some cases – a minority, but a significant minority – in which we also need to look at the higher prime numbers (from Eleven onwards) in order to find out what really makes the person tick. For instance, I feel that we cannot really understand Fred Astaire without looking at his Elevenness; or Jean Sibelius without looking at his Nineteenness; or Dylan Thomas without looking at his Twenty-threeness. Thus, it would seem to be desirable that astrologers have the tools to look at these numbers, in case they should turn out to be important in particular cases.

I therefore hope that other astrologers will take up the study of the spirit of numbers, and will develop it further than I have been able to in

254   The Spirit of Numbers

this book. They may use different methods from the ones I have used: for instance, they may go back to drawing separate harmonic charts for each prime number, as I did in my previous book *Harmonic Charts*. They may look at other prime numbers beyond 31. They may apply harmonics to synastry and to transits. They may develop computer programs which enable large-scale research. Above all, they may develop and refine the indications that I have given about the meanings of each of the numbers, and turn them into more subtle and sensitive tools for interpretation.

* * * * *

Before I end the book, there are two issues that I would like to raise. The first is the issue of celestial latitude and parallax, and the second is the issue of divination.

Firstly, latitude and parallax. In this book, we (in common with other astrologers) have been looking at the positions of the planets on the circle of the ecliptic, which is the path that the Sun follows (or appears to follow) around the Earth. But the problem is that, at any given time, most of the planets are not actually on the ecliptic. They have celestial latitude, which is defined as the angular distance between the actual position of the planet and its nearest point on the ecliptic. In the case of Pluto this distance can be as much as 14 degrees, and for the Moon it can be more than 5 degrees. (I believe that it can be very high for Chiron also, but I do not have figures for this.) In this book we have actually been looking at the angular distances, not between the planets themselves, but between their nearest points on the ecliptic. If we were to correct for celestial latitude, we might arrive at different conclusions.

And then there is the additional problem of parallax, which affects only the Moon (because the other planets are too far away to be affected). The Moon's position as given in the ephemeris is its position as seen (if it could be seen!) from the centre of the Earth. If we are to alter this to its position as seen from the point on the Earth's surface where the birth (or other event) took place, we have to correct for parallax. This again can make a substantial difference to the angular distance between the Moon and other planets.

In my article about the Silent Twins[2] (whom we discussed in Chapter 7), I did in fact correct for latitude (but not for parallax) before calculating the twins' harmonic aspects. I found that most of the harmonic aspects were unaffected by latitude correction, but that there were two aspects – JU–7–PL and SO–21–PL – which were brought into being by the latitude correction. Both of these aspects seem to be appropriate for the twins' personality and behaviour.

I feel that this should be one of the most important areas for research. Latitude and parallax correction require extra work, but this work could easily be done if the right computer programs were available, and it is important to discover whether latitude and parallax correction results in a better 'fit' between the chart and the person (or event) that it describes. Logically, it would seem to be more appropriate to study the angular distances between the planets themselves (as seen from the place of birth), rather than the angular distances between their nearest points on the ecliptic (as seen from the centre of the Earth).

The other issue that I want to raise is the issue of divination. Is there really a connection (whether causal or otherwise) between the pattern of the planets at the time of a person's birth and the personality and behaviour of that person? Or is the astrological chart nothing but a tool for divination (comparable to, for instance, the Tarot pack or the I Ching), a set of symbols which enable the astrologer to use his or her intuition and insight to 'divine' meaningful statements about the subject of the chart?

If we take the latter view, then (it seems to me) it does not matter whether the chart that we have chosen to use is the 'right' one. It would be perfectly reasonable to 'shuffle the pack' (just as a Tarot reader does) by using random numbers to generate a random chart, rather than going to great lengths to ensure that the person *really was* born at this time or that the event *really did* happen at this time. No matter what chart we use, we can trust that it will aid us in the process of divination.

The contrast between these two models of astrology (which we can call the empirical model and the divinatory model) was set out by Garry Phillipson in an article in *Correlation* (the journal devoted to astrological research).[3] In response, Roy Gillett argued[4] (and Garry Phillipson agreed with him) that all astrologers who practise divination are reluctant to 'shuffle the pack'. They are keen to work with the 'right' chart if this is possible, and are often sticklers for accuracy when calculating the chart. Although the 'wrong' chart may yield valid information because of the astrologer's divinatory skills, it is far better to work with the 'right' chart. Thus, there needs to be a 'middle way' which combines both the empirical and the divinatory aspects of astrology.

I entirely agree with this. If 'divination' means anything, it means 'allowing the Divine to speak through you'. For me this is the essence of Sevenness, which is about the search for the hidden meanings which lie beneath the surface of things. An astrology which contained no Sevenness would be one which rigidly followed rules based on empirical data. The astrologer would be saying, "This is what Neptune in this position has been found to mean, so this is what I am saying". There would be no room for the leap of faith, for the intuition that in this case Neptune may be saying something that has never been said before. There would be no room for the fact that we all have choices about how we *use* the birth chart, and some of us may use it in original and startling ways.

But Sevenness has to be tempered with Fiveness if it is not to lose touch with reality. Fiveness is about the building of sound and watertight structures that will stand the test of time, and that will act as safe containers for the Sevenness (and maybe also the other numbers) that may be flying around inside them. An astrology that contained no Fiveness would be one in which the astrologer would be free to say whatever he wished, according to how the Spirit guided him, without being constrained by the factual details of the chart or by all the astrological lore that has accumulated over time. It might well be inspirational, but it would not be reliable.

Thus there does need to be a 'middle way' that combines both Fiveness and Sevenness. But, so long as we acknowledge that there is a Fiveness element in astrology, we also have to acknowledge that there *is* a connection between the pattern of the planets at the time of a person's birth and the way in which that person's life develops. No one, so far as I know, has ever proposed a satisfactory explanation of *how* this connection works. Do the planets in some way *cause* a person to think, feel and behave in certain ways? Or is the true explanation non-causal, and something to do with the mysterious workings of synchronicity? Or is it all the product of the human mind, so that the planets affect us *because we think that they do*, and this thinking somehow becomes a reality? My own tendency is to believe the last of these: I would suggest that consciousness is a property of the whole universe, and that we have somehow affected the consciousness of the planets, which in turn affects our own. But, of course, this is all conjecture. We don't know how astrology works. We simply have to take it on trust.

As I said in the Preface, certainty is an illusion, and I am not *certain* of the truth of anything that I have said in this book. We cannot be certain that God (as some kind of universal consciousness beyond ourselves) exists, and we cannot be certain that He/She/It does not exist; in the same way, we as astrologers cannot be certain that astrology is true, but also the militant detractors of astrology (such as Stephen Fry and Brian Cox) cannot be certain that astrology is false. (If they think they are certain, they are deluded.) Nevertheless, we have to make choices, and to act on the assumption that some things are true. In this book I have to chosen to act on the assumption that astrology is true, and that it can bring great benefits to mankind.

Appendix I

How to Do It

I am including this Appendix (together with Appendices II and III) for the benefit of those astrologers who wish to follow the methods that I have used for identifying the harmonic aspects in a chart, without drawing harmonic charts. As I said in Chapter 1, I am hoping that before long a computer program will be available that will replicate this method. For the time being, however, astrologers will have to do the calculations themselves, armed only with a pocket calculator.

When I started to learn astrology in the late 1960s, there were no computers, and all the work of calculating the positions of the planets and the cusps of the houses had to be done by hand. There were, however, pocket calculators (which then were a marvellous new invention), and there were printed aids (such as ephemerides and tables of houses) which greatly facilitated the calculation. But even with these aids, it could take the best part of an hour to set up a chart. Nowadays, however, astrologers expect a chart to be instantly delivered to them by computer. All one has to do is enter the time and the place, and the chart magically appears.

I am now asking astrologers to go back to those times, since there are at present no computer programs which will calculate aspects for all the harmonics up to 32 in the way that I am proposing. (It is true that some computer packages, such as those of Astrocalc, contain programs for harmonic analysis; but these are programs for setting up harmonic charts, which I am not using in this book, and there are certain difficulties about translating the information from these programs into a form that we can use; also, the Astrocalc harmonic program does not include Chiron.) I am therefore asking astrologers to do some calculating. But once again, one can be helped by using a pocket calculator (provided that it has a ° ' " key which calculates in degrees, minutes and seconds), and once again I am providing a table which will greatly aid the calculation. With these aids, and with practice, the calculation should take less than an hour for any one chart. That is to say, the calculation can be done in the same length of time that (before the advent of computers) it took to calculate the basic chart.

Before I describe the method, I need to discuss the *width of orbs*, i.e. the extent to which an aspect is allowed to deviate from exactitude. Traditionally, astrologers have used an orb of 8° for the conjunction, the opposition, the square and the trine, and a lesser orb for other aspects. This means that two planets are regarded as being conjunct if they are within 8 degrees of each other, but, if the distance between them is more than 8°, they are not conjunct.

In this book, however, we are using *harmonic orbs*. This means that, once we have determined the orb for the conjunction, the orb for all other aspects will be *the conjunction orb divided by the number of the harmonic*. Thus, if the conjunction orb is 12°, the orb for the opposition will be 6° (12° divided by 2), the orb for the trine will be 4° (12° divided by 3), and so on. Thus, the orb for the 30th harmonic will be 12° divided by 30, which is 24 minutes.

Following this principle, I use a conjunction orb of 12°, which, if we are including all the harmonics up to 32, is wide enough to ensure that every planet is aspected to every other planet. But also (because, as I said in Chapter 1, an aspect is stronger if it is closer to exactitude), I use the principle of *close orbs* and *very close orbs*. For *close orbs* I have divided the basic orb by 2, and for *very close orbs* I have divided the basic orb by 6. Thus, since the conjunction orb is 12°, the *close orb* for the conjunction is 6°, and the *very close orb* is 2°. (Thus, if two planets are within two degrees of each other, they are regarded as being in a 'very close' conjunction.) Similarly, for the 30th harmonic, the basic orb is 24', the close orb is 12', and the very close orb is 4'.

Our task, then, for any individual chart, is to identify the harmonic (or harmonics) in which each pair of planets come together, and (in each case) to determine whether the aspect is very close, close, or wide. The method of doing this is as follows:

First, you need to have a form on which you can record your workings. A blank Aspect Form is printed at the end of this first Appendix, and it is suggested that you should photocopy these pages or (better) create your own version of the Aspect Form. (If you create your own form, I suggest that you use squared paper, which can be bought in a pad from stationers.) Also included is the same Aspect Form completed for Tony Blair's birth chart (which we discussed in Chapter 18). The blank Aspect Form contains:

1. A blank space on the left.

2. A list of all the 55 pairs of planets, from Sun-Moon to Pluto-Chiron.

3. A blank column in which you can record the angular distance between each pair of planets.

4. Twelve columns headed by the prime numbers from 1 to 31, in which you can enter the aspects pertaining to each prime number.

5. An empty space on the right.

When you are armed with this form, with a calculator, and with the actual chart (which you will have printed from your computer), the procedure is as follows:

1. In the blank space on the left, enter the name of the chart, the time and place, and the positions of the planets and of the Ascendant and Midheaven. For instance, Tony Blair's Sun is at Taurus 15° 23' in the 12th house. (I have used Placidus houses, but you are welcome to use whatever house system you prefer.[1]) I suggest that you should underline the house figure if the planet is within 8 degrees of one of the Angles (Ascendant, Descendant, Midheaven, I.C.). For instance, Tony Blair's Mars and Jupiter are in the 12th house within 8 degrees of the Ascendant, so the figure '12' is underlined, and his Chiron is in the 9th house within 8 degrees of the Midheaven, so the figure '9' is underlined.

Also, you can, if you wish, enter in the left-hand space the source of the data, and any other notes about the person (or event) whose chart it is. If you wish, you can also enter other factors such as the Moon's Nodes, the Part of Fortune, the position of asteroids such as Ceres and Vesta, and so on.

2. In the first column (to the right of the list of pairs of planets), enter the angular distance between each pair of planets. For instance, Tony Blair's Sun is at Taurus 15° 23' and his Moon is at Aquarius 11° 29'. From Aquarius to Taurus is 3 signs. Enter into your calculator (using the

sign ° for the ° ' " key): 3° 15° 23° – 0° 11° 29° =, and you will get the answer 3° 3° 54°. Enter these three figures (3, 3, 54) into the space on the form next to the sign for Sun-Moon.

Note that you always have to take the *shorter* of the two angular distances between the two planets: i.e. you have to calculate the distance from Aquarius to Taurus, rather than the long way round from Taurus to Aquarius.

However, a difficulty arises because there are only 30 degrees in a sign, whereas the calculator thinks there are 60. Thus, when you are calculating the distance from Tony Blair's Sun (Taurus 15° 23') to his Mercury (Aries 26° 24'), you will enter 1° 15° 23° – 0° 26° 24° =, and you will get the answer 0° 48° 59°. You then have to *subtract 30* from the figure 48, to get the true answer which is 0° 18° 59°. The rule is: *Whenever you get a figure of 30 or above for degrees within a sign, subtract 30 from this figure.* (But do not do this for minutes, because there are 60 minutes within a degree.)

When you have calculated the angular distances for all of the 55 pairs of planets, you can go on to the next step:

3. Turn to the Table of Harmonic Aspects, which is printed as Appendix II of this book. Use this Table to discover the aspect or aspects which correspond to each angular distance. For instance, Tony Blair's Sun-Moon (3s. 3° 54') comes within the range 3s. 3° 50' – 3s. 4° 00, and you will see from the Table that this corresponds to a *very close* Twenty-threeness aspect. Enter this figure (23) in the column headed '23', on the level of the sign for Sun-Moon (with a ring round it to show that it is very close). Do the same for all the other pairs of planets.

In the Table, *wide* (not-close) aspects are printed in the normal way, *close* aspects are <u>underlined</u>, and *very close* aspects are printed in ***<u>bold underlined italics</u>***. However, it is suggested that, in entering very close aspects onto the Aspect Form, rather than attempting bold underlined italics, you should draw a ring round the aspect figure. (Alternatively, you can give the figure a double underlining.)

Aspects should be entered onto the Aspect Form according to the *largest prime number which is a factor of the number to be entered.* Thus, the figures which should be entered in each column are as follows:

1: 1
2: 2, 4, 8, 16, 32
3: 3, 6, 9, 12, 18, 24, 27
5: 5, 10, 15, 20, 25, 30
7: 7, 14, 21, 28
11: 11, 22
13: 13, 26
17: 17
19: 19
23: 23
29: 29
31: 31

4. When you have entered all the aspects onto the Aspect Form, the next step is to list the most important aspects (that is to say, the ones that will be the most useful for interpretation) in the blank space on the right-hand side of the Form. I suggest that you should list here:

a. all *very close* aspects (which can be entered with a double underlining).

b. all *close* aspects involving the Sun (and also the Moon if the time of birth [or of the mundane event] is known to be accurate).

c. all *clusters* of three or more aspects (i.e. cases in which three or more planets are all aspected to one another). The suggested method of entering clusters is shown on the form which I have completed for Tony Blair. Clusters may be what I call *trios* (groups of 3 planets), *quartets* (groups of 4), or *quintets* (groups of 5). In rare cases, even *sextets* (6) or *septets* (7) may be found.

The majority of clusters can be found by simply looking down a particular column on the Aspect Form and finding three or more planets that are all aspected to one another. Thus, in the '2' column, Tony Blair has VE–4–UR, VE–8–JU, and JU–8–UR: this adds up to a trio of (VE–4–UR)–8–JU. Also he has ME–32–VE and ME–32–UR: together with VE–4–UR, this adds up to a trio of (VE–4–UR)–32–ME.

Sometimes, however, clusters can only be found by comparing information from two (or occasionally even three) columns. In Tony Blair's case, he has a very close Saturn-Neptune conjunction

(SA–_1_–NE), and this forms clusters with planets in several columns: (SA–_1_–NE)–2–ME, (SA–_1_–NE)–_5_/5–JU, (SA–_1_–NE)–_25_/25–VE, ((SA–_1_–NE)–_13_/_13_–MA)–_26_/26/26–UR, and ((SA–_1_–NE)–23/_23_–SO)–23/_23_/23–MO. Also there is a quartet which spreads across three columns: ((SA–_1_–NE)–_4_–CH)–6/6/_12_–PL.

The task of identifying clusters may seem difficult, but I assure you that with practice you will soon be able to do it much more quickly and confidently. However, it may be a good idea to write clusters at first on rough paper, on which you can do crossings-out and amendments, before entering them neatly onto the Form.

5. When you have entered all the clusters that you can find, it is time to go on to the final stage, which is interpretation. Interpretation is an art, not a science, and you need to do it in your own way, rather than letting me tell you how. However, I can perhaps offer some general hints:

- Quartets and quintets are always important (especially if the aspects within them are close or very close), and can offer the strongest clues to the person's character or to the nature of the event. Also, trios in which all the aspects are close or very close are always important.

- Sometimes a number of trios need to be considered together. Thus, Tony Blair has a trio of (VE–_4_–UR)–8–JU and a trio of (VE–_4_–UR)–_12_/_6_–SO. Although these are separate trios, they clearly form part of a single pattern centred on VE–_4_–UR.

- Wide (not close) aspects can usually be ignored if they do not form part of a cluster. This is particularly true if (as often happens) a pair of planets comes within orbs on more than one harmonic. For instance, Tony Blair's MA–UR comes within orbs for both 17 and 26: but the '26' is part of a quartet involving SA and NE, whereas the '17' is isolated. This means that the '17' can, in my view, be ignored.

- However, a close or very close aspect is sometimes important even if it does not form part of a cluster. Thus, Tony Blair has a close MA–_14_–PL. Even though it is not in a cluster, this aspect is probably important as an indication of how Sevenness operates in Blair's character, especially since Mars is on his Ascendant.

In interpreting the aspects, we need to keep referring back to the chart to note the signs and houses in which the planets are placed, since this will colour the interpretation. Sometimes we may want to make a copy of the chart on which we can draw lines connecting all the planets which are linked by aspects pertaining to a particular prime number. For instance, we could make a 'Fiveness' chart for Tony Blair, on which all the aspects in the '5' column were shown by lines connecting the planets. This would give an overall picture of the way Fiveness operates in his character.

I would like to end this Appendix by stressing the importance of accuracy in birth times (or in the timing of whatever event is being studied). When we come to the higher-numbered harmonics, which have a much shorter orb span, the planets can move very rapidly in and out of orb, and an error of (say) an hour in the birth time can make quite a difference to the Table of Aspects. This is especially true of the Moon, which moves more than 30 minutes (half a degree) in a single hour.

Therefore I feel that the methods proposed in this book should only be used for births (or other events) for which an accurate time is available. If one was tempted to use these methods for an event for which one had only the date and no time, it would be necessary to exclude the Moon: but the Moon is, of course, a very important factor in any chart, and an analysis which excluded it would be very incomplete.

Tony Blair
6 May 1953 06.10 (-1.00)
Edinburgh 55N57 3W13

				1	2	3	5	7	11	13	17	19	23	29	31	
☉☽	3	3	54										(23)			☉☽
☉☿	0	18	59									(19)				☉☿
☉♀	1	0	22				12									☉♀
☉♂	0	18	5				(20)									☉♂
☉♃	0	3	49						(26)							☉♃
☉♄	5	6	58		16							23				☉♄
☉♅	1	29	54			(6)										☉♅
☉♆	5	6	31										(23)			☉♆
☉♇	3	5	25					15								☉♇
☉☋	3	24	10						22			19				☉☋
☽☿	2	14	55			(24)										☽☿
☽♀	2	3	32							(17)						☽♀
☽♂	3	21	59		16								29			☽♂
☽♃	3	17	43				10									☽♃
☽♄	3	19	8				10					23				☽♄
☽♅	5	3	48					7								☽♅
☽♆	3	19	35										(23)			☽♆
☽♇	5	20	41								19					☽♇
☽☋	0	20	16			18										☽☋
☿♀	0	11	23	1	32										31	☿♀
☿♂	1	7	4					10					29			☿♂
☿♃	1	2	48						(11)							☿♃
☿♄	5	25	57		2											☿♄
☿♅	2	18	53		32	9										☿♅
☿♆	5	25	30		2											☿♆
☿♇	3	24	24						22							☿♇
☿☋	3	5	11									19				☿☋
				1	2	3	5	7	11	13	17	19	23	29	31	

☉ ♉ 15 23	12	♂ ♊ 3 28	12/1	♆ ♎ 2 54	6		
☽ ♒ 11 29	10	♃ ♉ 29 12	12	♇ ♌ 20 48	4	Asc ♊ 5
☿ ♈ 26 24	12	♄ ♎ 22 21	6	☋ ♑ 21 13	9	MC ♑ 26
♀ ♈ 15 1	11	♅ ♋ 15 17	3			

				1	2	3	5	7	11	13	17	19	23	29	31	
♀♂	1	18	27				15									♀♂
♀♃	1	14	11		8											♀♃
♀♄	5	22	40				25						23			♀♄
♀♅	3	0	16		4											♀♅
♀♆	5	23	7			27	25									♀♆
♀♇	4	5	47				20									♀♇
♀⚷	2	23	48				30			13						♀⚷
♂♃	0	4	16	1												♂♃
♂♄	4	18	53							13						♂♄
♂♅	1	11	49							26	17					♂♅
♂♆	4	18	26							13						♂♆
♂♇	2	17	20					14								♂♇
♂⚷	4	12	15				30					19				♂⚷
♃♄	4	23	9				5									♃♄
♃♅	1	16	5		8										31	♃♅
♃♆	4	22	42				5									♃♆
♃♇	2	21	36						22						31	♃♇
♃⚷	4	7	59					14							31	♃⚷
♄♅	3	7	4							26						♄♅
♄♆	0	0	27	1												♄♆
♄♇	2	1	33			6										♄♇
♄⚷	2	28	52		4											♄⚷
♅♆	3	6	37				15			26						♅♆
♅♇	1	5	31				10									♅♇
♅⚷	5	24	4		2									29	31	♅⚷
♆♇	2	1	6			6										♆♇
♆⚷	2	29	19		4											♆⚷
♇⚷	5	0	15			12										♇⚷
				1	2	3	5	7	11	13	17	19	23	29	31	

Harmonic Aspects in Tony Blair's Chart

①

♂ – 1 – ♃
♄ – 1 – ♆

⑦

☽ – 7 – ♅
♂ – 14 – ♆

⑲

(☉ – 19 – ☿) – 19 – ⛢
☽ – 19 – ♆

②

(♄ – 1 – ♆) – 2 – ☿
      – 4 – ⛢
(♀ – 4 – ♅) – 8 – ♃
      – 32 – ☿

⑪

(☿ – 11 – ♃) – 22 – ♇

㉓

(♄ – 1 – ♆) – 23/23/23/23
    – (☉ – 23 – ☽)

③

(♀ – 4 – ♆)
    – 12/6 – ☉
☽ – 24 – ☿
☽ – 18 – ⛢
♀ – 27 – ♆
♇ – 12 – ⛢

⑬

☉ – 26 – ♃
((♄ – 1 – ♆) – 13/13 – ♂)
    – 26/26/26 – ♅

㉙

☿ – 29 – ♂

⑤

☉ – 20 – ♂
(♄ – 1 – ♆) – 5/5 – ♃
      – 25/25 – ♀
(♃ – 5 – ♄) – 10/10 – ☽
(♀ – 4 – ♆) – 20/10 – ♇
(♀ – 15 – ♂) – 30/30 – ⛢

⑰

☽ – 17 – ♀

㉛

(♅ – 31 – ⛢) – 31 – ♃

Blank Aspect Forms

	1	2	3	5	7	11	13	17	19	23	29	31	
☉☽													☉☽
☉☿													☉☿
☉♀													☉♀
☉♂													☉♂
☉♃													☉♃
☉♄													☉♄
☉♅													☉♅
☉♆													☉♆
☉♇													☉♇
☉⚷													☉⚷
☽☿													☽☿
☽♀													☽♀
☽♂													☽♂
☽♃													☽♃
☽♄													☽♄
☽♅													☽♅
☽♆													☽♆
☽♇													☽♇
☽⚷													☽⚷
☿♀													☿♀
☿♂													☿♂
☿♃													☿♃
☿♄													☿♄
☿♅													☿♅
☿♆													☿♆
☿♇													☿♇
☿⚷													☿⚷
	1	2	3	5	7	11	13	17	19	23	29	31	

				1	2	3	5	7	11	13	17	19	23	29	31	
♀♂																♀♂
♀♃																♀♃
♀♄																♀♄
♀♅																♀♅
♀♆																♀♆
♀♇																♀♇
♀⚷																♀⚷
♂♃																♂♃
♂♄																♂♄
♂♅																♂♅
♂♆																♂♆
♂♇																♂♇
♂⚷																♂⚷
♃♄																♃♄
♃♅																♃♅
♃♆																♃♆
♃♇																♃♇
♃⚷																♃⚷
♄♅																♄♅
♄♆																♄♆
♄♇																♄♇
♄⚷																♄⚷
♅♆																♅♆
♅♇																♅♇
♅⚷																♅⚷
♆♇																♆♇
♆⚷																♆⚷
♇⚷																♇⚷
				1	2	3	5	7	11	13	17	19	23	29	31	

Appendix II

Table of Harmonic Aspects

0s. 0°00' – 0s. 2°00'	*1*	0s. 13°57' – 0s. 14°05'	25, 26
0s. 2°01' – 0s. 6°00'	1	0s. 14°06' – 0s. 14°09'	25, 26
0s. 6°01' – 0s. 10°51'	1	0s. 14°10' – 0s. 14°18'	25, 26
0s. 10°52' – 0s. 11°03'	1, 32	0s. 14°19'	25, 26
0s. 11°04' – 0s. 11°10'	1, 32	0s. 14°20' – 0s. 14°29'	25
0s. 11°11' – 0s. 11°13'	1, *32*	0s. 14°30' – 0s. 14°38'	24, 25
0s. 11°14' – 0s. 11°19'	1, 31, *32*	0s. 14°39' – 0s. 14°44'	24, 25
0s. 11°20' – 0s. 11°24'	1, 31, 32	0s. 14°45' – 0s. 14°53'	24, 25
0s. 11°25' – 0s. 11°26'	1, 31, 32	0s. 14°54'	24
0s. 11°27' – 0s. 11°32'	1, 31, 32	0s. 14°55' – 0s. 15°05'	24
0s. 11°33' – 0s. 11°35'	1, *31*, 32	0s. 15°06' – 0s. 15°07'	24
0s. 11°36' – 0s. 11°38'	1, 30, *31*, 32	0s. 15°08' – 0s. 15°15'	23, 24
		0s. 15°16' – 0s. 15°22'	23, 24
0s. 11°39' – 0s. 11°41'	1, 30, *31*	0s. 15°23' – 0s. 15°30'	23, 24
0s. 11°42' – 0s. 11°47'	1, 30, 31	0s. 15°31' – 0s. 15°33'	23
0s. 11°48' – 0s. 11°49'	1, 30, 31	0s. 15°34' – 0s. 15°44'	*23*
0s. 11°50' – 0s. 11°55'	1, 30, 31	0s. 15°45' – 0s. 15°48'	23
0s. 11°56' – 0s. 12°00'	1, *30*, 31	0s. 15°49' – 0s. 15°55'	22, 23
0s. 12°01' – 0s. 12°04'	29, *30*	0s. 15°56' – 0s. 16°05'	22, 23
0s. 12°05' – 0s. 12°12'	29, 30	0s. 16°06' – 0s. 16°10'	22, 23
0s. 12°13' – 0s. 12°20'	29, 30	0s. 16°11' – 0s. 16°16'	22
0s. 12°21' – 0s. 12°24'	*29*, 30	0s. 16°17' – 0s. 16°27'	22
0s. 12°25' – 0s. 12°29'	28, *29*	0s. 16°28' – 0s. 16°34'	22
0s. 12°30' – 0s. 12°37'	28, *29*	0s. 16°35' – 0s. 16°38'	21, 22
0s. 12°38' – 0s. 12°46'	28, 29	0s. 16°39' – 0s. 16°51'	21, 22
0s. 12°47' – 0s. 12°50'	*28*, 29	0s. 16°52' – 0s. 16°55'	21, 22
0s. 12°51' – 0s. 12°52'	*28*	0s. 16°56' – 0s. 17°02'	21
0s. 12°53' – 0s. 12°55'	27, *28*	0s. 17°03' – 0s. 17°15'	*21*
0s. 12°56' – 0s. 13°04'	27, 28	0s. 17°16' – 0s. 17°23'	21
0s. 13°05' – 0s. 13°06'	27, 28	0s. 17°24' – 0s. 17°26'	20, 21
0s. 13°07' – 0s. 13°15'	27, 28	0s. 17°27' – 0s. 17°41'	20, 21
0s. 13°16' – 0s. 13°17'	*27*, 28	0s. 17°42' – 0s. 17°43'	20, 21
0s. 13°18' – 0s. 13°22'	*27*	0s. 17°44' – 0s. 17°53'	20
0s. 13°23' – 0s. 13°24'	26, *27*	0s. 17°54' – 0s. 18°06'	*20*
0s. 13°25' – 0s. 13°33'	26, 27	0s. 18°07' – 0s. 18°18'	20
0s. 13°34' – 0s. 13°36'	26, 27	0s. 18°19' – 0s. 18°36'	19, 20
0s. 13°37' – 0s. 13°45'	26, 27	0s. 18°37'	19
0s. 13°46' – 0s. 13°47'	*26*, 27	0s. 18°38' – 0s. 18°50'	19
0s. 13°48' – 0s. 13°54'	*26*	0s. 18°51' – 0s. 19°03'	*19*
0s. 13°55' – 0s. 13°56'	25, *26*	0s. 19°04' – 0s. 19°16'	19

0s. 19°17' – 0s. 19°19'	19	0s. 25°53' – 0s. 26°09'	<u>14</u>
0s. 19°20' – 0s. 19°35'	18, 19	0s. 26°10' – 0s. 26°12'	14
0s. 19°36' – 0s. 19°39'	18	0s. 26°13' – 0s. 26°26'	14, 27
0s. 19°40' – 0s. 19°52'	<u>18</u>	0s. 26°27' – 0s. 26°34'	14, <u>27</u>
0s. 19°53' – 0s. 20°07'	***<u>18</u>***	0s. 26°35'	<u>27</u>
0s. 20°08' – 0s. 20°20'	<u>18</u>	0s. 26°36' – 0s. 26°44'	***27***
0s. 20°21' – 0s. 20°28'	18	0s. 26°45' – 0s. 26°46'	<u>27</u>
0s. 20°29' – 0s. 20°40'	17, 18	0s. 26°47' – 0s. 26°53'	13, <u>27</u>
0s. 20°41' – 0s. 20°50'	17	0s. 26°54' – 0s. 27°07'	13, 27
0s. 20°51' – 0s. 21°03'	<u>17</u>	0s. 27°08' – 0s. 27°13'	13
0s. 21°04' – 0s. 21°18'	***<u>17</u>***	0s. 27°14' – 0s. 27°32'	<u>13</u>
0s. 21°19' – 0s. 21°32'	<u>17</u>	0s. 27°33' – 0s. 27°51'	***13***
0s. 21°33' – 0s. 21°44'	17	0s. 27°52' – 0s. 28°10'	<u>13</u>
0s. 21°45' – 0s. 21°53'	16, 17	0s. 28°11' – 0s. 28°18'	13
0s. 21°54' – 0s. 22°06'	16	0s. 28°19' – 0s. 28°33'	13, 25
0s. 22°07' – 0s. 22°22'	<u>16</u>	0s. 28°34' – 0s. 28°37'	13, <u>25</u>
0s. 22°23' – 0s. 22°38'	***<u>16</u>***	0s. 28°38' – 0s. 28°43'	<u>25</u>
0s. 22°39' – 0s. 22°50'	<u>16</u>	0s. 28°44' – 0s. 28°53'	***25***
0s. 22°51' – 0s. 22°53'	<u>16</u>, 31	0s. 28°54' – 0s. 28°59'	<u>25</u>
0s. 22°54' – 0s. 23°01'	16, 31	0s. 29°00' – 0s. 29°02'	12, <u>25</u>
0s. 23°02' – 0s. 23°10'	16, <u>31</u>	0s. 29°03' – 0s. 29°17'	12, 25
0s. 23°11'	16, ***<u>31</u>***	0s. 29°18' – 0s. 29°29'	12
0s. 23°12' – 0s. 23°15'	15, 16, ***<u>31</u>***	0s. 29°30' – 0s. 29°49'	<u>12</u>
0s. 23°16' – 0s. 23°18'	15, ***<u>31</u>***	0s. 29°50' – 1s. 0°10'	***12***
0s. 23°19' – 0s. 23°26'	15, <u>31</u>	1s. 0°11' – 1s. 0°30'	<u>12</u>
0s. 23°27' – 0s. 23°35'	15, 31	1s. 0°31' – 1s. 0°46'	12
0s. 23°36' – 0s. 23°37'	<u>15</u>, 31	1s. 0°47' – 1s. 1°00'	12, 23
0s. 23°38' – 0s. 23°51'	<u>15</u>	1s. 1°01'	23
0s. 23°52' – 0s. 24°08'	***<u>15</u>***	1s. 1°02' – 1s. 1°12'	<u>23</u>
0s. 24°09' – 0s. 24°24'	<u>15</u>	1s. 1°13' – 1s. 1°23'	***23***
0s. 24°25' – 0s. 24°37'	15, 29	1s. 1°24' – 1s. 1°34'	<u>23</u>
0s. 24°38' – 0s. 24°45'	15, <u>29</u>	1s. 1°35' – 1s. 1°38'	23
0s. 24°46' – 0s. 24°48'	15, ***29***	1s. 1°39' – 1s. 1°49'	11, 23
0s. 24°49' – 0s. 24°51'	***29***	1s. 1°50' – 1s. 2°10'	11
0s. 24°52' – 0s. 24°54'	14, ***29***	1s. 2°11' – 1s. 2°32'	<u>11</u>
0s. 24°55' – 0s. 25°02'	14, <u>29</u>	1s. 2°33' – 1s. 2°55'	***11***
0s. 25°03' – 0s. 25°15'	14, 29	1s. 2°56' – 1s. 3°17'	<u>11</u>
0s. 25°16'	14	1s. 3°18' – 1s. 3°21'	11
0s. 25°17' – 0s. 25°33'	<u>14</u>	1s. 3°22' – 1s. 3°33'	11, 32
0s. 25°34' – 0s. 25°52'	***<u>14</u>***	1s. 3°34' – 1s. 3°40'	11, <u>32</u>

1s. 3°41' – 1s. 3°42'	11, **_32_**	1s. 9°01' – 1s. 9°19'	9
1s. 3°43' – 1s. 3°49'	11, 21, **_32_**	1s. 9°20' – 1s. 9°46'	<u>9</u>
1s. 3°50' – 1s. 3°56'	21, **_32_**	1s. 9°47' – 1s. 10°13'	**_<u>9</u>_**
1s. 3°57' – 1s. 3°59'	21, 32	1s. 10°14' – 1s. 10°40'	<u>9</u>
1s. 4°00' – 1s. 4°08'	<u>21</u>, 32	1s. 10°41' – 1s. 11°03'	9
1s. 4°09' – 1s. 4°10'	<u>21</u>	1s. 11°04' – 1s. 11°17'	9, 26
1s. 4°11' – 1s. 4°23'	**_21_**	1s. 11°18' – 1s. 11°20'	9, <u>26</u>
1s. 4°24' – 1s. 4°26'	<u>21</u>	1s. 11°21' – 1s. 11°26'	<u>26</u>
1s. 4°27' – 1s. 4°34'	<u>21</u>, 31	1s. 11°27' – 1s. 11°37'	**_<u>26</u>_**
1s. 4°35' – 1s. 4°37'	21, 31	1s. 11°38'	<u>26</u>
1s. 4°38' – 1s. 4°45'	21, <u>31</u>	1s. 11°39' – 1s. 11°46'	17, <u>26</u>
1s. 4°46' – 1s. 4°47'	21, **_31_**	1s. 11°47' – 1s. 11°59'	17, 26
1s. 4°48' – 1s. 4°51'	10, 21, **_31_**	1s. 12°00'	<u>17</u>, 26
1s. 4°52' – 1s. 4°53'	10, **_31_**	1s. 12°01' – 1s. 12°13'	<u>17</u>
1s. 4°54' – 1s. 5°02'	10, <u>31</u>	1s. 12°14' – 1s. 12°28'	**_17_**
1s. 5°03' – 1s. 5°13'	10, 31	1s. 12°29' – 1s. 12°42'	<u>17</u>
1s. 5°14' – 1s. 5°23'	10	1s. 12°43' – 1s. 12°57'	17, 25
1s. 5°24' – 1s. 5°47'	<u>10</u>	1s. 12°58' – 1s. 13°03'	17, <u>25</u>
1s. 5°48' – 1s. 6°12'	**_10_**	1s. 13°04' – 1s. 13°06'	<u>25</u>
1s. 6°13' – 1s. 6°36'	<u>10</u>	1s. 13°07' – 1s. 13°17'	**_<u>25</u>_**
1s. 6°37' – 1s. 6°48'	10	1s. 13°18' – 1s. 13°26'	<u>25</u>
1s. 6°49' – 1s. 7°01'	10, 29	1s. 13°27' – 1s. 13°29'	25
1s. 7°02' – 1s. 7°09'	10, <u>29</u>	1s. 13°30' – 1s. 13°41'	8, 25
1s. 7°10' – 1s. 7°12'	10, **_29_**	1s. 13°42' – 1s. 14°14'	8
1s. 7°13' – 1s. 7°15'	**_29_**	1s. 14°15' – 1s. 14°44'	<u>8</u>
1s. 7°16' – 1s. 7°18'	19, **_29_**	1s. 14°45' – 1s. 15°15'	**_8_**
1s. 7°19' – 1s. 7°26'	19, <u>29</u>	1s. 15°16' – 1s. 15°45'	<u>8</u>
1s. 7°27' – 1s. 7°34'	19, 29	1s. 15°46' – 1s. 16°03'	8
1s. 7°35' – 1s. 7°39'	<u>19</u>, 29	1s. 16°04' – 1s. 16°14'	8, 31
1s. 7°40' – 1s. 7°47'	<u>19</u>	1s. 16°15' – 1s. 16°22'	8, <u>31</u>
1s. 7°48' – 1s. 8°00'	**_19_**	1s. 16°23' – 1s. 16°25'	8, **_31_**
1s. 8°01' – 1s. 8°07'	<u>19</u>	1s. 16°26' – 1s. 16°30'	8, 23, **_<u>31</u>_**
1s. 8°08' – 1s. 8°13'	<u>19</u>, 28	1s. 16°31'	23, **_<u>31</u>_**
1s. 8°14' – 1s. 8°20'	19, 28	1s. 16°32' – 1s. 16°39'	23, <u>31</u>
1s. 8°21' – 1s. 8°29'	19, <u>28</u>	1s. 16°40' – 1s. 16°42'	23, 31
1s. 8°30' – 1s. 8°32'	19, **_28_**	1s. 16°43' – 1s. 16°50'	<u>23</u>, 31
1s. 8°33' – 1s. 8°38'	**_28_**	1s. 16°51'	<u>23</u>
1s. 8°39'	<u>28</u>	1s. 16°52' – 1s. 17°02'	**_23_**
1s. 8°40' – 1s. 8°47'	9, <u>28</u>	1s. 17°03' – 1s. 17°11'	<u>23</u>
1s. 8°48' – 1s. 9°00'	9, 28	1s. 17°12' – 1s. 17°13'	15, <u>23</u>

1s. 17°14' – 1s. 17°28'	15, 23	1s. 25°52' – 1s. 26°03'	13, 32
1s. 17°29' – 1s. 17°35'	15	1s. 26°04' – 1s. 26°10'	13, _32_
1s. 17°36' – 1s. 17°51'	_15_	1s. 26°11' – 1s. 26°12'	13, **_32_**
1s. 17°52' – 1s. 18°08'	**_15_**	1s. 26°13' – 1s. 26°18'	13, 19, **_32_**
1s. 18°09' – 1s. 18°24'	_15_	1s. 26°19'	19, **_32_**
1s. 18°25' – 1s. 18°31'	15	1s. 26°20' – 1s. 26°26'	19, _32_
1s. 18°32' – 1s. 18°48'	15, 22	1s. 26°27' – 1s. 26°31'	19, 32
1s. 18°49' – 1s. 18°59'	_22_	1s. 26°32' – 1s. 26°38'	_19_, 32
1s. 19°00' – 1s. 19°10'	**_22_**	1s. 26°39' – 1s. 26°44'	_19_
1s. 19°11' – 1s. 19°13'	_22_	1s. 26°45' – 1s. 26°57'	**_19_**
1s. 19°14' – 1s. 19°21'	_22_, 29	1s. 26°58' – 1s. 27°06'	_19_
1s. 19°22' – 1s. 19°26'	22, 29	1s. 27°07' – 1s. 27°10'	_19_, 25
1s. 19°27' – 1s. 19°34'	22, _29_	1s. 27°11' – 1s. 27°21'	19, 25
1s. 19°35' – 1s. 19°38'	22, **_29_**	1s. 27°22' – 1s. 27°29'	19, _25_
1s. 19°39' – 1s. 19°42'	**_29_**	1s. 27°30'	_25_
1s. 19°43'	7, **_29_**	1s. 27°31' – 1s. 27°40'	**_25_**
1s. 19°44' – 1s. 19°51'	7, _29_	1s. 27°41'	**_25_**, 31
1s. 19°52' – 1s. 20°04'	7, 29	1s. 27°42' – 1s. 27°50'	_25_, 31
1s. 20°05' – 1s. 20°35'	7	1s. 27°51' – 1s. 27°52'	25, 31
1s. 20°36' – 1s. 21°08'	_7_	1s. 27°53' – 1s. 27°59'	25, _31_
1s. 21°09' – 1s. 21°43'	**_7_**	1s. 28°00' – 1s. 28°05'	6, 25, **_31_**
1s. 21°44' – 1s. 22°17'	_7_	1s. 28°06' – 1s. 28°08'	6, **_31_**
1s. 22°18' – 1s. 22°52'	7	1s. 28°09' – 1s. 28°16'	6, _31_
1s. 22°52' – 1s. 23°06'	7, 27	1s. 28°17' – 1s. 28°27'	6, 31
1s. 23°07' – 1s. 23°09'	7, _27_	1s. 28°28' – 1s. 28°59'	6
1s. 23°10' – 1s. 23°15'	_27_	1s. 29°00' – 1s. 29°39'	_6_
1s. 23°16' – 1s. 23°23'	**_27_**	1s. 29°40' – 2s. 0°20'	**_6_**
1s. 23°24'	20, **_27_**	2s. 0°21' – 2s. 1°00'	_6_
1s. 23°25' – 1s. 23°33'	20, _27_	2s. 1°01' – 2s. 1°38'	6
1s. 23°34' – 1s. 23°41'	20, 27	2s. 1°39' – 2s. 1°51'	6, 29
1s. 23°42' – 1s. 23°47'	_20_, 27	2s. 1°52' – 2s. 1°59'	6, _29_
1s. 23°48' – 1s. 23°53'	_20_	2s. 2°00'	6, **_29_**
1s. 23°54' – 1s. 24°06'	**_20_**	2s. 2°01' – 2s. 2°05'	**_29_**
1s. 24°07' – 1s. 24°18'	_20_	2s. 2°06' – 2s. 2°08'	23, **_29_**
1s. 24°19' – 1s. 24°27'	20	2s. 2°09' – 2s. 2°16'	23, _29_
1s. 24°28' – 1s. 24°36'	13, 20	2s. 2°17' – 2s. 2°20'	23, 29
1s. 24°37' – 1s. 24°54'	13	2s. 2°21' – 2s. 2°29'	_23_, 29
1s. 24°55' – 1s. 25°13'	_13_	2s. 2°30' – 2s. 2°32'	_23_
1s. 25°14' – 1s. 25°32'	**_13_**	2s. 2°33' – 2s. 2°42'	**_23_**
1s. 25°33' – 1s. 25°51'	_13_	2s. 2°43' – 2s. 2°49'	_23_

2s. 2°50' – 2s. 2°53'	17, <u>23</u>	2s. 9°29' – 2s. 9°35'	26, **_31_**
2s. 2°54' – 2s. 3°08'	17, 23	2s. 9°36'	5, 26, <u>31</u>
2s. 3°09' – 2s. 3°10'	17	2s. 9°37' – 2s. 9°42'	5, 26, **_31_**
2s. 3°11' – 2s. 3°24'	<u>17</u>	2s. 9°43' – 2s. 9°45'	5, **_31_**
2s. 3°25' – 2s. 3°39'	**_17_**	2s. 9°46' – 2s. 9°53'	5, <u>31</u>
2s. 3°40' – 2s. 3°50'	<u>17</u>	2s. 9°54' – 2s. 10°04'	5, 31
2s. 3°51' – 2s. 3°53'	<u>17</u>, 28	2s. 10°05' – 2s. 10°47'	5
2s. 3°54' – 2s. 4°03'	17, 28	2s. 10°48' – 2s. 11°35'	<u>5</u>
2s. 4°04' – 2s. 4°12'	17, <u>28</u>	2s. 11°36' – 2s. 12°24'	**_5_**
2s. 4°13' – 2s. 4°14'	17, **_28_**	2s. 12°25' – 2s. 13°12'	<u>5</u>
2s. 4°15' – 2s. 4°21'	**_28_**	2s. 13°13' – 2s. 14°03'	5
2s. 4°22' – 2s. 4°30'	11, <u>28</u>	2s. 14°04' – 2s. 14°16'	5, 29
2s. 4°31' – 2s. 4°43'	11, 28	2s. 14°17' – 2s. 14°24'	5, <u>29</u>
2s. 4°44' – 2s. 4°53'	11	2s. 14°25' – 2s. 14°29'	**_29_**
2s. 4°54' – 2s. 5°15'	<u>11</u>	2s. 14°30' – 2s. 14°34'	24, **_29_**
2s. 5°16' – 2s. 5°38'	**_11_**	2s. 14°35' – 2s. 14°41'	24, <u>29</u>
2s. 5°39' – 2s. 5°59'	<u>11</u>	2s. 14°42' – 2s. 14°44'	24, 29
2s. 6°00' – 2s. 6°12'	11	2s. 14°45' – 2s. 14°54'	<u>24</u>, 29
2s. 6°13' – 2s. 6°26'	11, 27	2s. 14°55' – 2s. 15°05'	**_24_**
2s. 6°27' – 2s. 6°32'	11, <u>27</u>	2s. 15°06' – 2s. 15°08'	<u>24</u>
2s. 6°33' – 2s. 6°35'	<u>27</u>	2s. 15°09' – 2s. 15°15'	19, <u>24</u>
2s. 6°36' – 2s. 6°44'	**_27_**	2s. 15°16' – 2s. 15°27'	19, 24
2s. 6°45' – 2s. 6°53'	16, <u>27</u>	2s. 15°28' – 2s. 15°30'	<u>19</u>, 24
2s. 6°54' – 2s. 7°06'	16, 27	2s. 15°31' – 2s. 15°40'	<u>19</u>
2s. 7°07'	<u>16</u>, 27	2s. 15°41' – 2s. 15°53'	**_19_**
2s. 7°08' – 2s. 7°21'	<u>16</u>	2s. 15°54' – 2s. 16°06'	<u>19</u>
2s. 7°22' – 2s. 7°38'	**_16_**	2s. 16°07' – 2s. 16°17'	19
2s. 7°39' – 2s. 7°53'	<u>16</u>	2s. 16°18' – 2s. 16°25'	14, 19
2s. 7°54' – 2s. 7°59'	16	2s. 16°26' – 2s. 16°42'	14
2s. 8°00' – 2s. 8°15'	16, 21	2s. 16°43' – 2s. 16°59'	<u>14</u>
2s. 8°16'	21	2s. 17°00' – 2s. 17°18'	**_14_**
2s. 8°17' – 2s. 8°27'	<u>21</u>	2s. 17°19' – 2s. 17°35'	<u>14</u>
2s. 8°28' – 2s. 8°40'	**_21_**	2s. 17°36' – 2s. 17°44'	14
2s. 8°41' – 2s. 8°45'	<u>21</u>	2s. 17°45' – 2s. 17°59'	14, 23
2s. 8°46' – 2s. 8°51'	<u>21</u>, 26	2s. 18°00'	14, <u>23</u>
2s. 8°52' – 2s. 8°59'	21, 26	2s. 18°01' – 2s. 18°10'	<u>23</u>
2s. 9°00' – 2s. 9°08'	21, <u>26</u>	2s. 18°11' – 2s. 18°21'	**_23_**
2s. 9°09' – 2s. 9°17'	**_26_**	2s. 18°22' – 2s. 18°32'	<u>23</u>, 32
2s. 9°18' – 2s. 9°19'	**_26_**, 31	2s. 18°33'	23, 32
2s. 9°20' – 2s. 9°28'	<u>26</u>, 31	2s. 18°34' – 2s. 18°39'	23, <u>32</u>

2s. 18°40'	9, 23, _32_	2s. 25°09' – 2s. 25°24'	17, 21
2s. 18°41' – 2s. 18°47'	9, 23, **_32_**	2s. 25°25'	21
2s. 18°48' – 2s. 18°49'	9, **_32_**	2s. 25°26' – 2s. 25°36'	_21_
2s. 18°50' – 2s. 18°56'	9, _32_	2s. 25°37' – 2s. 25°49'	**_21_**
2s. 18°57' – 2s. 19°08'	9, 32	2s. 25°50' – 2s. 25°54'	_21_
2s. 19°09' – 2s. 19°19'	9	2s. 25°55' – 2s. 26°00'	_21_, 25
2s. 19°20' – 2s. 19°46'	_9_	2s. 26°01' – 2s. 26°09'	21, 25
2s. 19°47' – 2s. 20°13'	**_9_**	2s. 26°10' – 2s. 26°17'	21, _25_
2s. 20°14' – 2s. 20°40'	_9_	2s. 26°18'	_25_
2s. 20°41' – 2s. 20°53'	9	2s. 26°19' – 2s. 26°28'	**_25_**
2s. 20°54' – 2s. 21°04'	9, 31	2s. 26°29'	**_25_**, 29
2s. 21°05' – 2s. 21°12'	9, _31_	2s. 26°30' – 2s. 26°38'	_25_, 29
2s. 21°13' – 2s. 21°15'	9, **_31_**	2s. 26°39' – 2s. 26°41'	25, 29
2s. 21°16' – 2s. 21°20'	9, 22, **_31_**	2s. 26°42' – 2s. 26°49'	25, _29_
2s. 21°21'	22, **_31_**	2s. 26°50' – 2s. 26°53'	25, **_29_**
2s. 21°22' – 2s. 21°29'	22, _31_	2s. 26°54' – 2s. 26°58'	**_29_**
2s. 21°30' – 2s. 21°32'	22, 31	2s. 26°59'	_29_
2s. 21°33' – 2s. 21°40'	_22_, 31	2s. 27°00' – 2s. 27°06'	4, _29_
2s. 21°41' – 2s. 21°43'	_22_	2s. 27°07' – 2s. 27°19'	4, 29
2s. 21°44' – 2s. 21°54'	**_22_**	2s. 27°20' – 2s. 28°29'	4
2s. 21°55' – 2s. 22°05'	_22_	2s. 28°30' – 2s. 29°29'	_4_
2s. 22°06' – 2s. 22°09'	22	2s. 29°30' – 3s. 0°30'	**_4_**
2s. 22°10' – 2s. 22°22'	13, 22	3s. 0°31' – 3s. 1°30'	_4_
2s. 22°23' – 2s. 22°36'	13	3s. 1°31' – 3s. 2°30'	4
2s. 22°37' – 2s. 22°55'	_13_	3s. 2°31' – 3s. 2°41'	4, 31
2s. 22°56' – 2s. 23°14'	**_13_**	3s. 2°42' – 3s. 2°49'	4, _31_
2s. 23°15' – 2s. 23°33'	_13_	3s. 2°50' – 3s. 2°52'	4, **_31_**
2s. 23°34' – 2s. 23°35'	13	3s. 2°53' – 3s. 2°58'	4, 27, **_31_**
2s. 23°36' – 2s. 23°47'	13, 30	3s. 2°59' – 3s. 3°00'	4, 27, _31_
2s. 23°48' – 2s. 23°55'	13, _30_	3s. 3°01' – 3s. 3°06'	27, _31_
2s. 23°56' – 2s. 23°59'	13, **_30_**	3s. 3°07' – 3s. 3°15'	_27_, 31
2s. 24°00'	13, 17, **_30_**	3s. 3°16' – 3s. 3°17'	_27_, 31
2s. 24°01' – 2s. 24°04'	17, **_30_**	3s. 3°18' – 3s. 3°23'	**_27_**
2s. 24°05' – 2s. 24°12'	17, _30_	3s. 3°24'	23, **_27_**
2s. 24°13' – 2s. 24°20'	17, 30	3s. 3°25' – 3s. 3°33'	23, _27_
2s. 24°21' – 2s. 24°24'	_17_, 30	3s. 3°34' – 3s. 3°35'	23, 27
2s. 24°25' – 2s. 24°34'	_17_	3s. 3°36' – 3s. 3°47'	_23_, 27
2s. 24°35' – 2s. 24°49'	**_17_**	3s. 3°48' – 3s. 3°49'	_23_
2s. 24°50' – 2s. 25°03'	_17_	3s. 3°50' – 3s. 4°00'	**_23_**
2s. 25°04' – 2s. 25°08'	17	3s. 4°01' – 3s. 4°05'	_23_

Range	Values	Range	Values
3s. 4°06' – 3s. 4°11'	19, _23_	3s. 10°43' – 3s. 10°51'	**_25_**
3s. 4°12' – 3s. 4°24'	19, 23	3s. 10°52' – 3s. 10°53'	_25_, 32
3s. 4°25' – 3s. 4°26'	_19_, 23	3s. 10°54' – 3s. 11°02'	_25_, 32
3s. 4°27' – 3s. 4°37'	_19_	3s. 11°03'	25, 32
3s. 4°38' – 3s. 4°50'	**_19_**	3s. 11°04' – 3s. 11°07'	25, _32_
3s. 4°51' – 3s. 5°03'	_19_	3s. 11°08' – 3s. 11°10'	7, 25, _32_
3s. 5°04' – 3s. 5°11'	19	3s. 11°11' – 3s. 11°17'	7, 25, **_32_**
3s. 5°12' – 3s. 5°22'	15, 19	3s. 11°18' – 3s. 11°19'	7, **_32_**
3s. 5°23' – 3s. 5°35'	15	3s. 11°20' – 3s. 11°26'	7, _32_
3s. 5°36' – 3s. 5°51'	_15_	3s. 11°27' – 3s. 11°38'	7, 32
3s. 5°52' – 3s. 6°08'	**_15_**	3s. 11°39' – 3s. 11°59'	7
3s. 6°09' – 3s. 6°24'	_15_	3s. 12°00' – 3s. 12°33'	_7_
3s. 6°25' – 3s. 6°26'	15	3s. 12°34' – 3s. 13°08'	**_7_**
3s. 6°27' – 3s. 6°40'	15, 26	3s. 13°09' – 3s. 13°42'	_7_
3s. 6°41' – 3s. 6°48'	15, _26_	3s. 13°43' – 3s. 14°07'	7
3s. 6°49'	_26_	3s. 14°08' – 3s. 14°18'	7, 31
3s. 6°50' – 3s. 7°00'	**_26_**	3s. 14°19' – 3s. 14°26'	7, _31_
3s. 7°01' – 3s. 7°05'	_26_	3s. 14°27' – 3s. 14°29'	7, **_31_**
3s. 7°06' – 3s. 7°09'	11, _26_	3s. 14°30' – 3s. 14°34'	7, 24, **_31_**
3s. 7°10' – 3s. 7°23'	11, 26	3s. 14°35'	24, **_31_**
3s. 7°24' – 3s. 7°37'	11	3s. 14°36' – 3s. 14°43'	24, _31_
3s. 7°38' – 3s. 7°59'	_11_	3s. 14°44'	24, 31
3s. 8°00' – 3s. 8°22'	**_11_**	3s. 14°45' – 3s. 14°54'	_24_, 31
3s. 8°23' – 3s. 8°44'	_11_	3s. 14°55' – 3s. 15°05'	**_24_**
3s. 8°45' – 3s. 8°53'	11	3s. 15°06' – 3s. 15°08'	_24_
3s. 8°54' – 3s. 9°06'	11, 29	3s. 15°09' – 3s. 15°15'	17, _24_
3s. 9°07' – 3s. 9°14'	11, _29_	3s. 15°16' – 3s. 15°30'	17, 24
3s. 9°15' – 3s. 9°16'	11, **_29_**	3s. 15°31'	17
3s. 9°17' – 3s. 9°19'	**_29_**	3s. 15°32' – 3s. 15°45'	_17_
3s. 9°20' – 3s. 9°23'	18, **_29_**	3s. 15°46' – 3s. 16°00'	**_17_**
3s. 9°24' – 3s. 9°31'	18, _29_	3s. 16°01' – 3s. 16°12'	_17_
3s. 9°32' – 3s. 9°39'	18, 29	3s. 16°13' – 3s. 16°14'	_17_, 27
3s. 9°40' – 3s. 9°44'	_18_, 29	3s. 16°15' – 3s. 16°26'	17, 27
3s. 9°45' – 3s. 9°52'	_18_	3s. 16°27' – 3s. 16°35'	17, _27_
3s. 9°53' – 3s. 10°07'	**_18_**	3s. 16°36' – 3s. 16°44'	**_27_**
3s. 10°08' – 3s. 10°18'	_18_	3s. 16°45' – 3s. 16°47'	_27_
3s. 10°19' – 3s. 10°20'	_18_, 25	3s. 16°48' – 3s. 16°53'	10, _27_
3s. 10°21' – 3s. 10°33'	18, 25	3s. 16°54' – 3s. 17°07'	10, 27
3s. 10°34' – 3s. 10°40'	18, _25_	3s. 17°08' – 3s. 17°23'	10
3s. 10°41' – 3s. 10°42'	_25_	3s. 17°24' – 3s. 17°47'	_10_

3s. 17°48' – 3s. 18°12'	**<u>10</u>**	3s. 25°07' – 3s. 25°16'	**<u>25</u>**
3s. 18°13' – 3s. 18°36'	<u>10</u>	3s. 25°17'	**<u>25</u>**, 28
3s. 18°37' – 3s. 19°02'	10	3s. 25°18' – 3s. 25°26'	<u>25</u>, 28
3s. 19°03' – 3s. 19°12'	10, 23	3s. 25°27' – 3s. 25°29'	25, 28
3s. 19°13' – 3s. 19°17'	23	3s. 25°30' – 3s. 25°38'	25, <u>28</u>
3s. 19°18' – 3s. 19°28'	<u>23</u>	3s. 25°39' – 3s. 25°41'	25, **<u>28</u>**
3s. 19°29' – 3s. 19°39'	**<u>23</u>**	3s. 25°42' – 3s. 25°43'	**<u>28</u>**
3s. 19°40' – 3s. 19°50'	23	3s. 25°44' – 3s. 25°47'	<u>28</u>, 31
3s. 19°51' – 3s. 20°05'	13, 23	3s. 25°48' – 3s. 25°54'	<u>28</u>, 31
3s. 20°06' – 3s. 20°17'	13	3s. 25°55' – 3s. 25°56'	<u>28</u>, <u>31</u>
3s. 20°18' – 3s. 20°37'	<u>13</u>	3s. 25°57' – 3s. 25°59'	28, <u>31</u>
3s. 20°38' – 3s. 20°55'	**<u>13</u>**	3s. 26°00' – 3s. 26°02'	3, 28, <u>31</u>
3s. 20°56' – 3s. 21°14'	<u>13</u>	3s. 26°03' – 3s. 26°09'	3, 28, **<u>31</u>**
3s. 21°15' – 3s. 21°17'	13	3s. 26°10' – 3s. 26°11'	3, **<u>31</u>**
3s. 21°18' – 3s. 21°30'	13, 29	3s. 26°12' – 3s. 26°19'	3, <u>31</u>
3s. 21°31' – 3s. 21°38'	13, <u>29</u>	3s. 26°20' – 3s. 26°30'	3, 31
3s. 21°39' – 3s. 21°41'	13, **<u>29</u>**	3s. 26°31' – 3s. 27°59'	3
3s. 21°42' – 3s. 21°44'	**<u>29</u>**	3s. 28°00' – 3s. 29°19'	<u>3</u>
3s. 21°45' – 3s. 21°47'	16, **<u>29</u>**	3s. 29°20' – 4s. 0°40'	**<u>3</u>**
3s. 21°48' – 3s. 21°55'	16, <u>29</u>	4s. 0°41' – 4s. 2°00'	<u>3</u>
3s. 21°56' – 3s. 22°06'	16, 29	4s. 2°01' – 4s. 3°21'	3
3s. 22°07' – 3s. 22°08'	<u>16</u>, 29	4s. 3°22' – 4s. 3°33'	3, 32
3s. 22°09' – 3s. 22°21'	<u>16</u>	4s. 3°34' – 4s. 3°40'	3, <u>32</u>
3s. 22°22' – 3s. 22°38'	**<u>16</u>**	4s. 3°41' – 4s. 3°42'	3, **<u>32</u>**
3s. 22°39' – 3s. 22°53'	<u>16</u>	4s. 3°43' – 4s. 3°49'	3, 29, **<u>32</u>**
3s. 22°54' – 3s. 23°02'	16	4s. 3°50' – 4s. 3°55'	3, 29, <u>32</u>
3s. 23°03' – 3s. 23°15'	16, 19	4s. 3°56'	3, <u>29</u>, <u>32</u>
3s. 23°16' – 3s. 23°21'	19	4s. 3°57' – 4s. 4°00'	3, <u>29</u>, 32
3s. 23°22' – 3s. 23°34'	<u>19</u>	4s. 4°01' – 4s. 4°03'	<u>29</u>, 32
3s. 23°35' – 3s. 23°47'	**<u>19</u>**	4s. 4°04' – 4s. 4°08'	**<u>29</u>**, 32
3s. 23°48' – 3s. 23°59'	<u>19</u>	4s. 4°09' – 4s. 4°12'	26, **<u>29</u>**
3s. 24°00'	<u>19</u>, 22	4s. 4°13' – 4s. 4°20'	26, <u>29</u>
3s. 24°01' – 3s. 24°16'	19, 22	4s. 4°21' – 4s. 4°22'	26, 29
3s. 24°17' – 3s. 24°19'	19, <u>22</u>	4s. 4°23' – 4s. 4°31'	<u>26</u>, 29
3s. 24°20' – 3s. 24°27'	<u>22</u>	4s. 4°32' – 4s. 4°33'	**<u>26</u>**, 29
3s. 24°28' – 3s. 24°38'	**<u>22</u>**	4s. 4°34' – 4s. 4°41'	**<u>26</u>**
3s. 24°39' – 3s. 24°42'	<u>22</u>	4s. 4°42'	23, **<u>26</u>**
3s. 24°43' – 3s. 24°49'	<u>22</u>, 25	4s. 4°43' – 4s. 4°51'	23, <u>26</u>
3s. 24°50' – 3s. 24°57'	22, 25	4s. 4°52' – 4s. 4°56'	23, 26
3s. 24°58' – 3s. 25°06'	22, <u>25</u>	4s. 4°57' – 4s. 5°05'	<u>23</u>, 26

4s. 5°06' – 4s. 5°07'	_23_	4s. 11°36' – 4s. 11°47'	11, 30
4s. 5°08' – 4s. 5°18'	**_23_**	4s. 11°48' – 4s. 11°55'	11, _30_
4s. 5°19' – 4s. 5°23'	_23_	4s. 11°56' – 4s. 11°59'	11, **_30_**
4s. 5°24' – 4s. 5°29'	20, _23_	4s. 12°00'	11, 19, **_30_**
4s. 5°30' – 4s. 5°42'	20, 23	4s. 12°01' – 4s. 12°04'	19, **_30_**
4s. 5°43' – 4s. 5°44'	_20_, 23	4s. 12°05' – 4s. 12°12'	19, _30_
4s. 5°45' – 4s. 5°53'	_20_	4s. 12°13' – 4s. 12°18'	19, 30
4s. 5°54' – 4s. 6°06'	**_20_**	4s. 12°19' – 4s. 12°24'	_19_, 30
4s. 6°07' – 4s. 6°18'	_20_	4s. 12°25' – 4s. 12°31'	_19_
4s. 6°19' – 4s. 6°21'	20	4s. 12°32' – 4s. 12°44'	**_19_**
4s. 6°22' – 4s. 6°36'	17, 20	4s. 12°45' – 4s. 12°52'	_19_
4s. 6°37' – 4s. 6°43'	17	4s. 12°53' – 4s. 12°57'	_19_, 27
4s. 6°44' – 4s. 6°56'	_17_	4s. 12°58' – 4s. 13°06'	19, 27
4s. 6°57' – 4s. 7°11'	**_17_**	4s. 13°07' – 4s. 13°15'	19, _27_
4s. 7°12' – 4s. 7°21'	_17_	4s. 13°16'	19, **_27_**
4s. 7°22' – 4s. 7°25'	_17_, 31	4s. 13°17' – 4s. 13°24'	**_27_**
4s. 7°26' – 4s. 7°32'	17, 31	4s. 13°25' – 4s. 13°29'	27
4s. 7°33' – 4s. 7°40'	17, _31_	4s. 13°30' – 4s. 13°33'	8, _27_
4s. 7°41' – 4s. 7°42'	17, **_31_**	4s. 13°34' – 4s. 13°47'	8, 27
4s. 7°43' – 4s. 7°46'	14, 17,**_31_**	4s. 13°48' – 4s. 14°14'	8
4s. 7°47' – 4s. 7°49'	14, **_31_**	4s. 14°15' – 4s. 14°44'	_8_
4s. 7°50' – 4s. 7°57'	14, _31_	4s. 14°45' – 4s. 15°15'	**_8_**
4s. 7°58' – 4s. 8°07'	14, 31	4s. 15°16' – 4s. 15°45'	_8_
4s. 8°08'	_14_, 31	4s. 15°46' – 4s. 16°07'	8
4s. 8°09' – 4s. 8°24'	_14_	4s. 16°08' – 4s. 16°20'	8, 29
4s. 8°25' – 4s. 8°43'	**_14_**	4s. 16°21' – 4s. 16°28'	8, _29_
4s. 8°44' – 4s. 9°00'	_14_	4s. 16°29' – 4s. 16°30'	8, **_29_**
4s. 9°01' – 4s. 9°06'	14	4s. 16°31' – 4s. 16°34'	**_29_**
4s. 9°07' – 4s. 9°21'	14, 25	4s. 16°35' – 4s. 16°37'	21, **_29_**
4s. 9°22' – 4s. 9°25'	14, _25_	4s. 16°38' – 4s. 16°45'	21, _29_
4s. 9°26' – 4s. 9°30'	_25_	4s. 16°46' – 4s. 16°51'	21, 29
4s. 9°31' – 4s. 9°41'	**_25_**	4s. 16°52' – 4s. 16°58'	_21_, 29
4s. 9°42' – 4s. 9°49'	_25_	4s. 16°59' – 4s. 17°02'	_21_
4s. 9°50'	11, _25_	4s. 17°03' – 4s. 17°15'	**_21_**
4s. 9°51' – 4s. 10°05'	11, 25	4s. 17°16' – 4s. 17°26'	_21_
4s. 10°06' – 4s. 10°21'	11	4s. 17°27' – 4s. 17°32'	21
4s. 10°22' – 4s. 10°43'	_11_	4s. 17°33' – 4s. 17°43'	13, 21
4s. 10°44' – 4s. 11°06'	**_11_**	4s. 17°44' – 4s. 17°59'	13
4s. 11°07' – 4s. 11°28'	_11_	4s. 18°00' – 4s. 18°18'	_13_
4s. 11°29' – 4s. 11°35'	11	4s. 18°19' – 4s. 18°37'	**_13_**

Range	Numbers	Range	Numbers
4s. 18°38' – 4s. 18°56'	<u>13</u>	4s. 26°43' – 4s. 26°44'	22, ***27***
4s. 18°57'	13	4s. 26°45' – 4s. 26°53'	22, <u>27</u>
4s. 18°58' – 4s. 19°08'	13, 31	4s. 26°54' – 4s. 26°59'	22, 27
4s. 19°09' – 4s. 19°16'	13, <u>31</u>	4s. 27°00' – 4s. 27°07'	<u>22</u>, 27
4s. 19°17' – 4s. 19°19'	13, ***31***	4s. 27°08' – 4s. 27°10'	<u>22</u>
4s. 19°20' – 4s. 19°23'	13, 18, <u>***31***</u>	4s. 27°11' – 4s. 27°21'	***22***
4s. 19°24' – 4s. 19°25'	18, ***31***	4s. 27°22' – 4s. 27°31'	22
4s. 19°26' – 4s. 19°37'	18, <u>31</u>	4s. 27°32'	17, 22
4s. 19°38' – 4s. 19°39'	18, 31	4s. 27°33' – 4s. 27°49'	17, 22
4s. 19°40' – 4s. 19°43'	<u>18</u>, 31	4s. 27°50' – 4s. 27°52'	17
4s. 19°44' – 4s. 19°52'	<u>18</u>	4s. 27°53' – 4s. 28°06'	<u>17</u>
4s. 19°53' – 4s. 20°07'	***18***	4s. 28°07' – 4s. 28°21'	***17***
4s. 20°08' – 4s. 20°20'	<u>18</u>	4s. 28°22' – 4s. 28°32'	<u>17</u>
4s. 20°21' – 4s. 20°35'	18, 23	4s. 28°33' – 4s. 28°35'	<u>17</u>, 29
4s. 20°36' – 4s. 20°40'	18, <u>23</u>	4s. 28°36' – 4s. 28°45'	17, 29
4s. 20°41' – 4s. 20°46'	<u>23</u>	4s. 28°46' – 4s. 28°53'	17, <u>29</u>
4s. 20°47' – 4s. 20°57'	***23***	4s. 28°54' – 4s. 28°56'	17, ***29***
4s. 20°58' – 4s. 20°59'	<u>23</u>	4s. 28°57' – 4s. 28°59'	***29***
4s. 21°00' – 4s. 21°08'	23, 28	4s. 29°00' – 4s. 29°02'	12, ***29***
4s. 21°09' – 4s. 21°12'	23, 28	4s. 29°03' – 4s. 29°10'	12, <u>29</u>
4s. 21°13' – 4s. 21°21'	23, <u>28</u>	4s. 29°11' – 4s. 29°23'	12, 29
4s. 21°22' – 4s. 21°23'	23, ***28***	4s. 29°24' – 4s. 29°29'	12
4s. 21°24' – 4s. 21°30'	***28***	4s. 29°30' – 4s. 29°49'	<u>12</u>
4s. 21°31' – 4s. 21°35'	<u>28</u>	4s. 29°50' – 5s. 0°10'	***12***
4s. 21°36' – 4s. 21°39'	5, <u>28</u>	5s. 0°11' – 5s. 0°30'	<u>12</u>
4s. 21°40' – 4s. 21°52'	5, 28	5s. 0°31' – 5s. 0°34'	12
4s. 21°53' – 4s. 22°47'	5	5s. 0°35' – 5s. 0°45'	12, 31
4s. 22°48' – 4s. 23°35'	<u>5</u>	5s. 0°46' – 5s. 0°53'	12, <u>31</u>
4s. 23°36' – 4s. 24°24'	<u>***5***</u>	5s. 0°54' – 5s. 0°56'	12, ***31***
4s. 24°25' – 4s. 25°12'	<u>5</u>	5s. 0°57' – 5s. 1°00'	12,19, ***31***
4s. 25°13' – 4s. 25°51'	5	5s. 1°01' – 5s. 1°02'	19, ***31***
4s. 25°52' – 4s. 26°03'	5, 32	5s. 1°03' – 5s. 1°10'	19, <u>31</u>
4s. 26°04' – 4s. 26°10'	5, <u>32</u>	5s. 1°11' – 5s. 1°15'	19, 31
4s. 26°11' – 4s. 26°12'	5, ***32***	5s. 1°16' – 5s. 1°21'	<u>19</u>, 31
4s. 26°13' – 4s. 26°19'	5, 27, ***32***	5s. 1°22' – 5s. 1°28'	<u>19</u>
4s. 26°20' – 4s. 26°24'	5, 27, <u>32</u>	5s. 1°29' – 5s. 1°41'	***19***
4s. 26°25' – 4s. 26°26'	27, <u>32</u>	5s. 1°42' – 5s. 1°49'	<u>19</u>
4s. 26°27' – 4s. 26°35'	<u>27</u>, 32	5s. 1°50' – 5s. 1°54'	<u>19</u>, 26
4s. 26°36' – 4s. 26°38'	***27***, 32	5s. 1°55' – 5s. 2°03'	19, 26
4s. 26°39' – 4s. 26°42'	***27***	5s. 2°04' – 5s. 2°12'	19, <u>26</u>

Range	Numbers	Range	Numbers
5s. 2°13'	19, 26	5s. 10°58' – 5s. 11°10'	9, 29
5s. 2°14' – 5s. 2°23'	26	5s. 11°11' – 5s. 11°18'	9, 29
5s. 2°24' – 5s. 2°32'	26	5s. 11°19' – 5s. 11°20'	9, 29
5s. 2°33'	26	5s. 11°21' – 5s. 11°23'	29
5s. 2°34' – 5s. 2°46'	7, 26	5s. 11°24' – 5s. 11°27'	20, 29
5s. 2°47' – 5s. 3°26'	7	5s. 11°28' – 5s. 11°35'	20, 29
5s. 3°27' – 5s. 3°59'	7	5s. 11°36' – 5s. 11°41'	20, 29
5s. 4°00' – 5s. 4°34'	7	5s. 11°42' – 5s. 11°48'	20, 29
5s. 4°35' – 5s. 5°08'	7	5s. 11°49' – 5s. 11°53'	20
5s. 5°09' – 5s. 5°35'	7	5s. 11°54' – 5s. 12°06'	20
5s. 5°36' – 5s. 5°47'	7, 30	5s. 12°07' – 5s. 12°11'	20
5s. 5°48' – 5s. 5°55'	7, 30	5s. 12°12' – 5s. 12°18'	20, 31
5s. 5°56' – 5s. 5°59'	7, 30	5s. 12°19' – 5s. 12°22'	20, 31
5s. 6°00'	7, 23, 30	5s. 12°23' – 5s. 12°30'	20, 31
5s. 6°01' – 5s. 6°04'	23, 30	5s. 12°31' – 5s. 12°32'	20, 31
5s. 6°05' – 5s. 6°12'	23, 30	5s. 12°33' – 5s. 12°36'	11, 20, 31
5s. 6°13' – 5s. 6°14'	23, 30	5s. 12°37' – 5s. 12°39'	11, 31
5s. 6°15' – 5s. 6°24'	23, 30	5s. 12°40' – 5s. 12°47'	11, 31
5s. 6°25'	23	5s. 12°48' – 5s. 12°58'	11, 31
5s. 6°26' – 5s. 6°36'	23	5s. 12°59' – 5s. 13°04'	11
5s. 6°37' – 5s. 6°44'	23	5s. 13°05' – 5s. 13°26'	11
5s. 6°45' – 5s. 6°47'	16, 23	5s. 13°27' – 5s. 13°49'	11
5s. 6°48' – 5s. 7°02'	16, 23	5s. 13°50' – 5s. 14°11'	11
5s. 7°03' – 5s. 7°06'	16	5s. 14°12' – 5s. 14°29'	11
5s. 7°07' – 5s. 7°21'	16	5s. 14°30' – 5s. 14°43'	11, 24
5s. 7°22' – 5s. 7°38'	16	5s. 14°44'	24
5s. 7°39' – 5s. 7°53'	16	5s. 14°45' – 5s. 14°54'	24
5s. 7°54'	16	5s. 14°55' – 5s. 15°05'	24
5s. 7°55' – 5s. 8°09'	16, 25	5s. 15°06' – 5s. 15°13'	24
5s. 8°10' – 5s. 8°15'	16, 25	5s. 15°14' – 5s. 15°15'	13, 24
5s. 8°16' – 5s. 8°18'	25	5s. 15°16' – 5s. 15°30'	13, 24
5s. 8°19' – 5s. 8°29'	25	5s. 15°31' – 5s. 15°41'	13
5s. 8°30' – 5s. 8°38'	25	5s. 15°42' – 5s. 15°59'	13
5s. 8°39'	25	5s. 16°00' – 5s. 16°18'	13
5s. 8°40' – 5s. 8°53'	9, 25	5s. 16°19' – 5s. 16°37'	13
5s. 8°54' – 5s. 9°19'	9	5s. 16°38' – 5s. 16°42'	13
5s. 9°20' – 5s. 9°46'	9	5s. 16°43' – 5s. 16°55'	13, 28
5s. 9°47' – 5s. 10°13'	9	5s. 16°56' – 5s. 17°04'	13, 28
5s. 10°14' – 5s. 10°40'	9	5s. 17°05' – 5s. 17°11'	28
5s. 10°41' – 5s. 10°57'	9	5s. 17°12' – 5s. 17°13'	15, 28

5s. 17°14' – 5s. 17°22'	15, _28_	5s. 22°54' – 5s. 23°02'	_25_, 27
5s. 17°23' – 5s. 17°35'	15, 28	5s. 23°03' – 5s. 23°06'	25, 27
5s. 17°36' – 5s. 17°51'	_15_	5s. 23°07' – 5s. 23°15'	25, _27_
5s. 17°52' – 5s. 18°08'	_**15**_	5s. 23°16' – 5s. 23°17'	25, _**27**_
5s. 18°09' – 5s. 18°21'	_15_	5s. 23°18' – 5s. 23°22'	_**27**_
5s. 18°22' – 5s. 18°24'	_15_, 32	5s. 23°23' – 5s. 23°24'	_**27**_, 29
5s. 18°25' – 5s. 18°33'	15, 32	5s. 23°25' – 5s. 23°33'	_27_, 29
5s. 18°34' – 5s. 18°40'	15, _32_	5s. 23°34' – 5s. 23°35'	27, 29
5s. 18°41' – 5s. 18°42'	15, _**32**_	5s. 23°36' – 5s. 23°43'	27, _29_
5s. 18°43' – 5s. 18°48'	15, 17, _**32**_	5s. 23°44' – 5s. 23°47'	27, _**29**_
5s. 18°49'	17, _**32**_	5s. 23°48'	_**29**_
5s. 18°50' – 5s. 18°56'	17, _32_	5s. 23°49' – 5s. 23°52'	_**29**_, 31
5s. 18°57' – 5s. 19°03'	17, 32	5s. 23°53' – 5s. 23°59'	_29_, 31
5s. 19°04' – 5s. 19°08'	_17_, 32	5s. 24°00'	2, 29, 31
5s. 19°09' – 5s. 19°17'	_17_	5s. 24°01' – 5s. 24°07'	2, 29, _31_
5s. 19°18' – 5s. 19°32'	_**17**_	5s. 24°08' – 5s. 24°13'	2, 29, _**31**_
5s. 19°33' – 5s. 19°46'	_17_	5s. 24°14' – 5s. 24°16'	2, _**31**_
5s. 19°47' – 5s. 19°53'	17	5s. 24°17' – 5s. 24°24'	2, _31_
5s. 19°54' – 5s. 20°07'	17, 19	5s. 24°25' – 5s. 24°35'	2, 31
5s. 20°08' – 5s. 20°12'	19	5s. 24°36' – 5s. 26°59'	2
5s. 20°13' – 5s. 20°25'	_19_	5s. 27°00' – 5s. 28°59'	_2_
5s. 20°26' – 5s. 20°38'	_**19**_	5s. 29°00' – 6s. 0°00'	_**2**_
5s. 20°39' – 5s. 20°51'	_19_		
5s. 20°52' – 5s. 21°08'	19, 21		
5s. 21°09' – 5s. 21°10'	19, _21_		
5s. 21°11' – 5s. 21°21'	_21_		
5s. 21°22' – 5s. 21°32'	_**21**_		
5s. 21°33' – 5s. 21°38'	_21_		
5s. 21°39' – 5s. 21°43'	_21_, 23		
5s. 21°44' – 5s. 21°53'	21, 23		
5s. 21°54' – 5s. 22°00'	21, _23_		
5s. 22°01' – 5s. 22°04'	_23_		
5s. 22°05' – 5s. 22°15'	_**23**_		
5s. 22°16' – 5s. 22°18'	_23_		
5s. 22°19' – 5s. 22°26'	_23_, 25		
5s. 22°27' – 5s. 22°33'	23, 25		
5s. 22°34' – 5s. 22°41'	23, _25_		
5s. 22°42'	_25_		
5s. 22°43' – 5s. 22°52'	_**25**_		
5s. 22°53'	_**25**_, 27		

Appendix III
Harmonic Aspects for charts given in Chapters 3-16

Here I list the harmonic aspects for all the charts discussed in Chapters 3-16, in the order in which they were discussed, so that readers can interpret them using the methods shown in Chapter 18. To save space I have omitted some aspects that are less important for interpretation, so these lists are slightly shorter than those given in Chapter 18.

Chapter 3: Oneness

Padre Pio
1: ((SO-*1*-PL)-1/*1*-ME)-1/1/1/1/1-(MA-*1*-NE)
   MO-1-VE
   VE-1-SA
2: (SO-*1*-PL)-8/8-SA
3: ((SO-*1*-PL)-*9*/9-VE)-18/*18*/18-CH
   (MO-9-VE)-27/27-CH
   (MA-*1*-NE)-12/12-JU
5: ((SO-*1*-PL)-1/*1*-ME)-5/*5*/5-JU
7: (SA-7-NE)-14/*14*-CH)-28-MO
11: (SO-*1*-PL)-11/11-MO
   (MA-*1*-NE)-11/*11*-UR
13: SO-26-UR
17: (ME-*17*-VE)-17/*17*-UR

Josemaria Escriva
1: (SO-*1*-MO-*1*-SA)-1-(ME-*1*-JU)
   -1-CH
3: (SO-*1*-MO-*1*-SA)-*9*/9/*9*/9/-(VE-*3*-NE)
   -12/*12*/*12*-JU
   (ME-*1*-JU)-*27*-CH
5: (ME-*1*-JU)-*5*-PL)-10/10/*10*-VE
   -10/*30*/10/30-(VE-*3*-NE)
7: (SO-*1*-MO-*1*-SA)-21/*21*/21-MA
   (ME-*1*-JU)-28-MA
   -21-*UR*
17: (SO-*1*-MO-*1*-SA)-17/17/*17*-PL

Pierre Teilhard de Chardin
1: ((VE-*1*-NE)-1-SO)-1-(JU-*1*-SA)
   -1/1/1-CH
2: (JU-16-PL)-32-ME
3: (VE-*1*-NE)-*12*/12-MO
   (JU-*1*-SA)-*9*/9-MO
7: (MO-7-ME)-21/21-PL
   (VE-*1*-NE)-28/*28*-UR
   (UR-7-PL)-21-MO
   -28/*28*-UR
11: (SO-11-MO)-*22*/22-PL
13: (MO-*13*-MA)-26-SA
29: SO-*29*-MA
   (ME-*29*-CH)-29-UR

Helen Duncan
1: (SO-*1*-MA-*1*-SA)-1-(MO-*1*-ME)
   -1-UR)-1-CH

2: (MO-*1*-ME)-*2*/2-PL
   (MO-*2*-PL)-16/*16*-CH
3: (SO-*1*-SA)-18/*18*-VE
   -6-*JU*
   ((MO-*1*-ME)-*2*/2-PL)-12/12/12-VE
5: (SO-*1*-SA)-20-NE
7: (JU-*7*-NE)-28-VE
17: (SO-*1*-SA)-17/*17*-PL
19: (VE-19-MA)-19/*19*-*JU*
31: ((SO-*1*-SA)-*31*/31-*JU*)-*31*/31/*31*-CH

Meurig Morris
1: (((VE-*1*-MA)-1-UR)-1/1/1-CH)-1/1/1/1-ME
   ((ME-1-CH)-1/*1*-VE)-1/1/1-SA
   SO-1-JU
2: (((VE-*1*-MA)-1-CH)-1/1/*1*-ME)-2/2/*2*/2-PL
   (SO-1-JU)-*2*/2-MO
3: MO-*9*-VE
11: (VE-*1*-MA)-11/*11*-*NE*
13: SO-*13*-SA
19: (VE-*1*-MA)-*19*-JU
23: (VE-*1*-MA)-*23*/23-SO
29: (SO-*29*-UR)-29-*NE*

Matthew Manning
1: ((SO-*1*-MA)-1-(MO-*1*-VE))-1/1/*1*/1-JU
   -1/1/*1*-PL
   (SO-1-PL)-1-ME
2: (SO-*1*-MA)-16-CH
5: (SO-*1*-MA)-30/*15*/30/15-(ME-*10*-UR)
   (JU-*5*-NE)-*25*/25-UR
   -30/*6*-PL
   -15-CH
29: (SO-*1*-MA)-29/*29*-NE
31: ((SO-*1*-MA)-*31*/31-SA)-31/31/*31*-ME

Lucky Luciano
1: ((*SO-1*-MO-*1*-MA-*1*-SA)-1-*UR*)-1-CH
   -1-*ME*
2: (PL-*16*-CH)-32-*SO*
3: *SO-18*-VE
   (*MO-1*-SA)-6-JU
5: *SO-25*-JU
   (*MO-1*-SA)-20/30/20/*30*-(NE-12-CH)
17: ((*MO-1*-SA)-17/*17*-PL)-17/17/*17*-VE
19: (VE-19-*MA*)-19/*19*-JU
31: (JU-*31*-CH)-*31*/31-VE

Henri Landru
1: ((SO-*1*-MO)-1/*1*-JU)-1/1/1/1/1-(VE-*1*-NE)
(ME-*1*-CH)-1-VE
3: (SO-*1*-MO)-9-*UR*
((VE-*1*-NE)-3/*3*-MA)-3/*3*/*3*-SA
(MA-*3*-SA-*3*-NE)-*27*/*27*/27-CH
((MA-*3*-SA)-3-VE)-*4*/12/12-*PL*
5: (MA-*3*-SA-*3*-NE)-30/10/*30*-ME
7: SO-*21*-ME
11: SO-*22*-MA
(ME-*11*-*UR*)-11-MA
17: (MO-17-SA)-17-CH
(*PL*-*17*-CH)-17-MO

Charles Baudelaire
1: (VE-*1*-JU-*1*-CH)-1-(SO-1-SA)
              -1-(MA-*1*-PL)
(ME-*1*-PL)-1/*1*-MA)-1-VE
UR-*1*-NE
2: SO-4-MO
(UR-*1*-NE)-4-MA
5: (UR-*1*-NE)-15-JU-30/30/*30*-ME
7: ((VE-*1*-JU-*1*-CH)-7/*7*/7-MO
(UR-*1*-NE)-*21*-PL
13: (UR-*1*-NE)-*26*-CH
19: SO-19-MA
(UR-*1*-NE)-19-VE
29: (UR-*1*-NE)-29-(MO-29-MA)

Algernon Swinburne
1: (SO-*1*-MO-*1*-PL)-1-(ME-*1*-*VE*)
MA-*1*-JU
2: (MA-*1*-JU)-2/*2*-NE
(SO-*1*-PL)-16/*16*/16/16/*16*/16-
              -((JU-*2*-NE)-*8*-*CH*)
3: (SO-*1*-PL)-12-SA
7: (SO-*1*-PL)-*28*/28-UR
13: (ME-*1*-*VE*)-13/*13*/13/13-(SA-*13*-UR)
19: (SO-*1*-PL)-19-MA

Eva Marie Saint
1: (SO-*1*-ME-*1*-PL)-1-VE
2: SA-2-CH
(JU-8-SA)-16-NE
3: (SO-*1*-ME-*1*-PL)-*12*/12/12/*12*/12/12-
              -(MO-3-JU)
(MO-3-JU)-*9*/9-MA
5: (SO-*1*-ME-*1*-PL)-*10*/10/10-NE
(SA-2-CH)-5/*10*-MO)-*10*/5/10-VE
7: (SO-*1*-ME-*1*-PL)-*7*/7/7-SA
(ME-*1*-PL)-*14*/14-MA
(MA-7-CH)-*14*/14-ME
13: (SO-*1*-ME-*1*-PL)-13/13/*13*-UR
23: (SO-*1*-PL)-23-(23-CH
(MO-*23*-UR)-23-ME
29: SO-29-JU
(ME-*1*-PL)-*29*/29-NE

Sabine Dardenne
1: (SO-*1*-ME)-1-SA)-1/*1*/1-PL
VE-*1*-*MA*
2: (*VE*-*1*-*MA*)-*8*/8-*ME*
3: (*VE*-*1*-*MA*)-9/*9*-UR)-27-CH
(*MA*-*9*-UR)-*27*-MO
              -18-NE
5: (*VE*-*1*-*MA*)-*20*/20-MO
7: (SO-1-SA)-7-(NE-7-CH)
(MO-*7*-SA)-7-(NE-7-CH)
17: (*MA*-*17*-PL)-17/17/*17*/17-(JU-*17*-CH)
23: SO-*23*-*MA*
29: (*VE*-*1*-*MA*)-*29*/29-NE

Mata Hari
1: ((SO-*1*-MA)-1/*1*-ME)-1-UR
MO-1-*SA*
2: (MO-*16*-ME)-32/*32*-VE
3: (SO-*1*-MA)-9-*SA*
(*SA*-*6*-*NE*)-9/*18*-SO
5: (JU-*2*-PL)-*10*/5-MO
(VE-*5*-CH)-*10*-UR
7: (MO-*7*-CH)-7-SO
(ME-*1*-MA)-*7*/7-*NE*
(ME-*7*-*NE*)-21/*21*-VE
(JU-*7*-*SA*)-*14*/14-VE
13: (ME-*1*-MA)-*13*/13-PL
17: (ME-*1*-MA)-*17*/17-CH
23: (SO-*23*-VE)

Christine Keeler
1: (MO-*1*-UR)-**1**-(MA-*1*-SA)
              (MA-*1*-SA is exact)
ME-1-*VE*
2: (ME-1-VE)-*2*/2-CH
(PL-1-CH)-*2*/2-VE
3: (MA-*1*-SA)-9-SO
ME-*3*-JU
5: (MO-*1*-UR)-5/*5*-CH
((MA-*1*-SA)-*5*-PL)-*25*/*25*/25-ME
7: (ME-*3*-JU)-*7*/21-MO
(JU-*7*-PL)-21/*21*-MO
(MA-*1*-SA)-*14*-CH
11: (SO-*11*-JU)-22/*22*-MO
13: (SO-*13*-VE)-13-UR

King George III
1: ((VE-*1*-SA)-1/*1*-ME)-*1*/1/1-NE
2: MO-2-*CH*
3: (ME-*1*-SA)-9/*9*-MA
(VE-*1*-NE)-3/*3*-PL
7: (SO-*7*-JU)-7-MO
11: SO-22-NE
13: (SO-13-*CH*)-13-PL
              -26/*26*-SA
23: ((ME-*23*-PL)-23/23-*CH*)-23/23/*23*-MA
SO-*23*-VE
29: (VE-29-UR)-29/*29*-*CH*

Storming of the Bastille
1: SO-*1*-ME-*1*-CH
   (*VE*-*1*-UR)-1-*JU*
2: (SO-*1*-ME-*1*-CH)-4-NE
   -8/*8*/8-MA
   ((*VE*-*1*-UR)-*16*/16-MO)-
   -32/*32*/32/*32*/32/32-(ME-*8*-MA)
3: (SO-*1*-CH)-18-MO
   (SO-*1*-ME-*1*-CH)-*3*/*3*/3-SA
   (ME-*3*-SA)-*27*/27-JU
   -*8*/*24*-MA
5: (SO-*1*-CH)-25/*25*-JU
   -30/*30*/30/*30*-(*VE*-*1*-UR)
7: (SO-*1*-ME-*1*-CH)-*7*-*PL*

Breach of the Berlin Wall
1: (SO-*1*-ME)-1/*1*-PL
   (*VE*-*1*-UR)-1/*1*/1/1-(SA-*1*-NE)
   JU-1-CH
2: (SO-*1*-ME)-*8*/8-UR
   (SA-*1*-NE)-*2*/2/*2*/2-(JU-1-CH)
   (MO-*8*-PL)-32-*MA*
3: ((SO-*1*-ME)-1/*1*-PL)-3-CH
   (SO-*1*-ME)-27/*27*-MA
   (((SA-*1*-NE)-*9*-MO)-*27*/27/*27*-ME)-
   -27/*27*/27/*27*-MA
   ((SA-*1*-NE)-*2*-JU)-*9*/*9*/18-MO
   (VE-*1*-UR)-6-*MA*
7: (SA-*1*-NE)-7-SO
13: ((SA-*1*-NE)-*2*-JU)-13/*13*/*26*-PL
19: (SO-*1*-ME)-*19*/19-MO

La Belle Dame sans Merci
1: ((MO-*1*-SA-*1*-PL)-1-MA)-1-VE
   -1-CH
2: (MO-*1*-SA-*1*-PL)-4-NE
   (SA-*1*-PL)-*4*/4/4/4-(UR-1-NE)
5: (SA-*4*-UR)-10/20-SO
7: SO-21-PL
17: (VE-17-UR)-17-SO
19: SO-*19*-MA

Chapter 4: Twoness

R.D. Laing
1: SO-1-MA
   JU-1-*UR*
2: (((MO-*2*-NE)-8/*8*-SO)-16/*16*/*16*-ME)-
   -32/*32*/32/32-VE
   ME-2-CH
   MA-*4*-PL
   MA-8-SA
   JU-*16*-SA
3: SO-*9*-CH
11: ((MA-*11*-CH)-11-MO)-22/*22*/*2*-NE
   SO-11-*JU*
13: (MO-13-*JU*-13-PL)-*2*/26/26-NE
17: (VE-*17*-SA)-17-MO

Frida Kahlo
1: (SO-*1*-NE)-1-JU
   VE-*1*-PL
   MA-1-UR
2: (SO-*1*-NE)-*2*/2/*2*/2-(MA-1-UR)
   (SO-*2*-MA)-8-*MO*
   -16-ME
   -32-*CH*
3: (MA-*9*-PL)-27/*27*-JU
5: ((SO-*1*-NE)-*2*-UR)-5/5/10-*CH*
   (VE-*1*-PL)-15/*15*-*MO*
7: *MO*-7-JU-7-*CH*
   (ME-*7*-UR)-14-SA
11: (VE-*1*-PL)-*11*/11-UR
17: SO-*17*-SA
   (VE-*1*-PL)-17-*CH*)-17/*17*/*17*-ME
19: SO-*19*-VE
29: ((VE-*29*-SA)-29-*MO*)-29-MA

Václav Havel
1: MO-1-CH
2: (MO-1-CH)-2/2-JU
   (MO-2-JU)-*4*/*4*/4/*4*-(SA-*2*-NE)
   (VE-*2*-UR)-8/8-CH
3: (UR-*9*-*PL*)-9-MO
   (VE-*9*-JU)-27/*27*-SO
   -18-*PL*
5: (SO-5-*PL*)-*10*/10-MA
   (MA-*5*-CH)-10/*10*-*PL*
   (VE-*2*-UR)-10/*5*-ME
   (SA-*2*-NE)-15/30-MA
7: (SA-*7*-UR)-7/*7*-SO
   (VE-*2*-UR)-14/*7*/*7*/14-(SA-*2*-NE)
11: SO-*22*-MO
   (SA-11-*PL*)-11-ME
19: ME-*19*-JU
23: SO-*23*-CH
   ME-*23*-NE
   (MO-*23*-VE)-23-MA
29: SO-*29*-NE

Augustus John
1: (SO-*1*-JU)-1-MO
2: ((SO-*1*-JU)-*4*/4-*MA*)-8/*8*/8/8/8/*8*-
   -(VE-*2*-UR)
3: (SO-*1*-JU)-6/*6*-SA
   MA-*9*-PL
7: (VE-*21*-SA)-21-PL
11: (SA-*11*-UR)-22/22-NE
13: (SO-13-NE)-26-ME
23: ME-*23*-VE-*23*-CH

Françoise Sagan
1: SO-*1*-ME
2: (SO-*1*-ME)-*8*/*8*/8/*8*-(VE-*4*-JU)
   (*SA*-2-*NE*)-4-CH
   (*SA*-*4*-CH)-8/8-PL
3: (SO-*1*-ME)-3/*3*-*MO*

(UR-9-PL)-18/18-VE
(NE-4-CH)-12/3-MA
5: (MO-3-ME)-15/5-NE
((SA-2-NE)-4-CH)-10/5/20-SO
7: ((SO-1-ME)-7/7-MA)-14/14/14-PL
13: (SO-1-ME)-13/13-UR
VE-13-NE

Steve Fossett
2: ((ME-4-JU)-8/8-NE)-16/16/16/16/16/
16-(MO-8-CH)
((MO-8-CH)-16/16/16/16)-(ME-8-NE))-
-32/32/32/32-MA
3: (JU-8-NE)-24/12-SO
(MO-6-SA)-9/18-MA
(ME-9-PL)-18/6-UR
5: (SO-5-MA)-20/4-VE
7: (SO-7-SA)-21/21-VE
19: SO-19-PL
(MA-19-CH)-19-ME
31: (SO-31-UR)-31/31-CH

Cindy Sherman
1: (SO-1-ME-1-VE)-1/1/1-CH
2: (SO-1-ME-1-VE)-2/2/2-MO
(SO-1-VE)-4/4-NE
((MO-2-ME)-8/8-JU)-16/16/16-PL)-
-32/32/32/32-UR
3: SO-9-SA
5: (SO-1-ME)-5/5-MA
(MO-2-ME)-30/15-NE
7: SO-7-PL
13: SO-13-JU
(MO-2-ME)-26/13-ME
31: SO-31-NE
(MO-31-VE)-31/31-UR

Jürgen Bartsch
1: SO-1-JU
(VE-1-MA)-1/1-ME
SA-1-PL
2: (SO-4-PL)-16-ME)-32-NE
(JU-4-SA)-16-VE
3: (ME-1-VE)-3/3-MO
(VE-1-MA)-12/12-CH
5: ME-10-CH
7: (MO-7-CH)-14/14/14/14-(UR-7-PL)
(VE-1-MA)-7/7-NE
(VE-7-NE)-21/21-SO
11: SO-22-MA
13: (MA-13-SA)-26/26-MO
19: SO-19-SA
23: SO-23-MO

Mahatma Gandhi
1: VE-1-MA
JU-1-PL
2: (VE-1-MA)-2/2/2/2-(JU-1-PL)

((JU-1-PL)-2/2-MA)-4/4/4-MO)-
-8/8/8/8-CH
(MO-4-JU)-16/16-SA
3: ((MA-2-PL)-4-MO)-12/12/3-NE
(ME-12-CH)-24/24/8/24-(MA-12-NE)
5: MA-15-SA
7: (SO-14-UR)-28/28-PL
(VE-14-SA)-28/28-ME
11: SO-22-MO
(ME-11-JU)-11-NE
13: SO-13-JU
ME-13-PL
17: SO-17-SA
19: (SO-19-NE)-19-VE
29: (SO-29-ME)-29-VE

Charles de Foucauld
1: SO-1-ME
2: ((SO-1-ME)-2-NE)-4/4/4-JU
-8/8/8-PL
(SO-2-NE)-8/8/8/8/8/8-((VE-2-PL)-
-4/4-SA)
(MA-2-JU)-4/4-ME
(VE-4-SA)-32/32-CH
3: (MA-2-JU)-6/3-CH
5: SO-25-MA
(JU-25-PL)-25-MO
7: (MO-7-CH)-7-UR
-21-NE
11: (MA-11-SA)-11-NE
17: (ME-17-SA)-17/17-CH

Mary Baker Eddy
1: JU-1-SA
UR-1-NE
2: ((UR-1-NE)-4/4-PL)-8/8/8/8/8-
-(MO-2-ME)
(MO-2-ME)-8-NE)-16/16/16-SO
3: SO-24-VE
5: (MO-5-JU)-25/25-VE
(UR-1-NE)-4/4-PL)-20/20/5-MA
7: SO-21-JU
(UR-1-NE)-7-CH
(VE-7-SA)-14-PL)-28/28/4-UR
23: SO-23-UR
(ME-23-SA)-23-MA
31: MA-31-SA-31-UR

Saint Thérèse de Lisieux
2: (MA-2-NE)-4/4-SA
((SO-4-CH)-16/16/16/16-(ME-8-UR))-
-32/32/32/32-NE
3: (MA-2-NE)-6/3-ME
-3/6-VE
(ME-8-24/12)-MO
5: (SO-4-CH)-20/10-PL

(SO-**25**-NE)-25-UR
7: SO-**7**-MO
(JU-7-PL)-14-UR
11: SO-22-MA
19: (UR-**19**-PL)-19-MA
29: (MO-**29**-ME)-29-PL

My Lai massacre
1: SO-1-CH
ME-1-VE
UR-1-PL
2: (UR-1-PL)-2/2-SO
(SO-1-CH)-2-UR
(ME-**2**-JU)-4/4-NE)-8/8/**8**/**8**/8/8-
-(MO-**2**-SA)
3: (SO-2-UR)-3/6-PL
(ME-**2**-JU)-12/**12**/12/12-(UR-2-CH)
5: (MA-5-NE)-30/6-NE
(PL-**25**-CH)-25-SA
7: (VE-7-MA)-14/**14**-SO
13: (ME-**2**-JU)-13/**26**-SO
(MO-**13**-CH)-13/13-VE
29: SO-**29**-VE

Nuneaton rail crash
1: MO-1-CH
MA-1-JU
2: (MO-1-CH)-**2**-UR
((MO-2-UR)-**4**/4-VE)-**8**/8/**8**-SO
(VE-4-UR)-16/16-PL
(JU-**4**-SA)-32/**32**-UR
3: (PL-**9**-CH)-9-SA
-27/27-VE
5: (VE-**10**-MA)-**30**/15-SA
7: (MO-1-CH)-**7**-ME
(MO-7-**ME**)-14/**14**-SA
(JU-**4**-SA)-28/**14**-ME
11: SO-**11**-SA
17: (**ME**-**17**-UR)-17-JU
19: SO-19-JU
29: SO-**29**-PL

Chapter 5: Threeness

Jerry Lewis
1: SO-**1**-UR
VE-**1**-JU
MO-1-CH
2: MA-**4**-CH
ME-4-**PL**
3: (((SO-**1**-UR)-**3**-SA)-**6**/**6**/6-MA)-
-**9**/9/9/9/**9**/**9**/18/18-(VE-**1**-JU)
-**12**/**12**/12/**4**-CH
(JU-**9**-SA)-27/27/**27**/**27**-(NE-**9**-PL)
5: (VE-**1**-JU)-25-ME
(ME-25-NE)-25/**25**-VE
((SO-**1**-UR)-10-(MO-**5**-PL))-
-**20**/20/20/**4**-ME

11: (SO-**1**-UR)-**22**/22-NE
29: (MO-29-JU)-29-NE

Pat Rodegast
1: SO-**1**-UR
VE-**1**-JU
2: (VE-**1**-JU)-**4**-MO
ME-4-PL
MA-4-CH
3: (((SO-**1**-UR)-**3**-SA)-**6**/6/**6**-**MA**)-
-**9**/**9**/9/9/**9**/**9**/18/18-(VE-**1**-JU)
-12/**12**/12/4-CH
(SA-**3**-UR)-**9**/9-JU)-
-27/**27**/27/27/27/27-(NE-**9**-PL)
5: (VE-**1**-JU)-25/**25**-**ME**
7: (**MA**-7-NE)-14/**14**-**ME**
17: SO-17-PL
31: (**ME**-**31**-VE)-31/**31**-CH

Phyllis Diller
1: (SA-**1**-NE)-1-ME)-1/1/**1**-SO
(MO-**1**-PL)-1-MA
3: (MO-**1**-PL)-18/**18**-SO
(ME-1-SA)-**3**/3-CH
((MA-**3**-UR)-**9**-SA)-27-**VE**
((SA-**1**-NE)-**6**-**JU**)-12/12/**12**-MO
-12-(MO-**1**-PL)
5: (**VE**-5-**JU**)-25/**25**-**UR**
7: (MO-**1**-PL)-**14**/14-ME
11: (MO-**1**-PL)-**11**/11-**UR**
13: (MA-13-CH)-**26**/26-NE
17: (MO-**1**-PL)-**17**/17-PL
19: SO-19-**UR**
23: SO-23-MA

Benny Hill
2: SO-**8**-UR
MA-**8**-CH
(JU-**16**-NE)-32/32-**MA**
3: (SO-6-**MA**)-9/**18**-PL
(VE-**3**-SA)-9-JU)-18/**18**/18-MO
(JU-**9**-SA)-27-UR
5: ((ME-**5**-NE)-5-SA)-15/15/**3**-VE
7: (UR-**7**-NE)-**28**/28/28/**28**-(VE-14-PL)
11: (SO-11-VE)-**22**/22-ME
31: (JU-**31**-UR)-31-PL

Michael Palin
1: ME-**1**-UR
2: (ME-**1**-UR)-**8**/8-JU
3: (ME-**1**-UR)-**9**-MA)-9/**9**/**9**-CH
(ME-**1**-UR)-**18**/6/18/6-(SO-9-**PL**)
(MA-**9**-UR)-9-CH)-18/18/**6**-VE
(MO-27-JU)-27/**27**-VE
5: MA-**20**-JU
7: MA-**28**-PL
11: (SO-**11**-JU)-11-CH
13: SO-**13**-SA

Cynthia Payne
2: (ME-4-NE)-16/16-SO
   VE-8-UR
   MA-16-CH
3: (SO-9-PL)-18/6-JU
   (SO-9-PL)-27/27-MA)-27/27/27-UR
   (MO-2-CH)-3/6-PL
   (JU-3-CH)-6/6-PL
5: (VE-5-JU)-30/6-PL
17: (VE-17-CH)-17-NE
23: SO-23-CH

Linda McCartney
1: SO-1-NE
   SA-1-UR
2: VE-4-CH
3: (SO-1-NE)-3/3/3-(SA-1-UR)
   (((SO-3-UR)-9/9-VE)-9/9/9-MA)-
                    -18/18/18/6-JU
   (ME-9-PL)-27-SA
5: (SO-3-UR)-15/5-ME
   (SA-1-UR)-5-CH
   (ME-5-UR)-5/5-CH
7: (MO-7-PL)-7/7-MA
                -7/7-NE
13: (ME-13-NE)-26-JU
23: ME-23-VE
   (MA-23-CH)-23-JU

Frank Farrelly
1: (SO-1-VE)-1/1-NE
2: SO-8-SA
3: (SO-9-MO)-9/9-PL
             -27-UR
   (ME-9-JU)-27/27/27/27-(MA-9-NE)
             -18-VE
5: MO-5-ME
13: VE-13-SA
29: SO-29-CH
31: SO-31-JU

Adi Da
2: (SO-8-NE)-16/16-ME
   (SO-16-ME)-32/32-MO
   MA-4-UR
3: (ME-1-VE)-3-(MO-3-JU)
   ((MO-1-PL)-3/3-ME)-3/3/3-JU
   (ME-3-PL)-27-JU
   (JU-2-NE)-3/6-VE
   (MA-4-UR)-12/6-CH
5: ((ME-3-PL)-5/15-SA)-15/5/15-UR
7: (ME-3-PL)-21/7-NE
   (MA-4-UR)-14/28-ME
13: ((SO-13-CH)-13-SA)-13-JU
31: SO-31-JU

Caril Ann Fugate
1: SO-1-JU-1-PL

2: (MA-8-NE)-16-UR
3: ((SO-1-JU-1-PL)-9-VE)-27/27/27/27/
                    27/27/27/27-(ME-9-NE)
                    -6-UR
   (VE-3-MA)-9/9-JU
5: (SO-1-JU-1-PL)-15/15/15-CH
   (ME-5-UR)-25/25-MO)-25/25/25-SA
11: VE-11-UR
23: (SO-1-JU-1-PL)-23/23/23-MO

George W. Bush
1: (MO-1-JU)-1/1-CH
   (MO-1-CH)-1-NE
   (ME-1-PL)-1-VE
2: (MO-1-CH)-4-SO
3: (MO-9-SA)-27/27-ME
   (JU-3-UR)-9/9-MA
   (MA-9-UR)-27/27-NE
5: (MA-10-CH)-20/20-VE
   (MA-25-PL)-25-SA
7: SO-14-ME
   SO-28-SA
   (JU-3-UR)-21/7-ME
13: SO-13-MA
   (NE-13-PL)-13-SO
19: (SO-19-VE)-19/19-JU
31: SO-31-MO
   ME-31-VE

Paddington rail crash
2: (ME-2-JU)-4-NE
3: (SO-3-UR)-9/9-JU
   (MO-3-MA)-9-NE)-27/27/27-PL
   (JU-9-UR)-27-SA
5: (MA-5-SA)-5-SO
   (JU-5-PL)-10-MO
7: (ME-7-MA-7-UR)-21/3/21-MO
   (SO-7-CH)-7-MO
11: (SA-11-CH)-11-ME
19: (SO-19-PL)-19/19-ME

Selby rail crash
2: MA-16-CH
3: (MO-9-ME)-18/18/18/6-(SA-9-PL)
   (VE-3-PL)-6-ME
             -9/9-SA
5: (ME-6-UR)-15/10-SO
   (SO-10-VE)-20/20-UR
11: SO-11-NE
13: (MO-13-JU)-13-SO
17: SO-17-PL
31: SO-31-MA

Chapter 6: Sixness

Charles Harvey
1: ((ME-1-MA)-1/1-PL)-1/1/1-CH
   JU-1-SA

2: (ME-_1_-PL)-2/_2_-MO
(MO-16-VE)-_32_/32-_SA_
3: (MO-_2_-PL)-12-SO
((UR-_3_-NE)-6/_6_-MA)-8/_24_/_24_-VE
(VE-_6_-JU)-_24_/_24_/24/_8_-(MA-_6_-NE)
5: (MA-_5_-SA_)-25/25-MO
((_JU_-_5_-CH)-_6_/30-VE)-30/_30_/15-PL
7: NE-_7_-PL
11: (_SA_-11-NE)-22/_22_-SO
19: SO-_19_-CH
ME-_19_-NE
29: (SO-29-_SA_)-29/_29_-ME

Rolf Harris
1: (SO-_1_-MO-_1_-ME)-_1_/_1_/_1_-UR
2: SA-_4_-UR
3: (SA-_3_-CH)-18/6/18/6-(VE-9-MA)
(SA-_3_-CH)-6/_12_/6/_12_-(MA-4-JU)
(SA-_3_-CH)-_12_/_4_/_12_/_12_-(JU-_6_-UR)
(JU-_6_-UR)-_9_/_18_-_NE_
5: (SO-_1_-ME)-_5_/5-_NE_
(SA-_3_-CH)-30/10-ME
(JU-_6_-UR)-_10_/15-PL
7: ME-_14_-MA
11: (SO-_11_-CH)-11-PL
29: ((SO-_29_-SA)-_29_-VE)-29-PL

Luciano Pavarotti
2: (MA-_2_-CH)-4/_4_-NE
((NE-_4_-CH)-_8_-ME)-32/_32_/32-SA
3: SO-_2_-MO)-_6_/3/3/_6_-(MA-_2_-CH)
(SO-_6_-MA)-_9_/18-PL
(MA-_2_-CH)-4/_4_-NE)-3/_6_/_12_-MO
(NE-_4_-CH)-_8_-ME)-_12_/_6_/24-MO
(ME-2-UR)-3/_6_-SA
(SA-_6_-UR)-_18_/_9_-JU
5: (SO-_6_-MA)-_10_/15-JU
(MO-_5_-VE)-_6_/_30_-CH
7: (ME-_7_-VE)-_28_/28-SO
11: (SO-_11_-UR)-11-NE
13: (UR-_13_-PL)-_26_/26-CH
29: SO-29-SA

Amy Johnson
1: SO-_1_-NE
ME-1-PL
2: SO-_8_-VE
(JU-_4_-UR)-_8_-SA
3: (SO-_9_-MO)-27-MA
(SO-_8_-VE)-_24_/_24_/_12_/12/_3_/24-
-((JU-_4_-UR)-_8_-SA)
5: (JU-_4_-UR)-_20_/_5_-MA
7: (VE-_3_-UR)-21/21-MO
ME-_21_-NE
SO-28-_CH_
11: (MO-_11_-PL)-11-SA
31: SO-_31_-MA

Meher Baba
1: NE-_1_-PL
2: (VE-_4_-JU)-_8_/8-MA
(NE-_1_-PL)-8-sa
3: ((SO-_3_-MO)-6/_6_-MA)-4/12/12-PL
(MO-_6_-MA)-_24_/_8_-VE
(ME-_6_-JU)-_12_/12-SA
(VE-_3_-SA)-_4_/12-JU
(SA-8-PL)-12/_24_-JU
5: SO-_20_-ME
VE-_10_-NE
7: ((UR-_7_-NE)-7-MA)-14-ME
11: (MO-_11_-JU)-_22_/22-NE
13: (SO-_13_-CH)-_13_-UR
-26-VE
29: (MO-_29_-ME)-_29_/_29_-PL

Reginald Kray
1: VE-1-MA
2: SO-8-VE
ME-_8_-JU
(MO-8-CH)-16/_16_-SA
(MA-4-NE)-8-UR
(UR-_4_-PL)-8-MA
3: SO-_9_-MA
(ME-_3_-PL)-_8_/24/24/_24_-(JU-_3_-SA)
((ME-_3_-PL)-12/_4_-UR)-24/_24_/24-SA
((JU-_3_-SA)-6-MA)-_24_/_24_/8-PL
5: ME-5-NE
17: SO-_17_-JU
23: (VE-_23_-NE-_23_-PL)-23-MO
29: (UR-_29_-NE-_29_-CH)-29-SO

Chapter 7: Fiveness

June Gibbons
1: MO-_1_-NE
VE-_1_-CH
3: (MO-_1_-NE)-_3_/3/_3_/3-(VE-_1_-CH)
(ME-3-UR)-12/_12_-JU
5: ((((MO-_1_-NE)-_3_-VE)-15/_15_/_5_-MA)-
-15/15/15/_15_/_15_/_15_-(ME-_5_-_SA_)-
-30/30/_10_/10/_30_/_6_-SO
((MO-_1_-NE)-_5_/5-UR)-15/15/3-ME
JU-25-PL
7: (VE-_1_-CH)-_21_/21-JU
11: SO-_11_-UR
17: MA-_17_-JU
19: SO-_19_-JU-_19_-CH
23: SO-_23_-MO
31: SO-_31_-PL

Bahá-u-Lláh
1: (JU-_1_-UR)-1-NE
PL-_1_-CH
2: (NE-_4_-PL)-32/_32_-_SO_

((MA-*2*-NE)-4/*4*/4-(PL-*1*-CH)-
-8/8/*8*/8-ME
3: (JU-*1*-UR)-24/*24*-SA
SO-*18*-SA
5: (*SO*-*5*-MA)-25/*25*/25/25-(MO-*5*-VE)
(MA-*4*-CH)-5/20-*SO*
((JU-*1*-UR)-*10*/10-ME)-
-20/*20*/20/20/20/*20*-(MO-*5*-VE)
(MO-*25*-MA)-25-*SA*
SA-*15*-PL
7: (JU-*1*-UR)-14/14-*SO*
(PL-*1*-CH)-7/*7*-VE
((VE-*7*-CH)-14/*14*-*SA*)-*28*/*4*/28-MA
13: ME-*13*-SA
17: (JU-*1*-UR)-17/*17*-MA
29: (*SO*-29-UR)-29-PL

Frank Buchman
1: (NE-*1*-CH)-1-ME
-1-VE
2: (NE-*1*-CH)-4/*4*-*JU*
UR-*4*-PL
5: (SO-*5*-SA-*5*-UR)-10/*10*/10/*10*/10/*10*-
-(NE-*1*-CH)
-10/10/*10*-CH)-
-20/20/*4*/20-PL
-15/*15*/15-ME
-*25*/*25*/25-VE
((SO-*5*-SA)-*10*-CH)-20/20/20/*20*/4/20-
-(*JU*-10-PL)
7: ME-*7*-*JU*
29: (MA-29-*JU*)-29/*29*-UR
31: (MA-*31*-NE)-31-SO

Aurobindo
2: SA-*4*-CH)-*8*/8-VE
3: (MO-*3*-NE)-*12*/4-MA
(ME-*3*-SA)-*24*/*8*-VE
5: (ME-*3*-SA)-15/*5*-SO
(SA-*4*-CH)-*5*/20-SO
-20/10-MO
((UR-*5*-PL)-*5*-MO)-15/15/*3*-NE
-25-ME
7: (MA-*4*-NE)-14/28-SO
VE-21-*JU*
13: (VE-*13*-UR)-26-NE
17: (UR-17-CH)-17-ME
23: (SO-*23*-MO)-23-CH
31: SO-*31*-ME-*31*-NE

Percy Bysshe Shelley
1: (SO-*1*-VE)-*1*/1-UR
(*MA*-*1*-*JU*)-1-NE
2: (SO-*16*-ME)-32-*SA*
3: (*MA*-*1*-*JU*)-3-PL
-18-MO
(SO-*1*-VE)-18-CH
(*SA*-*3*-CH)-27/27-UR

5: ((SO-*1*-VE)-*5*-(*MA*-*1*-*JU*)-
-25/25/*25*/25-*SA*
7: (ME-*7*-NE)-*28*/28-PL
(*MA*-*1*-*JU*)-7-CH
11: (SO-*1*-VE)-22-MO
19: (SO-*19*-PL)-19-CH
29: (SO-*1*-VE)-29/*29*-NE

Sylvia Plath
2: (ME-*4*-MA)-16/*16*-SA
MO-*16*-JU
3: SO-9-VE
(ME-*4*-MA)-12/*3*-UR
(VE-*6*-PL)-24/*24*-MO
5: (SO-*5*-MA)-*15*/15-JU
(ME-*4*-MA)-*5*/20-NE
(ME-*5*-NE)-25/*25*-MO)-25/25/25-VE
(MA-*3*-UR)-15/*15*-MO
-15/*5*-JU
(UR-10-CH)-15/*30*-MO
7: SO-*14*-MO
SO-21-ME
11: ME-*11*-JU
13: (UR-13-NE)-13-SO
MA-*13*-PL
17: SO-17-SA
MA-*17*-CH
29: MA-*29*-JU

Graham Greene
1: MO-*1*-NE
2: (MO-*1*-NE)-4/*4*-SO
3: (VE-6-MA)-9/18-*ME*
5: ((*ME*-*5*-JU)-*5*/5-SA)-5/*5*/5/5/5-
-(MO-*1*-NE))-*20*/20/*20*/4/4-SO
(*ME*-*5*-JU)-*5*/5-SA)-5-NE)-
-15/*3*/15/*15*-UR
-*20*/4/20/20-(SO-10-PL)
7: VE-*7*-SA
(SO-*14*-UR)-28/*28*-MA
11: (NE-*11*-CH)-22-PL
17: SO-*17*-CH
19: VE-*19*-NE
29: SO-*29*-JU
31: SO-*31*-VE
(MO-*31*-JU)-31-CH

Thomas Hardy
1: (ME-1-MA)-1-SO
-*1*/1-VE
2: MA-*8*-PL
3: (MO-*3*-JU)-9-ME
-9-*PL*
(NE-*9*-CH)-27-ME
(SA-*3*-*PL*)-*4*/12-UR
5: (((SA-*5*-CH)-*25*/25-SO)-
-*25*/25/*25*-VE)-25/25/*25*/25-MO
(MO-*3*-JU)-*10*/30-MA

(SA-4-UR)-20/5-ME
(SA-3-PL)-5/15-CH
7: VE-7-NE
11: SO-22-UR
13: (MO-13-UR)-26/26-CH
(MA-13-SA)-13/13-NE
19: (VE-19-PL)-19-CH
29: SO-29-NE

Henri Matisse
1: MO-1-SA
ME-1-MA
JU-1-PL
2: (ME-1-MA)-2/2-UR
3: (SO-3-JU)-24/8-MO
((MO-6-JU)-12/12-MA)-8/24/24-JU
5: (SO-3-JU)-15/15-NE
(SA-5-PL)-20/20-SO
(MO-6-VE)-15/10-CH
((ME-2-UR)-10/5-VE)-5/10/10-CH
(SA-5-PL)-25/25-ME
(ME-5-CH)-25-NE
(ME-25-SA)-25-NE
7: (ME-2-UR)-14/7-MO
-28/28-PL
11: (MA-11-CH)-22/22-SO
23: SO-23-MA

Laurence Olivier
1: MA-1-UR
JU-1-NE
2: (JU-1-NE)-2-UR
(UR-2-NE)-8/8-ME
SO-16-PL
3: (JU-1-NE)-9-SO
-27/27-MA
-24/24-SA
5: ((JU-1-NE)-2-UR)-5/5/10-VE)-
-5/5/10/5-CH
-25-(ME-25-MA)
-20/20-PL
7: (JU-1-NE)-21-MO
SO-7-CH
SO-28-SA
13: ME-13-VE
19: SO-19-MA
29: ((ME-29-CH)-29-MO)-29-SA

Barry Humphries
1: ME-1-MA
2: SO-4-CH
(JU-2-UR)-4/4-PL
3: (MA-8-UR)-12/24-VE
5: (ME-5-CH)-5/5-JU
-10/10-VE
(ME-10-VE)-20-SO
(JU-4-PL)-20/10-MO
(MO-10-PL)-30/15-NE

7: (ME-14-SA)-28/28-UR
(UR-4-PL)-28/7-SA
(NE-7-CH)-21/21-UR
13: (SO-13-NE)-26-JU
19: (SO-19-UR)-19-MO
29: SO-29-MA

Richard Branson
1: MA-1-NE
2: (MO-8-MA)-16-VE
SA-4-CH
3: (PL-3-CH)-6/6-MA
((JU-3-UR)-9/9-CH)-18/18/6-MA
5: (MA-1-NE)-5/5-ME
((ME-5-NE)-25/25-PL)-25/25/25-MO
(SA-25-NE)-25/25-PL)-25-MO
7: (SA-4-CH)-7/28-SO
ME-28-VE
11: SO-22-MA
13: SO-13-JU
(MO-13-UR)-26/26-SA

Alexander Fleming
1: ((JU-1-CH)-1/1/1/1-(MA-1-PL)
-1/1/1/1-(SA-1-NE)
2: (SA-1-NE)-4-SO
3: (JU-1-CH)-9-SO
-6/6-ME
SA-3-UR
5: (SO-5-MA)-25/25-UR
(SA-3-UR)-5/15-ME
-15/5-VE
(JU-1-CH)-10/10/10/10-(VE-5-UR)
(VE-5-UR)-25/25-MA)-25/25-NE
7: (UR-7-PL)-28/28-NE
13: ME-13-PL
19: SO-19-ME
29: (SO-29-PL)-29-NE

Sinking of the Titanic
1: SO-1-ME
2: SO-8-CH
MO-4-PL
MA-8-SA
ME-16-VE
3: MA-9-JU
VE-6-UR
5: (SO-1-ME)-5-MA
((JU-5-NE)-10-VE)-15/15/30/15/15/
/30/6/30/15-((UR-5-PL)-10-CH)
((JU-5-NE)-25/25-SO)-25-MO
7: (SO-1-ME)-21/21-NE
29: (SO-29-SA)-29/29-PL
31: (MA-31-CH)-31-ME

Ufton Nervet rail crash
1: VE-1-JU
2: (MO-2-UR)-4/4-ME

MA-*4*-SA
3:   (UR-*9*-CH)-18-*NE*
5:   (MO-2-UR)-10/*5*-*PL*
     (JU-*5*-UR-*5*-*PL*)-*5*-SA)-*1*/5/5/5-VE
                   -10/*10*/10/10-SO)-
                   -20/20/*4*/20/20/20/20/*4*
                   -(ME-*10*-MA)
7:   (VE-*1*-JU)-*7*/7-CH
     (VE-*7*-CH)-21/21-SO
     (MA-*21*-CH)-21-SO
11: VE-*22*-MA
29: (MO-*29*-JU)-29-*NE*
31: SO-31-*PL*

Chapter 8: Sevenness

Walk-in from Sirius
1:   SO-*1*-UR
     ME-*1*-*VE*
2:   (SO-*1*-UR)-2/*2*-JU
     SO-*8*-PL
     (*ME*-*1*-*VE*)-*8*/8-CH
     (SA-*4*-CH)-8/*8*-ME
5:   (SO-*1*-UR)-5/*5*-CH
     (*ME*-*1*-*VE*)-5/*5*-MO
     (MO-5-*ME*)-10/10-PL
7:   (((SO-*1*-UR)-7/*7*-MO)-*7*/7/7-SA)-
                   -7/7/*7*/*7*-NE
     ((SO-*7*-SA)-*7*/*7*-NE)-14/*14*/*14*-MA
19: *ME*-19-NE-19-PL
23: (MA-*23*-UR)-23-PL

Alice Bailey
3:   MO-*9*-ME
5:   SO-*25*-*MA*
     (ME-*25*-NE)-25/*25*-PL
     (UR-*10*-CH)-20/*20*-ME
7:   ((MO-*7*-VE)-*7*/*7*-SA)-*7*/7/7-*MA*)-
                   -*21*/21/21/21-NE
                   -14/*14*/*14*-UR
13: SO-*13*-PL
     ME-*13*-*MA*
17: SO-*17*-NE
19: SO-*19*-MO
23: SO-*23*-ME
     (VE-*23*-*JU*)-23-CH
31: (ME-*31*-VE)-31-NE

George Van Tassel
1:   ME-*1*-CH
2:   (ME-*1*-CH)-4/*4*-*MA*
     (*MA*-*4*-CH)-16/16-SO
3:   SO-*18*-ME
5:   (MO-*5*-UR)-10-ME
7:   SO-*28*-NE
     (ME-*1*-CH)-*7*/7-SA
     (VE-*7*-*MA*)-7-MO
     (VE-*7*-*MA*)-*14*/14-PL)-28/*4*/*28*-CH)

     (JU-*21*-CH)-21/*21*-NE
19: SO-*19*-UR
23: (SO-*23*-PL)-23/*23*-MO
     (MO-*23*-SA)-*23*/23-PL
31: SO-*31*-VE

Jean Miguères
1:   SO-*1*-UR
     (MO-*1*-CH)-1-*VE*
     (ME-*1*-SA)-1-*JU*
2:   (SO-*1*-UR)-16-JU
3:   (SO-*1*-UR)-*3*-NE
5:   (SO-*25*-SA)-25-*VE*
     (*JU*-*5*-NE)-25/*25*-*MA*
7:   (SO-*1*-UR)-7/*7*-MO
     (MO-*7*-UR)-*21*-*MA*)-21-PL
31: SO-*31*-PL)-31/*31*-*JU*
     (ME-*31*-PL)-31-*MA*

Anita McKeown
1:   MA-1-PL
2:   (MA-1-PL)-2/*2*-CH
     (SO-*8*-VE)-*32*-*ME*
3:   SO-*9*-UR
     (VE-*3*-SA)-*9*/9-NE
                   -*8*/24-SO
5:   (VE-*3*-SA)-15/*5*-MA
     (SO-*25*-JU)-25-NE
7:   (MA-1-PL)-*7*/7-SO
     (VE-*3*-SA)-21/*7*-UR
     ((*ME*-*7*-SA-*7*-UR)-*28*/*28*/*28*/*28*/28/
                   28-(PL-*2*-CH))-
                   -*14*/14/*14*/28/28-MO
11: (PL-*2*-CH)-*11*/*22*-VE
23: MO-*23*-NE-*23*-PL

Roger Federer
1:   SO-1-ME
     MO-1-UR
     JU-*1*-SA
2:   (JU-*1*-SA)-*8*/8-CH
     (MO-1-UR)-*2*/2-CH
     (MO-2-CH)-*8*/8-SA
3:   (JU-*8*-CH)-*24*/12-NE
     (NE-*6*-PL)-12/*12*-CH
5:   (MO-*25*-JU)-*25*/25-PL
7:   (JU-*1*-SA)-*7*/7-SO
     (ME-*7*-UR)-7-SA
                   -*14*/14-NE
                   -*21*/21-*VE*)-21/21/*21*-PL
11: (MA-*11*-PL)-11-SO
13: (JU-*1*-SA)-*13*/13-MA
17: (MO-*17*-MA)-17/*17*-*VE*
19: (*VE*-*19*-NE)-19/*19*-SA

Bruce Chatwin
1:   (*SO*-*1*-*UR*)-1-*ME*
2:   JU-*4*-PL

3: (*SO*-*1*-UR)-*3*/3-NE
5: (MA-10-*UR*)-20/20-CH
    (JU-5-NE)-25/25-*ME*
7: (*SO*-*1*-*UR*)-14/*14*-MO
    (*ME*-*7*-VE)-*21*-MO
    (*ME*-*7*-VE)-14/14/14/*14*-(NE-7-PL)
    (UR-3-NE)-21/7-PL
11: VE-*11*-JU
31: (*SO*-*31*-JU)-31/*31*-MA

Herman Melville
1: (MO-1-UR)-1/*1*-NE
    (SA-1-PL)-*1*/1-CH
2: (NE-4-PL)-8/8-JU
    ((JU-8-PL)-16/*16*-ME)-*32*/32/32-MO
3: (ME-8-VE)-24/*12*-VE
7: (ME-*7*-SA)-*14*-SO
                -7-MO
    SO-21-NE
    MO-*21*-MA
    MA-28-UR
17: SO-17-MO
29: (ME-29-MA)-29-NE
                -29-CH

Hector Berlioz
1: (SO-*1*-MA)-1-ME
    MO-1-NE
2: *VE*-*4*-SA
3: (*VE*-*4*-SA)-24/24-MA
    (ME-6-UR)-18/9-NE
    VE-*18*-CH
5: (ME-*5*-SA)-15-MO
    SO-*25*-VE
7: (SA-7-NE)-7-*PL*
                -14/*14*-JU)-*4*/28/*28*-VE
                -*4*/*28*/28/28-(*VE*-14-UR)
    SO-*21*-CH
    ME-28-CH
17: ((MO-*17*-*PL*)-*17*/17-*VE*)-17-JU
    SO-17-UR
23: (UR-*23*-*PL*)-23-MA

James Ensor
1: VE-*1*-UR
2: SO-4-MO
3: (VE-*1*-UR)-*6*/6-ME
    (ME-*6*-VE)-*18*/*9*-JU
    (*NE*-*9*-PL)-*27*/27-CH
5: (VE-*1*-UR)-5/*5*-MA)-*5*/5/5-SA
    (VE-*5*-SA)-15/*15*-CH
    ((MO-*5*-ME)-10-CH)-30/*6*/15-VE

7: (SO-7-MA)-*14*/14-*NE*)-*28*/28/*28*-SA
                -*7*/7-CH
    (MO-*7*-PL)-7-SA
    SO-4-(MO)-*28*/7-SA
11: SO-22-ME

13: (SO-13-JU)-26/26/*26*/*26*-(UR-*13*-PL)
    MO-*26*-MA
23: (MO-*23*-JU)-23-*NE*

Martin Heidegger
1: (MO-*1*-UR)-1-ME
    (VE-*1*-SA)-1-MA
    NE-1-PL
2: ((MO-*1*-UR)-4/*4*-CH)-8/8/*8*-*PL*
3: (*NE*-1-*PL*)-3/3-*SO*
    ((VE-*1*-SA)-*1*-MA)-*3*-JU
    (VE-*1*-SA)-*3*-JU)-*6*/*6*/6-ME
5: (SO-*5*-CH)-*25*-JU
    (UR-4-CH)-20/5-*SO*
    (*NE*-1-*PL*)-5/5-ME
    (ME-*5*-*NE*)-15/15-CH
7: ((MO-*1*-UR)-*7*/*7*/7-(VE-*1*-SA)-
                -*21*/21/*21*/21-*SO*
    (JU-*7*-*NE*)-21/21-UR
17: (VE-*1*-SA)-*17*/17-*NE*
23: *SO*-23-MA
31: *SO*-31-SA

Ira Einhorn
1: (SO-1-UR)-1/*1*-ME
2: JU-4-PL
3: (SO-1-UR)-3/*3*-NE
    ((MO-*3*-SA)-*6*-*VE*)-*24*/24/8-UR
5: (MO-*3*-SA)-10/30-PL
    (JU-4-PL)-*20*/5-ME
    (UR-*3*-NE)-10/*30*-*MA*
7: ((SO-*7*-CH)-*7*/*7*-MO)-21/*21*/21-*MA*
    (MO-*7*-SA)-21/*3*/*21*/21-(*MA*-7-SA)
    (UR-*3*-NE)-*21*/7-PL
13: SO-*26*-*VE*
23: MO-*23*-ME-*23*-NE
29: SO-*29*-JU

Charles Starkweather
2: ((VE-*4*-JU)-8-CH)-16/16/*16*-PL
    MO-2-CH
    ME-*4*-*NE*
3: SO-*3*-PL
    ((VE-*4*-JU)-12/*6*-ME)-8/8/24-CH
5: (SO-*5*-CH)-25/*25*-CH
    (ME-4-*NE*)-*10*/20-SA
7: (*NE*-*7*-PL)-*7*/7-MO
    ((MO-7-*NE*)-14/*14*/14/14-(MA-*7*-UR)-
                -*28*/4/28/28-ME
13: SO-*26*-*NE*
23: ((MA-*23*-SA)-23/*23*-JU)-23/23/23-PL
29: (*NE*-*29*-CH)-29-SA

Ian Brady
1: (ME-*1*-VE)-1-*SO*
3: *SO*-3-*UR*
    (ME-*1*-VE)-12-JU
    (SA-*3*-PL)-18/9/18/9-(MA-*6*-*UR*)

5: (ME-*1*-VE)-<u>20</u>-<u>UR</u>
((JU-*5*-CH)-*10*-MA)-30/30/<u>15</u>-NE
7: (((ME-*1*-VE)-*7*-PL)-<u>7</u>/*7*/7-NE)-
-*21*/21/*3*/21-SA
11: ((ME-*1*-VE)-*11*/11-MA)-22-<u>MO</u>
13: <u>SO</u>-<u>13</u>-NE
17: <u>SO</u>-<u>17</u>-JU

Chapter 10: Elevenness

Fred Astaire
2: (<u>UR</u>-1-<u>CH</u>)-*2*/2-<u>MO</u>
(<u>MO</u>-1-PL)-2/2-<u>CH</u>
SA-*2*-NE
3: (SA-*2*-NE)-<u>3</u>/6-ME
MA-3-<u>CH</u>
5: (MA-3-<u>CH</u>)-10/*15*/30/15-(ME-<u>6</u>-NE)
7: (<u>MO</u>-*2*-<u>UR</u>)-*28*/28-MA
11: (((SO-*11*-<u>UR</u>)-11/*11*-NE)-<u>11</u>/11/11-JU)-
-11/11/11/<u>11</u>-VE)-22/22/*2*/*22*/22-SA
((SO-*11*-<u>UR</u>)-11/*11*-NE)-
-22/22/*2*/22/22/22-(MO-11-SA)
(VE-11-JU)-<u>22</u>/22/22/*22*-(MA-11-SA)
19: (ME-<u>19</u>-JU)-19-<u>CH</u>
23: SA-<u>23</u>-<u>UR</u>-<u>23</u>-PL

Richard Pryor
1: VE-*1*-MA
JU-1-SA
2: (VE-*1*-MA)-*2*/2/*2*/2-(JU-1-SA)
(VE-*2*-JU)-4-PL
3: SO-<u>18</u>-ME
SO-<u>12</u>-SA
((VE-*1*-MA)-*2*-JU)-9/*9*/9-18-<u>NE</u>
(MA-*9*-<u>NE</u>)-27/*27*-PL
5: SO-*5*-<u>NE</u> (exact)
7: (MO-<u>7</u>-ME)-7/*7*-<u>NE</u>
11: ((VE-*1*-MA)-*2*-JU)-11/*11*/*22*-UR)-
-11/11/22/<u>11</u>-SO
-*11*/11-MO)-11/*11*/11-UR)-
-11/11/<u>11</u>/11-SO
17: (ME-*17*-SA)-17/<u>17</u>-PL
23: SO-*23*-PL

Donald Trump
1: SO-<u>1</u>-UR
VE-*1*-SA
(JU-<u>1</u>-CH)-1-NE
2: SO-*16*-CH
3: JU-*3*-UR
ME-*24*-SA
5: MO-<u>5</u>-VE
(ME-*15*-<u>MA</u>)-15-CH
((SA-*5*-NE)-*10*-UR)-30/30/*3*-JU
(VE-*1*-SA)-5/*5*-NE
7: SO-*7*-NE
(UR-<u>7</u>-PL)-21-<u>MA</u>
11: (SO-*11*-VE)-22/*22*/22/22-(ME-11-JU)

((PL-*11*-CH)-<u>11</u>-MO)-<u>22</u>-SA
17: SO-<u>17</u>-<u>MA</u>
19: VE-*19*-UR
23: (ME-*23*-PL)-<u>23</u>-SO

Humphrey Lyttelton
1: ME-<u>1</u>-MA
2: (ME-<u>1</u>-MA)-*2*/2-MO
(MO-*2*-ME)-*4*/4-SA
((JU-*2*-UR)-4-MA)-8-VE
3: (NE-*3*-CH)-<u>6</u>/*6*-MA
(JU-*2*-UR)-6/*3*-<u>PL</u>
5: (VE-*5*-PL)-*10*-SO
((NE-*3*-CH)-<u>6</u>/*6*-MA)-10/30/*15*-SA
7: (ME-*7*-VE)-28-CH
11: ((SO-*11*-MO)-<u>11</u>-JU)-
-22/22/*22*/22/*2*/*22*-(UR-*11*-CH)
13: (JU-*2*-UR)-*13*/*26*-ME
(ME-*13*-JU)-13-NE
17: (VE-*17*-NE)-17-MO
31: SO-*31*-NE
(VE-*31*-MA)-<u>31</u>-MO

Princess Grace
2: (<u>ME</u>-*2*-<u>CH</u>)-16/*16*-NE
<u>VE</u>-*8*-JU
3: (SO-*3*-PL)-3-MO
(<u>VE</u>-<u>6</u>-SA)-9/<u>18</u>-UR
5: (MO-*5*-<u>VE</u>)-30/<u>6</u>-SA
(JU-<u>10</u>-PL)-20/*20*-MA
7: (SO-*3*-PL)-*21*-<u>CH</u>
SO-*28*-SA
11: (MO-<u>11</u>-<u>ME</u>)-22/*22*/*22*/*2*-(UR-11-<u>CH</u>)
((UR-*11*-CH)-11/<u>11</u>-JU)-<u>22</u>/*22*/22-MO
13: SO-*13*-UR
<u>VE</u>-*13*-NE
(JU-<u>13</u>-SA)-13-MO

Vincent Van Gogh
1: MO-<u>1</u>-JU
(ME-<u>1</u>-PL)-1-UR
<u>VE</u>-*1*-<u>MA</u>
3: (<u>VE</u>-*1*-<u>MA</u>)-9/*9*-UR
(ME-*3*-JU)-12/4-<u>CH</u>
5: (MO-5-SA)-10/<u>10</u>-SO
<u>VE</u>-*15*-SA
7: (UR-<u>7</u>-<u>CH</u>)-28-<u>VE</u>
11: ((MO-*11*-<u>CH</u>)-11-(<u>VE</u>-*11*-PL))-22-NE
13: (SO-13-NE)-13-UR
-26/*26*-<u>MA</u>
17: SO-*17*-PL
19: SO-<u>19</u>-<u>CH</u>
23: (<u>VE</u>-23-JU)-<u>23</u>/23-NE
31: SO-*31*-<u>VE</u>

Paul Gauguin
2: (<u>MO</u>-*2*-<u>NE</u>)-4/<u>4</u>/4/4-(VE-2-CH)
JU-*4*-UR

3: MO-**9**-JU
MA-**3**-CH
(JU-**4**-UR)-24/24-ME
SO-**24**-MO
5: (MA-**3**-CH)-15/**5**-ME
11: (SO-**11**-CH)-22/22/22/**22**-(SA-**11**-PL)
(MA-11-UR)-22-NE
(MO-**2**-NE)-11/22-UR
13: SO-**13**-UR
(MO-13-ME)-26/26-PL
29: SO-**29**-VE

Paul Cézanne
1: MO-1-UR
(VE-1-NE)-1-SO
2: (SO-**8**-MO)-16/16-ME
3: SO-**3**-MA
SO-**18**-JU
(MO-1-UR)-3-CH
5: (MO-1-UR)-5/5-JU
((MO-**5**-JU)-10/10-VE)-3/15/30-CH
(ME-**25**-PL)-25-CH
7: (SO-**7**-SA)-14/**14**-PL
11: (MO-**11**-MA)-11-NE)-11/11/11-PL
JU-**22**-SA
13: SO-**26**-UR
ME-**13**-SA
(JU-13-NE)-26/**26**-CH
31: (SO-**31**-ME)-31-NE

David Carpenter
1: SO-1-CH
MO-1-NE
ME-1-VE
MA-1-UR
2: ME-**8**-PL
(MO-16-CH)-**32**/32-MA
3: VE-**9**-PL
5: SO-**10**-MA
(JU-**5**-NE)-10-CH
7: MO-14-JU
11: (SO-**11**-JU-**11**-UR)-22-ME
MA-**11**-PL
SA-**11**-NE
23: (ME-**23**-SA)-23-JU
29: (SO-**29**-SA)-29/**29**-PL

Dennis Nilsen
1: MO-1-SA
JU-**1**-CH
2: (JU-**1**-CH)-**4**/4-MO
3: SO-**3**-MA
(JU-**1**-CH)-3/3-UR
5: SO-**20**-SA
7: (SO-**3**-MA)-21/7-VE
11: (MO-**11**-UR)-11-SO)-**22**/22/22-VE
(ME-11-CH)-11/11-PL

(ME-11-CH)-**22**/22-SA
13: SO-**26**-JU
17: (SO-**17**-ME)-17-JU
31: (ME-**31**-UR)-31-MA

Winston Churchill
2: (MA-1-JU)-2-CH
SO-**16**-UR
3: (MO-**3**-NE)-**9**/9-SA
(JU-2-CH)-6/**3**-VE
SO-**18**-ME
5: SO-**25**-VE
(MO-**25**-UR)-**25**/25-CH
ME-**15**-JU
7: SO-**7**-MA
11: SO-**11**-MO-**11**-PL
VE-**11**-MA
ME-**22**-SA
19: SO-**19**-CH
23: SO-**23**-NE
(MO-**23**-MA)-23/**23**-ME
29: SO-**29**-SA

Chapter 11: Thirteenness

Catherine the Great
1: (SO-**1**-CH)-1-MA
(MO-**1**-VE)-1-JU
2: (MO-**1**-VE)-**8**/8-MA
3: (SO-**1**-CH)-**27**-PL
(MO-**8**-MA)-**24**/12-PL
(ME-**9**-SA)-27/**27**-VE
(MA-**6**-SA)-18/**9**-ME
5: (SO-**1**-CH)-**15**-ME
7: (SO-**1**-CH)-**7**/7-JU)-28/28/28-SA
11: (MO-**1**-VE)-**11**/11-ME
13: ((SO-**1**-CH)-**13**-UR-**13**-NE)-**26**-MO
MA-**13**-JU
17: (SO-**1**-CH)-**17**-VE
19: (ME-**19**-JU)-19-PL

Antoine de Saint-Exupéry
1: MO-1-ME
2: MA-**2**-JU
3: (VE-**9**-SA)-27/**27**-MO
(MA-**2**-JU)-6/**3**-ME
                      -**12**/12-SA
(MA-**12**-SA)-24/24-PL
5: (MA-**2**-JU)-10/**5**-SO
7: (MA-**2**-JU)-**14**/7-VE
11: (MA-**2**-JU)-22/**11**-VE
13: (SO-**13**-MO)-**26**/**26**/26/26-(VE-**13**-UR)
ME-13-CH
29: (MO-**29**-CH)-29-NE
VE-**29**-MA
31: SO-**31**-SA
(NE-**31**-CH)-31-UR

Amelia Earhart
1: (MO-_1_-VE-_1_-PL)-1/_1_/1-NE
   MA-_1_-JU
   SA-_1_-UR
2: (MA-_1_-JU)-4-MO
                -32/_32_-NE
   (SO-_8_-VE)-_16_/16-UR
3: (SA-_1_-UR)-_9_/9-PL
   (MA-_1_-JU)-6-_CH_
                -_24_/24-UR
5: (PL-_5_-_CH_)-_15_-SO
7: (SA-_1_-UR)-7/_7_-ME)-7/_7_/_7_-NE
   (MA-_1_-JU)-21/21-PL
   (ME-_7_-NE)-21/21-_CH_
11: (MO-_11_-UR)-22/22-_CH_
13: ((MA-_1_-JU)-13/_13_-ME)-13/13/_13_-VE
19: (MA-_1_-JU)-19/_19_-SO
29: SO-_29_-SA

Basel air crash
1: (SO-_1_-VE)-_1_-CH
   MA-_1_-JU
2: ((SO-_1_-VE)-_1_-CH)-_2_/_2_/2-UR
3: (SO-_1_-VE)-27/_27_-NE
   (MO-_3_-ME)-24/8-JU
5: (SO-_1_-VE)-5/_5_/5/_5_-(MA-_1_-JU)
   (((SO-_1_-VE)-_2_-UR)-_5_/_5_/10-JU)-
                -20/_20_/20/10-PL
   (MO-_3_-ME)-10/15/30/_15_-(SA-_6_-CH)
13: ((SO-_1_-VE)-_13_-ME)-13/13/_13_-SA
19: (ME-_19_-UR)-19-PL
31: (MO-_31_-MA-_31_-PL)-31-SO

Bahrain air crash
1: SO-_1_-ME
   (MO-_1_-JU)-1-SA
2: (SO-_1_-ME)-_4_/4-SA
   (MO-_1_-JU)-2/_2_/2/2-(PL-_1_-CH)
5: (MO-_2_-CH)-_9_/18-ME
   (VE-_10_-MA)-20/_20_-ME
7: (SO-_4_-SA)-_7_/28-NE
   (SO-_7_-NE)-7/_7_-CH
   (MO-_2_-CH)-14/_7_-NE
11: (MO-_11_-VE)-22/_2_/22/_22_-(UR-_11_-CH)
13: ((JU-_13_-UR)-13-ME)-_26_/_26_/26-NE
23: SO-_23_-MO
29: SO-_29_-PL
31: (SA-_31_-NE)-31-MO

Dalian air crash
1: (VE-_1_-MA-_1_-SA)-1-ME
2: (VE-_1_-MA-_1_-SA)-2/_2_/2-_PL_
3: (_MA_-_2_-_PL_)-12/_12_-SO
5: (MO-_5_-CH)-_20_/20-SO
                -15/_15_/15/15-(NE-_5_-_PL_)
   (_MA_-10-UR)-30/_15_-CH
7: (VE-_1_-_MA_-_1_-SA)-_7_/7/_7_-CH
11: (VE-_1_-SA)-22-MO

Peter Sellers
1: _SO_-_1_-_MA_
   ME-_1_-JU
2: ME-_8_-JU
   (MO-_16_-MA)-_32_/32-VE
3: ME-_3_-CH
   (MO-_27_-ME)-27-VE
   (JU-_2_-PL)-3/_6_-_SO_
5: ME-_5_-SA
7: (ME-_7_-UR)-7-VE
                -21/21-_SO_
   (SA-_14_-NE)-_28_/28/28/28-(PL-_14_-CH)
13: ((_SO_-_13_-MO)-_13_/13-SA)-13-CH
   UR-_13_-PL
31: (JU-_31_-CH)-31-_MA_)-31/31/31-NE

Truman Capote
1: VE-_1_-NE
2: (VE-_1_-NE)-_8_/8-SO
   (ME-_2_-UR)-8/8-MO
3: (MO-_9_-JU)-27/27-SO
   ((VE-_1_-NE)-_3_/3-CH)-_8_/8/_24_-SO
5: ((VE-_1_-NE)-_3_/3-CH)-5/_5_/15-MO
   (SA-_10_-PL)-15/_30_-SO
   MA-_5_-JU
7: SO-_21_-ME
13: (SO-_13_-MA)-13-(MO-_13_-PL)
   (VE-_1_-NE)-_13_/13-ME
   (ME-_13_-VE)-_26_-SA
19: (SA-_19_-CH)-_19_-MA
29: (SO-_29_-UR)-29-SA

Rainer Werner Fassbinder
1: SO-_1_-_UR_
2: SO-_8_-MO
3: SO-_6_-PL
   (SO-_8_-MO)-12/_24_-SA
   ME-_12_-MA
   (JU-_3_-PL)-_27_-MA
5: ((SO-_10_-CH)-15/30-MA)-20/20/_12_-ME
   (ME-_15_-SA)-_30_-NE
   (ME-_12_-MA)-_30_/20-NE
7: (MA-_7_-_UR_)-7-CH
11: SO-_22_-NE
13: (_UR_-_13_-NE-_13_-PL)-13-MO
   (NE-_13_-PL)-13-SA
17: (ME-_17_-_UR_
   MO-_17_-SA
31: VE-31-_UR_-31-CH
   ME-_31_-JU

Hermann Hesse
1: NE-*1*-CH
2: MO-4-*JU*
   (*ME*-8-NE)-32-VE
   (VE-8-MA)-32-*ME*
   SA-*8*-CH
3: (SO-3-MA)-24/8-VE
   (MO-3-VE)-9-NE
5: SO-20-*ME*
   (MO-*5*-UR)-10-CH
   VE-20-SA
   MA-20-PL
7: SO-*7*-MO
11: SO-*11*-CH
13: ((SO-*13*-JU)-13/*13*-SA)-*26*/26/26-UR
   ME-*13*-PL
   MA-*13*-NE
31: (VE-*31*-*JU*)-31-CH

Janis Joplin
1: ME-1-VE
   SA-1-*UR*
2: ME-8-MA
3: SO-*9*-MO
   (*UR*-3-NE)-9-SO
5: MO-5-VE
   (*UR*-3-NE)-15/5-JU
7: VE-7-JU
11: (MO-11-*SA*)-22/22-*CH*
13: ((MO-*13*-MA)-*13*/13-NE)-13/*13*/13-PL
17: SO-17-*SA*
19: SO-19-JU
23: (VE-*23*-PL)-23-SO
29: (VE-29-*SA*)-29-MA
31: (*SA*-*31*-NE)-31-ME

Che Guevara
1: VE-1-CH
2: MO-8-JU
3: (SO-27-NE)-27-VE
   (((JU-3-NE)-9-ME)-*9*/9/9-PL)-
          -18/18/*6*/18-*UR*
   (ME-*6*-*UR*)-12/12-CH
5: SO-*5*-MO
   (ME-*6*-*UR*)-15/10-SA
   (SA-10-*UR*)-30/15-SO
7: (SO-*7*-PL)-21/21-CH
   (ME-14-VE)-28/*28*-SO
13: (SO-*13*-JU)-13-MA
   ((MO-*13*-CH)-13-SA)-13/13/*13*-NE
          -26/*26*/26-PL
17: VE-17-MA-17-NE
23: SO-23-*UR*
29: SO-29-ME
   (*UR*-*29*-PL)-29/29-MO

Roberta Cowell
1: (MO-*1*-VE)-1/1-UR

2: (MO-*1*-VE)-*8*-SO
   (SA-1-NE)-*4*/4-*ME*
3: (MO-*1*-VE)-*3*/3-*PL*
5: (MO-*3*-PL)-*15*/15-JU
   MA-*5*-PL
7: (SO-*7*-JU)-*7*-UR
   (MO-*1*-VE)-*7*/7-SA
   (MO-*7*-SA)-28/28-MA
13: (MO-*1*-VE)-13/*13*-MA)-13/*13*/13-CH
   ((VE-*13*-MA)-*13*-CH)-
      -*26*/26/*26*/*26*/26/26-(JU-*13*-NE)
17: SO-17-MA
19: SO-19-*ME*-19-*PL*

Black Wednesday
1: SO-*1*-ME-*1*-JU
2: MO-4-SA
5: (SO-*1*-ME-*1*-JU)-10/*10*/10-CH
   ((ME-*1*-JU)-*10*-CH)-15/15/*6*-VE
7: SO-*14*-VE
   MO-*7*-*MA*
13: (SO-*1*-ME-*1*-JU)-*13*/13/13-SA
   (ME-*1*-JU)-13-(*MA*-*13*-*NE*-*13*-PL)
   (SO-*13*-SA)-*13*/13-*UR*
19: (SO-*19*-MO)-19-PL
29: (ME-*1*-JU)-29/29-*NE*
   (ME-29-*NE*)-29/29-VE
31: SO-31-*MA*

Chapter 12: Seventeenness

Madalyn Murray O'Hair
2: (MO-*2*-CH)-4/4-PL
3: (SO-3-SA)-*9*/9-MO
5: SO-*5*-PL
   (JU-25-SA)-25-VE
7: (SO-*7*-UR)-7-*NE*
11: (MA-11-*NE*)-11/11-PL
17: ((MO-*17*-VE)-17-ME)-17/17/*17*-JU
          -17/*17*/17-UR
19: (SO-*19*-CH)-19-JU
31: (ME-31-SA)-31/31-PL
   (MA-*31*-JU)-31-UR

L. Ron Hubbard
1: MA-*1*-UR
2: (MO-2-CH)-8-*VE*
   (ME-*8*-MA)-32/32/32/*32*-(NE-16-PL)
   (NE-*8*-CH)-16/*16*-PL
3: SO-9-MO
   SO-*27*-UR
   (ME-*3*-JU)-8/24-MA
7: (SO-*7*-MA)-14-*VE*
   (SA-*7*-PL)-21/21-*VE*
11: (MO-11-PL)-22/22-UR
   (ME-11-*VE*)-22/22-SA
13: (JU-*13*-PL)-26-VE

17: (JU-**17**-SA)-17-SO
(MO-**17**-NE)-17/**17**-MA

Nicolae Ceaușescu
1: (VE-**1**-UR)-1-*SO*
2: MA-4-PL
3: (VE-**1**-UR)-12/**12**-ME
    -18-MA
5: (VE-**1**-UR)-**20**/20-*NE*
(MO-5-PL)-10/10-*SA*
7: *SO*-14-MO
(VE-**1**-UR)-28/28-*SA*
11: (((VE-**1**-UR)-**11**-JU)-11-CH)-11/11/11/11-PL
13: (MO-**13**-PL)-13-ME
17: (*SO*-**17**-JU)-17-*NE*
(VE-**1**-UR)-17/**17**-MO

Roger Vadim
1: (*JU*-**1**-*UR*)-1-*MO*
2: (*MO*-**4**-*VE*)-32/32/**32**/32-(SA-**8**-CH)
3: (*VE*-**3**-NE)-3-CH
(*JU*-12-CH)-24/**24**/**8**/24-(SA-12-PL)
5: (*MO*-**4**-*VE*)-10/20-PL
7: (*JU*-**1**-*UR*)-7-SA
(*MO*-**4**-*VE*)-7/28-SO
13: (*JU*-**1**-*UR*)-13/13-SO
17: (((*JU*-**1**-*UR*)-17/**17**/**17**-*MA*)-17/17/**17**/**17**-NE)-
        -17/17/**17**/**17**-ME
(((*MA*-**17**-*UR*)-17-NE)-17/17/**17**/**17**-ME)-
        -17/17/**17**/**17**-PL
31: (*JU*-**1**-*UR*)-**31**/31-SA
(*VE*-31-UR)-31/31-SA

Harold Pinter
1: (*JU*-**1**-*PL*)-1-MA
MO-**1**-*CH*
2: (*JU*-**1**-*PL*)-8/8-NE
3: (*JU*-**1**-*PL*)-**6**/6-*MO*
(*MO*-**1**-*CH*)-6-JU   (SA-3-NE)-9/**9**-MA
5: (*MO*-**1**-*CH*)-10-NE
(*MO*-**6**-JU)-10/**15**-UR
(ME-**6**-VE)-15/**30**/30/15-(NE-10-*CH*)
7: (SO-**21**-*PL*)-21-ME
11: (*MO*-11-MA)-22/**22**-SO
13: (ME-13-UR)-**26**/26-SA
17: (SO-**17**-VE)-17-(*MO*-**17**-NE)
29: (VE-**29**-MA)-29-SA

Vanessa Redgrave
1: ME-1-JU
2: (MO-2-VE)-8/**8**-*MA*
(SA-2-NE)-4/4-CH
3: (MO-2-VE)-6/**3**-PL
(VE-**3**-PL)-9/**9**-CH
(SO-9-SA)-27/**27**-JU
(ME-3-NE)-12/4-CH
5: (SO-4-*MA*)-5/20-NE
(MO-2-VE)-10/5-ME

(MO-5-*UR*)-10/10-ME
7: (JU-**7**-CH)-7-MO
(VE-**3**-PL)-21/**7**-NE
13: (JU-**13**-PL)-13-SO
17: (SO-**17**-CH)-17-*UR*
((*MA*-**17**-SA)-17/**17**-ME)-17-PL

Diane Keaton
1: MA-1-SA
JU-1-CH
2: SO-**16**-MO
VE-4-NE
MA-**4**-JU
3: (ME-6-JU)-18/**9**-SO
(MO-**3**-NE)-4/12-VE
(VE-27-PL)-27-ME
5: ((MA-**5**-NE)-**15**-SO)-30-CH
        -25-PL
(VE-4-NE)-20/**5**-MA
7: VE-**14**-CH
11: (JU-**11**-UR)-22/**22**-NE
13: (VE-**13**-SA)-26/**26**-ME
17: ((MA-**17**-UR)-17-MO)-17/17/17/17/
        17/**17**-(ME-17-CH)
19: (UR-**19**-PL)-19-SA
        -19-ME
(ME-19-NE)-19-PL

Oscar Wilde
2: (ME-**2**-UR)-4/**4**-MO
(MO-**4**-UR)-**16**/16-SO
(*MA*-8-JU)-32/**32**-VE
(VE-**16**-SA)-**32**/**32**-JU
3: (MO-**4**-UR)-6/**12**-SA
(MO-6-JU)-9/18-CH
(ME-**2**-UR)-**3**/6-*NE*
5: ((ME-**2**-UR)-**3**/6-*NE*)-10/5/30-VE
((ME-**5**-CH)-**3**/15-*NE*)-10/**10**/30-VE
(ME-**5**-CH)-10/**10**-VE
(ME-**3**-*NE*)-**5**/15-CH
7: ((MO-**7**-JU)-**7**-PL)-7/7/**7**-VE
17: ((SO-**17**-PL)-17-SA)-**17**/**17**-ME
29: ((*MA*-29-PL)-29/**29**-UR)-29/29/**29**-*NE*

Dorothy Parker
1: (SO-1-MA)-1/1-CH
2: (SO-**4**-JU)-**16**/16-UR
MO-**4**-SA
3: (SO-**4**-JU)-**12**/**3**-VE
((SA-**3**-PL)-**9**/9-SO)-27/**27**/27-UR
(MO-**4**-SA)-**12**/**3**-PL
(MO-3-CH)-**12**/4-PL
(VE-**3**-JU)-**27**/27-NE
(NE-1-PL)-3/**3**-CH
5: (VE-**3**-JU)-15/**5**-ME
7: SO-14-NE
17: ((MO-**17**-ME)-**17**/17-UR)-17-MA

Bertrand Russell
1: (SO-*1*-MA)-1-PL
2: (JU-1-UR)-4/4-NE
3: (SO-*1*-MA)-*6*-UR
5: (SO-*1*-MA)-15/15-*ME*
            -20/20-MO
            -*25*/25-JU
7: (UR-*7*-CH)-21-PL
      VE-*21*-NE
11: (SO-*1*-MA)-11/*11*-NE
       (JU-11-PL)-22/22-*ME*
17: ((SO-*1*-MA)-*17*/17-SA)-17/*17*/17-CH
23: ((SO-*1*-MA)-23/*23*-*VE*)-23/23/23-MO

Neville Heath
1: ME-*1*-MA-*1*-JU
2: (ME-*1*-MA-*1*-JU)-4/*4*/4-UR
      MO-*2*-VE
3: (JU-*4*-UR)-12/6-MO
      (MO-*2*-VE)-6/3-UR
      (ME-*1*-MA)-*9*-PL
5: (MO-*2*-VE)-*5*/10-NE
7: (MA-*4*-UR)-28/*7*-SA
11: (MO-*2*-VE)-*22*/11-ME)-22/11/11-SA
13: (MA-*1*-JU)-13/13-CH
17: (SO-*17*-MO-*17*-MA)-17-SA
19: (SO-19-CH)-19-PL
23: (MO-*23*-PL)-23-CH
29: (VE-*29*-CH)-29-NE

Randall Woodfield
2: (*ME*-4-NE)-8/*8*-JU
3: SO-*27*-*VE*
      (SO-*6*-JU)-24/*8*-NE
      (NE-*6*-PL)-24/*8*-SO
5: (NE-*6*-PL)-30/*15*-MO
      (MO-*15*-PL)-*12*/20-CH
7: (MA-14-JU)-28-MO
17: ((*ME*-*17*-MA)-*17*/*17*-SA)-17/17/*17*-PL
             -*17*/17-CH
      SA-*17*-UR-*17*-PL
29: SO-29-NE
       (MA-*29*-UR)-29-JU

Chapter 13: Nineteenness

Jean Sibelius
1: ME-*1*-JU
2: (ME-*1*-JU)-2/2-*UR*
           -*4*/4-NE
      (ME-4-NE)-8/*8*-MO
3: ME-*9*-VE
      (MA-*3*-NE)-*12*/12-SA
            -*18*-CH
5: VE-*5*-*UR*
      ME-*5*-CH
      ME-*20*-PL
7: (MA-*7*-PL)-7-*UR*

Jane Austen
1: MO-1-SA
      MA-1-PL
2: (*SO*-*4*-*NE*)-8-VE
      (MA-*4*-SA)-*8*/8-UR
3: (*SO*-3-CH)-9/*9*-UR
             -*12*/4-PL
      (MO-*3*-JU)-*18*/18/18/18-(*NE*-*3*-PL)
5: (VE-*5*-JU)-5-MA
      (*NE*-*3*-PL)-15/*15*-SA
7: (MO-*3*-JU)-21/*7*-CH
11: *SO*-*11*-SA
       MO-*11*-UR
19: (*SO*-*19*-JU)-19-ME
       (MO-*19*-MA)-19/*19*-CH
       VE-*19*-PL
29: (JU-*29*-SA)-*29*/29-*NE*

Gerry Rafferty
1: ME-1-MA
2: (*MO*-*4*-JU)-*16*/16-UR
      (VE-4-UR)-16/*16*-*MO*
      (*MO*-*16*-UR)-32-ME
3: ((*MO*-*4*-JU)-*6*/12-SO)-24/*24*/24-PL
      (ME-1-MA)-*3*-SA
5: SO-*10*-VE
7: (VE-*4*-UR)-*28*/7-PL
      (*MO*-21-NE)-21/21-ME
19: (VE-*19*-JU-*19*-CH)-*19*/19/19-SA
31: (NE-*31*-PL)-31/*31*-MA

Gavin Maxwell
1: (SO-*1*-ME)-*1*-NE
2: (ME-*1*-NE)-4-MO
      (MO-4-NE)-*8*/8-MA
3: MO-*6*-SA
      VE-*9*-UR
5: (ME-*10*-VE)-20-*CH*
7: ME-*7*-JU
11: SO-*22*-MA
       (MO-*11*-JU)-11-PL
17: SO-*17*-PL
19: (SO-*19*-VE)-19-JU
       MO-*19*-UR-*19*-*CH*
29: SO-*29*-*CH*
       MO-29-VE
       MA-29-UR

Fred Kimball
1:   <u>MO-*1*-CH</u>
     VE-<u>1</u>-UR
2:   VE-<u>2</u>-PL
3:   ((<u>MO-*1*-CH</u>)-*3*-MA)-6-ME
     (VE-<u>2</u>-PL)-<u>3</u>/6-JU
5:   (<u>MO-*1*-CH</u>)-25/*25*-JU
                   -*20*/20-NE
     (ME-<u>5</u>-JU)-<u>30</u>/6-PL
     SO-*20*-MA
7:   (VE-<u>7</u>-SA)-<u>14</u>-ME
11: ((<u>MO-*1*-CH</u>)-<u>11</u>/*11*-VE)-<u>11</u>/*11*/*11*-SO
13: (<u>MO-*1*-CH</u>)-<u>13</u>/*13*-UR
17: (SO-*17*-SA)-17-PL
19: (SO-*19*-UR)-19-(JU-*19*-NE)
     (<u>MO-*1*-CH</u>)-*19*/19-SA
29: SO-<u>29</u>-PL
31: (ME-<u>31</u>-NE)-<u>31</u>/31-<u>CH</u>

Frank Skinner
1:   (MO-*1*-ME)-<u>1</u>-VE
2:   (MO-*1*-ME)-*8*/8-PL
3:   (MO-*1*-ME)-*9*/9-UR
     (<u>MA-*3*-PL</u>)-<u>18</u>-VE
5:   ((MO-*1*-ME)-*5*/5-<u>NE</u>)-15/15/*15*-<u>SO</u>
7:   (MO-*1*-ME)-<u>7</u>-JU
     VE-*14*-NE
11: (MO-*1*-ME)-*11*/11-SA
13: (MO-*1*-ME)-13/*13*-<u>CH</u>
17: SO-*17*-JU
     (MO-*1*-ME)-17/<u>17</u>-<u>MA</u>
19: (VE-*19*-SA)-<u>19</u>-<u>SO</u>
     <u>MA-*19*-JU</u>-*19*-UR

Norman Lamont
1:   SA-*1*-UR
2:   (SA-*1*-UR)-4-MO
                   -<u>16</u>/16-JU
     SO-<u>8</u>-<u>VE</u>
3:   <u>VE</u>-<u>3</u>-PL
5:   SO-<u>10</u>-JU
7:   MO-*7*-NE
17: ME-<u>17</u>-VE
19: (SO-<u>19</u>-MO)-19-ME
                   -19/<u>19</u>-PL
     ((SA-*1*-UR)-19/*19*-<u>MA</u>)-19/*19*/*19*-VE
29: (SA-*1*-UR)-<u>29</u>-SO
31: SO-*31*-CH

Chapter 14: Twenty-threeness

Dylan Thomas
1:   ME-<u>1</u>-MA
     <u>JU</u>-1-<u>UR</u>
     SA-*1*-PL
2:   ME-*16*-NE
3:   SO-<u>3</u>-PL
     ME-*9*-<u>JU</u>

5:   ((SA-*1*-PL)-5/*5*-<u>UR</u>)-*10*/*10*/10-CH
                   -<u>25</u>/25/25-VE
     ((<u>UR</u>-*5*-PL)-25/<u>25</u>-VE)-*25*/25/25-NE
7:   MO-<u>14</u>-ME
     MO-<u>21</u>-CH
     ME-<u>21</u>-VE
     (SA-*1*-PL)-21-MA
11: (SO-<u>11</u>-CH)-22/*22*-MA
13: ((SA-*1*-PL)-13-<u>JU</u>)-26/<u>26</u>/26-MO
19: (SO-*19*-MO)-<u>19</u>/19-ME
23: (SO-<u>23</u>-<u>UR</u>)-23/<u>23</u>-MA
     VE-*23*-JU-*23*-CH
     ((SA-*1*-PL)-<u>23</u>/*23*-ME)-23-MO
29: SO-*29*-JU

Marie Duplessis
2:   (SO-*8*-VE)-<u>16</u>/*16*-SA
     MO-<u>4</u>-CH
     MA-<u>4</u>-NE
3:   (MO-<u>4</u>-CH)-*6*/12-SA
     (MO-*27*-JU)-<u>27</u>-PL
7:   SO-<u>21</u>-NE
     MO-<u>7</u>-ME
     (MA-<u>4</u>-NE)-*28*/14-SA
11: (SO-*11*-PL)-22-CH
13: (VE-*13*-PL)-13-NE
17: (ME-*17*-VE)-<u>17</u>-CH
23: SO-<u>23</u>-MO
     ((ME-*23*-SA)-23-PL)-*23*/23/23-JU
     ((MA-*23*-CH)-23/*23*-UR)-23-PL
29: SO-<u>29</u>-UR

O. Henry
1:   SO-<u>1</u>-SA
     ME-<u>1</u>-JU
2:   ((SO-*8*-MO)-*16*/16-VE)-32/*32*/32-CH
     JU-*2*-NE
3:   ME-*12*-CH
     MA-<u>9</u>-CH
5:   VE-*5*-NE
7:   (JU-*7*-UR-*7*-CH)-*2*/14/14-NE
13: SO-*13*-NE
19: SO-<u>19</u>-ME
23: MO-*23*-MA-*23*-SA-*23*-NE
     (MO-*23*-SA-*23*-NE)-23-UR
31: SO-<u>31</u>-PL
     MO-*31*-UR
     VE-<u>31</u>-MA

Salvador Dali
1:   (ME-*1*-MA)-<u>1</u>-SO
2:   SO-*4*-SA
     VE-*8*-PL
3:   (SO-*4*-SA)-12/*3*-PL
     (VE-*8*-PL)-*6*/24-PL
     (ME-*1*-MA)-*9*/9-NE
5:   SO-<u>15</u>-<u>MO</u>
     (ME-*1*-MA)-*5*/5-UR

(ME-**5**-UR)-10-JU
7: (ME-**1**-MA)-**7**/7-MO
(*MO*-7-ME)-**14**/14-PL
(NE-**7**-*CH*)-**14**/14-JU
(JU-**14**-NE)-28-MA
SA-**7**-UR
19: (ME-**19**-VE)-19-*CH*
MA-19-SA
23: SO-**23**-VE-**23**-UR
MO-23-*CH*
JU-**23**-PL

Edward Gorey
1: SO-**1**-MO
2: (SO-**1**-MO)-**16**/16-MA
VE-2-NE
MA-2-SA
JU-2-PL
3: (SO-**1**-MO)-**24**/24-VE
(VE-2-NE)-6/**3**-CH
(MA-2-SA)-3/**6**/**6**/3-(JU-2-PL)
5: (NE-**3**-CH)-**5**/15-JU
7: (SO-**1**-MO)-28-NE
VE-**21**-JU
MA-7-*UR*
11: (SO-**1**-MO)-22/**22**-JU
(JU-11-*UR*)-22/22-SO
13: ME-**13**-CH
23: (SO-**1**-MO)-**23**/**23**/23/23-(SA-**23**-CH)
31: (SO-**1**-MO)-**31**/31-PL

Hans Christian Andersen
1: SO-**1**-ME
2: ((SO-**1**-ME)-2/**2**-SA)-8/**8**/**8**-NE
3: MO-**9**-UR
MO-**6**-PL
5: (SO-25-VE)-**25**/25-UR
UR-**10**-CH
7: (ME-**2**-SA)-**14**/7-MO
(MA-14-UR)-28/**28**-NE
11: (SO-**1**-ME)-11-(PL-**11**-CH)
13: (MO-**13**-MA)-13-SO
17: ME-**17**-JU
23: (JU-**23**-UR-**23**-PL)-23-SO
(VE-**23**-MA)-23-ME

Karl Marx
1: SO-1-MO
2: ((NE-**4**-PL)-**8**/8-MO)-**16**/16/16-ME
VE-8-JU
3: (SO-1-MO)-**3**-JU
(SO-27-MA)-27/**27**-VE
5: (SO-**5**-UR)-**3**/**15**/15/15-(JU-**5**-PL)
13: (MO-**13**-SA)-26-MA
17: SO-17-CH
23: (MA-**23**-JU)-23-ME)-**23**/**23**/23-SA)-
-**23**/**23**/23/**23**-CH
31: SO-**31**-SA

Timothy McVeigh
1: SO-**1**-ME
VE-**1**-SA
UR-1-PL
2: (SO-**1**-ME)-**8**/8-MO
(SO-**8**-MO)-**16**/16/16/16-(JU-**4**-NE)
(VE-**1**-SA)-**16**/16-UR
3: (VE-**1**-SA)-**12**/12-MO
(MO-2-PL)-6/**3**-MA
(*JU*-**4**-NE)-**12**/**6**-UR
5: (SO-**1**-ME)-5/**5**-UR
(ME-**5**-UR)-20-MA
-**25**/25-SA
-**30**/**6**-NE
(*JU*-5-CH)-15-MA
7: SO-**21**-PL
(VE-**1**-SA)-14/**14**-*JU*
11: SO-**11**-CH
13: (ME-13-PL)-**26**/26-VE
23: ((VE-**1**-SA)-**23**-SO)-**23**/23/23-MA

Charles Sobhraj
2: (JU-**8**-NE)-16/**16**-*CH*
(SA-**8**-PL)-32/**32**/**32**/32-(NE-16-*CH*)
3: SO-**3**-JU
(ME-**6**-MA)-**9**/18-VE
5: (SO-**3**-JU)-**5**/15-*CH*
(SO-**5**-CH)-**20**/20-ME
(VE-5-*UR*)-5/5-JU
(JU-**5**-*UR*)-10/10-*MO*
(VE-**25**-NE)-25-SA
11: SO-**11**-SA
VE-**11**-SA
MA-**11**-*CH*
13: SO-13-NE
17: SO-17-VE
23: ((*MO*-**23**-PL)-**23**-SO)-23/23/**23**-MA
((ME-**23**-SA)-**23**-*UR*)-23-*CH*

John Perkins
1: ME-**1**-MA
2: (SO-**2**-PL)-**32**/32-SA
(NE-1-CH)-**4**-SA
3: ((SO-**2**-PL)-**3**/**6**-UR)-18/**9**/18-ME
(SO-**3**-UR)-3-NE
(ME-**9**-PL)-**27**/27-VE
5: ((SO-**2**-PL)-**3**/**6**-UR)-30/**15**/**10**-JU
(MA-**25**-PL)-25-NE
7: ME-**7**-NE
(SA-**14**-UR)-28-MA
13: (ME-**13**-SA)-**26**/**26**-*MO*
17: SO-**17**-MA
23: (SO-**23**-*MO*)-23-VE-23-CH
29: *MO*-29-NE
VE-29-SA

Chapter 15: Twenty-nineness

Margaret Mead
1: (MA-*1*-JU-*1*-SA)-1-CH
   (ME-1-UR)-1-SO
2: (ME-1-UR)-2/*2*-PL
3: (MA-*1*-SA)-9/*9*-MO
   (MA-*1*-JU)-12-(UR-*2*-PL)
5: (MA-*1*-JU)-15/*15*-SO
7: (UR-*2*-PL)-28-NE
11: (MA-*1*-JU)-11-ME
23: SO-23-VE
29: ((MO-*29*-NE)-29-(PL-*29*-CH))-
               -29/29/29/29-SO
    VE-*29*-SA
31: (SO-*31*-MA)-31-VE
    ((NE-*31*-CH)-31-VE)-31/31/31-*JU*

Gertrude Stein
1: ((SO-*1*-ME)-1-VE)-1/1/*1*-SA
2: (VE-1-SA)-*2*-UR
3: (SO-*1*-ME)-9-MA
             -*27*-JU)-27-UR
   MO-12-UR
   VE-*18*-PL
   MA-12-NE
   SA-*9*-NE
5: ((SO-*2*-ME)-*5*-NE)-15/15/*15*-PL
   (MO-*10*-PL)-20-MA
             -30/15-NE
7: VE-*14*-JU
   (UR-*7*-NE)-7-JU
19: MA-*19*-UR
23: (SO-*1*-ME)-23-*MO*
29: ((SO-*1*-ME)-*29*-CH)-29-UR
    MA-29-SA

Edith Sitwell
1: *VE*-1-*UR*
   MA-1-SA
2: JU-*4*-SA
3: *VE*-*3*-PL
   (MO-3-ME)-12/12-*UR*
   (JU-3-CH)-4/*12*-SA
5: SO-*5*-CH
   (MO-3-ME)-5/15-*VE*
7: (ME-*7*-JU)-7/*7*-*NE*
            -*21*/21-MA
11: SO-22-JU
13: (PL-*13*-CH)-26/*26*-ME
17: (SO-*17*-SA)-17-*VE*
23: (*VE*-*23*-*NE*)-23-SA
29: ((MO-*29*-*PL*)-29-MA)-29/29/*29*-SO
31: SO-*31*-*NE*
    (*VE*-*31*-MA)-*31*/31CH

Elizabeth Taylor
1: (SO-*1*-ME)-1-MA

VE-*1*-*UR*
2: ((SO-*1*-ME)-1-MA)-*2*/*2*/2-NE
             -16/*16*/16/16-(MO-*4*-JU)
   (*VE*-*1*-*UR*)-*8*-MA
3: (SO-*1*-ME)-*9*/*9*/9/9-(*VE*-*1*-*UR*)
   (*VE*-*1*-*UR*)-3-JU
5: (((SO-*1*-ME)-*2*-NE)-5/5/*10*-CH)-
               -10/10/*5*/*10*-SA
7: (*VE*-*1*-*UR*)-14-SA
11: MA-*11*-JU
17: MO-*17*-MA
19: (SO-*1*-ME)-19/*19*-PL
    (*VE*-*1*-*UR*)-*19*/19-MO
23: (*VE*-*1*-*UR*)-*23*/23-CH
29: ((SO-*1*-ME)-*29*/29-MO)-29/*29*/29-SA
    (JU-29-PL)-29-CH
31: ((*VE*-*1*-*UR*)-*31*/31-NE)-31/31/*31*-PL

Lord Byron
1: MO-1-UR
   VE-*1*-*SA*
2: (SO-*8*-JU)-*32*/32-NE
3: (SO-9-*MA*)-27/27/*27*/*27*-(ME-*27*-PL)
   ((MO-*9*-PL)-27/*27*-ME)-27-*MA*
5: (SO-*25*-MO)-25-NE
7: (SO-*14*-*SA*)-28/28-PL
   MO-*21*-NE
11: MO-*22*-*SA*
13: (ME-13-*CH*)-26/*26*-SO
    (UR-*13*-NE)-26/26-*VE*
29: (*MA*-*29*-JU)-*29*-*VE*-29-NE
    MO-*29*-ME
    SA-29-PL
31: SO-31-*VE*

Michael Hutchence
1: *SO*-1-*ME*
   VE-*1*-JU
2: (VE-*1*-JU)-8/8-NE
3: MA-*3*-PL
5: *SO*-5-PL
   (VE-*1*-JU)-10-PL
   (VE-10-PL)-20/*20*-SA
   (MA-*3*-PL)-*30*/10-VE
7: (VE-*1*-JU)-7-MO
            -21-*ME*
11: *SO*-*22*-NE
17: MO-*17*-ME
19: (VE-*1*-JU)-19/19/*19*/19-(SO-*19*-SA)
23: (*ME*-*23*-SA)-23-NE
    (VE-*1*-JU)-23/*23*-CH
29: (((VE-*1*-JU)-29/*29*-CH)-29/29/*29*-SO)-
             -29/*29*/29/29-MA

Allen Ginsberg
1: SO-*1*-ME
   VE-*1*-CH
2: (SO-*1*-ME)-*4*-MO

(VE-*1*-CH)-16/16-NE
3: (*MA*-*3*-SA)-*9*/9-SO
              -12/4-NE
    (VE-*1*-CH)-9/*9*-SA
    (ME-9-VE)-9-SA
    SO-*24*-JU
5: (SO-*1*-ME)-5-*UR*)-5/*5*/5-NE
    (VE-*1*-CH)-5/5-PL
7: ME-7-JU
13: (VE-*1*-CH)-26/26-SO
17: (VE-*1*-CH)-*17*/17-JU
23: SO-23-PL
    ME-*23*-*MA*
    VE-23-*UR*
29: (VE-*29*-NE)-29-MO
    (*MA*-*29*-JU)-29/*29*-PL
31: (SA-*31*-*UR*)-31-PL

Luc Jouret
1: (MA-1-PL)-1/1-SA
    VE-1-CH
2: *UR*-8-CH
3: SO-3-*UR*
    (MA-1-PL)-3/3-MO
5: SO-15-ME
    (VE-*25*-MA)-25-*UR*
7: (JU-*21*-CH)-21-SO
13: SO-26-PL
17: SO-*17*-SA
29: (SO-*29*-MA)-29-MO
    (ME-*29*-VE)-29-NE
              -29-MO
31: (VE-*31*-PL)-31-SO

Steven Spielberg
1: SO-1-MA
    MO-*1*-CH
    SA-1-PL
2: MO-4-SA
3: (SO-*27*-PL)-27/*27*-UR
    (ME-*3*-SA)-18-JU
5: ((ME-*3*-SA)-15/*5*-MA)-*15*/15/*15*-UR
    (VE-*15*-PL)-30-MO
7: (SO-*7*-CH)-*28*/28-JU
11: (ME-*11*-CH)-22/22-PL

13: (MA-13-CH)-*13*/13-PL
              -26/*26*-VE
19: (SO-*19*-NE)-*19*-ME
29: SO-*29*-MO-*29*-VE
    JU-*29*-NE-*29*-CH
31: ME-31-MA

Suicide of Donald Crowhurst
1: (JU-*1*-UR)-1/1-PL
2: VE-2-NE
    ((SO-*8*-VE)-16/16-MO)-*32*/32/32-JU
    (ME-16-NE)-32-UR

3: MO-*6*-MA
    (JU-*1*-UR)-3-MO
              -9-SO
    VE-3-PL
5: (ME-*5*-UR)-15/*15*-VE
    (*SA*-5-UR)-20/*20*-VE
7: SO-*21*-NE
13: (PL-*13*-CH)-26-MA
23: SO-*23*-*SA*
29: ((ME-*29*-JU)-29-VE)-29/*29*/29-MO
    (UR-29-CH)-29-MA
    SO-29-NE
31: SO-*31*-CH

Chapter 16: Thirty-oneness

Sigmund Freud
1: (SO-1-UR)-1-ME
2: VE-16-MA
3: SO-*18*-VE
    MO-*9*-*PL*
    MO-3-*CH*
5: (MO-3-*CH*)-15/5-VE
    (MO-5-VE)-15-UR
    MA-15-SA
7: SO-*21*-MA
17: MO-*17*-NE
23: SO-23-JU
31: ((JU-*31*-*PL*)-*31*/31-*CH*)-31-ME-
              -31/31/31/*31*-SO

Carl Gustav Jung
1: ME-1-VE
2: *SO*-*4*-NE
    MO-4-UR
    SA-4-*PL*
    ME-*16*-MA
3: ((JU-*3*-SA)-9/9-*SO*)-*18*/18/18-ME
    (ME-1-VE)-6-MO
5: (MO-*5*-MA)-25/*25*-JU
    ((VE-5-SA)-15/*3*-JU)-*20*/4/12-*PL*
19: (ME-*19*-CH)-19-*SO*
29: MO-*29*-VE-*29*-NE
31: (UR-*31*-*PL*)-31-*SO*
    (MO-*31*-SA)-31-ME

Marquis de Sade
1: SO-1-JU
    (VE-1-SA)-*1*/1-CH
2: (SO-*4*-MO)-*8*/8-VE
    (VE-1-SA)-4-MA
    UR-*16*-*PL*
3: SO-*9*-SA
    (MO-*3*-UR)-9/9-CH
    VE-*9*-JU
5: (SO-*5*-*PL*)-15/15/*15*/*15*-(ME-*15*-MA)
    (MO-*25*-ME)-*25*/25-JU
7: (MO-*7*-SA)-7-*PL*

13: VE-13-UR
17: SO-17-UR
31: ((MO-31-VE)-31-NE)-31/31/31-MA
(JU-31-SA)-31-PL

Jack Smith
2: (ME-8-SA)-16-SO
VE-8-MA
3: (SO-3-PL)-24/8-MO
(ME-8-SA)-6/24-VE
5: (SO-5-NE)-10-VE
7: (MO-7-JU)-14-VE
11: SO-22-JU
17: (SO-17-UR)-17JU
29: SO-29-VE
31: ((MO-31-PL)-31-(VE-31-CH))-31-NE
-31/31-UR
((VE-31-CH)-31-NE)-31/31/31-SA

Federico García Lorca
1: (SO-1-PL)-1-NE
2: ((SO-1-PL)-1-NE)-2/2/2-MO
-8-MA)-16-ME
3: MO-9-JU
5: MA-20-NE
7: MO-14-MA
11: MA-22-UR
13: ((SO-1-PL)-13/13-VE)-13-UR
(JU-13-CH)-26/26-MA
17: SO-17-JU
19: (MO-19-UR)-19/19-ME
29: SO-29-CH
31: (((SO-1-PL)-31/31-MO)-31/31-SA)-
-31/31/31-ME
((SO-31-SA)-31/31-ME)-31-MA

Robert Mapplethorpe
1: (SO-1-JU)-1-CH
(ME-1-VE)-1/1-MA
2: (SO-1-JU)-4/4-SA
(JU-4-SA)-16-VE
3: (VE-9-UR)-18/18-SO
(SO-1-JU)-3/3-MO
(MO-3-JU)-18/18-MA
-12/4-SA
5: (VE-10-PL)-15/30-MO
7: (MO-7-UR)-7/7-PL
(JU-4-SA)-14/28-ME
13: (ME-13-NE)-13/13-PL
31: ((MO-31-SA)-31-(ME-31-CH)-31-SO

Marcel Marceau
1: ME-1-UR
2: SO-8-NE
(VE-2-NE)-4/4-JU
3: (ME-1-UR)-6/3/6/3-(MA-2-JU)
(NE-3-CH)-8/24-SO

(VE-3-SA)-4/12-JU
-9/27-ME
7: SO-7-MO
11: (ME-1-UR)-22/22/22/22-(SO-11-PL)
((SO-11-PL)-11-SA)-22-ME
13: (MA-13-CH)-13-PL
17: SO-17-VE-17-MA
19: (VE-19-CH)-19-MO
23: (ME-1-UR)-23/23-SO
31: (((ME-1-UR)-31/31-MA)-31/31/31-JU)-
-31/31/31/31-NE

Marc Dutroux
1: SO-1-ME
2: UR-2-CH
((MO-4-JU)-8/8-JU)-16-SA
3: ((UR-2-CH)-6/3-VE)-18/9/9-MA
5: ((UR-2-CH)-6/3-VE)-
-15/30/30/15/30/15-(JU-10-NE)
((VE-10-PL)-30/15/15/6-(JU-10-NE)-
-6/15/15/30-UR
11: SO-22-JU
ME-11-VE
13: (UR-2-CH)-26/13-SO
(MO-13-NE)-13-UR
17: SO-17-MO
19: (SO-19-SA)-19-VE
29: SO-29-VE
ME-29-CH
31: ((((ME-31-MA)-31/31-UR)-
-31/31-SA)-31/31/31/31-PL)-
-31/31/31/31-MO

Robert Black
1: ME-1-MA
2: ((ME-1-MA)-2/2-NE)-16/16/16-SO
(VE-8-PL)-32-MA
3: SO-18-PL
((ME-1-MA)-2/2-NE)-12/12/12-MO
VE-3-JU
5: (ME-1-MA)-5/5-UR
(MA-5-UR)-15/15-SO
7: VE-28-NE
(UR-7-PL)-21/21-CH
11: MA-22-SA
13: VE-13-UR
19: ((ME-1-MA)-19/19-CH)-19/19/19-SA
((ME-19-CH)-19-JU)-19/19/19-SA
31: SO-31-VE-31-MA-31-CH
JU-31-NE-31-PL

Jeffrey Dahmer
2: (PL-2-CH)-4/4-SO
-8/8-SA
JU-8-UR
3: (PL-2-CH)-3/6-JU
(JU-6-CH)-18/9-VE
-8/24-UR

5:   (JU-*6*-CH)-*10*/*15*-MO)-*15*/*10*/30-MA
7:   ME-7-JU
13:   (ME-13-_SA_)-*26*/26-VE
19:   SO-19-_SA_
23:   SO-23-NE
31:   SO-31-PL
        ((ME-*31*-MA)-31/*31*-NE)-31/31/31-_MO_

Gavrilo Princip

1:   ((_VE_-*1*-_NE_)-1-_PL_)-1-JU
2:   _MO_-8-SA
3:   (SO-*9*-_PL_)-27-_MO_
        (_MO_-3-ME)-24/8-CH
        (_MO_-8-SA)-24/12-CH
5:   (_VE_-*1*-_NE_)-10/10-CH
        _MO_-*15*-_VE_
7:   ME-*7*-_PL_
11:   ME-11-UR
13:   (JU-*13*-UR)-13-SO
17:   _MO_-17-_NE_
31:   (ME-*31*-_VE_-*31*-CH)-31-SO
        (JU-*31*-SA)-*31*/31-_PL_

Carol Burnett

1:   SO-*1*-VE
        MO-1-CH
        (MA-1-NE)-1-JU
2:   MO-8-ME
3:   (SO-*1*-VE)-3/*3*-NE
        (MA-1-NE)-3/3-SO
        (MO-8-ME)-12/24-UR
5:   SO-20-MO
        (SA-*25*-CH)-25-NE
7:   (VE-*3*-NE)-21/7-MO
        (ME-*7*-JU)-7-PL
                -14-SO
        VE-*28*-UR
11:   (MO-*11*-MA-*11*-SA)-22-VE
13:   ME-*13*-VE
17:   ME-*17*-NE
19:   SO-19-PL
31:   (SO-*31*-UR)-31-(MA-*31*-JU)

Notes and References

Preface

1. Iain McGilchrist, *The Master and his Emissary*, New Haven and London: Yale University Press, 2009, p.460.
2. Garry Phillipson, *Astrology in the Year Zero*, London: Flare Publications, 2000, pp.119-123.

Chapter 1: Introduction

1. John M. Addey, *Harmonics in Astrology*, Romford: L.N. Fowler, 1976.
2. David Hamblin, *Harmonic Charts*, Wellingborough: Aquarian Press, 1983.
3. Ward Rutherford, *Pythagoras, Lover of Wisdom*, Wellingborough: Aquarian Press, 1984, p.55.
4. Shirley Gotthold, *The Transformational Tarot*, Berkeley, CA: Foolscap Press, 1995.
5. Paul Wright, *A Multitude of Lives*, Edinburgh: Parlando Press, 2009.
6. Frank C. Clifford, *British Entertainers, the Astrological Profiles* (3rd edition), London: Flare Publications, 2003.
7. Frank C. Clifford, *The Astrologer's Book of Charts*, London: Flare Publications, 2009.

Chapter 2: The Planets

1. Robert Wadlow, born 22 February 1918, 06.30 (+06.00), Alton IL, USA (38N53. 90W10). Source: Letter from Alton Museum of History, via Steinbrecher (ADB). RR: A.
2. The name and birthdata of this "boy genius" are withheld to protect his privacy.
3. Earl of Arundel, born 7 September 1879, 08.00 (+00.00), London, England (51N30. 00W10). Source: from his father (ADB). RR: A. The quotation is from his AstroDatabank biography.
4. Some examples of major volcanic eruptions:
   Katmai eruption, 6 June 1912, 13.00 (+10.00), Katmai AK, USA (58N20. 154W59).
   Krakatoa eruption, 27 August 1883, 03.00 (+00.00), Krakatoa, Indonesia (6S10. 105E20).
   Mount Pelée eruption, 8 May 1902, 07.52 (+04.04), Martinique (14N40. 61W00).
   Mount St Helens eruption, 18 May 1980, 08.32 (+07.00), Mount St Helens WA, USA (46N29. 122W12).
   Pinatubo eruption, 15 June 1991, 13.42 (–08.00), Pinatubo, Philippines (15N13. 120E35).
   Tambora eruption, 10 April 1815, 19.00 (–07.52), Tambora, Indonesia (8S12. 118E05).

5.   Some examples of major earthquakes:
> Chile quake, 27 February 2010, 03.34 (+03.00), Concepcion, Chile (36S50. 73W03).
> Haiti quake, 12 January 2010, 16.53 (+05.00), Port-au-Prince, Haiti (18N32. 72W20).
> Indian Ocean quake (that caused the Boxing Day tsunami), 26 December 2004, 07.59 (–07.00), (05N00. 95E00).
> Sendai quake, 11 March 2011, 14.46 (–09.00), Sendai (Miyagi), Japan (38N15. 140E53).
> Sichuan quake, 12 May 2008, 14.28 (–08.00), Yingxin, China (31N02. 103E38).
> Tangshan quake, 27 July 1966, 03.42 (–08.00), Tangshan, China (39N38. 118E11).

6.   A possible exception to this is the Tunguska explosion (30 June 1908, 00.17 (+00.00), Vanavar, Siberia (60N55. 101E57)), which was probably caused by a giant meteorite hitting the Earth. This was an event that was not caused by human action, and yet the chart seems to describe the event very clearly. Perhaps we can speculate that, in the case of such violent and un-subtle events involving the collision of heavenly bodies, the influence of the planets is strong enough to be visible at the physical level.

7.   Demetra George and Douglas Bloch, *Asteroid Goddesses*, Lake Worth FL: Ibis Press, 2003.

Chapter 3: Oneness

1.   William M. Carrigan, *An Introduction to Padre Pio*, www.padrepio.net/Pio. Intro.html
2.   www.josemariaescriva.info (in the section headed *The Founding of Opus Dei*).
3.   Anodea Judith, *Teilhard de Chardin 1881-1955*, www.gaiamind.com/Teilhard.html
4.   Pierre Teilhard de Chardin, 'My Universe' (quoted in Ursula King, *Spirit of Fire, the Life and Vision of Teilhard de Chardin*, Maryknoll NY: Orbis Books, 2000, p.5).
5.   Nandor Fodor, in www.survivalafterdeath.org.uk/books/fodor/chapter25.htm
6.   www.time.com/time/time100/builder/profile.luciano2.html
7.   www.cosmicbaseball.com/swinbur7.html
8.   William Rossetti, *Some Reminiscences*, 1906.
9.   Pauline Collins, born 3 September 1940, 19.40 (–01.00), Exmouth, England (50N37. 03W23). Source: From her, from "mother's (excellent) memory," via Frank C. Clifford (FCC). RR: A.
10.   Chris Evert, born 21 December 1954, 04.30 (+05.00), Fort Lauderdale FL, USA (26N07. 80W08). Source: Birth certificate, via Robert Jansky (ADB). RR: AA.
11.   Jon Henley, *The Guardian*, Monday, April 18, 2005. Reprinted in www. guardian.co.uk/crime/article/0,2763,1462136.00.html?gusrc=rss

12. Robert Gittings (ed.), *Letters of John Keats*, Oxford and New York: Oxford University Press, 1970, p.244.

13. Robert Gittings, *John Keats*, London: Penguin Books, 2001, p.300. (Originally published in 1968.)

Chapter 4: Twoness

1. R.D. Laing, *The Divided Self*, London: Tavistock Publications, 1960.
2. Stephen Ticktin, *R.D.L. Biography*, http://laing.society.org/biograph.htm
3. R.D. Laing, *The Politics of Experience*, London: Tavistock Publications, 1967.
4. Walter H. Capps, *Interpreting Václav Havel*, www.aril.org/capps.htm
5. Václav Havel in his February 1990 address to the US Congress, quoted by Capps, op.cit.
6. *French literary icon Sagan dies*, http://news.bbc.co.uk/1/hi/world/europe/3688296.stm
7. Els Barents, introduction to *Cindy Sherman*, a publication accompanying an exhibition of Sherman's work in Amsterdam, 1982.
8. Alice Miller, *For Your Own Good: The Roots of Violence in Child-Rearing*, London: Virago Press, 1987.
9. For details see Miller, op.cit., pp.203-4.
10. Nathaniel Bar-Jonah, born 15 February 1957, 08.38 (+05.00), Worcester MA, USA (42N15. 71W48). Source: Birth certificate, via Frances McEvoy (ADB). RR: AA.
11. Ted Bundy, born 24 November 1946, 22.35 (+05.00), Burlington VT, USA (44N25. 73W12) (ADB). Source: Birth certificate, via T. Pat Davis. RR: AA.
12. Edward Gein, born 27 August 1906, 23.30 (+06.00), North La Crosse WI, USA (43N50. 91W14). Source: Birth certificate, via G.S. MacEwan (ADB). RR: AA.
13. Maria Swanenburg, born 9 September 1839, 22.00 (–00.18), Leiden, Netherlands (52N09. 04E30). Source: Birth certificate, via Ger Westenberg (ADB). RR: AA.
14. Kate White, *The Hidden Life of Charles de Foucauld*, http://ncronline.org/NCR_Online/archives2/2005d/111105/111105a.php
15. From her AstroDatabank biography.
16. Pierre Descouvement and Helmuth Nils Loose, *Thérèse and Lisieux*, Toronto: Novalis, 1996, p.53.
17. Thérèse de Lisieux, quoted in Wikipedia (no source given).
18. This was the instruction given by Colonel Oran K. Henderson before the offensive (see Wikipedia).
19. I say "he" because I feel that Two (like Five) is essentially a masculine number, related more to yang than to yin.
20. Eckhart Tolle, *A New Earth*, London: Michael Joseph, 2005.

21. Richard Evans, *McEnroe, a Rage for Perfection*, London: Sidgwick & Jackson, 1982. John McEnroe, born 16 February 1959, 22.30 (–01.00), Wiesbaden, Germany (50N05. 08E14). Source: Richard Evans, op.cit (ADB). RR: B.

Chapter 5: Threeness
1. *Robert Louis Martin, Artist*, http://artwerker.tripod.com/biography.html
2. John M. Addey, *Harmonics in Astrology*, Romford: Fowler, 1976, chapter 11.
3. *King of Comedy, the Jerry Lewis Page*, www.dhalgren.com/Jerry/
4. Chris Fujiwara, *Jerry Lewis*, www.sensesofcinema.com/contents/directors/03/lewis.html
5. http://en.wikipedia.org/wiki/Jerry_Lewis
6. AstroDatabank biography of Jerry Lewis.
7. Jerry Lewis and James Kaplan, *Dean and Me, a Love Story*, London: Macmillan, 2005, p.326.
8. www.jerrylewiscomedy.com/biography.htm
9. *Emmanuel's Book*, compiled by Pat Rodegast and Judith Stanton, New York: Bantam Books, 1987.
10. *Emmanuel's Book*, op.cit., p.ix.
11. www.wic.org/bio/pdiller.htm
12. http://en.wikipedia.org/wiki/Phyllis_Diller
13. John Cleese, born 27 October 1939, 03.15 (–01.00), Weston-super-Mare, England (51N21. 02W59). Source: From his mother, via Eve Jackson and David Fisher (FCC). RR: A.
14. Frank Farrelly and Jeff Brandsma, *Provocative Therapy*, Cupertino CA: Meta Publications, 1974.
15. Farrelly and Brandsma, op.cit., pp.167-8.
16. www.provocativetherapy.com
17. "Woundology" (attachment to one's own woundedness) is a word invented by Caroline Myss, a "medical intuitive" and spiritual teacher who also has a strong Threeness chart. Caroline Myss, born 2 December 1952, 08.00 (–06.00), Chicago IL, USA (41N51. 87W39). Source: From her, via Shelley Ackerman (ADB). RR: A.
18. http://en.wikipedia.org/wiki/Adi_Da
19. Ludwig (or Louis) Haeusser, 6 November 1881, 09.30 (–00.40), Bonnigheim, Germany (49N48. 09E56). From his devotees, via *Modern Astrology* 6/1921 (ADB). RR: A.
20. Roberto Assagioli, *Psychosynthesis*, London: Turnstone Books, 1975, pp.118-9.
21. Eckhart Tolle, *A New Earth*, London: Michael Joseph, 2005, p.56.

Chapter 6: Sixness
1. www.meherbaba.co.uk
2. http://en.wikipedia.org/wiki/Kray_twins
3. Ronnie Kray, *My Story*, quoted in Wikipedia.

Chapter 7: Fiveness

1. www.answers.com/topic/pentagram-2
2. http://irelandsown.net/penta2.html
3. Francis Bacon, quoted in Chris Clarke, *Living in Connection*, Warminster: Creation Spirituality Books, 2002, p.33.
4. I have elaborated on this at greater length in my book *Harmonic Charts*, op.cit., p.48.
5. Michael Harding and Charles Harvey, *Working with Astrology*, London: Arkana, 1990, p.185.
6. The next five paragraphs are taken from my article 'Harmonics and the Silent Twins', *Astrological Journal*, vol.29 no.4, June/July 1987, pp.165-173. All my information on the Silent Twins comes from Marjorie Wallace, *The Silent Twins*, London: Chatto & Windus, 1986, and from a later article by Marjorie Wallace, 'Dying to Live', *Sunday Times*, 3 July 1994; also from the AstroDatabank biography.
7. Wallace, *The Silent Twins*, op.cit., p.14.
8. June Gibbons, quoted by Wallace, *The Silent Twins*, op.cit., p.194. Reprinted by permission of The Random House Group Ltd.
9. Jennifer Gibbons died on 9 March 1993, 18.15 (+00.00), Bridgend, Wales (51N30. 03W35). Source: Marjorie Wallace, 'Dying to Live', *Sunday Times*, 3 July 1994.
10. David Hamblin, 'Harmonics and the Silent Twins', op.cit.
11. AstroDatabank gives this chart a rating of 'B', but I have my doubts. The original source is not stated, and there is a tendency for religious devotees to believe that their leaders were born at sunrise. However, the chart is very convincing.
12. http://info.bahai.org/bahaullah-teachings.html. Published by the Bahá'i International Community, and reproduced by kind permission of the National Spiritual Assembly of the Bahá'is of the United Kingdom.
13. http://en.wikipedia.wiki/Bahá-u-lláh
14. AstroDatabank biography of Frank Buchman.
15 www.iofc.org/index.php?LA=1&sn=2,2&sub=2
16. http://en.wikipedia.wiki/Frank_N_D_Buchman
17. www.orange-papers.org/orange-rroot060.html
18. http://en.wikipedia.wiki/Aurobindo
19. Charles E. Moore, quoted in www.miraura.org/bio.ot-on-sa.html
20. Steven Axelrod in http://litencyc.com/php/speople.php?rec=true&UID=3579
21. www.sylviaplath.de/plath/bio.html
22. Michelle Orange, "Not Easy Being Greene", *The Nation*, 15 April 2009, quoted by Wikipedia.
23. http://en.wikipedia.org/wiki/Thomas_Hardy
24. www.ibiblio.org/wm/paint/auth/matisse/

25. www.henri-matisse.net/quotes.html
26. http://en.wikipedia.org/wiki/Richard_Branson
27. See David Hamblin, *Harmonic Charts*, op.cit., p.49.
28. www.bl.uk/onlinegallery/features/beautifulminds/fleming.html
29. Wikipedia states: "Times are given in ship's time, the local time for Titanic's position in the Atlantic. On the night of the sinking, this was approximately ... three and a half hours behind GMT."
30. Thomas Berry, *The Dream of the Earth*, San Francisco: Sierra Club Books, 1988, p.210.

Chapter 8: Sevenness

1. In fact the numbers are not completely random, as we can see the sequence beginning to repeat itself: 0.142857142857... However, we can certainly say that Seven does not have a simple relationship to the decimal system.
2. www.deeptrance.now.com
3. AstroDatabank gives Alice Bailey's birthtime a rating of 'C' ("caution"), as the original source of the data is not known. However, Bailey was interested in astrology and was still alive when Rudhyar's article was published, so it seems very likely that she was herself the source of the birthtime given by Rudhyar.
4. http://en.wikipedia.org/wiki/Alice_Bailey
5. The crash occurred at 05.25 (–01.00) on 11 August 1969 in St Etienne-du-Vouvray, France (49N23. 01E06). Source: www.jean-migueres.com
6. www.jean-migueres.com
7. These details are from Anita McKeown's AstroDatabank biography, which also gives dates for several of her accidents. See also www.people/com/people/archive/article/0,,20091481,00.html, which gives precise times for some of the accidents.
8. The time of birth has now (2010) been withdrawn from Federer's website, but it was there when I found it in 2007.
9. Rafael Nadal, born 3 June 1986, 19.15 (–02.00), Manacor, Mallorca, Spain (39N34. 3E12). Source: From biography, via Paddy de Jabrun (ADB). RR: B.
10. www.newstatesman.com/199904190045.htm
11. "Bruce Chatwin: Spike looks at Bruce Chatwin's travel writing: In Search of the Miraculous": www.spikemagazine.com/0896chat.php
12. http://en.wikipedia.org/wiki/Moby-Dick
13. http://en.wikipedia.org/wiki/Hector_Berlioz
14. www.biographybase.com/biography/Ensor_James.html
15. http://en.wikipedia.org/wiki/James_Ensor
16. See also my comments about Ensor in my earlier book: David Hamblin, *Harmonic Charts*, op.cit., p.69.
17. Iain McGilchrist, *The Master and his Emissary*, New Haven and London: Yale University Press, 2009, pp.450-1.

18. AstroDatabank biography of Ira Einhorn.

19. http://en.wikipedia.org/wiki/Charles_Starkweather

20. Myra Hindley, born 23 July 1942, 02.45 (–02.00), Crumpsall, England (53N31. 02W15). Source: From biography by Jean Ritchie, *Inside the Mind of a Murderess*, "between 2.30 and 3.00 a.m." (ADB). RR: B. (Hindley is strong in Fiveness rather than Sevenness.)

21 Michael Harding and Charles Harvey, *Working with Astrology*, op.cit., Chapter 13.

Chapter 9: Introduction to the Higher Prime Numbers

1. David Hamblin, *Harmonic Charts*, op.cit., pp. 264-5.

Chapter 10: Elevenness

1. See for example: http://australis.com.au/hazz/number011.html; www.mystic-mouse.co.uk/Wisdom_Texts/G_Tucker/ElevenElevenAgain.htm; www.lightofisis.com/lp11.htm; www.theforbiddenknowledge.com/hardtruth/significance_of_11.htm.

2. Vincente Minnelli, quoted in Wikipedia.

3. www.brainyquote.com/quotes/authors/r/richard_pryor.html

4. www.brainyquote.com/quotes/authord/d/donald_trump.html

5. Shortly after Lyttelton's death in 2008, the BBC broadcast a programme celebrating his life, which included an extract from a televised episode of *I'm Sorry I Haven't a Clue*. During this extract Lyttelton said: "If, at seven in the morning on 23rd May 1921, I'd known that eighty-two years later I'd be sitting in this studio talking to you lot, I'd have crawled back into the womb". The place of birth is taken from the Cambridge Encyclopaedia.

6. www.expo-cezanne.com

7. http://en.wikipedia.org/wiki/Paul_Gauguin

8. www.vangoghgallery.com/misc/quotes.html

Chapter 11: Thirteenness

1. www.brainyquote.com/quotes/authors/a/antoine_de_saintexupery.html

2. www.brainyquote.com/quotes/author/a/amelia_earhart.html

3. Peter Evans, *Peter Sellers, the Mask Behind the Mask*, revised edition, London: New English Library, 1980, p.171.

4. www.newworldencyclopedia.org/entry/Truman_Capote

5. www.sensesofcinema.com/contents/directors/02/fassbinder.html

6. www.gss.ucsb.edu/projects/hesse/life/jennifer.html

7. www.brainyquote.com/quotes/authors/j/janis_joplin.html

8. Guevara's birth certificate states 14th June 1928, but his mother told the biographer that she had changed the date from the actual date of 14th May in order to hide the fact that she was unmarried when Che was conceived.

9. http://en.wikipedia.org/wiki/Che_Guevara
10. Wikipedia does not state the time at which the stock market opened for trading on Black Wednesday. However, it normally opens at 08.00, so I have taken this to be the correct time.
11. An example of a painter with strong Thirteenness links is Camille Corot. Unlike the painters whom we considered in the chapter on Elevenness, Corot found happiness and self-fulfilment through travelling the world and recording what he saw in his paintings. (Camille Corot, born 16 July 1796, 01.30 (–00.09), Paris, France (48N52. 02E20). Source: Birth certificate, via Gauquelin (ADB). RR: AA.))
12. The impersonator Rory Bremner has strong Thirteenness links. (Rory Bremner, born 6 April 1961, 21.05 (–01.00), Edinburgh, Scotland (55N53. 03W13). Source: Birth certificate, via Gerard (FCC). RR: AA.)
13. Jacqueline Kennedy Onassis, born 28 July 1929, 14.30 (+04.00), Southampton NY, USA (40N53. 72W23). Source: From her to mutual friends, via Frances McEvoy (ADB). RR: A.
14. Vivien Leigh, born 5 November 1913, 17.16 (–05.53), Darjeeling, India (27N02. 88E16). Source: From Laurence Olivier by Cottrell ("sunset") (ADB). RR: B.
15. Mary Shelley, born 30 August 1797, 23.20 (+00.01), London, England (51W30. 00W10). Source: From father's diary, via Barbara Lynne Devlin (ADB). RR: AA.

Chapter 12: Seventeenness
1. www.brainyquote.com/quotes/authors/m/madalyn_murray_ohair.html
2. William J. Murray, quoted in http://en.wikipedia.org/wiki/Madalyn_Murray_O'Hair
3. Quoted in http://en.wikipedia.org/wiki/L_Ron_Hubbard
4. www.brainyquote.com/quotes/authors/r/roger_vadim.html
5. http://en.wkipedia.org/wiki/Harold_Pinter
6. Samuel Beckett, born 13 April 1906, 20.14 (+00.25), Stillorgan, Ireland (53N18. 06W12). Source: From Beckett by Deidre Bair ("At 8.00 p.m. [my] father went for a walk, and when he returned I had been born") (ADB). RR: B.
7. Quoted by Frank C. Clifford, British Entertainers, op.cit., p.248.
8. Michael McWilliams, TV Sirens, Perigee 1987, quoted by F.C. Clifford, op.cit., p.249.
9. http://en.wikipedia.org/wiki/Diane_Keaton
10. www.phrases.org.uk/meanings/191400.html casts doubt on whether Oscar Wilde actually said this, but provides some examples of his fully authenticated witticisms, e.g. "To love oneself is the beginning of a life-long romance".
11. http://listverse.com/2008/02/05/top-20-quotes-of-dorothy-parker lists 20

of Dorothy Parker's best-known witticisms, e.g.: "I don't care what people say about me so long as it isn't true"; "If you want to know what God thinks of money, just look at the people he gave it to".

12. Bertrand Russell, *In Praise of Idleness*, London: George Allen and Unwin, 1935, quoted in http://grammar.about.com/od/classicessays/a/praiseidleness.htm

13. It would seem to be doubtful whether Fagan obtained the data from Heath, since Fagan published the data in 1954 (A.A., 9/1954) and Heath had been hanged in 1946. However, AstroDatabank gives the data a rating of 'A'.

14. This spirit of revolutionary fervour is of course also present in Che Guevara, whom we considered in the chapter on Thirteenness; but then Guevara has a cluster of VE–17–MA–17–NE in addition to his Thirteenness aspects.

15. It is interesting to note that Julian Assange, the founder of Wikileaks (the organization devoted to uncovering official secrets), has strong Seventeenness aspects: ((SO–**17**–MA)–17–ME)–17–JU, also SA–**17**–UR, NE–17–PL, and MO–17–CH. However, I have not included him as one of my case studies, because of the unreliability of the birthdata. (Julian Assange, born 13 July 1971, 14.05 (–10.00), Townsville, Australia (19S16. 146E48). Source: allegedly from birth certificate, via an anonymous (but questionable) source. RR: C.)

Chapter 13: Nineteenness

1. Santeri Levas, *Sibelius, a personal portrait*, London: J.M. Dent and Sons, 1972, p.47.
2. Jean Sibelius, quoted by Jalmari Finne, 26 June 1905.
3. Jean Sibelius, quoted in Cecil Gray, *Sibelius, the Symphonies*, Oxford University Press, 1935, p.56.
4. Santeri Levas, op.cit., p.135.
5. Michael Gray, obituary of Gerry Rafferty, *The Guardian*, 5 January 2011.
6. Gerry Rafferty (interviewed by Charlotte Heathcote), *Sunday Express*, 22 November 2009.
7. www.highlandnaturalists.com/biography/gavin-maxwell
8. *Dictionary of National Biography 1961-70*, Oxford University Press, 1981, (quoted by Paul Wright, *A Multitude of Lives*, Edinburgh: Parlando Press, 2009, p.112).
9. http://ingridkarazincir.com/psychic-abilities
10. www.koratworld.com/sunan.html
11. Review in *The Times*, quoted in www.frankskinnerlive.com/press.php
12. *Los Angeles Times*, December 7, 1990: http://articles.latimes.com/1990-12-07/news/mn-6172_1_black-eye

Chapter 14: Twenty-threeness

1. http://en.wikipedia.org/wiki/Under_Milk_Wood
2. http://en.wikipedia.org/wiki/Salvador_Dali

3. Friedrich Engels, born 28 November 1820, 21.00 (–00.29), Barmen, Germany (51N17. 07E13). Source: Birth certificate, via Steinbrecher (ADB). RR: AA.
4. http://allthingshorror.tripod.com/mcveigh.html
5. http://en.wikipedia.org/wiki/Charles_Sobhraj
6. John Perkins, *Confessions of an Economic Hit Man*, San Francisco: Berrett-Koehler, 2004 (published in the UK by Ebury Press, London, 2006).
7. www.beyondtheordinary.net/johnperkins.shtml
8. www.dreamchange.org

Chapter 15: Twenty-nineness

1. www.goodreads.com/author/quotes/65646.Edith_Sitwell
2. Sam Kashner and Nancy Schoenberger, *Furious Love*, London: JR Books, 2011 (reprinted in *The Sunday Times*, 27 March 2011).
3. Michael Schumacher in www.allenginsberg.org/index.php?page=bio
4. Joseph Di Mambro, born 19 August 1924, 23.00 (–01.00), Pont St Esprit, France (44N15. 04E39). Source: Birth certificate, via Cadran no.23 (ADB). RR: AA.
5. A fuller description of the Order's practices can be found at http://blog.templarhistory.com/2010/04/the-tragedy-of-the-solar-temple-cult
6. Jim Jones, born 13 May 1931, 22.00 (+06.00), Lynn IN, USA (40N03. 84W56). Source: from official birth records, via F.C. Clifford (ADB). RR: AA.
7. David Koresh, born 17 August 1959, 08.49 (+06.00), Houston TX, USA (29N46. 95W22). Source: from his mother, via Joyce Mason (ADB). RR: A.
8. Crowhurst was using British Summer Time (–01.00), "because it was convenient for BBC broadcasts" (Nicholas Tomalin and Ron Hall, *The Strange Last Voyage of Donald Crowhurst*, London: Adlard Coles Nautical, 1970. p.265).
9. Nicholas Tomalin and Ron Hall, *The Strange Last Voyage of Donald Crowhurst*, op.cit.

Chapter 16: Thirty-oneness

1. Jay Harris and Jean Harris in their book *The One Eyed Doctor Sigmund Freud* have argued that the records were falsified and that Freud was born on 6 March. However, Michael Harding in *Astrological Journal* July-Aug 2000 has reviewed the evidence and concluded that the correct date is 6 May.
2. Jung is said to have told an astrologer that he was born "when the last rays of the setting sun lit the room". To fit in with this, the time of 19.32 given by his daughter has been calculated for local mean time, rather than for Berne time which was officially in use.

3. Sigmund Freud, *New Introductory Lectures on Psychoanalysis* (1933), London: Penguin Freud Library 2, pp.105-6.
4. www.kheper.net/topics/Jung/collective_unconscious.html
5. http://en.wikiquote.org/wiki/Quills
6. www.brainyquote.com/quotes/authors/m/marquis_de_sade.html
7. www.jahsonic.com/SadeBio.html
8. www.brightlightsfilm.com/29/jacksmith.php
9. Robert Pring-Mill in http://boppin.com/lorca
10. www.brainyquote.com/quotes/quotes/r/robertmapp312625.html
11. Marcel Marceau in *Wall Street Journal*, 19 November 1965.
12. www.webalice.it/filibertomaida/orgasm.htm states that Dahmer said this to a psychiatrist.
13. Assassination of Franz Ferdinand: 28 June 1914, 11.00 (–01.00), Sarajevo, Bosnia (43N52. 18E26). Source: AstroDatabank.
14. Vladimir Dedijek, *The Road to Sarajevo*, London: Simon and Schuster, 1966, quoted in Wikipedia.
15. Well, not quite the only one. Marie Antoinette, the Queen of France who allegedly said "Let them eat cake" and who was guillotined during the French Revolution, has three clusters of Thirty-oneness. Marie Antoinette, born 2 November 1755, 19.30 (–01.05), Vienna, Austria (48N13. 16E20). Source: From biography by A. Asquith (ADB). RR: B.

Chapter 18: Interpreting the Whole Chart

1. At 10.17 a.m. on the day of Tony Blair's birth (6 May 1953), at Porton Down near Salisbury, England, an RAF engineer named Ronald Maddison was given a lethal dose of sarin (an extremely toxic substance) by scientists who were testing the effects of chemical weapons. It has now been officially ruled that Maddison was "unlawfully killed". I have written an article in which I looked at the two charts (for the birth of Tony Blair and the killing of Ronald Maddison) and compared the actions and motivations of the Porton Down scientists with those of Tony Blair at the time of the invasion of Iraq. David Hamblin, 'Tony Blair and the killing at Porton Down', *Astrological Journal*, vol.52 no.6, November/December 2010, pp.56-60.
2. Paul Wright in *A Multitude of Lives* gives the same time, but gives the birthplace as Glasgow (55N53. 04W15). This makes virtually no difference to the planets and angles.
3. Alice Miller, *For Your Own Good: The Roots of Violence in Child-Rearing*, op.cit., p.157.
4 Hermann Rauschning, *The Voice of Destruction*, New York: G.P. Putnam's Sons, 1940, quoted by Alice Miller, op.cit., p.174.
5. www.sriramanamaharshi.org/selfrealisation.html
6. Paula Marvelly, *The Teachers of One*, London: Watkins Publishing, 2002, p.265.

Chapter 20: Conclusion: Astrology

1. Since the Moon's Nodes are regarded as so important by many astrologers, the omission of them from this book is sure to cause adverse comment. I have omitted them because they do not form part of my own system of interpretation, but I have no objection to other astrologers using them. However, it needs to be emphasized that the Nodes are not planets: they are intersections between two great circles, and as such are more similar to the Ascendant and Midheaven than to the planets. It would, in my view, be inappropriate to calculate harmonic aspects between the Nodes and the planets.

2. David Hamblin, 'Harmonics and the Silent Twins', *Astrological Journal*, vol.29 no.4, June/July 1987, pp.165-173. In that article I said that I had used a computer program for latitude correction developed by Astrocalc, but I no longer have access to that program.

3. Garry Phillipson, 'Modern Science, Epistemology and Astrology', *Correlation*, vol.23(2), 2005-2006.

4. Roy Gillett, 'The "middle way" model of astrology: a response to Garry Phillipson's article', *Correlation*, vol.24(1), 2006.

Appendix 1: How to Do It

1. I do not favour the Equal House system, as I feel that the Midheaven is important and needs to be the cusp of the 10th house. But it is difficult to choose between the other house systems (Placidus, Koch, Regiomontanus, etc.) on either theoretical or empirical grounds. Although for most of my astrological career I have followed Placidus, I am inclined now to think that the best house system may well be Porphyry, in which the arc between the Ascendant and the Midheaven, and also the arc between the Midheaven and the Descendant, is divided into three equal arcs. But I believe that the houses need to be seen as gradually merging into each other, rather than as separated by sharp boundaries.

Index

(* indicates pages on which the person's birthdata, or the time of the mundane event, is presented)

Also by The Wessex Astrologer

Patterns of the Past
Karmic Connections
Good Vibrations
The Soulmate Myth: A Dream Come True or Your Worst Nightmare?
The Book of Why
Judy Hall

The Essentials of Vedic Astrology
Lunar Nodes - Crisis and Redemption
Personal Panchanga and the Five Sources of Light
Komilla Sutton

Astrolocality Astrology
From Here to There
Martin Davis

The Consultation Chart
Introduction to Medical Astrology
Wanda Sellar

The Betz Placidus Table of Houses
Martha Betz

Astrology and Meditation
Greg Bogart

The Book of World Horoscopes
Nicholas Campion

Life After Grief : An Astrological Guide to Dealing with Loss
AstroGraphology: The Hidden Link between your Horscope and your Handwriting
Darrelyn Gunzburg

The Houses: Temples of the Sky
Deborah Houlding

Through the Looking Glass
The Magic Thread
Richard Idemon

Temperament: Astrology's Forgotten Key
Dorian Geiseler Greenbaum

Nativity of the Late King Charles
John Gadbury

Declination - The Steps of the Sun
Luna - The Book of the Moon
Paul F. Newman

www.wessexastrologer.com

Astrology, A Place in Chaos
Star and Planet Combinations
Bernadette Brady

Astrology and the Causes of War
Jamie Macphail

Flirting with the Zodiac
Kim Farnell

The Gods of Change
Howard Sasportas

Astrological Roots:The Hellenistic Legacy
Joseph Crane

The Art of Forecasting using Solar Returns
Anthony Louis

Horary Astrology Re-Examined
Barbara Dunn

Living Lilith
M. Kelley Hunter

Your Horoscope in Your Hands
Lorna Green

Primary Directions
Martin Gansten

Classical Medical Astrology
Oscar Hofman

The Door Unlocked: An Astrological Insight into Initiation
*Dolores Ashcroft Nowicki and
Stephanie V. Norris*

Understanding Karmic Complexes
Patricia L. Walsh

Pluto Volumes 1 & 2
Jeff Green

Essays on Evolutionary Astrology
Jeff Green Edited by Deva Green

Planetary Strength
Bob Makransky

All the Sun Goes Round
Reina James

The Moment of Astrology
Geoffrey Cornelius

The Tapestry of Planetary Phases
Christina Rose